AF580878

THE PUBLIC LAW OF WALES

Administrative Law and the Administrative Court in Wales

David C. Gardner LLB (Hons),
Administrative Court Office Lawyer for Wales,
Barrister of Lincoln's Inn, Solicitor of the Senior Courts

UNIVERSITY OF WALES PRESS
2016

The views expressed in this text are those of the author, and do not necessarily reflect those of Her Majesty's Courts and Tribunals Service or the Ministry of Justice.

www.uwp.co.uk

British Library CIP Data
A catalogue record for this book is available from the British Library.

ISBN 978-1-78316-932-0
eISBN 978-1-78316-933-7

Typeset by Marie Doherty
Printed by CPI Antony Rowe, Melksham

Series Preface

For several centuries after the union of the two countries under the Tudors, the laws which applied in England and the laws which applied in Wales were almost exactly identical. Although administered differently in Wales by the courts of Great Session, the laws were not different. Only in the nineteenth century, barely half a century after the abolition of the Great Sessions in 1830, did laws begin to be made for Wales which did not apply in neighbouring England. The number of such laws however remained small when compared with those which were common to both countries. England and Wales was a single law district with a single law – the law of England and Wales, which was in reality English law.

Devolution has changed that situation significantly. The creation of the National Assembly for Wales and its subsequent acquisition of primary law-making powers has meant that there is now a growing number of differences between the laws which apply in Wales and those which apply in England. Although in the majority of cases, the laws of the two countries remain the same, there is an increasing divergence in the rules relating to those matters which have been devolved. In truth, there are now three bodies of law in England and Wales: one which applies only in Wales; a second which applies only in England, and a third which applies in both countries. Whenever the National Assembly legislates for Wales or the United Kingdom Parliament legislates only for England, the divergence increases. As that divergence increases, so does the importance that lawyers, law students and the public should be able to inform themselves of what the law is in Wales. People need to know the laws which govern their lives from the perspective of the society in which they live. In both countries, lawyers need to know what the law is on either side of the border

The temptation has been to present the law which applies in Wales in terms of the law which applies in England, while merely noting the differences. As divergence increases, that approach becomes not merely unhelpful from a Welsh perspective, but unacceptable. The purpose of this series therefore is to present to the professions and to the public an account of the law as it applies in Wales in the areas where there is now divergence, and in so doing to both redress the deficit and provide the foundation for a legal literature to serve the distinct needs of Wales.

Thomas Glyn Watkin

Contents

Series Preface v
Foreword xi
Preface xiii
Acknowledgements xix
Note on the Text xxi

List of UK Statutes xxiii
List of UK Statutory Instruments xxix
List of Acts of the National Assembly xxxv
List of Assembly Measures xxxv
List of Welsh Statutory Instruments xxxvi
List of Conventions xxxvi
List of European Treaties xxxvii
List of Cases xxxviii
Practice Directions, Notes and Statements lv

1 **Historical Introduction 1**
Introduction 1
Prehistory and the Romans 1
The Welsh Princes 3
After the Welsh Princes 7
The Legal Union of England and Wales 9
The Establishment of the Current Judicial System in England and Wales 11
Modern Development of Administrative Law and the Crown Office/Administrative Court Office 21
The European Element 23
The Road to Devolution 25
The Government of Wales Act 1998 26
The Government of Wales Act 2006 29
Conclusion 32
2 **The Administrative Court in Wales: Creation and Jurisdiction 33**
Introduction 33
Creating the Administrative Court in Wales 33
The Current Arrangement for the Administrative Court in Wales 38
The Jurisdiction of the Administrative Court in Wales 42
The Western Circuit 50
Conclusion 51

3 **Administrative Law** **53**
Introduction 53
Overview 54
Unlawfulness 57
Unreasonableness 71
Procedural Impropriety 77
Human Rights 84
Conclusion 95
4 **Public Law Defendants in Wales** **97**
Introduction 97
Public Bodies – Defendants in Administrative Court Cases 98
United Kingdom Government 101
The National Assembly for Wales 102
The Welsh Government and the Welsh Ministers 118
Local Government 122
Other Welsh Public Body Defendants 127
Conclusion 133
5 **Judicial Review** **135**
Introduction 135
Establishing the Parties 135
Pre-Action Considerations 138
Representation, Funding and Advice 147
An Overview of the Judicial Review Procedure 151
Lodging the Claim 151
Interim, Urgent, and Pre-Action Applications 154
The Acknowledgement of Service 160
Permission to Apply for Judicial Review 161
The Substantive Judicial Review 167
Remedies 172
The Role of the Upper Tribunal in Judicial Review Proceedings 182
The Planning Court 189
Conclusion 190
6 **Non-Judicial Review Administrative Court Procedures** **191**
Introduction 191
Pre-Action Conduct 191
Statutory Applications 192
General Statutory Appeals 197
Appeals By Way of Case Stated 202
Habeas Corpus 206
Committal for Contempt 211
Devolution Issues in Court Proceedings: Part 2 of Schedule 9 to the Government of Wales Act 2006 217
Conclusion 224

7 Consequential and Ancillary Orders in the Administrative Court 225

Introduction 225
Ending a Case 225
Costs 230
References to the Court of Justice of the European Union 247
Appeals 249
Enforcing After Non-Compliance with an Order of the Court 252
Conclusion 256

Annex A – Part 54 Civil Procedure Rules 257
Annex B – ACO Wales Listing Policy 277
Annex C – Contact Details 282
Annex D – Addresses for Service of Central Government Departments .. 285
Annex E – Judicial Review Checklist 287
Annex F – ACO Wales Statistics 288
Annex G – Pro Formas 291
Annex H – The Legal System of England and Wales 293

Bibliography 295
Index 303

Foreword

Judicial review, the mainstay work of the Administrative Court, derives from the ancient prerogative writs whereby citizens directly petitioned the monarch for relief against the acts done in the monarch's name. As a result, the jurisdiction of the court has historically been particularly metrocentric. Until very recently, all claims had to be brought, and heard, in London.

That has now changed. From 1999, claimants were able to issue claims in Cardiff – although they were still generally managed and heard in London. More fundamentally, in 2009, four out-of-London Administrative Court Offices were opened, where claims concerning the relevant circuits can be issued, managed and heard. Two Queen's Bench Division High Court Judges were appointed to administer this work, and, with other High Court Judges and Deputies, to hear it. Each of the English centres – in Birmingham, Manchester and Leeds – has, in its own way, been successful. About one-quarter of Administrative Court cases are now dealt with outside London. Many have a high level of local public interest, and these offices not only enable parties to have their cases managed and heard locally, but also enable all those with an interest in the case conveniently to attend hearings. This has been an important initiative in favour of access to justice.

The fourth office to open was that of the Administrative Court in Wales. However, whilst it too offers local access to justice, this office is in a somewhat different position to the regional offices in England. Devolution in Wales – a process which appears not yet to have run its full course – made it imperative that challenges to decisions of the Welsh Ministers and other devolved institutions could be made in Wales; hence, the setting up of the post box facility in 1999. From 2009, that became a fully fledged Administrative Court Office, with, in addition to staff, a dedicated High Court Liaison Judge. It is now inconceivable that the challenge to a Welsh decision, made in Wales by a Welsh institution and affecting the people of Wales, is heard anywhere but in Wales. Furthermore, although the court office is in Cardiff, in recognition of the geography of Wales, the Administrative Court in Wales sits throughout the country, in any court appropriate to the subject matter, North or South.

As with the Masters and lawyers who assist with the Administrative Court in London, each of the out-of-London centres has a dedicated lawyer, who is vital to the efficient working of the office. David Gardner has been the Administrative Court lawyer in Cardiff since the office opened. The judges and users of the centres outside London owe him – and his colleagues in the English regional offices – a substantial debt for their contribution to the success of the initiative to enable public law work to be issued and heard outside London. David has a unique perspective of where the Administrative Court in Wales now stands – and how it has got there – as well as what the future might hold. This invaluable book covers past, present and future; and will be invaluable for all those who practise in public law in Wales, or who have an interest in it.

The Hon Mr Justice Hickinbottom
Former Queen's Bench Division Liaison Judge for Wales
October 2014

Preface

I had the honour of being present on 21 April 2009 when the architect of the decentralised Administrative Court, Sir Anthony May, attended Cardiff Civil Justice Centre and formally opened the Administrative Court in Wales. He told the story of his vision of the decentralised Courts which arose out of the recommendation in his Justice Outside London report.[1] In the tale Sir Anthony opened his diary in 2007, turned to 21 April 2009, and wrote that this was the date on which the out-of-London Courts would open. It represented for him an unshakable goal. It represented for Wales a step towards legal and judicial autonomy and a decentralised check on devolved powers.

Two years later, the Administrative Court sat in Cardiff Civil Justice Centre and heard the case of *R (Brynmawr Foundation School Governors)* v *Welsh Ministers*.[2] The claimants challenged the decision of the Welsh Ministers to enter into an arrangement with Blaenau Gwent County Borough Council, pursuant to s. 83(1)(a) of the Government of Wales Act 2006, under which the Council would exercise the function of consulting upon and making proposals about the provision of sixth-form education. The Council was restructuring sixth-form education in its area and wished to close the sixth-form at Brynmawr School. In that case, Mr Justice Beatson (as he then was) was called upon to determine whether the Welsh Ministers were entitled to delegate their statutory power to consult upon and make proposals about the provision of sixth-form education to a Welsh local authority. It was a particularly Welsh issue that, on the one hand, dealt with the provision of education in Wales but, on the other, dealt with the limits of the statutory powers of the Welsh Government.

Five years after decentralisation a Divisional Court[3] sat in Cardiff Civil Justice Centre and heard the case of *R (Welsh Language Commissioner)* v *National Savings and Investments*.[4] As with the aforementioned *Brynmawr* case, this case embodied the need for an Administrative Court in Wales. In the claim the Welsh Language Commissioner, a Welsh public office based in Wales, challenged the decision of National Savings and Investments, a UK-wide public body, to withdraw its Welsh language scheme. These two public bodies had equally valid, yet competing interests. The Commissioner represented the distinctly Welsh goal of promoting the use of the Welsh language. NS&I represented a UK-wide goal of public bodies cutting

[1] Which is further discussed in chapter 2.

[2] [2011] EWHC 519 (Admin).

[3] One of many Divisional Courts that have sat in Wales.

[4] [2014] PTSR D8.

spending to aid the financial recovery of the UK. It was a case that had public policy implications that affected Welsh speakers, a big issue for a relatively small number of people.[5] It was also the first Administrative Court case to be conducted in both Welsh and English (at the speaker's preference);[6] a right held by Welsh speakers in Welsh Courts pursuant to s. 22 of the Welsh Language Act 1993.

These two cases are wonderfully illustrative of the need for an Administrative Court and an Administrative Court Office in Wales. The Court represents the ability to bring distinctly Welsh issues in a distinctly Welsh way to challenge the decisions of the Governments in Westminster and Cardiff, as well as other public bodies. It would be contrary to the principles behind the legislative and executive autonomy brought by the devolution settlement if these judicial checks were still conducted in London.

The Administrative Court in Wales also has the potential to be the focal point around which the local legal professions can develop an administrative law practice. In his address as part of the Cardiff Law School Public Lecture Series on 7 May 2009, Carwyn Jones outlined the potential that arises out of the Administrative Court in Wales:

> [T]here are wider benefits of the expansion of the Administrative Court office in Cardiff, such as encouraging the development of public law practices in Wales – something the Welsh Assembly Government is strongly in favour of.
>
> The enhancement of the Administrative Court in Wales and the growing body of law particular to Wales both create the need for a greater span of lawyers located in Wales, who understand the law as it applies in Wales, and have the knowledge and experience to take on the most complex and sensitive of cases ... [W]hat this means is great opportunities for lawyers in Wales – a devolution dividend for the legal professions. I know that changes are happening. We are now seeing the establishment of specialist criminal and civil chambers in Cardiff. However, we need more advocates who are prepared to branch out into areas such as administrative and employment law. I very much hope that the legal professions in Wales will demonstrate that they have the ambition and the will to broaden their horizons, and ensure that centres of legal expertise in a wide range of areas can be found here in Wales.
>
> We also need public bodies and local authorities in Wales to ask themselves why they are instructing counsel from outside Wales. If they are getting a better service elsewhere then we need to know so that the situation in Wales can be improved. Over the next ten years however, I would want to see advocates from

[5] In 2012 NS&I had 107 customers who corresponded with them in Welsh, representing 0.007% of the 1,549,577 customers who live in Wales, and only 0.06% of Welsh deposits.

[6] As well as counsel for the Commissioner speaking in Welsh at the hearing, the Commissioner's papers were written in Welsh.

> Wales getting the lion's share of the work. The challenge for the Bar particularly is to structure itself to compete for that work.[7]

Sadly a strong public law practice has not developed in Wales. The majority of the public law advocates in Wales travel out from chambers in London. In 2014 only 13 per cent of the advocates appearing in the Administrative Court in Wales came from chambers in Wales.[8] In his *Report: The Future of Legal Services in Wales*,[9] Professor Dermot Cahill analysed what can be done to encourage a stronger local legal profession. Two passages from his report are of particular interest:

> A new vision is needed, and Welsh Law Firms and Chambers need to adopt a longer term practice development view ... The Welsh Government can play its part by reviewing the appropriateness of the supports it currently has on offer for practice expansion and development. Existing supports are not meeting the development needs of Law Firms. Law Firms and Chambers should be looked on as a distinct [small- and medium-sized enterprises] sector, with supports tailored towards those seeking to develop high growth potential in new areas of practice. Tailored supports should be considered to help support sector growth. Supports should not remain confined to supporting indigenous firms, but should also seek to attract firms from outside Wales in order to foster innovation, competition and attract in seasoned practices with already-established client bases.[10]

> Much of the specialist public procurement Bar is currently situated in London. As public sector bodies are located throughout Wales, and given that Cardiff is now one of the Administrative Court Centres, this is a practice area ripe for development.[11]

The potential is there, the cases are there, but more encouragement is needed from Welsh public bodies, the profession itself, and those responsible for legal education in building a strong, local public law profession. Just as the Administrative Court in Wales is vital to the constitutional settlement in Wales, a strong legal profession is a vital component in maintaining a check on executive power in Wales.

Having outlined the importance of the Administrative Court in Wales I should like to say something about the importance of this book, and indeed the Public Law of Wales series. When I took on the role of the Administrative Court Office lawyer for Wales in 2009 I immediately looked for a text on the subject. Wales had enjoyed the benefits of devolution for around ten years and I reasoned that the law

[7] C. Jones, *Getting the Devolution Dividend: Legal Wales in the next ten years*, 7 May 2009, Cardiff Law School Public Lecture Series.

[8] Statistics provided by the Administrative Court Office in Wales.

[9] Professor Dermot Cahill, *Report: The Future of Legal Services in Wales*, 8 July 2013, Bangor University.

[10] Ibid, pp. 2–3.

[11] Ibid, p. 7.

of England and the law of Wales would have been slowly diverging. Thus, surely a text existed to guide me through the subtle differences between English and Welsh administrative law. I discovered that such a text did not exist. After three years in the role I had become acutely aware of two points. First, the administrative law of England and the administrative law of Wales were very similar, but not identical. Secondly, in the short time I had been in the role, there were more differences than when I started. The gap was widening. It occurred to me that if a book was to be written on administrative law in Wales, now was the time. I contacted the University of Wales Press and discovered, as seems to be the case with all good ideas, that someone had already had it. Sarah Lewis and Professor Thomas Watkin had also recognised this gap in the market and had resolved to create the Public Law of Wales series. To my good fortune, they invited me to write the inaugural text.

To my mind there was already a demand for a Public Law of Wales series and a text on Administrative Law in Wales. If we look to the future, the case is even stronger. At the Legal Wales Conference held in Cardiff on 7 October 2011 Carwyn Jones, announced that a Green Paper would be produced that would start the debate as to a separate legal jurisdiction for Wales. He pointed to the fact that whilst Wales has distinct Welsh law, the law of England and Wales still applies in Wales which, if nothing else, provides for complex questions over present jurisdiction. The Welsh Government Consultation, *A Separate Legal Jurisdiction for Wales*, was published on 27 March 2012. In its response to the twelve-week consultation in 2012, the Welsh government said no purpose would be usefully served in seeking immediate responsibility for the whole of administration of justice. In 2014, the Silk Commission agreed with the reasoning of the Welsh Government, but did not remove the idea of a separate legal jurisdiction from the agenda:

> We are not therefore convinced of the case for devolving the court system or creating a Welsh judiciary and legal profession at present. We also recognise that there seems from our opinion poll to be limited public appetite for devolution in this area. However, given the emergence of a distinct body of Welsh law that will need to be adequately administered, a separate Welsh courts system and a separate Welsh judiciary is something that must be contemplated in the future. We recommend that the two Governments review the case for this within the next ten years.[12]

The final sentence of the above quote can be seen as much a challenge as a recommendation. It may be that over the next ten years the people of Wales and the authorities in Wales decide that a separate legal jurisdiction is not warranted. If that is the case then the laws of Wales will continue to diverge as they are now. This book and the series it appears in will still be invaluable as an aid to practitioners and students in Wales. If, however, the people and the authorities in Wales truly

[12] Paragraph 10.3.36, *Empowerment and Responsibility: Legislative Powers to Strengthen Wales (The Second Report of the Silk Commission)*, March 2014 Commission on Devolution in Wales.

wish to take up 'the challenge' and a separate legal jurisdiction for Wales is to be a reality within ten years, the Government, the legal profession, and the universities in Wales must act now. The public authorities must show that they are capable of setting up and maintaining an infrastructure, the legal profession must show that it has the capability and breadth of experience to conduct legal proceedings, and the universities must show that they can train suitable lawyers for the future. In those circumstances, I hope the Public Law of Wales series, and from a personal perspective, this text, is received and utilised in the spirit of the challenge.

David C. Gardner
October 2015

Acknowledgements

Had I known, when I started writing this book, how long it would take or how many people would be of such assistance I would have allocated more than 500 words to this section. I apologise in advance to those I have forgotten. I have separated my acknowledgements into three sections: publishing, professional, and personal.

The publishing acknowledgements must start with my eternal gratitude to Professor Thomas Watkin. From his initial review of my proposal right through to publication he has been a constant source of encouragement as well as a sound guide and mentor. His intellect and eye for detail have properly steered me in the right direction, from correction of typos (some hilarious) to discussion of the niche details of the National Assembly's legislative process. Thomas, thank you. My thanks also to Tom Haworth (ACO lawyer, Birmingham), Ian Freer (UTIAC lawyer, London), the judges of the Administrative Court in Wales (you can find a list of them in chapter two), and Upper Tribunal Judge Edward Mitchell for comments on earlier drafts. Finally, thank you to all at the University of Wales Press for having the foresight to publish this series and for helping me through the publishing process.

My professional thanks must start with the Judges of the Administrative Court in Wales, as well as the two liaison Judges I have worked with, Mr Justice Beatson (now Lord Justice Beatson) and Mr Justice Hickinbottom. I can say without exception that our Judges possess the enviable combination of keen, quick, considered thought and an affable manner. We in the Administrative Court Office ("ACO") in Wales consider ourselves very lucky. I would also like to thank the ACO Wales managers I have had the pleasure of working with, Simon Jenkins, Becky Logar, and Beth Weaver. Each has brought his or her own style to the administration of the ACO and contributed much to its strategic direction. A book about Courts in Wales cannot fail but thank the infamous Annette Parsons. As diary manager for Wales she ensures that we have sufficient time in the lists for our cases to be heard expeditiously and efficiently, which maintains the good reputation the ACO in Wales has acquired. I would finally like to thank the ACO Wales caseworkers. There have been too many to mention them all, but thank you to each of you.

As for personal thanks, there could be many. First should be thanks to my mother and late father, Elaine and Chris, whose upbringing shaped three keen young minds in me, my brother Rich, and my sister Claire, to whom thanks are also due. No small part was also played by my grandparents, Harold, Sheila, Roma and Ron. Thanks to you all for all your help and support. As with the caseworkers, there are too many helpful and supportive (more often fun and distracting) friends to thank. You know who you are and my thanks to you. The biggest personal thank you, and the one with which I shall end, is for my wife, Re. Since I started writing this book in 2012 I have lost two close relatives, become a world record holder, had major knee surgery twice, and climbed Mount Fuji. I have been at my figurative lowest and literal highest. Re has been by my side for every moment. Her love and support never wavered and was a constant source of happiness, just as it has been since we started our relationship in our mid-teens. Thank you for everything.

David C. Gardner
October 2015

Note on the Text

The law in this text and annexes and any addresses mentioned in the text and annexes are accurate as far as I am aware, up to 1 October 2015 although some elements have been included to incorporate known future changes.

A number of public sector licensed sources are reproduced/referenced with permission under the Open Government License v.3.0. All judgments handed down after 1 January 2003 and quoted in this text are quoted from the judgments as they appear on *www.bailii.org*, despite the fact that the footnotes may not refer to the bailii neutral citation in accordance with Practice Direction – Citation of Authorities [2012] 2 All ER 255. Use is made of an extract from a publication by Cardiff University, quoted under fair dealing. Permission has been granted from the following publishers to quote extracts under fair dealing:

- Cambridge University Press;
- European Union Publishing Office: *http://eur-lex.europa.eu*, © European Union, 1998–2015;
- The Incorporated Council of Law Reporting;
- Legal Action Group;
- Lexis Nexis (All England Law Reports and Justice of the Peace Reports). Reproduced by permission of Reed Elsevier (UK) Limited, trading as LexisNexis;
- Reproduced by permission of Thomson Reuters (Professional) UK Limited: Administrative Law Reports, Administrative Court Digest, Crown Office Digest, Entertainment and Media Law Reports, European Human Rights Reports, European Law Review, Public Law (Nason, S., and Sunkin, M., The Regionalisation of Judicial Review: Constitutional Authority, Access to Justice and Specialisation of Legal Services in Public Law) © 2015 Thomson Reuters (Professional) UK Limited and contributors; and
- Wiley Publishing; © 2013 Nason, S., and Sunkin, M., The Modern Law Review © 2013 The Modern Law Review Limited (2013) 76(2) MLR 223–53.

List of UK Statutes

Abergavenny Improvement Act 1854 **3-4**
  28 **3-4**
The Act for Certain Ordinances in the King's Dominion and Principality of Wales of 1542/3 **1-17**
The Act for Law and Justice to be Ministered in Wales in like Form as it is in this Realm of 1535/6 **1-17**
Acquisition of Land Act 1981 **4-31**
  23(1) **4-31**
Administration of Justice Act 1960 **1-30, 7-33**
  1(2) **7-33**
  2(1) **7-33**
Administration of Justice Act 1969 **7-29**
  12 **7-29**
  13 **7-29**
  15 **7-29**
Administration of Justice Act 1970 **1-29**
Administration of Justice (Miscellaneous Provisions) Act 1938 **1-32**
Agricultural Wages Act 1948 **4-11**
Anti-terrorism, Crime and Security Act 2001 **5-53**
  23 **5-53**
Architects Act 1997 **6-6, 7-31**
  22 **6-6, 7-31**
  (7) **7-31**
Asylum and Immigration Act 1996 **5-63**
Asylum and Immigration Appeals Act 1993 **5-63**
Asylum and Immigration (Treatment of Claimants, etc.) Act 2004 **5-63**
Children Act 1989 **3-7**
  23(1) **3-7**
Chiropractors Act 1994 **6-6**
  31 **6-6**
Civil Procedure Act 1997 **5-36**
  Sch.1 para.2 **5-36**
Companies Act 2006 **5-2**
  16(2) **5-2**
Constitutional Reform Act 2005
  23(1) **1-31**
  38(1) **1-31**
  40(2) **1-31, 4-31**
    (5) **1-31**
  42(1) **1-31**
Contempt of Court Act 1981 **6-17, 6-20**
  16 **6-20, 7-38**
Coroners Act 1988 **6-3**
  13 **6-3**
County Courts Act 1846 **1-22**
County Courts Act 1984 **1-22**
  A1 **1-22**
  5 **1-22**
Courts Act 1971 **1-28**
Crime and Courts Act 2013 **1-22**
  17(1) **1-22**
    (3) **1-23**
Criminal Appeal Act 1968 **1-30**
Criminal Injuries Compensation Act 1995 **5-62**
  5(1) **5-62**
Criminal Justice Act 2003 **6-21**
  258 **6-21**
Criminal Justice and Courts Act 2015
  87(3) **7-17**
    (4) **7-17**
    (5) **7-17**
    (6) **7-17**
    (9) **7-17**
    (10) **7-17**

Criminal Justice and Courts Act 2015 (contd)
87(11) **7-17**
88(3) **7-21, 7-23**
(4) **7-21**
(6) **7-22**
(7) **7-22**
(8) **7-22**
89(1) **7-22**
(2) **7-22**
Criminal Procedure and Investigations Act 1996 **6-3**
54(3) **6-3**
Crown Proceedings Act 1947 **4-5, 5-30, 5-53, 5-59**
40 **5-59**

Dentists Act 1984 **6-6**
29 **6-6**
44 **6-6**
Enterprise and Regulatory Reform Act 2013 **4-11**
Environment Act 1995 **4-35**
65(5) **4-35**
66(1) **4-35**
Equality Act 2010 **3-10**
149 **3-10**
Sch.19, part 2 **3-10**
European Communities Act 1972 **1-35, 1-37**
1(2) **1-37**
3(1) **1-37**
Sch.1 Pt II **1-37**
Extradition Act 2003 **6-6**

Forestry Act 1967 **4-34**
46(1) **4-34**
(4C) **4-34**

Government of Wales Act 1998 **1-39**
22 **4-21**
(1) **1-39**
Sch.2 **1-39**

Government of Wales Act 2006 **1-41**
1(1) **1-41**
22 **1-44**
27(1) **1-44**
(5) **1-44**
41(1) **4-18**
(2), **4-19**
(3) **4-18**
(4) **4-19**
(5) **4-18, 4-19**
45(1) **1-44**
(2) **5-3**
48(1) **1-44**
51(1) **1-44, 4-20**
57(1) **4-26**
(4) **4-26**
58(1) **4-21**
(4) **4-21**
93(1) **1-41**
94 **1-41**
103(1) **1-42**
(8) **-1-42**
107 **1-42**
(1) **1-42**
(5) **4-7**
108 **1-42**
(1) **1-43, 4-7**
(2) **1-43, 4-7**
(4) **4-11, 4-12**
(4)(a) **4-7**
(4)(b) **4-7**
(5) **4-7, 4-12**
(6) **3-25, 4-12**
(6)(a) **4-7**
(6)(b) **4-7**
(6)(c) **4-7**
(7) **4-8, 4-11**
109(1) **4-7**
(4) **4-7**
110 **1-42**
112 **4-19**
(1) **4-9, 4-13, 4-14**
(2) **4-14**
(3) **4-14**

114 **4-19**
(1) **4-17**
(2) **4-17**
(3) **4-17**
(4) **4-17**
(5) **4-17**
(8) **4-17, 4-19**
115 **1-42**
(2) **4-14**
(3) **4-16**
154 **4-11**
(1) **4-8**
(2) **4-8, 4-10**
(3) **4-8**
161(5) **4-21**
162(1) **4-21**
Sch.2 **1-44**
Sch.3 **1-44, 4-21**
Sch.5 **1-41, 1-42**
Sch.7, Part 1 **1-43, 4-7, 4-8, 4-11**
Paragraph 9 **4-12**
Part 2
Paragraph 1 **4-2**
Paragraph 2 **4-2**
Paragraph 3 **4-7**
Paragraph 4 **4-7**
Paragraph 5 **4-7**
Part 3
Paragraph 6(1)(b) **4-10**
Sch.9 **6-22**
Paragraph 1 **5-30, 6-22**
Paragraph 2 **6-23**
Paragraph 5 **6-23**
Paragraph 6 **6-26**
Paragraph 7 **6-26**
Paragraph 8 **6-26**
Paragraph 9 **6-26**
Paragraph 10 **6-26**
Paragraph 11 **6-26, 7-36**
Sch.11
Paragraph 30 **4-21**

Human Rights Act 1998 **1-35**
2(1) **3-11, 3-30**
3(1) **3-11**
4 **5-52, 5-63**
(1) **5-52**
(2) **5-52**
(3) **5-52**
(4) **5-52**
(6) **5-52**
5(1) **5-53**
(2) **5-53**
6(1) **3-11, 3-25**
(3) **4-2**
8(1) **5-55**
21(1) **3-4**

Immigration Act 1971 **5-63**
Immigration Act 1988 **5-63**
Immigration Act 2014 **5-63**
Immigration and Asylum Act 1999 **5-63**
Immigration, Asylum and Nationality Act 2006 **5-63**
Interpretation Act 1978
5 **1-37**
21(1) **3-4**
Sch.1 **1-37, 5-62**

Judicature Acts 1873-5 **1-29**

Law Terms Act 1830 **1-18**
Legal Aid, Sentencing, and Punishment of Offenders **5-25**
14(a) **5-25**
(b) **5-25**
(c) **5-25**
(d) **5-25**
(e) **5-25**
(f) **5-25**
(g) **5-25**
16 **5-25**
19 **5-25**
Legal Services Act 2007 **5-26**
20 **5-26**
Sch.3
Paragraph 1(6) **5-26**

Legal Services Act 2007 (contd)
Sch.4
Paragraph 1 **5-26**
Local Government Act 1972 **4-27**, **4-28**, **4-30**
20 **4-27**
21 **4-27**
101(1) **4-29**
222 **5-2**
235(1) **4-30**
(2) **4-30**
236(4) **4-30**
(5) **4-30**
Sch.4 **4-27**
Local Government Act 1974 **4-28**
Local Government Act 2000 **4-28**, **4-29**, **4-33**
Part II **4-29**
11(3) **4-29**
(8) **4-29**
13 **4-29**
25 **4-29**
(1)(b) **4-29**
(2) **4-29**
(6)(a) **4-29**
26 **4-29**
27 **4-29**
38(1) **4-29**
48(6) **4-29**
68 **4-33**
69 **4-33**
70 **4-33**
71 **4-33**
72 **4-33**
73 **4-33**
74 **4-33**
79(15) **6-6**, **6-8**, **6-26**
(16) **6-6**
Local Government Act 2003
87(2) **3-4**
Local Government Finance Act 1988 **4-28**
Local Government (Wales) Act 1994 **4-27**
58(2)(d) **3-4**
Magistrates' Courts Act 1980 **6-11**
111(1) **6-11**
(2) **6-11**
113(1) **6-11**
114 **6-12**
Matrimonial and Family Proceedings Act 1984 **1-23**
31A **1-23**
31C **1-23**
31E(1)(a) **1-23**
Medical Act 1983
40 **6-6**, **6-8**
(5) **6-3**
41A(6) **6-3**
(14) **6-3**
Medicines Act 1968 **6-6**
82(3) **6-6**
83(2) **6-6**
Mental Capacity Act 2005 **6-15**
2 **6-15**
3 **6-15**
Mental Health Act 1983 **6-3**
Part II **6-3**
29 **6-3**

National Health Service (Wales) Act 2006 **3-24**
183(1) **3-24**
National Parks and Access to the Countryside Act 1949 **4-35**
4A(1), **4-35**
(2) **4-35**
5(1) **4-35**
(3) **4-35**
7(1) **4-35**
11A(1) **4-35**
(2) **4-35**
21 **3-9**
Nationality, Immigration and Asylum Act 2002 **5-63**
Nurses, Midwives and Health Visitors Act 1997 **6-6**
12 **6-6**

Opticians Act 1989 **6-6**
  23 **6-6**
Osteopaths Act 1993 **6-6**
  31 **6-6**

Pharmacy Act 1954 **6-6**
  10 **6-6**
Planning and Compulsory Purchase Act 2004
  113 **6-3**
Planning (Consequential Provisions) Act 1990 **4-35**, **5-20**
Planning (Hazardous Substances) Act 1990 **4-35**, **5-20**
  22 **6-3**
Planning (Listed Buildings and Conservation Areas) Act 1990 **4-35**, **5-20**
  63 **6-3**
  65(5) **6-6**
Proceeds of Crime Act 2002 **6-3**
Prevention of Terrorism Act 2005 **6-3**
Public Health Act 1875 **3-9**
  164 **3-9**
Public Services Ombudsman (Wales) Act 2005 **4-33**
  7(1)(a) **4-33**
    (b) **4-33**
    (c) **4-33**
  11(2) **4-33**
  28(2) **4-33**
  Sch.3 **4-33**

Rehabilitation of Offenders Act 1974 **5-53**
Road Traffic Regulation Act 1984 **3-5**, **4-31**
  Sch.9 **4-31**, **6-5**
    Paragraph 34 **4-31**
    Paragraph 35 **4-31**
    Paragraph 36 **4-31**
    Paragraph 37 **4-31**

Scotland Act 1998 **4-19**
  40 **4-19**
Senior Courts Act 1981
  1 **1-28**, **5-13**
  5(1) **1-29**
  9 **1-29**, **2-9**, **5-39**
  15(2) **1-30**
  16(1) **4-31**
  18(1)(a) **7-33**, **7-34**
  19(2) **1-29**
  28 **6-11**
    (2)(a) **4-2**
  28A(3) **6-13**
  29(3) **1-28**, **5-13**
  30(1) **5-54**
  31 **1-32**
    (1) **5-7**, **5-47**
    (2), **5-52**, **5-54**
    (2A) **5-57**
    (2B) **5-57**
    (3) **5-10**, **5-29**, **5-30**
    (3C) **5-39**
    (3E) **5-39**
    (3F) **5-39**
    (4) **5-47**, **5-55**
    (5)(a) **5-49**
    (5)(b) **5-49**
    (5A) **5-49**
    (6) **5-58**
    (6)(a) **5-20**
  31A **5-61**
  42 **6-3**
  46(1) **1-28**, **5-13**
  51(1) **6-5**, **6-10**, **7-08**, **7-18**
    (3) **7-18**
  53(1) **1-30**
    (2) **1-30**
    (3) **1-30**
  66 **1-29**, **2-9**, **5-41**
  81(1)(e) **6-11**
  Sch.1 **1-29**
Statutory Instruments Act 1946 **3-5**
  1 **3-5**
  1A **3-5**

Sunday Closing (Wales) Act 1881
1-19
Supreme Court of Judicature Act 1873
1-30

Town and Country Planning Act 1990
4A(2) **4-35**
58(1)(b) **4-31**
78 **4-31**
287 **6-3**
288 **4-24, 4-31, 6-3, 6-5**
(4A) **6-5**
289 **6-8, 7-31**
(6) **6-6, 6-9**
336 **4-35, 5-20**
Tribunals Courts and Enforcement Act 2007
3(5) **1-20**
5 **5-61**
6 **5-61**
11(2) **1-26**
(5) **5-62**
13(1) **1-26**
(8) **1-26**
15(1) **5-61**
(3) **5-61**
(4) **5-61**
(5) **5-61**
16(6) **5-61**
18(6) **5-62**

UK Borders Act 2007 **5-63**
61 **5-63**

Wales Act 2014
4(1) **1-44, 4-20**
Welsh Intermediate Education Act 1889 **1-19**
Welsh Language Act 1993 **2-5, 5-15, 5-45**
22 **2-5, 5-15, 5-45**
Wildlife and Countryside Act 1981
4-31, 6-5
Sch.15, Paragraph 12 **4-31, 6-5**

List of UK Statutory Instruments

Administrative Justice and Tribunals Council (Listed Tribunals) (Wales) Order 2007 **1-27**
Civil Legal Aid (Financial Resources and Payment for Services) Regulations 2013 **5-24**
Civil Legal Aid (Merits Criteria) Regulations 2013 **5-24**
Civil Procedure Rules 1998
1.1(1) **6-18**
2.8(3) **5-41**
2.11 **5-18, 7-11**
3.1(2) **5-41**
(a) **5-20, 5-37**
3.7(1)(d) **5-41**
(2) **5-41**
(3) **5-41**
(4) **5-41**
6.14 **5-40**
6.17(2)(a) **5-30**
8.2 **6-5**
8.3 **6-5**
8.5 **6-5**
19.4A **5-53**
(1) **5-53**
(2) **5-53**
19.6(1) **5-2**
(4)(b) **5-2**
21.1(2)(c) **6-15**
(2)(d) **6-15**
22 **6-5**
23.3(1) **5-32**
23.4(1) **5-32**
23.8
25.2(2)(b) **5-32, 5-34**
(3) **5-32**
25.3(2) **5-32**
(3) **5-32**
31.12(1) **5-16**
38.2(1) **7-04**
(2)(i) **7-04**
(2)(ii) **7-04**
(3) **7-04**
38.5(1) **7-04**
38.6(1) **7-04**
39.2 **5-44, 6-20**
(1) **5-44**
(3) **5-44**
(4) **5-44**
39.6(2) **5-26**
40.6(7)(b) **7-05**
(7)(c) **7-05**
40.20 **5-52**
44.2(1) **7-08**
(2)(a) **7-09**
44.3(1) **7-10**
(2) **7-10**
(2)(a) **7-04**
(3) **7-10**
(4)(a) **7-10**
(5) **7-10**
44.4(1) **7-10**
(2) **7-10**
(3) **7-10**
44.6(1) **7-11**
44.7(1)(a) **7-11**
44.9(1)(c) **7-04**
44.10(1)(a)(i) **7-13**
(2) **7-13**
(3) **7-13**
45.43(1) **7-25**
45.44 **7-25**
46.15(2) **7-17**
47
52.3(1)(a)(i) **7-35**
(1)(a)(ii) **7-34**
(2)(a) **7-29**
(3) **7-29**
52.4(2)(b) **6-7, 7-29**

Civil Procedure Rules 1998 (contd)
52.5(4)(b) **6-7**
52.10(2) **6-10**
52.11(2) **6-10**
(3) **6-8**
(3)(a)
52.15(1A) **7-29**
(2) **7-29**
54.1(2)(a)(ii) **4-2**
(2)(f) **5-4**
54.1A **2-18, 5-36**
(1) **5-36, 5-61**
(5) **5-36**
(6) **5-36**
(7) **5-36**
54.2 **5-30**
(a) **5-47**
(b) **5-47**
(c) **5-47**
54.3 **5-30**
(1)(a) **5-47**
(1)(b) **5-47**
(2) **5-47, 5-55**
54.4 **5-29, 5-30**
54.5(1) **5-14, 5-20, 5-61**
(1)(a) **5-17**
(1)(b) **5-17**
(2) **5-18**
(5) **5-20**
(6) **5-20**
54.6 **5-61**
(1)(b) **5-30**
(1)(c) **5-30**
54.7 **5-30, 5-61**
(b) **5-4**
54.7A **5-64**
(2) **5-64**
(3) **5-20, 5-64**
(7) **5-64**
(8) **5-64**
(9) **5-64**
54.8(2) **5-37, 5-61**
(2)(a) **5-37**
(3) **5-37**
(4)(a)(i) **5-37**
(4)(a)(ia) **5-37**
(4)(a)(ii) **5-37**
(4)(b) **5-37**
54.9(1)(a) **5-37**
(2) **5-37**
54.10(1) **5-41**
(2)(a) **5-41**
(2)(b) **5-41**
54.11A **5-39**
54.12(2) **5-39**
(3) **5-39, 5-61, 5-64**
(4) **5-40, 5-61**
(5) **5-40**
(7) **5-39, 5-61**
54.13 **5-39**
54.14(1) **5-41, 5-61**
54.15 **5-41**
54.16(2) **5-41**
54.17 **7-17**
(1) **5-5**
(2) **5-5**
54.18 **5-44**
54.19(2)(a) **5-49**
(2)(b) **5-49**
54.20 **5-55**
54.21(2) **5-65**
54.22(1) **5-65**
(2) **5-65**
(3) **5-65**
66 **4-5, 5-53**
68.2 **7-27**
68.3(1) **7-27**
(3) **7-27**
68.4 **7-27**
76.18 **6-3**
81.2(1) **6-17**
81.4(1) **7-37**
(3) **7-41**
81.5(1) **7-39**
81.6 **7-39**
81.8(1) **7-39**
(2) **7-39**
81.9(1) **7-41**

81.10(1) **7-42**
(3)(a) **7-42**
(3)(b) **7-42**
(4) **7-42**
(5) **7-42**
81.12(1) **6-17**
(2) **6-17**
(3) **6-18**
81.13(1) **6-17**
(2) **6-17**
81.14 **6-18**
(1) **6-18**
(2) **6-18**
(3) **6-18**
(4) **6-18**
(5) **6-18**
81.17(5) **6-17**
81.28 **6-19**, **7-44**
(1) **6-19**
(2) **6-19**
(3) **6-19**
(4) **6-19**
(5) **6-20**
81.29(1) **6-20**
81.30(2) **6-20**
(3) **6-20**
81.31(1) **6-21**
(2) **6-21**
87.2(1)(a) **6-14**
(1)(b) **6-14**
(2) **6-14**
(3) **6-14**
(4) **6-14**
(5) **6-14**
(6) **6-14**
87.3(1) **6-15**
(2)(a) **6-15**
(2)(b) **6-15**
87.4(1) **6-15**
(2) **6-15**
(3) **6-15**
(4) **6-15**
87.5 **6-15**
(g) **6-15**
87.7 **6-15**
87.8(1) **6-16**
(2) **6-16**
87.9(1) **6-16**
(2) **6-16**
87.10(1) **6-16**
87.11(a) **6-16**
87.12 **6-14**
Practice Direction 2A, Paragraph 2.1 **5-33**
Practice Direction 4 **6-14**, **6-16**
Practice Direction 7A **1-22**
Paragraph 2.4A(1) **1-22**
Paragraph 4A.1 **1-22**
Practice Direction 7C **1-22**
Practice Direction 8A
Paragraph 9.4 **6-3**
Paragraph 16.1 **6-3**
Paragraph 19.1 **6-3**
Paragraph 22 **6-5**, **7-30**
22.3 **6-5**
22.8 **6-5**
22.9 **6-5**
22.10 **6-5**
Practice Direction 8C **6-3**, **7-30**
Practice Direction 16 **5-53**
Paragraph 15.1(2)(a) **5-53**
(c)(i) **5-53**
(d) **5-53**
Practice Direction 19A **5-53**
Paragraph 6.1 **5-53**
6.4(1) **5-53**
6.4(2) **5-53**
6.4(3) **5-53**
6.4(4) **5-53**
6.5 **5-53**
Practice Direction 23A, Paragraph 2.1 **5-32**
Practice Direction 39A
Paragraph 5.2 **5-26**
5.3 **5-26**
Practice Direction 40E **5-46**
Paragraph 2.3 **5-46**
2.8 **5-46**

Civil Procedure Rules 1998 (contd)
Practice Direction 40E **5-46**
Paragraph 3.1 **5-46**
4.1 **5-46**
4.2 **5-46**
5.1 **5-46**
Practice Direction 44
Paragraph 8.2 **7-11**
9.5 **7-11**
9.5(4)(b) **7-11**
9.9 **7-11**
Practice Direction 45, Paragraph 5.1 **7-25**
Practice Direction 52A
Paragraph 3.5 **1-22**
6.1 **7-04**
6.2 **7-04**
6.3 **7-04**
Practice Direction 52D
Paragraph 3.4(1) **6-7**
3.5 **6-7**
4.1 **6-6**
19.1 **6-6**
21.1 **6-6**
26.1 **6-6**
27.1 **6-6**
27A.1 **6-6**
Practice Direction 52E, Paragraph 3 **6-11**
Practice Direction 54A **5-53**
Paragraph 5.1 **5-4, 5-30**
5.4 **5-30**
5.5 **5-30**
5.6 **5-30**
5.7 **5-30**
5.9 **5-30, 5-61**
6.1 **5-30**
6.2(b) **5-30**
8.2 **5-53**
8.5 **5-40**
15.1 **5-41, 5-61**
15.2 **5-61**
15.3 **5-41, 5-42, 5-61**
16.1 **5-41, 5-61**
16.2 **5-41, 5-61**
Practice Direction 54D
Paragraph 2.1 **2-11**
3.1 **2-12, 5-3**
3.1(1) **6-3**
3.1(2) **6-3**
3.1(3) **6-3**
3.1(4) **6-6**
3.1(5) **2-12, 6-3**
3.1(6) **2-12, 6-6**
3.2 **2-12**
4.1 **2-13**
4.2 **2-13, 5-33**
5.2 **2-11, 2-18**
5.4 **2-18**
Practice Direction 54E:
Paragraph 3.1 **5-65**
Practice Direction 68 **7-27**
Practice Direction 81
Paragraph 1 **7-40**
5.2 **6-18**
9 **6-19**
11(2) **6-18**
11(3) **6-18**
12(4) **6-18**
13.1 **7-42**
13.2(2) **7-42**
13.2(3) **7-43**
13.2(4) **7-43**
15.1 **7-43**
15.2 **6-18**
15.4 **6-19**
16.1 **6-17**
16.2 **6-17, 6-18, 7-42**
16.3 **6-17**

Civil Procedure (Amendment No. 3) Rules 2014/610 **5-65**
Civil Procedure (Amendment No. 4) Rules (SI/2000/2092) **1-34, 2-3**
Civil Procedure (Amendment No. 8) Rules 2014 **6-14**

2(c) **6-14**
15 **6-14**
Sch.2 **6-14**
Council Tax (Alteration of Lists and Appeals) Regulations 1993
32(1) **4-31**
Criminal Legal Aid (Determinations by a Court and Choice of Representative) Regulations 2013 **5-25**
7(1) **5-25**
Criminal Legal Aid (General) Regulations 2013 **5-25**
20(2)(a) **5-25**
21(b) **5-25**
Criminal Procedure Rules 2015 **3-21**, **6-11**
35 **6-11**
35.2(1)(a) **6-11**
(2) **6-11**
(2)(b) **6-11**
35.3 **6-12**
Crown Court Rules 1982 **6-11**
26 **6-11**
(1) **6-11**
(11) **6-12**

Equality Act 2010 (Statutory Duties) (Wales) Regulations 2011
3(1) **3-10**

Family Court (Composition and Distribution of Business) Rules 2014 **1-23**
Sch.1 **1-23**
First-tier Tribunal and Upper Tribunal (Chambers) Order 2008 **1-25**
2 **1-25**
6 **1-26**

General Teaching Council for Wales (Disciplinary Functions) Regulations 2001 **6-6**
24 **6-6**

Health Professions Order 2001 **6-6**
38 **6-6**
High Court (Distribution of Business) Order 2014 **6-14**
3 **6-14**
Higher Rights of Audience Regulations 2000 **5-26**
Human Rights Act 1998 (Commencement No. 2) Order (SI/2000/1851)
2 **3-25**

Magistrates' Courts Rules 1981 **6-11**
76 **6-11**
77 **6-11**
78 **6-11**
79 **6-11**
80 **6-11**
81 **6-11**

National Assembly for Wales (Transfer of Functions) Order 1999 **1-39**, **4-21**
Sch.2 **1-39**
National Park Authorities (Wales) Order 1995 **4-35**
3 **4-35**
4 **4-35**
Sch.1 **4-35**
Nursing and Midwifery Order 2001 **6-6**
38 **6-6**

Pharmacy Order 2010 **6-6**
58 **6-6**
Public Bodies (Abolition of Administrative Justice and Tribunals Council) Order 2013 **1-27**
Public Contracts Regulations 2015
92(2) **5-20**

Rehabilitation of Offenders Act 1974 (Exceptions) Order 1975 **5-53**

Rules of the Supreme Court Order 1981 ("RSC Ord")
53 **1-32**
54 **6-14**
115 **6-3**
Rules of the Supreme Court (Amendment No.3) 1977 **1-32**

Supreme Court Rules 2009 **4-13**
3(2) **4-15**
41 **4-15**
(1) **4-15**
(2) **4-15**
(3) **4-15**
(4) **4-15**
Practice Direction 10 - Devolution Jurisdiction **4-13**
Paragraph 10.2.2 **4-15**
10.2.3 **4-15**
10.2.4 **4-15**
10.2.5 **4-15**
10.2.6 **4-15**

Town and Country Planning (Development Management Procedure) (Wales) Order 2012 **3-21**
Town and Country Planning (Environmental Impact Assessment) (England and Wales) Regulations 1999
3(2) **3-12**
Tribunal Procedure (Upper Tribunal) Rules 2008
4(1) **5-61**, **7-06**
(3) **5-61**
10(5) **7-06**
(6) **7-06**
(7)(a) **7-06**
17(1) **7-06**
(1)(a) **7-06**
(2) **7-06**
(3) **7-06**
(4) **7-06**
(5) **7-06**
22 **3-23**
28(2) **5-61**
(4) **5-61**
(5) **5-61**
(6) **5-61**
28A(2) **5-61**
29(1) **5-61**
30 **3-23**
(3) **5-61**
(4) **5-61**
(4A) **5-61**
(5) **5-61**
31(2) **5-61**
39(1) **7-05**
40 **3-23**

Welsh Ministers (Transfer of Functions) Order 2008 **4-21**

List of Acts of the National Assembly

Local Government Bye Laws (Wales) Act 2012 **4-10, 4-30**
- 6 **4-10, 4-30**
- 7(11) (a) **4-30**
- 8 **4-30**
- 9 **4-10**
- Sch.1
  - Part 1 **4-30**

List of Assembly Measures

Housing (Wales) Measure 2011 **3-4**
- 5(3) **3-4**
  - (a) **3-4**
  - (b) **3-4**

Welsh Language (Wales) Measure 2011 **6-6**
- 59 **6-6**

List of Welsh Statutory Instruments

Animal Welfare (Electronic Collars) (Wales) Regulations 2010 **4-25**

Natural Resources Body for Wales (Establishment) Order 2012 **4-34**
- 3(1) **4-34**
- 4(1) **4-34**
- 5A(1) **4-34**
- 5B(1) **4-34**
- 5C(1) **4-34**
- 5D(1) **4-34**
- 5E(1) **4-34**
- 10 **4-34**

Natural Resources Body for Wales (Functions) Order 2013 **4-34**

List of Conventions

Convention on Access to Information, Public Participation in Decision Making and Access To Justice in Environmental Matters ('the Aarhus Convention') **7-24**
- Article 2(3) **7-24**
- Article 9(3) **7-24**

Convention for the Protection of Human Rights and Fundamental Freedoms (European Convention on Human Rights) 1950 **1-36, 3-11, 3-25, 3-26**
- 1 **1-36**
- 2(1) **3-26**
- 2(2) **3-26**
- 3 **3-26**
- 4(1) **3-26**
- 4(2) **3-27**
- 4(3) **3-27**
- 5 **3-27, 5-53**
- 6(1) **3-27**
- 6(3) **3-27**
- 7 **3-26**
- 8 **3-28, 5-48**
- 9 **3-28**
- 10(1) **3-28**
- 10(2) **3-28**
- 11(1) **3-28**
- 11(2) **3-28**
- 12 **3-27**
- 14 **3-28, 5-53**
- 34 **1-36**
- *FIRST PROTOCOL*
- 1 **3-28, 4-12, 4-25**
- 2 **3-27**
- 3 **3-28**

List of European Treaties

Treaty of Lisbon amending the Treaty on European Union and the Treaty establishing the European Community, signed at Lisbon, 13 December 2007 **1-37**

Treaty on the Functioning of the European Union (Treaty of Rome), 1957 – Formerly known as Treaty Establishing the European Community **1-37**

5 **3-19**

10(5) **1-37**, **3-12**

226 **1-37**

227 **1-37**

267 **7-27**

Treaty on European Union 1992 (The Maastricht Treaty) **1-37**

List of Cases

A v Secretary of State for the Home Department [2004] UKHL 56; [2005] 2 A.C. 68; [2005] 2 W.L.R. 87; [2005] 3 All E.R. 169; [2005] H.R.L.R. 1; [2005] U.K.H.R.R. 175; 17 B.H.R.C. 496; [2005] Imm. A.R. 103; (2005) 155 N.L.J. 23; (2005) 149 S.J.L.B. 28; Times, December 17, 2004; Independent, December 21, 2004 **5-53**

Abraham v Jutsun [1963] 1 W.L.R. 658; [1963] 2 All E.R. 402; (1963) 107 S.J. 357 **3-16**

Adesina v Nursing and Midwifery Council [2013] EWCA Civ 818; [2013] 1 W.L.R. 3156; (2013) 133 B.M.L.R. 196; Times, July 22, 2013 **6-4**

Al-Rawi v Security Service [2011] UKSC 34; [2012] 1 A.C. 531; [2011] 3 W.L.R. 388; [2012] 1 All E.R. 1; [2011] U.K.H.R.R. 931; (2011) 108(30) L.S.G. 23; (2011) 155(28) S.J.L.B. 31; Times, July 15, 2011 **3-16**

Ali v United Kingdom [2011] 53 E.H.R.R. 12; 30 B.H.R.C. 44; [2011] E.L.R. 85 **3-27**

American Cyanamid Company v Ethicon Limited [1975] A.C. 396; [1975] 2 W.L.R. 316; [1975] 1 All E.R. 504; [1975] F.S.R. 101; [1975] R.P.C. 513; (1975) 119 S.J. 136 **5-31**

Anisminic Ltd v Foreign Compensation Commission (No2) [1969] 2 A.C. 147; [1969] 2 W.L.R. 163; [1969] 1 All E.R. 208, H.L.(E.)..**3-3**

Argos Ltd v Office Fair Trading [2006] EWCA Civ 1318; [2006] U.K.C.L.R. 1135; (2006) 103(42) L.S.G. 32; (2006) 150 S.J.L.B. 1391 **3-6**

Associated Provincial Picture Houses Ltd. v. Wednesbury Corporation [1948] 1 K.B. 22; [1947] 2 All E.R. 680; (1947) 63 T.L.R. 623; (1948) 112 J.P. 55; 45 L.G.R. 635; [1948] L.J.R. 190; (1947) 177 L.T. 641; (1948) 92 S.J. 26 **3-17**

Aston Cantlow and Wilmcote with Billesley Parochial Church Council v Wallbank [2003] UKHL 37; [2004] 1 A.C. 546; [2003] 3 W.L.R. 283; [2003] 3 All E.R. 1213; [2003] H.R.L.R. 28; [2003] U.K.H.R.R. 919; [2003] 27 E.G. 137 (C.S.); (2003) 100(33) L.S.G. 28; (2003) 153 N.L.J. 1030; (2003) 147 S.J.L.B. 812; [2003] N.P.C. 80; Times, June 27, 2003 **4-2**

AXA General Insurance Ltd v Lord Advocate [2011] UKSC 46; [2012] 1 A.C. 868; [2011] 3 W.L.R. 871; 2012 S.C. (U.K.S.C.) 122; 2011 S.L.T. 1061; [2012] H.R.L.R. 3; [2011] U.K.H.R.R. 1221; (2011) 122 B.M.L.R. 149; (2011) 108(41) L.S.G. 22; Times, October 19, 2011 **4-18**

Azzam v General Medical Council [2008] EWHC 2711 (Admin); [2009] LS Law Medical 28; (2009) 105 B.M.L.R. 142 **6-8**

B v W [1979] 1 W.L.R. 1041; [1979] 3 All E.R. 83; (1979) 123 S.J. 536 **3-16**

Berry Piling Systems Limited v. Sheer Projects Limited [2013] EWHC 347 (TCC); [2013] B.L.R. 232; [2013]

T.C.L.R. 4; 147 Con. L.R. 215; [2013] C.I.L.L. 3324 **6-18**

Boddington v British Transport Police [1999] 2 A.C. 143, HL; [1998] 2 All ER 203, [1999]162 JP 455 **3-3**

Boland v Welsh Ministers [2011] EWHC 629 (Admin) **4-31**

Brecon Beacons National Park Authority v National Assembly for Wales [2010] EWHC 3780 (Admin) **3-18**

British Oxygen Co. Ltd. v Minster of Technology [1971] A.C. 610; [1969] 2 W.L.R. 892; [1970] 3 W.L.R. 488; [1970] 3 All E.R. 165 **3-22**

Cala Homes (South) Limited v Chichester District Council [2000] C.P. Rep. 28; (2000) 79 P. & C.R. 430; [1999] 4 P.L.R. 77; [2000] P.L.C.R. 205; (1999) 96(33) L.S.G. 33; Times, October 15, 1999 **6-1**

Campbell and Cosans v United Kingdom [1982] 4 E.H.R.R. 293 **3-28**

Chahal v United Kingdom (22414/93) [1997] 23 E.H.R.R. 413; 1 B.H.R.C. 405; Times, November 28, 1996; Independent, November 20, 1996 **3-26**

Cheatle v General Medical Council [2009] EWHC 645 (Admin); [2009] LS Law Medical 299 **6-8**

Council of Civil Service Unions v. Minister for the Civil Service [1985] A.C. 374; [1984] 3 W.L.R. 1174; [1984] 3 All E.R. 935, H.L.(E.) **3-2, 3-3, 3-17, 3-20, 3-21, 3-25**

Daniels v Monmouth School [2009] EWHC 2720 (Admin) **4-31**

Daniels v Nursing and Midwifery Council [2015] EWCA Civ 225; [2015] Med. L.R. 255 **6-4**

Devine v Welsh Ministers [2011] EWCA Civ 1328 **4-31, 6-5**

Devine v Welsh Ministers [2011] EWHC 358 (Admin) **4-31, 6-5**

Devon County Council v Secretary of State for Communities and Local Government [2010] EWHC 1456 (Admin); [2011] B.L.G.R. 64; [2010] A.C.D. 83 **3-24**

Director General of Fair Trading v Proprietary Association of Great Britain [2001] 1 WLR 700 (CA); [2001] U.K.C.L.R. 550; [2001] I.C.R. 564; [2001] H.R.L.R. 17; [2001] U.K.H.R.R. 429; (2001) 3 L.G.L.R. 32; (2001) 98(7) L.S.G. 40; (2001) 151 N.L.J. 17; (2001) 145 S.J.L.B. 29; Times, February 2, 2001; Independent, January 12, 2001 **3-15**

Dudgeon v United Kingdom [1982] 4 E.H.R.R. 149 **3-29**

E v Secretary of State for the Home Department [2004] EWCA Civ 49; [2004] Q.B. 1044; [2004] 2 W.L.R. 1351; [2004] I.N.L.R. 268; [2004] B.L.G.R. 463; (2004) 101(7) L.S.G. 35; (2004) 148 S.J.L.B. 180; Times, February 9, 2004; Independent, February 4, 2004 **3-2**

Eckle v Federal Republic of Germany (1983) 5 E.H.R.R. 1 **3-27**

Emezie v The Secretary of State for the Home Department [2013] EWCA Civ 733, (2013) 157(26) S.J.L.B. 27 **7-09**

First Secretary of State v Sainsbury's Supermarkets Ltd [2005] EWCA Civ 520; [2005] N.P.C. 60 **3-6**

Gard v Commissioners of Sewers for the City of London [1885] 28 Ch.D. 486 **3-14**

Goodwin v United Kingdom [2002] I.R.L.R. 664; [2002] 2 F.L.R. 487; [2002] 2 F.C 577; (2002) 35 E.H.R.R. 18; 13 B.H.R.C. 120;

(2002) 67 B.M.L.R. 199; [2002] Fam. Law 738; (2002) 152 N.L.J. 1171; Times, July 12, 2002 **3-27**

Grainger plc v Nicholson [2010] 2 All E.R. 253; [2010] I.C.R. 360; [2010] I.R.L.R. 4; (2009) 159 N.L.J. 1582; Times, November 11, 2009 **3-28**

Hamer v United Kingdom [1982] 4 E.H.R.R. 139 **3-27**

Handyside v United Kingdom [1979-80] 1 E.H.R.R. 737 **3-29**

Hatton v United Kingdom [2002] 1 F.C.R. 732; (2002) 34 E.H.R.R. 1; 11 B.H.R.C. 634; Times, October 8, 2001 **3-28**

Hazell v Hammersmith and Fulham London Borough Council [1992] 2 A.C. 1; [1991] 2 W.L.R. 372; [1991] 1 All E.R. 545; 89 L.G.R. 271; (1991) 3 Admin. L.R. 549; [1991] R.V.R. 28; (1991) 155 J.P.N. 527; (1991) 155 L.G. Rev. 527; (1991) 88(8) L.S.G. 36; (1991) 141 N.L.J. 127; Times, January 25, 1991; Independent, January 25, 1991; Financial Times, January 29, 1991; Guardian, January 25, 1991; Daily Telegraph, February 4, 1991 **4-29**

Heesom v Public Services Ombudsman for Wales [2014] EWHC 1504 (Admin) **6-6, 6-28**

Hollis v Secretary of State for the Environment [1984] 47 P. & C.R. 351; [1983] 265 E.G. 476; [1983] J.P.L. 164 **3-2**

Horseferry Road Justices & Ors v The Lord Mayor and the Citizens of the City of Westminster [2003] EWCA Civ 1007; [2004] 1 W.L.R. 195; [2004] C.P. Rep. 1; (2003) 100(34) L.S.G. 31; (2003) 147 S.J.L.B. 817; Times, August 21, 2003; Independent, July 16, 2003 **7-32**

Huang v Secretary of State for the Home Department [2007] UKHL 11; [2007] 2 A.C. 167; [2007] 2 W.L.R. 581; [2007] 4 All E.R. 15; [2007] 1 F.L.R. 2021; [2007] H.R.L.R. 22; [2007] U.K.H.R.R. 759; 24 B.H.R.C. 74; [2007] Imm. A.R. 571; [2007] I.N.L.R. 314; [2007] Fam. Law 587; (2007) 151 S.J.L.B. 435; Times, March 22, 2007 **3-25**

Inland Revenue Commissioners v National Federation of Self-Employed and Small Businesses Ltd [1982] A.C. 617; [1981] 2 W.L.R. 722; [1981] 2 All E.R. 93; [1981] S.T.C. 260; 55 T.C. 133; (1981) 125 S.J. 325 **5-10**

Internationale Handelsgesellschaft mbH v Einfuhr- und Vorratsstelle fur Getreide und Futtermittel (Case 11/70) [1970] E.C.R. 1125; [1972] C.M.L.R. 255 **1-37, 3-12, 3-19**

James v The United Kingdom [1986] 8 E.H.R.R. 123; [1986] R.V.R. 139 **3-27, 3-28**

Jones v Director of Public Prosecutions [2011] EWHC 50 (Admin); (2011) 175 J.P. 129; [2012] R.T.R. 3 **2-14**

Kay v Lambeth London Borough Council [2006] UKHL 10; [2006] 2 A.C. 465; [2006] 2 W.L.R. 570; [2006] 4 All E.R. 128; [2006] 2 F.C.R. 20; [2006] H.R.L.R. 17; [2006] U.K.H.R.R. 640; 20 B.H.R.C. 33; [2006] H.L.R. 22; [2006] B.L.G.R. 323; [2006] 2 P. & C.R. 25; [2006] L. & T.R. 8; [2006] 11 E.G. 194 (C.S.); (2006) 150 S.J.L.B. 365; [2006] N.P.C. 29; Times, March 10, 2006; Independent, March 14, 2006 **5-9**

King's Lynn and West Norfolk BC v Bunning [2013] EWHC 3390 (QB); [2015] 1 W.L.R. 531; [2014] 2 All E.R. 1095; [2014] 1 Costs L.O. 85 **5-25**
Kirk v. Walton [2008] EWHC 1780 (QB); [2009] 1 All E.R. 257 **6-18**
KJM Superbikes Limited v. Hinton [2008] EWCA Civ 1280; [2009] 1 W.L.R. 2406; [2009] 3 All E.R. 76; [2009] C.I.L.L. 2645; (2008) 158 N.L.J. 1683 **6-18**
Laker Airways Inc v FLS Aerospace Ltd [2000] 1 W.L.R. 113; [1999] 2 Lloyd's Rep. 45; [1999] C.L.C. 1124; Times, May 21, 1999; Independent, May 24, 1999 **3-14**
Lautsi v Italy [2012] 54 E.H.R.R. 3; 30 B.H.R.C. 429; [2011] Eq. L.R. 633; [2011] E.L.R. 176 **3-28**
Lingens v Austria [1986] 8 E.H.R.R. 407 **3-28**
Lloyd v Jones [1769] 1 Dougl. 213, n. 10 **1-18**
Lloyd v McMahon [1987] A.C. 625; [1987] 2 W.L.R. 821; [1987] 1 All E.R. 1118; 85 L.G.R. 545; [1987] R.V.R. 58; (1987) 84 L.S.G. 1240; (1987) 137 N.L.J. 265; (1987) 131 S.J. 409 **3-21**
London & Henley (Middle Brook Street) Ltd v Secretary of State for Communities and Local Government [2013] EWHC 4207 (Admin) **5-65**
Maaouia v France (39652/98) [2001] 33 E.H.R.R. 42; 9 B.H.R.C. 205 **3-27**
M v M (Breaches of Orders: Committal) [2005] EWCA Civ 1722; [2006] 1 F.L.R. 1154; [2006] Fam. Law 259; Times, August 24, 2005 **7-35**
Mackman v Secretary of State for Communities and Local Government [2013] EWHC 4435 (Admin) **7-26**
Malgar Limited v. RE Leach (Engineering) Limited [2000] C.P. Rep. 39; [2000] F.S.R. 393; (2000) 23(1) I.P.D. 23007; Times, February 17, 2000 **6-18**
Marleasing SA v La Comercial Internacional de Alimentacion SA [1990] E.C.R. I-4135 **1-37**, **3-12**
McKenzie v McKenzie [1971] P. 33; [1970] 3 W.L.R. 472; [1970] 3 All E.R. 1034; (1970) 114 S.J. 667 **5-28**
Mucelli v Government of Albania [2009] UKHL 2; [2009] 1 W.L.R. 276; [2009] 3 All E.R. 1035; [2009] Extradition L.R. 122; (2009) 153(4) S.J.L.B. 28; Times, January 27, 2009 **6-4**
National Provincial Bank Ltd v Ainsworth [1965] A.C. 1175; [1965] 3 W.L.R. 1; [1965] 2 All E.R. 472; (1965) 109 S.J. 415 **3-28**
Newcombe v Crown Prosecution Service [2013] EWHC 2160 (Admin) **5-49**
Niemietz v Germany [1993] 16 E.H.R.R. 97 **3-28**
Office of Fair Trading v IBA Health Ltd [2004] All E.R. 1103, [2004] EWCA Civ 142 **3-4**
O'Reilly v. Mackman [1983] 2 A.C. 237, HL, [1982] 3 All ER 1124; [1982] 3 All ER 680, [1982] 3 All ER 680 **3-1**, **3-3**, **4-2**
Padfield v Minister for Agriculture, Fisheries and Food [1968] A.C. 997 **3-4**
Phillips v Symes [2003] EWCA Civ 1769; (2003) 147 S.J.L.B. 1431 **6-19**
Plattform 'Ärzte für das Leben' v Austria [1991] 13 E.H.R.R. 204; Times, June 30, 1988 **3-28**

Pomiechowski v Poland [2012] UKSC 20; [2012] 1 W.L.R. 1604; [2012] 4 All E.R. 667; [2012] H.R.L.R. 22; [2013] Crim. L.R. 147; (2012) 162 N.L.J. 749; Times, June 7, 2012 **6-4**

Porter v Magill [2001] UKHL 67; [2002] 2 A.C. 357; [2002] 2 W.L.R. 37; [2002] 1 All E.R. 465; [2002] H.R.L.R. 16; [2002] H.L.R. 16; [2002] B.L.G.R. 51; (2001) 151 N.L.J. 1886; [2001] N.P.C. 184; Times, December 14, 2001; Independent, February 4, 2002; Daily Telegraph, December 20, 2001 **3-15**

PR (Sri Lanka) v Secretary of State for the Home Department [2011] EWCA Civ 988; [2012] 1 W.L.R. 73; [2011] C.P. Rep. 47; [2011] Imm. A.R. 904; [2012] I.N.L.R. 92 **5-64**

Prashar v Secretary of State for the Environment, Transport and the Regions [2001] 3 PLR 116;[2001] 3 P.L.R. 116 **7-31**

Pretty v the United Kingdom [2002] 2 F.L.R. 45; [2002] 2 F.C.R. 97; (2002) 35 E.H.R.R. 1; 12 B.H.R.C. 149; (2002) 66 B.M.L.R. 147; [2002] Fam. Law 588; (2002) 152 N.L.J. 707 **3-28**

Public Services Ombudsman for Wales v Heesom [2015] EWHC 3306 (QB) **7-11**

R. v A [2001] UKHL 25; [2002] 1 A.C. 45; [2001] 2 W.L.R. 1546; [2001] 3 All E.R. 1; [2001] 2 Cr. App. R. 21; (2001) 165 J.P. 609; [2001] H.R.L.R. 48; [2001] U.K.H.R.R. 825; 11 B.H.R.C. 225; [2001] Crim. L.R. 908; (2001) 165 J.P.N. 750; Times, May 24, 2001; Independent, May 22, 2001; Daily Telegraph, May 29, 2001 **5-53**

R. v Advertising Standards Authority Ex p. Insurance Services (1990) 2 Admin. L.R. 77; (1990) 9 Tr. L.R. 169; [1990] C.O.D. 42; (1989) 133 S.J. 1545 **4-3**

R. v Athoe [1723] Strange 553 **1-18, 2-14**

R. v Birmingham City Council, Ex Parte Ferrero Ltd [1993] 1 All ER 530; [1991] 155 J.P. 721; 89 L.G.R. 977; (1991) 3 Admin. L.R. 613; (1991) 10 Tr. L.R. 129; [1991] C.O.D. 476; (1991) 155 J.P.N. 522; (1991) 155 L.G. Rev. 645; Times, May 30, 1991; Independent, May 24, 1991 **5-9**

R. v Birmingham Licensing Planning Committee Ex Parte Kennedy [1972] 2 Q.B. 140; [1972] 2 W.L.R. 939; [1972] 2 All E.R. 305 **3-14**

R v Brent LBC Ex parte Gunning (1985) 84 LGR **3-24**

R. v Chancellor of St. Edmundsbury and Ipswich Diocese. Ex Parte White [1948] 1 K.B. 195; [1947] 2 All E.R. 170; 63 T.L.R. 523; 177 L.T. 488; (1947) 91 S.J. 369 **1-20, 5-13**

R. v Commissioner for Administration, Ex Parte Turpin [2001] EWHC Admin 503; [2003] B.L.G.R. 133; [2002] J.P.L. 326; [2001] A.C.D. 90 **4-33**

R. v Cotswold District Council Ex Parte Barrington Parish Council [1998] 75 P. & C.R. 515; [1997] E.G. 66 (C.S.); [1997] N.P.C. 70; [1998] Env. L.R. D3 **5-17**

R. v Darlington BC Ex p. Association of Darlington Taxi Owners [1994] C.O.D. 424; Times, January 19,

1994; Independent, January 13, 1994 **5-2**

R. v Department of Transport Ex p. Presvac Engineering [1992] 4 Admin. L.R. 121; Times, July 10, 1991; Independent, June 26, 1991 **5-19**

R v Derbyshire County Council Ex Parte The Times Supplement Ltd [1991] 3 Admin. L.R. 241; [1991] C.O.D. 129; [1991] 155 L.G. Rev. 123; [1990] 140 N.L.J. 1421; Times, July 19, 1990 **3-14**

R. v Devon County Council, Ex Parte Baker [1995] 1 All E.R. 73; 91 L.G.R. 479; (1994) 6 Admin. L.R. 113; [1993] C.O.D. 253; Times, January 21, 1993; Independent, February 22, 1993 **3-20**, **3-24**

R. v. Disciplinary Committee of the Jockey Club, ex p Aga Khan [1993] 1 W.L.R. 909; [1993] 2 All E.R. 853; [1993] C.O.D. 234; (1993) 143 N.L.J. 163; Times, December 9, 1992; Independent, December 22, 1992 **4-2**, **4-3**

R. v Dudley Magistrates Court Ex p. Gillard [1986] A.C. 442; [1985] 3 W.L.R. 936; [1985] 3 All E.R. 634; (1986) 82 Cr. App. R. 186; (1986) 150 J.P. 45; [1986] Crim. L.R. 185 **5-50**

R. v East Berkshire Health Authority Ex Parte Walsh [1985] Q.B. 152; [1984] 3 W.L.R. 818; [1984] 3 All E.R. 425; [1984] I.C.R. 743; [1984] I.R.L.R. 278 **4-2**

R. v Epping and Harlow General Commissioners Ex p. Goldstraw [1983] 3 All E.R. 257; [1983] S.T.C. 697; 57 T.C. 536 **5-9**

R. v Falmouth and Truro Port HA Ex p. South West Water Ltd[2001] Q.B. 445; [2000] 3 W.L.R. 1464; [2000] 3 All E.R. 306; [2000] Env. L.R. 658; [2000] E.H.L.R. 306; (2000) 2 L.G.L.R. 1061; [2000] J.P.L. 1174 (Note); [2000] E.G. 50 (C.S.); (2000) 97(23) L.S.G. 41; [2000] N.P.C. 36; Times, April 24, 2000 **5-9**

R. v Gough [1993] A.C. 646; [1993] 2 W.L.R. 883; [1993] 2 All E.R. 724; (1993) 97 Cr. App. R. 188; (1993) 157 J.P. 612; [1993] Crim. L.R. 886; (1993) 157 J.P.N. 394; (1993) 143 N.L.J. 775; (1993) 137 S.J.L.B. 168; Times, May 24, 1993; Independent, May 26, 1993; Guardian, May 22, 1993 **3-15**

R. v Governor of Durham Prison, ex p Hardial Singh [1984] 1 WLR 704; [1984] 1 All E.R. 983; [1983] Imm. A.R. 198; (1984) 128 S.J. 349 **5-55**

R. v Governor of Risley Remand Centre Ex p. Hassan [1976] 1 W.L.R. 971; [1976] 2 All E.R. 123; (1976) 120 S.J. 333 **3-23**, **6-14**, **6-16**

R. v Hillingdon London Borough Council Ex parte Puhlhofer [1986] A.C. 484; [1986] 2 W.L.R. 259; [1986] 1 All E.R. 467; [1986] 1 F.L.R. 22; (1986) 18 H.L.R. 158; [1986] Fam. Law 218; (1986) 83 L.S.G. 785; (1986) 136 N.L.J. 140; (1986) 130 S.J. 143 **3-2**

R. v Hillingdon London Borough Council Ex parte Royco Homes Ltd [1974] Q.B. 720; [1974] 2 W.L.R. 805; [1974] 2 All E.R. 643; 72 L.G.R. 516; (1974) 28 P. & C.R. 251; (1974) 118 S.J. 389 **3-19**

R. v Higher Education Funding Council Ex p. Institute of Dental Surgery [1994] 1 W.L.R. 242; [1994] 1 All E.R. 651; [1994]

C.O.D. 147; Independent, September 28, 1993 **3-23**

R. v HM Coroner for Inner London South District Ex parte Douglas-Williams [1999] 1 All E.R. 344; (1998) 162 J.P. 751; [2003] Lloyd's Rep. Med. 317; [1998] C.O.D. 358; Times, September 4, 1998 **5-58**

R. v Hull University Visitor Ex. Parte Page [1993] A.C. 682, HL **3-3**

R. v Huntingdon District Council ex parte Cowan [1984] 1 W.L.R. 501; [1984] 1 All E.R. 58; 82 L.G.R. 342; (1984) 148 J.P.N. 332 **5-9**

R. v Independent Television Commission Ex parte TSW Broadcasting Ltd [1996] E.M.L.R. 291; Times, March 30, 1992; Independent, March 27, 1992; Guardian, April 2, 1992 **3-2**

R. v Inland Revenue Commissioners Ex parte MFK Underwriting Agents Ltd [1990] 1 W.L.R. 1545; [1990] 1 All E.R. 91; [1990] S.T.C. 873; 62 T.C. 607; [1990] C.O.D. 143; (1989) 139 N.L.J. 1343; Times, July 17, 1989; Independent, August 4, 1989; Independent, August 7, 1989; Financial Times, July 19, 1989; Guardian, July 20, 1989 **3-20**

R. v Knightsbridge Crown Court Ex parte Marcrest Properties [1983] 1 W.L.R. 300; [1983] 1 All E.R. 1148; (1983) 127 S.J. 87 **5-58**

R. v Lambeth London Borough Council ex parte Crookes (1997) 29 H.L.R. 28; [1996] C.O.D. 398 **5-9**

R. v Leicestershire CC Ex parte Blackfordby and Boothorpe Action Group Ltd [2001] Env. L.R. 2; [2000] E.H.L.R. 215; [2000] J.P.L. 1266 **5-2**

R. v Lincolnshire CC Ex parte Atkinson [1996] 8 Admin. L.R. 529; [1997] J.P.L. 65; (1996) 160 L.G. Rev. 580; [1995] E.G. 145 (C.S.); [1995] N.P.C. 145; Times, September 22, 1995; Independent, October 3, 1995 **5-58**

R. v Local Commissioner for Administration for the North and East Area of England Ex parte Bradford City Council [1979] Q.B. 287; [1979] 2 W.L.R. 1; [1979] 2 All E.R. 881; 77 L.G.R. 305; [1978] J.P.L. 767; (1978) 122 S.J. 573 **4-33**

R. v Manchester Crown Court Ex parte DPP [1993] 1 W.L.R. 1524; [1993] 4 All E.R. 928; (1994) 98 Cr. App. R. 461; [1994] 1 C.M.L.R. 457; (1993) 143 N.L.J. 1711; Times, November 26, 1993; Independent, December 7, 1993 **5-13**

R. v Minister for Agriculture, Fisheries, and Food Ex. Parte FEDESA [1988] 3 C.M.L.R. 661, HC **3-12**

R. v North and East Devon Health Authority ex parte. Coughlan [2001] Q.B. 213; [2000] 2 W.L.R. 622; [2000] 3 All E.R. 850; (2000) 2 L.G.L.R. 1; [1999] B.L.G.R. 703; (1999) 2 C.C.L. Rep. 285; [1999] Lloyd's Rep. Med. 306; (2000) 51 B.M.L.R. 1; [1999] C.O.D. 340; (1999) 96(31) L.S.G. 39; (1999) 143 S.J.L.B. 213; Times, July 20, 1999; Independent, July 20, 1999 **3-24**

R. v North West Suffolk (Mildenhall) Magistrates Court Ex p. Forest Heath District Council [1997] 161 J.P. 401; [1998] Env. L.R. 9; [1997] C.O.D. 352; (1997) 161 J.P.N. 602; Times, May 16, 1997 **6-11**

R. v North West Thames RHA Ex parte Daniels [1993] 4 Med. L.R. 364; [1994] C.O.D. 44; Times, June 22, 1993; Independent, June 18, 1993; Guardian, June 21, 1993 **5-58**

R. v Panel on Takeovers and Mergers Ex Parte Datafin PLC [1987] Q.B. 815; [1987] 2 W.L.R. 699; [1987] 1 All E.R. 564; (1987) 3 B.C.C. 10; [1987] B.C.L.C. 104; [1987] 1 F.T.L.R. 181; (1987) 131 S.J. 23 **4-2**, **4-3**

R. v Parliamentary Commissioner for Standards Ex parte Al-Fayed [1998] 1 W.L.R. 669; [1998] 1 All E.R. 93; (1998) 10 Admin. L.R. 69; [1998] C.O.D. 139; (1997) 94(42) L.S.G. 31; (1997) 147 N.L.J. 1689; Times, November 13, 1997; Independent, October 29, 1997 **4-18**

R. v Poplar MBC Ex p. London CC (No.2) [1922] 1 K.B. 95 **5-60**

R. v Secretary of State for Foreign and Commonwealth Affairs Ex parte World Development Movement Ltd [1995] 1 W.L.R. 386; [1995] 1 All E.R. 611; [1995] C.O.D. 211; (1995) 145 N.L.J. 51; Times, December 27, 1994; Independent, January 11, 1995 **5-16**

R. v The Secretary of State for the Home Department Ex parte Begum [1990] Imm. A.R. 1; [1990] C.O.D. 107; Times, April 3, 1989; Independent, March 27, 1989 **5-39**

R. v Secretary of State for the Home Department Ex parte Chinoy [1992] 4 Admin. L.R. 457; [1991] C.O.D. 381; Times, April 16, 1991; Independent, April 22, 1991 **5-39**

R. v Secretary of State for the Home Department Ex parte Doody [1994] 1 A.C. 531; [1993] 3 W.L.R. 154; [1993] 3 All E.R. 92; (1995) 7 Admin. L.R. 1; (1993) 143 N.L.J. 991; Times, June 29, 1993; Independent, June 25, 1993 **3-23**

R. v Secretary of State for the Home Department Ex parte Leech (No.2) [1994] Q.B. 198; [1993] 3 W.L.R. 1125; [1993] 4 All E.R. 539; (1993) 137 S.J.L.B. 173; Times, May 20, 1993; Independent, May 20, 1993 **3-19**

R. v Secretary of State for the Home Department ex parte Salem [1999] I AC 450; [1999] 2 W.L.R. 483; [1999] 2 All E.R. 42; (1999) 11 Admin. L.R. 194; [1999] C.O.D. 486; (1999) 96(9) L.S.G. 32; (1999) 143 S.J.L.B. 59; Times, February 12, 1999 **5-12**

R. v Secretary of State for Social Services and Another, Ex parte Child Poverty Action Group and Others [1990] 2 Q.B. 540; [1989] 3 W.L.R. 1116; [1989] 1 All E.R. 1047; (1989) 86(41) L.S.G. 41; (1989) 133 S.J. 1373; Times, October 10, 1988; Independent, October 24, 1988; Independent, October 11, 1988; Guardian, October 12, 1988 **5-10**

R. v Secretary of State for Transport Ex parte Factortame Ltd (C-48/93) [1996] Q.B. 404; [1996] 2 W.L.R. 506; [1996] All E.R. (EC) 301; [1996] E.C.R. I-1029; [1996] 1 C.M.L.R. 889; [1996] C.E.C. 295; [1996] I.R.L.R. 267; Times, March 7, 1996 **1-37**, **5-55**

R. v Secretary of State for Transport Ex parte Factortame Ltd (C-213/89) [1991] 1 All E.R. 70; [1990] 2 Lloyd's Rep. 351; [1990] E.C.R. I-2433; [1990] 3 C.M.L.R. 1; (1990) 140 N.L.J. 927 **1-37**, **3-12**

R. v Secretary of State for Transport Ex parte Factortame Ltd (No.2) [1991] 1 A.C. 603; [1990] 3 W.L.R. 818; [1991] 1 All E.R. 70; [1991] 1 Lloyd's Rep. 10; [1990] 3 C.M.L.R. 375; (1991) 3 Admin. L.R. 333; (1990) 140 N.L.J. 1457; (1990) 134 S.J. 1189 **1-37, 3-12**

R. v Shropshire County Council Ex Parte Jones [1997] 9 Admin. L.R. 625; [1997] E.L.R. 357; [1997] C.O.D. 116; (1997) 161 J.P.N. 1080 **3-20**

R. v Solicitor General Ex parte Taylor and Taylor [1996] 1 F.C.R. 206; [1996] C.O.D. 61; Times, August 14, 1995; Independent, August 3, 1995 **3-23**

R. v Somerset County Council Ex. Parte Fewings [1995] 1 W.L.R. 1037 **3-5**

R. (on the application of A) v Chief Constable of Kent [2013] EWCA Civ 1706; (2014) 135 B.M.L.R. 22 **3-25**

R. (on the application of A) v Croydon London Borough Council [2009] UKSC 8; [2009] 1 W.L.R. 2557; [2010] 1 All E.R. 469; [2010] P.T.S.R. 106; [2010] 1 F.L.R. 959; [2009] 3 F.C.R. 607; [2010] H.R.L.R. 9; [2010] U.K.H.R.R. 63; [2010] B.L.G.R. 183; (2009) 12 C.C.L. Rep. 552; [2010] Fam. Law 137; (2009) 159 N.L.J. 1701; (2009) 153(46) S.J.L.B. 34; Times, November 30, 2009 **5-61**

R. (on the application of A) v Partnerships in Care Ltd [2002] EWHC 529 (Admin); [2002] 1 W.L.R. 2610; (2002) 5 C.C.L. Rep. 330; [2002] M.H.L.R. 298; (2002) 99(20) L.S.G. 32; (2002) 146 S.J.L.B. 117; Times, April 23, 2002 **4-3**

R. (on the application of Alansi) v Newham London Borough Council [2013] EWHC 3722 (Admin); [2014] P.T.S.R. 948; [2014] H.L.R. 25; [2014] B.L.G.R. 138 **3-20**

R. (on the application of Albert Court Residents' Association) v Westminster City Council [2011] EWCA Civ 430; [2012] P.T.S.R. 604; [2011] B.L.G.R. 616; [2011] 2 E.G.L.R. 49; [2011] 24 E.G. 110; [2011] L.L.R. 240; [2011] 16 E.G. 79 (C.S.); (2011) 108(17) L.S.G. 14; (2011) 155(15) S.J.L.B. 38; Times, April 21, 2011 **3-20**

R. (on the application of Allwin) v Snaresbrook Crown [2005] EWHC 742 (Admin) **6-11**

R. (on the application of Al-Sweady) v Secretary of State for Defence [2009] EWHC 2387 (Admin); [2010] H.R.L.R. 2; [2010] U.K.H.R.R. 300; Times, October 14, 2009 **5-16**

R. (on the application of Anufrijeva) v Southwark LBC [2003] EWCA Civ 1406; [2004] Q.B. 1124; [2004] 2 W.L.R. 603; [2004] 1 All E.R. 833; [2004] 1 F.L.R. 8; [2003] 3 F.C.R. 673; [2004] H.R.L.R. 1; [2004] U.K.H.R.R. 1; 15 B.H.R.C. 526; [2004] H.L.R. 22; [2004] B.L.G.R. 184; (2003) 6 C.C.L. Rep. 415; [2004] Fam. Law 12; (2003) 100(44) L.S.G. 30; Times, October 17, 2003; Independent, October 23, 2003 **5-55**

R. (on the application of Bahta) v Secretary of State for the Home Department [2011] EWCA Civ 895; [2011] C.P. Rep. 43; [2011] 5 Costs L.R. 857; [2011] A.C.D. 116 **7-19**

R. (on the application of Baker) v Police Appeals Tribunal [2013] EWHC 718 (Admin) **5-49**, **5-58**

R. (on the application of BAPIO Action Ltd) v Secretary of State for the Home Department [2007] EWCA Civ 1139; [2008] A.C.D. 7 **3-24**

R (on the application of Boxall) v Waltham Forest LBC [2001] 4 CCLR 258 **7-09**

R. (on the application of Boyle) v Haverhill Pub Watch [2009] EWHC 2441 (Admin) **4-3**

R. (on the application of British Bankers Association) v Financial Services Authority [2011] EWHC 999 (Admin); [2011] Bus. L.R. 1531; [2011] A.C.D. 71; (2011) 108(18) L.S.G. 20 **4-33**

R. (on the application of Brown) v Work and Pensions Secretary [2008] EWHC 3158 (Admin); [2009] P.T.S.R. 1506 **3-10**

R. (on the application of Brynmawr Foundation School Governors) v Welsh Ministers [2011] EWHC 519 (Admin) **2-19**

R (on the application of BT3G Limited) v The Secretary of State for Trade and Industry [2001] Eu. L.R. 325 **3-18**

R. (on the application of Buglife: The Invertebrate Conservation Trust) v Thurrock Thames Gateway Development Corp [2008] EWCA Civ 1209; [2009] C.P. Rep. 8; [2009] 1 Costs L.R. 80; [2009] Env. L.R. 18; [2009] J.P.L. 1045; [2008] 45 E.G. 101 (C.S.); (2008) 152(43) S.J.L.B. 29; [2008] N.P.C. 118; Times, November 18, 2008 **7-23**

R. (on the application of Butt) v Secretary of State for the Home Department [2014] EWHC 264 (Admin) **5-33**

R. (on the application of Carson) v Secretary of State for Work and Pensions [2005] UKHL 37; [2006] 1 A.C. 173; [2005] 2 W.L.R. 1369; [2005] 4 All E.R. 545; [2005] H.R.L.R. 23; [2005] U.K.H.R.R. 1185; 18 B.H.R.C. 677; Times, May 27, 2005 **3-28**

R. (on the application of Cart) v Upper Tribunal [2011] UKSC 28; [2012] 1 A.C. 663; [2011] 3 W.L.R. 107; [2011] 4 All E.R. 127; [2011] P.T.S.R. 1053; [2011] S.T.C. 1659; [2012] 1 F.L.R. 997; [2011] Imm. A.R. 704; [2011] M.H.L.R. 196; [2012] Fam. Law 398; [2011] S.T.I. 1943; (2011) 161 N.L.J. 916; (2011) 155(25) S.J.L.B. 35; Times, June 23, 2011 **4-2**, **5-3**, **5-64**

R. (on the application of Clive Rees Associates) v Swansea Magistrates' Court [2011] EWHC 3155 (Admin); (2012) 176 J.P. 39; [2012] A.C.D. 25 **5-52**

R. (on the application of Committee of Care North East Newcastle) v Newcastle City Council [2012] EWHC 2655 Admin **3-24**

R. (on the application of Condron) v Merthyr Tydfil County Borough Council [2009] EWHC 1621 (Admin) **2-14**

R. (on the application of Condron) v National Assembly for Wales [2005] EWHC 3007 (Admin); [2006] Env. L.R. 35 **3-14**

R. (on the application of Condron) v National Assembly for Wales [2006] EWCA Civ 1573; [2007] B.L.G.R. 87; [2007] 2 P. & C.R. 4; [2007] J.P.L. 938; [2006] 49 E.G. 94 (C.S.); [2006] N.P.C. 127; [2007] Env.

L.R. D7; Times, December 13, 2006; Independent, November 29, 2006 **2-14, 3-24**

R. (on the application of Corner House Research) v Secretary of State for Trade and Industry [2005] EWCA Civ 192; [2005] 1 W.L.R. 2600; [2005] 4 All E.R. 1; [2005] C.P. Rep. 28; [2005] 3 Costs L.R. 455; [2005] A.C.D. 100; (2005) 102(17) L.S.G. 31; (2005) 149 S.J.L.B. 297; Times, March 7, 2005; Independent, March 4, 2005 **7-21, 7-22, 7-23**

R. (on the application of Daly) v Secretary of State for the Home Department [2001] UKHL 26; [2001] 2 A.C. 532; [2001] 2 W.L.R. 1622; [2001] 3 All E.R. 433; [2001] H.R.L.R. 49; [2001] U.K.H.R.R. 887; [2001] Prison L.R. 322; [2001] A.C.D. 79; (2001) 98(26) L.S.G. 43; (2001) 145 S.J.L.B. 156; Times, May 25, 2001; Daily Telegraph, May 29, 2001 **3-25**

R. (on the application of Deepdock Ltd) v Welsh Ministers [2007] EWHC 3347 (Admin) **2-14**

R. (on the application of Dempsey) v Sutton London Borough Council [2013] EWCA Civ 863 **7-09**

R. (on the application of Edwards) v Environment Agency [2013] UKSC 78; [2014] 1 W.L.R. 55; [2014] 1 All E.R. 760 **7-26**

R. (on the application of Ewing) v Office of the Deputy Prime Minister [2005] EWCA Civ 1583; [2006] 1 W.L.R. 1260; [2005] N.P.C. 146; Independent, January 20, 2006 **7-15**

R. (on the application of Federation of Technological Industries) v Customs and Excise Commissioners [2004] EWCA Civ 1020; [2004] S.T.C. 1424; [2004] 3 C.M.L.R. 41; [2005] Eu. L.R. 110; [2004] B.T.C. 5623; [2004] B.V.C. 682; [2004] S.T.I. 1763; (2004) 101(36) L.S.G. 35; (2004) 148 S.J.L.B. 977 **7-27**

R. (on the application of FH) v Secretary of State for the Home Department [2007] EWHC 1571 (Admin) **3-19**

R. (on the application of Friends Provident Life & Pensions Ltd) v Secretary of State for Transport, Local Government and the Regions [2001] EWHC Admin 820; [2002] 1 W.L.R. 1450; [2002] J.P.L. 958; [2001] 44 E.G. 147 (C.S.); [2001] N.P.C. 152 **3-27**

R (on the application of FZ) v London Borough of Croydon [2011] EWCA Civ 59; [2011] P.T.S.R. 748; [2011] 1 F.L.R. 2081; [2011] H.L.R. 22; [2011] B.L.G.R. 445; (2011) 14 C.C.L. Rep. 289; [2011] Fam. Law 355; (2011) 108(7) L.S.G. 16 **5-39, 5-61**

R. (on the application of G) v Barnett London Borough Council [2003] UKHL 57; [2004] 2 A.C. 208; [2003] 3 W.L.R. 1194; [2004] 1 All E.R. 97; [2004] 1 F.L.R. 454; [2003] 3 F.C.R. 419; [2004] H.R.L.R. 4; [2004] H.L.R. 10; [2003] B.L.G.R. 569; (2003) 6 C.C.L. Rep. 500; [2004] Fam. Law 21; (2003) 100(45) L.S.G. 29; [2003] N.P.C. 123; Times, October 24, 2003; Independent, October 29, 2003 **3-7**

R. (on the application of Garner) v Elmbridge Borough Council [2010] EWCA Civ 1006; [2011] 3 All E.R. 418; [2012] P.T.S.R. 250; [2011] 1 Costs L.R. 48; [2011] Env. L.R. 10;

[2010] 3 E.G.L.R. 137; [2011] J.P.L. 289; [2011] A.C.D. 7 **7-26**
R. (on the application of Gifford) v Governor of Bure Prison [2014] EWHC 911 (Admin) **5-9**
R. (on the application of Griffiths) v Secretary of State for Justice [2013] EWHC 4077 (Admin) **3-10**
R. (on the application of Grace) v Secretary of State for the Home Department [2014] EWCA Civ 1091; [2014] 1 W.L.R. 3432; [2015] Imm. A.R. 10 **5-39**
R. (on the application of Hamid) v Secretary of State for the Home Department [2012] EWHC 3070 (Admin); [2013] C.P. Rep. 6; [2013] A.C.D. 27 **5-33**
R. (on the application of Hicks) v Commissioner of Police of the Metropolis [2014] EWCA Civ 3; [2014] 1 W.L.R. 2152; [2014] 2 Cr. App. R. 4; [2014] H.R.L.R. 11; [2014] Crim. L.R. 681 **3-30**
R. (on the application of Horvarth) v Secretary of State for the Environment, Food and Rural Affairs [2007] EWCA Civ 620; [2007] Eu. L.R. 770; [2007] N.P.C. 83; Times, July 30, 2007 **4-10**
R. (on the application of the Howard League for Penal Reform) v Secretary of State for the Home Department (No.2) [2002] EWHC 2497 (Admin); [2003] 1 F.L.R. 484; (2003) 6 C.C.L. Rep. 47; [2003] Prison L.R. 128; [2003] Fam. Law 149; (2003) 100(3) L.S.G. 30; (2003) 147 S.J.L.B. 61; Times, December 5, 2002 **5-10**
R. (on the application of HS2 Action Alliance Ltd) v Secretary of State for Transport [2015] EWCA Civ 203; [2015] 2 Costs L.R. 411 **7-25**
R. (on the application of Jackley) v Secretary of State for Justice [2015] EWHC 342 (Admin) **3-20**
R. (on the application of Jackson) v Attorney General [2005] UKHL 56; [2006] 1 A.C. 262; [2005] 3 W.L.R. 733; [2005] 4 All E.R. 1253; (2005) 155 N.L.J. 1600; [2005] N.P.C. 116; Times, October 14, 2005; Independent, October 20, 2005 **4-3**
R. (on the application of Jenkins) v Marsh Farm Community Development Trust [2011] EWHC 1097 (Admin) **4-3**
R (on the application of JM) v Croydon London Borough Council [2009] EWHC 2474 (Admin); [2010] 1 W.L.R. 1658; [2010] P.T.S.R. 866; [2010] A.C.D. 1 **7-41**
R. (on the application of JM) v Isle of Wight Council [2011] EWHC 2911 Admin; [2012] Eq. L.R. 34; (2012) 15 C.C.L. Rep. 167 **3-24**
R. (on the application of Jones) v Nottingham City Council [2009] EWHC 271 (Admin); [2009] A.C.D. 42 **7-19**
R. (on the application of Khatun) v Newham London Borough Council [2004] EWCA Civ 55; [2005] Q.B. 37; [2004] 3 W.L.R. 417; [2004] Eu. L.R. 628; [2004] H.L.R. 29; [2004] B.L.G.R. 696; [2004] L. & T.R. 18; (2004) 148 S.J.L.B. 268; [2004] N.P.C. 28; Times, February 27, 2004; Independent, March 4, 2004 **3-19**
R. (on the application of Kides) v South Cambridgeshire District Council [2002] EWCA Civ 1370; [2003] 1 P. & C.R. 19; [2002] 4 P.L.R. 66; [2003] J.P.L. 431; [2002] 42 E.G. 160 (C.S.); (2002) 99(43) L.S.G. 35; (2002) 146 S.J.L.B.

230; [2002] N.P.C. 121; Times, October 15, 2002; Independent, October 16, 2002 **5-10**

R. (on the application of KR) v Secretary Of State for the Home Department [2012] EWCA Civ 1555 **7-09**

R. (on the application of Kumar and Another) v Secretary of State for the Home Department (acknowledgement of service; Tribunal arrangements) (IJR) [2014] UKUT 104 **5-61**

R. (on the application of Laporte) v Newham London Borough Council [2004] EWHC 227 (Admin) **5-58**

R. (on the application of LH) v Shropshire Council [2014] EWCA Civ 404; [2014] P.T.S.R. 1052; (2014) 17 C.C.L. Rep. 216 **3-24**

R. (on the application of Long) v Welsh Ministers [2012] EWHC 3131 (Admin) **3-4**

R. (on the application of M) v Croydon London Borough Council [2012] EWCA Civ 595; [2012] 1 W.L.R. 2607; [2012] 3 All E.R. 1237; [2012] 4 Costs L.R. 689; [2012] 3 F.C.R. 179; [2012] B.L.G.R. 822 **7-09**, **7-14**

R. (on the application of M) v Isleworth Crown Court [2005] EWHC 363 (Admin) **6-11**

R. (on the application of M) v Kingston Crown Court [2014] EWHC 2702 (Admin); [2015] 1 Cr. App. R. 3; (2014) 178 J.P. 438; (2014) 158(31) S.J.L.B. 37 **5-13**

R. (on the application of Mavalon Care Ltd) v Pembrokeshire County Council [2011] EWHC 3371 (Admin); (2012) 15 C.C.L. Rep. 229; [2012] A.C.D. 45 **5-49**

R. (on the application of MD (Afghanistan)) v Secretary of State for the Home Department [2012] EWCA Civ 194; [2012] 1 W.L.R. 2422; [2012] C.P. Rep. 24 **5-35**

R. (on the application of Medical Justice) v Secretary of State for the Home Department [2010] EWHC 1425 (Admin); [2010] A.C.D. 70 **5-31**

R. (on the application of Moreton) v Medical Defence Union Ltd [2006] EWHC 1948 (Admin); [2007] LS Law Medical 180; [2006] A.C.D. 102; (2006) 156 N.L.J. 1253 **4-3**

R. (on the application of Moseley) v Haringey London Borough Council [2014] UKSC 56; [2014] 1 W.L.R. 3947; [2014] P.T.S.R. 1317; [2014] B.L.G.R. 823; Times, November 5, 2014 **3-24**

R. (on the application of Mount Cook Land Ltd) v Westminster City Council [2003] EWCA Civ 1346; [2004] C.P. Rep. 12; [2004] 2 Costs L.R. 211; [2004] 2 P. & C.R. 22; [2004] 1 P.L.R. 29; [2004] J.P.L. 470; [2003] 43 E.G. 137 (C.S.); (2003) 147 S.J.L.B. 1272; [2003] N.P.C. 117; Times, October 16, 2003 **7-16**

R. (on the application of Munjaz) v Mersey Care NHS Trust [2005] UKHL 58; [2006] 2 A.C. 148; [2005] 3 W.L.R. 793; [2006] 4 All E.R. 736; [2005] H.R.L.R. 42; [2006] Lloyd's Rep. Med. 1; (2005) 86 B.M.L.R. 84; [2005] M.H.L.R. 276; Times, October 18, 2005; Independent, October 18, 2005 **3-6**

R. (on the application of Nadarajah) v Secretary of State for the Home Department [2005] EWCA Civ 1363; Times, December 14, 2005 **3-24**

R. (on the application of National Association of Memorial Masons) v Cardiff City Council [2011] EWHC 922 (Admin); [2011] A.C.D. 77 **3-19**

R. (on the application of Newport City Council) v Welsh Ministers [2009] EWHC 3149 (Admin); [2010] Env. L.R. 27 **4-23**

R. (on the application of Newsmith Stainless Ltd) v Secretary of State for the Environment, Transport and the Regions [2001] EWHC Admin 74 **6-5**

R. (on the application of Petsafe Ltd) v Welsh Ministers [2010] EWHC 2908 (Admin); [2011] Eu. L.R. 270 **4-7**, **4-25**

R (on the application of PG) v London Borough of Ealing [2002] EWHC 250 (Admin); [2002] M.H.L.R. 140; [2002] A.C.D. 48; (2002) 99(17) L.S.G. 37; (2002) 146 S.J.L.B. 68; (2002) 146 S.J.L.B. 209; Times, March 18, 2002 **5-44**

R. (on the application of Plantagenet Alliance Ltd) v Secretary of State for Justice [2014] EWHC 1662 Admin **3-24**

R. (on the application of Purdy) v Director of Public Prosecutions [2009] UKHL 45; [2010] 1 A.C. 345; [2009] 3 W.L.R. 403; [2009] 4 All E.R. 1147; [2010] 1 Cr. App. R. 1; [2009] H.R.L.R. 32; [2009] U.K.H.R.R. 1104; 27 B.H.R.C. 126; (2009) 12 C.C.L. Rep. 498; [2009] LS Law Medical 479; (2009) 109 B.M.L.R. 153; (2009) 179 N.L.J. 1175; (2009) 153(31) S.J.L.B. 28; Times, July 31, 2009 **5-48**

R (on the application of Razgar) v Secretary of State for the Home Department (No.2) [2003] EWCA Civ 840; [2003] Imm. A.R. 529; [2003] I.N.L.R. 543; [2003] A.C.D. 81 **3-17**

R. (on the application of Roberts) v Welsh Ministers [2011] EWHC 3416 (Admin) **4-24**

R. (on the application of Sharma) v Upper Tribunal [2012] EWHC 3930 (Admin) **5-64**

R (on the application of Springhall) v Richmond on Thames London Borough Council [2006] EWCA Civ 19, [2006] B.L.G.R. 419; [2007] 1 P. & C.R. 30; [2006] J.P.L. 970; [2006] A.C.D. 50; [2006] 103(8) L.S.G. 26; [2006] 150 S.J.L.B. 165; [2006] N.P.C. 7; Times, February 13, 2006 **3-6**

R. (on the application of South Wales Sea Fisheries Committee) v Welsh Assembly [2001] EWHC Admin 1162; [2002] R.V.R. 134 **2-3**

R. (on the application of Swami Suryananda) v Welsh Ministers [2007] EWHC 1736 **2-3**

R. (on the application of Swami Suryananda) v Welsh Ministers [2007] EWCA Civ 893 2-3

R. (on the application of T) v Chief Constable of Greater Manchester [2014] UKSC 35; [2014] 3 W.L.R. 96; [2014] 2 Cr. App. R. 24; Times, June 23, 2014 **5-53**

R. (on the application of TA Gwillim & Sons) v Welsh Ministers [2009] EWHC 2946 (Admin); [2009] N.P.C. 136 **3-12**

R. (on the application of TA Gwillim & Sons) v Welsh Ministers [2010] EWCA Civ 1048; [2011] 1 W.L.R. 966; [2010] N.P.C. 97; Times, November 2, 2010 **3-12**

R. (on the application of Tecle) v Secretary of State for the Home Department [2013] EWHC 3823 (Admin) **3-19**
R. (on the application of Thomas) v Hywel Dda University Health Board [2014] EWHC 4044 (Admin) **3-24**
R. (on the application of Thompson) v Law Society [2004] EWCA Civ 167; [2004] 1 W.L.R. 2522; [2004] 2 All E.R. 113; (2004) 101(13) L.S.G. 35; (2004) 154 N.L.J. 307; (2004) 148 S.J.L.B. 265; Times, April 1, 2004; Independent, March 29, 2004 **3-27**
R. (on the application of Umo) v Commissioner for Local Administration in England [2003] EWHC 3202 (Admin); [2004] E.L.R. 265 **5-9**
R. (on the application of Usk Valley Conservation Group) v Brecon Beacons National Park Authority [2010] EWHC 71 (Admin); [2010] 2 P. & C.R. 14; [2010] N.P.C. 9 **4-35**, **5-2**
R. (on the application of the Vale of Glamorgan Council v The Lord Chancellor and Secretary of State for Justice [2011] EWHC 1532 (Admin) **4-27**
R. (on the application of Van Hoogstraten) v Governor of Belmarsh Prison [2002] EWHC 1965 (Admin); [2003] 1 W.L.R. 263; [2003] 4 All E.R. 309; [2003] Prison L.R. 6; [2003] A.C.D. 19; (2002) 99(42) L.S.G. 38; (2002) 152 N.L.J. 1531; (2002) 146 S.J.L.B. 213; Times, November 5, 2002; Independent, November 25, 2002 **5-48**
R. (on the application of Welsh Language Commissioner) v National Savings and Investments [2014] EWHC 488 (Admin); [2014] P.T.S.R. D8 **5-45**
R. (on the application of Willford) v Financial Services Authority [2013] EWCA Civ 677 **5-9**
R. (on the application of Y) v Aylesbury Crown Court [2012] EWHC 1140 (Admin); [2012] E.M.L.R. 26; [2012] Crim. L.R. 893; [2012] A.C.D. 70 **5-13**
R (on the application of Zoolife International Ltd v The Secretary of State for Environment, Food and Rural Affairs [2007] EWHC 2995 (Admin); [2008] A.C.D. 44 **5-12**
Re Agricultural Sector (Wales) Bill [2014] UKSC 43; [2014] 1 W.L.R. 2622; Times, July 14, 2014 **4-10**, **4-12**
Re Amand [1941] 2 K.B. 239 **6-15**
Re Corke [1954] 1 W.L.R. 899; [1954] 2 All E.R. 440; (1954) 98 S.J. 406 **6-14**
Re F [1990] 2 A.C. 1; [1989] 2 W.L.R. 1025; [1989] 2 All E.R. 545; [1989] 2 F.L.R. 376; (1989) 139 N.L.J. 789; (1989) 133 S.J. 785 **4.52**
Re Hastings (No 3); [1959] Ch 368; [1959] 1 All ER 698; [1959] 3 All ER 221; [1959] 1 WLR 807, CA **1-29**
Re Local Government Byelaws (Wales) Bill 2012 [2012] UKSC 53; [2013] 1 A.C. 792; [2012] 3 W.L.R. 1294; [2013] 1 All E.R. 1013; Times, December 31, 2012 **4-10**, **4-12**, **4-13**, **4-15**, **4-18**
Re M. [1994] 1 A.C. 377; [1993] 3 W.L.R. 433; [1993] 3 All E.R. 537; (1995) 7 Admin. L.R. 113; (1993) 90(37) L.S.G. 50; (1993) 143 N.L.J. 1099; (1993) 137 S.J.L.B. 199; Times, July 28, 1993; Independent, July 28, 1993 **5-60**

Re Poh [1983] 1 W.L.R. 2; [1983] 1 All E.R. 287; (1983) 127 S.J. 16 **7-33**

Re Poyser and Mills' Arbitration [1963] 2 W.L.R. 1309; [1964] 2 Q.B. 467 **3-23**

Re Recovery of Medical Costs for Asbestos Diseases (Wales) Bill [2015] UKSC 3; [2015] A.C. 1016; [2015] 2 W.L.R. 481; [2015] 2 All E.R. 899; [2015] H.R.L.R. 9; (2015) 143 B.M.L.R. 1 **3-25**, **4-12**

Ridge v Baldwin [1963] 1 Q.B. 539; [1962] 2 W.L.R. 716; [1962] 1 All E.R. 834; (1962) 126 J.P. 196; 60 L.G.R. 229; (1962) 106 S.J. 111 **3-14**

Royal Mail Group Plc v The Postal Services Commission [2007] EWHC 1205 (Admin); [2007] A.C.D. 81 **3-6**

Sadler v Whiteman [1910] 1 KB 868 **5-2**

Shadrokh-Cigari v Shadrokh-Cigari [2010] EWCA Civ 21; [2010] 1 W.L.R. 1311; [2010] Fam. Law 342; (2010) 107(6) L.S.G. 20 **7-40**

Sharma v Brown-Antoine [2006] UKPC 57; [2007] 1 W.L.R. 780 **5-39**

South Buckinghamshire District Council v Flanagan [2002] EWCA Civ 690; [2002] 1 W.L.R. 2601; [2002] 3 P.L.R. 47; [2002] J.P.L. 1465; (2002) 99(25) L.S.G. 35; (2002) 146 S.J.L.B. 136; [2002] N.P.C. 71 **3-20**

South Buckinghamshire DC v Porter (No.2) [2004] UKHL 33; [2004] 1 W.L.R. 1953; [2004] 4 All E.R. 775; [2005] 1 P. & C.R. 6; [2004] 4 P.L.R. 50; [2004] 28 E.G. 177 (C.S.); (2004) 101(31) L.S.G. 25; (2004) 148 S.J.L.B. 825; [2004] N.P.C. 108; Times, July 2, 2004; Independent, July 6, 2004 **3-23**

South Wales Fire and Rescue Service v Smith [2011] EWHC 1749 (Admin) **6-17**

Stefan v General Medical Council (No.1) [1999] 1 W.L.R. 1293; [2000] H.R.L.R. 1; 6 B.H.R.C. 487; [1999] Lloyd's Rep. Med. 90; (1999) 49 B.M.L.R. 161; (1999) 143 S.J.L.B. 112; Times, March 11, 1999 **3-23**

Stobart Group Ltd v Elliott [2014] EWCA Civ 564 **6-18**, **6-19**

Streames v Copping [1985] Q.B. 920; [1985] 2 W.L.R. 993; [1985] 2 All E.R. 122; (1985) 81 Cr. App. R. 1; (1985) 149 J.P. 305; [1985] R.T.R. 264; (1985) 82 L.S.G. 1709; (1985) 129 S.J. 299 **6-11**

The Sunday Times v The United Kingdom (1979-80) 2 E.H.R.R. 245; (1979) 76 L.S.G. 328 **3-29**

Symphony Group Plc v Hodgson [1994] Q.B. 179; [1993] 3 W.L.R. 830; [1993] 4 All E.R. 143; [1997] Costs L.R. (Core Vol.) 319; (1993) 143 N.L.J. 725; (1993) 137 S.J.L.B. 134; Times, May 4, 1993; Independent, May 14, 1993 **7-18**

Taylor v Lancashire County Council [2005] EWCA Civ 284; [2005] 1 W.L.R. 2668; [2005] H.R.L.R. 17; [2005] U.K.H.R.R. 766; [2005] L. & T.R. 26; [2005] 2 E.G.L.R. 17; [2005] 23 E.G. 142; [2005] N.P.C. 43; Times, March 31, 2005 **5-53**

Tesco Stores Ltd v Dundee City Council [2012] UKSC 13; [2012] P.T.S.R. 983; 2012 S.C. (U.K.S.C.) 278; 2012 S.L.T. 739; [2012] 2 P. & C.R. 9; [2012] J.P.L. 1078; [2012] 13 E.G. 91 (C.S.); 2012 G.W.D. 12-235 **3-6**

Telford and Wrekin Council v Secretary of State for Communities and Local Government [2013] EWHC 1638 (Admin) **6-5**

Tesco Stores Ltd. v Secretary of State for the Environment [1995] 1 W.L.R. 759; [1995] 2 All E.R. 636; 93 L.G.R. 403; (1995) 70 P. & C.R. 184; [1995] 2 P.L.R. 72; [1995] 2 E.G.L.R. 147; [1995] 27 E.G. 154; [1995] E.G. 82 (C.S.); (1995) 92(24) L.S.G. 39; (1995) 145 N.L.J. 724; (1995) 139 S.J.L.B. 145; [1995] N.P.C. 89A; Times, May 13, 1995 **3-18**

Test Claimants in the FII Group Litigation v Revenue and Customs Commissioners [2012] UKSC 19; [2012] 2 A.C. 337; [2012] 2 W.L.R. 1149; [2012] 3 All E.R. 909; [2012] Bus. L.R. 1033; [2012] S.T.C. 1362; [2012] B.T.C. 312; [2012] S.T.I. **5-55**

Trail Riders Fellowship v Powys County Council [2013] EWHC 3144 (Admin) **3-5**, **4-31**, **6-5**

Tuthill v Director of Public Prosecutions [2011] EWHC 3760 (Admin); [2012] A.C.D. 26 **6-12**

Venn v Secretary of State for Communities and Local Government [2013] EWHC 3546 (Admin) **7-26**

Venn v Secretary of State for Communities and Local Government [2014] EWCA Civ 1539 **7-26**

Walsall Metropolitan Borough Council v Secretary of State for Communities and Local Government [2013] EWCA Civ 370; [2013] J.P.L. 1183 **7-31**

Western Power Distribution Investments Ltd v Cardiff County Council [2011] EWHC 300 (Admin); [2011] N.P.C. 25 **3-9**

Whaley v Lord Watson of Invergowrie 2000 S.C. 340; 2000 S.L.T. 475; 2000 S.C.L.R. 279; 2000 G.W.D. 8-272; Times, March 21, 2000 **4-19**

Wiener S.I. GmbH v Hauptzollamt Emmerich (Case C-338/95) [1997] E.C.R. I-6495; [1998] 1 C.M.L.R. 1110 **7-27**

Wood v United Kingdom [2004] Po. L.R. 326; Times, November 23, 2004 **3-28**

Yell Limited v Garton [2004] EWCA Civ 87; [2004] C.P. Rep. 29; (2004) 148 S.J.L.B. 180; Times, February 26, 2004; Independent, February 11, 2004 **7-07**

YL v Birmingham City Council [2007] UKHL 27; [2008] 1 A.C. 95; [2007] 3 W.L.R. 112; [2007] 3 All E.R. 957; [2007] H.R.L.R. 32; [2008] U.K.H.R.R. 346; [2007] H.L.R. 44; [2008] B.L.G.R. 273; (2007) 10 C.C.L. Rep. 505; [2007] LS Law Medical 472; (2007) 96 B.M.L.R. 1; (2007) 104(27) L.S.G. 29; (2007) 157 N.L.J. 938; (2007) 151 S.J.L.B. 860; [2007] N.P.C. 75; Times, June 21, 2007 **4-2**

Practice Directions, Notes and Statements

Guidance as to how the parties should assist the Court when applications for costs are made following settlement of claims for judicial review - December 2013 *http://www.justice.gov.uk/downloads/courts/administrative-court/aco-costs-guidance-dec-13.pdf* [Accessed 9th March 2015] **7-05**

Judicial Review Pre-Action Protocol **5-14**

Lord Chief Justice's Practice Direction; Jurisdiction of the Upper Tribunal under s.18 of the Tribunals, Courts and Enforcement Act 2007 and Mandatory Transfer of Judicial Review applications to the Upper Tribunal under s. 31A(2) of the Senior Courts Act 1981 29th August 2013. *http://www.judiciary.gov.uk/Resources/JCO/Documents/Practice%20Directions/Tribunals/lcj-direction-jr-iac-21-08-2013.pdf* [Accessed 4th January 2014] **5-63**

Practice Direction (Administrative Court: Establishment) [2000] 1 W.L.R. 1654; [2000] 4 All E.R. 1071; [2000] 2 Lloyd's Rep. 445; [2000] 2 Cr. App. R. 455; [2000] C.O.D. 290; Times, July 27, 2000 **1-34, 5-6**

Practice Direction (Administrative Court: Uncontested Proceedings) [2008] 1 W.L.R. 1377; [2009] 1 All E.R. 651; Times, July 17, 2008 **7-05**

Practice Direction – Civil Recovery Proceedings **6-3**

Practice Direction (Committal for Contempt: Open Court) [2015] 1 W.L.R. 2195 **6-18, 6-20, 7-43**

Practice Direction: Immigration Judicial Review in the Immigration and Asylum Chamber of the Upper Tribunal (1st November 2013) *http://www.judiciary.gov.uk/wp-content/uploads/2013/11/utiac-immigration-claim-01112013.pdf* [accessed 07/09/2014] **5-61**

Practice Direction – Pre-Action Conduct **6-2**

Practice Direction Relating to the Use of the Welsh Language in Cases in the Civil Courts in Wales **5-45**

Practice Direction (Trials in London) [1981] 1 W.L.R. 1296 **1-33**

Practice Direction (Sen Cts: Upper Tribunal: Judicial Review Jurisdiction) [2012] 1 W.L.R. 16; [2012] P.T.S.R. 325 **5-63**

Practice Direction (Supreme Court: Devolution) [1999] 1 W.L.R. 1592; [1999] 3 All E.R. 466; [2000] 1 Cr. App. R. 101; [1999] 2 Cr. App. R. 486; Times, July 5, 1999 **2-3, 6-22**

Practice Direction (Upper Tribunal: Judicial Review Jurisdiction) [2009] 1 W.L.R. 327; [2009] P.T.S.R. 95 **5-62**

Practice Note (Sen Cts: McKenzie Friends: Civil and Family Courts) [2010] 1 W.L.R. 1881; [2010] 4 All E.R. 272; [2010] 2 F.L.R. 962; [2010] 2 F.C.R. 625; [2010] B.P.I.R. 1204 **5-28**

Practice Statement (Administrative Court: Listing and Urgent Cases) [2002] 1 W.L.R. 810; [2002] 1 All E.R. 633; [2002] A.C.D. 64 **5-33**

Chapter 1 1-1

Historical Introduction

INTRODUCTION

A chapter that discusses Welsh history in a legal textbook must be a chapter about context. The primary purpose of this chapter is to give the reader the background knowledge to understand the following chapters in their proper context. However, whilst it is not discussed in great length in this chapter, an analysis of Welsh history can serve a secondary purpose for this book. It is important to keep in mind that Welsh legal autonomy is currently on an upward trend. The primary legislative powers possessed by the National Assembly for Wales in the current devolution settlement represent greater legal autonomy for Wales than has been present for centuries, but the present position is not the high or low water mark. Any scholar should keep in mind that the power to make its own laws is something that, over time, Wales has entirely possessed and entirely lost. This chapter will touch on this point, but only briefly, the point not being integral to the understanding of the working of administrative law and the Administrative Court in Wales.

PREHISTORY AND THE ROMANS 1-2

Prehistory

A theory of the twelfth-century cleric and historian Geoffrey of Monmouth, which is as well known as it is discredited, is that the first people to populate the British Isles were descendants of Troy.[1] Whether we believe Geoffrey of Monmouth's creative study or not there have been human beings in the land we would call Wales for hundreds of thousands of years. From around 1000 BC, due to increasing population growth, the competition for land became fiercer. This era is also the time of the first archaeological evidence of the spread of the Celts across Europe.[2] The exact date that the Celts came to Wales is unknown, but archaeological finds certainly indicate a presence from around 600 BC. There is some evidence to suggest that tribal kingship existed alongside rule by aristocracy.

[1] For an outline of the ancient, yet likely fictional, Kings of Britain based on the writings of Geoffrey of Monmouth, see T. Venning, *The Kings and Queens of Wales* (Amberley Publishing, 2012).

[2] The term Celt is used for ease of reference. There is academic debate as to the extent to which 'The Celts' existed. The term may be oversimplification of the diversity of Iron Age Western Europe. The term 'early Britons' would serve just as well for the tribes in Wales in this period.

1-3 The Romans

In AD 43 the Roman army invaded mainland Britain. By AD 48 battle had begun with the tribes that inhabited the land that would one day be Wales. There were, broadly speaking, six Celtic tribes that covered the area (although it seems likely that there were some smaller tribes the names of which have been lost to history), the *Dobunni*, the *Silures*, the *Demetae*, the *Ordovices*, the *Cornovii*, and the *Deceangli*.[3] After thirty years and at least thirteen separate military campaigns, the conquest of the area that would become Wales was complete.

Not all areas were deemed sufficiently civilised in Britain to obtain *civitas* status.[4] There is evidence to suggest that some tribes integrated more effectively than others. The *Dematae* and the *Silures* in what would become South Wales blended effectively with the Roman occupiers. The *Ordovices* and the *Deceangli* in what would become North Wales remained largely opposed to the occupation, never obtaining *civitas* status and being subject to military supervision for the majority of the Roman occupation. An important distinction must be made at this point. The Roman model of occupation was different from that of the Anglo-Saxons (in England) and the Normans (in England and Wales). The *civitas* structure allowed two separate national identities, British and Roman, to intertwine and form a single structure. It did not overrule, oppress, or subvert the local laws and customs, it simply provided a better administrative structure and access to Roman law, albeit that where conflict arose Roman law took priority. The system was Roman, the law was, to a large extent, local. The Celtic identity, therefore, continued to have a presence in what was almost four hundred years of Romano-British culture.

The Roman civil law system was complex. Roman private law made provision for a number of areas of law. Roman public law made provision for criminal law and rules governing property that the public had access to (such as rivers, seas, the shore, ports, bridges, harbours which were deemed not to be owned by anyone, not even the Romans). It is of note that Roman criminal law was based on penalty rather than restitution, which, whilst common in modern day society, was not the case in post-Roman Britain.

From the late fourth century and into the early fifth century the Roman presence in Britain gradually reduced. In 410 the remaining British authorities, lacking the support of a single Roman legion, sent word to Emperor Honorius and requested military support against the surrounding raiders, raiders that were staying longer and becoming invaders. The Emperor's response signalled the formal end of the Roman occupation – the Britons were to fend for themselves.

[3] For a discussion of the likely territories of these tribes based on the works of primary sources such as *Tacitus* and *Ptolemy* see G. Jarrett and J. Mann, 'The Tribes of Wales', *Welsh History Review*, 4/2 (1968), 161–74.

[4] *Civitas* status involved the local population effectively self governing whilst subject to overall Roman rule.

After the Empire 1-4

The Roman system of governance and law making did not disappear with the Romans. The tribes that inhabited the area now known as Wales (as well as Britain generally) were still heavily influenced by the institutional systems imposed by the Romans. It appears likely that the system of Roman governance declined slowly over the century that followed the Roman withdrawal. Lacking a central system of government, the Britons succumbed to two problems. Without the military might of Rome to deter them, the invading Angles, Saxons and Jutes slowly encroached upon what would become England, ultimately overrunning the native Britons and installing their respective legal systems. In what would become Wales, the lack of central government allowed the Romano-British ruling class to assert greater power. The most successful of these families would go on to form the Welsh (or perhaps properly at this stage, *Brythonic*) dynasties that would rule Wales for hundreds of years.

In the late seventh and early eighth centuries, on the border of Wales the Mercian (Anglo Saxon) Kings Aethelbald and Offa built dykes to prevent incursions by the tribes in what would become Wales. Offa's dyke ran for two hundred and forty kilometres, from Prestatyn to Chepstow, albeit in places utilising natural boundaries. On the other side it marked the edge of Wales. The dykes are significant in Welsh history as they mark a clear boundary for Wales and thus gave a physical definition to the extent of the power of the Welsh rulers and the influence of their laws. It should be noted that a distinctly Welsh national identity and legislative system had still not formed at this stage in Wales' history. The Welsh were to continue to refer to themselves as *Brytaniaid* until the late twelfth century, and they also referred to the land in which they lived as the Romans had done, Britannia.

THE WELSH PRINCES 1-5

Whilst the Welsh of the Middle Ages ran their own affairs, Welsh law carried with it an inherent problem that inhibited the development of a single legal code extending over all of Wales. Land rights on the death of the landowner would be divided between the sons of the landowner. The sons would jointly own the land but would divide the land in practical terms for administration. A King (or Prince)[5] would inherit a kingdom and enlarge it throughout his life by adding other lands by marriage, conquest or further inheritance. On his death the kingdom would be divided between his sons, although the regal title itself would pass to a single son as nominated by the monarch in his own lifetime. Incidentally, the system of primogeniture practised by the Normans (who would invade England in the eleventh century), under which the eldest son would inherit lands, was a system which allowed a succession of English Kings to acquire the majority of modern Britain.

[5] Often the Princes would prefer the term 'Prince' as opposed to 'King' as there were so many kings in Wales during this period. Prince came from the Latin for Principal Ruler.

During this period there were some Welsh princes that shaped the constitutional and legal context of their time by acquiring large areas of Wales.

1-6 Rhodri Mawr (the Great)

We know little of Rhodri, but we can be fairly sure that, having inherited the Crown of Gwynedd in North Wales in 844, he had an illustrious premiership that began with defeating Scandinavian invaders. Rhodri went on to acquire a large part of the lands that comprised what would become Wales, from Prestatyn in the North to the borders of Gwent and Pembrokeshire in the South. He was the first Welsh Prince to control an area as large as he did and he is generally considered to be the father of all the Welsh Princes, with all later Princes coming from his bloodline.

1-7 Hywel Dda (the Good)

During the reign of one of Rhodri the Great's grandsons, Hywel ap Cadell (later known as Hywel Dda) (910–49), an even larger part of Wales came together under one kingdom. Hywel Dda's kingdom was a kingdom that by the time of his death incorporated virtually all of Wales. It was also during this period that the native laws of Wales are traditionally thought to have been reduced to writing. Hywel Dda is said to have called together a great assembly consisting of representatives from all over the country. After forty days' debate and examination of the various laws that governed the various areas of Wales, they brought together a revised and substantive law for all of Wales. At around the same time the Anglo-Saxon kingdoms of England, under the Kings of Wessex, were consolidating into an English kingdom with their own set of laws, thus representing a split in national identity and laws – from the Roman influenced Brytaniaid and tribal customs, to distinct and separate Welsh and English laws. This said, there was still a distinct link between the thrones. Hywel Dda attended the English King's council (the Witan) and did homage. He was named in treaties of the time with the title 'under king'.

Public law, under the laws of Hywel Dda, did not represent the system of obligations, judicial checks and balances that it does today. One of the King's citizens could not challenge the decisions of the king and his officers. It did, however, incorporate a system whereby the state would protect its citizens, including a criminal code. The criminal law was detailed and largely based on a principle of restitution by compensation for offences against the person and criminal damage. Some offences, such as theft, did fall into a punitive system with capital punishment, the removal of limbs, or fines being imposed.

1-8 Gruffudd ap Llywelyn

Gruffudd assumed the control of all of Wales through conquest. He began his campaign in 1039 and by around 1057 he assumed control of all of Wales. He was the first Welsh Prince to assume a kingdom large enough to present a direct threat to the English Crown. In 1063 the ill-fated Harold Godwinson, who was not yet King of England, struck to remove this threat and Gruffudd was killed near Snowdonia on 5 August 1063. The seven years during which he ruled the whole of Wales, nonetheless, represent the one occasion in history where all of Wales was united under a single ruler and subject to no outside authority. It was perhaps the period of greatest constitutional freedom.

The Welsh Princes, the Normans and the Plantagenets 1-9

In the years following the Norman conquest of England, Wales retained its identity. The law with its roots in the laws of Hywel Dda was still in force. After the death of William I (the Conqueror) the Norman Lords who were granted the land on the edge of Wales began to encroach. In South and East Wales areas were taken by force and Norman Lords took the place of Welsh Princes. The conquered areas became known as 'the Marches'. The Marcher Lords were outside Royal authority but were nonetheless dependent on it. They were the legislative, executive and judicial authority for their land, not the King of England. It was in the Lord's court that justice was done. The Marches operated not under the Welsh law or the English law but in a third way. Welsh customs were retained but the courts often used common law procedures and allowed access to the writs that were a feature of English law.[6]

In his extensive work, *The Acts of Welsh Rulers: 1120–1283*, Huw Pryce identifies nine Welsh dynasties that made laws for Wales during the titular years; Arwystli, Cedewain, Deheubarth, Maelienydd, Glamorgan, Gwynedd, Gwynllwg, Powys, and Senghennydd. Some of these houses had only fleeting periods of independence. Arwystli and Cedewain in Mid Wales were largely subject to the authority of other dynasties, predominantly Powys and Gwynedd. Conversely, Glamorgan, Gwynllwg, and Senghennydd in South Wales were mainly controlled by the Marcher Lords.

Gwynedd and Llywelyn ap Gruffudd 1-10

Gwynedd, with its ancestral homeland lying in what is now North West Wales, is the dynasty most worthy of note as it was the most consistently powerful of the medieval Welsh dynasties.

In 1246 the leadership of the house of Gwynedd came to Llywelyn ap Gruffudd, perhaps the most famous Welsh Prince of this era. His reign began in a time of almost constant battle with the English. In 1267 Llywelyn ap Gruffudd was formally recognised by Henry III as the most powerful of the Welsh Princes and granted precedence over the other Welsh kingdoms. The Treaty of Montgomery, by which this precedence was granted, also granted Llywelyn the title 'Prince of Wales' – the first and last Welsh ruler to be formally granted the title.[7]

[6] See 1-14 and 5-47 for details of the public law based prerogative writs.

[7] Some of Llywelyn's ancestors were self proclaimed.

1-11 Laws of the later Welsh Princes

Before reaching the end of the narrative that is Wales' greatest era of legal autonomy, it may be useful to pause and conduct a quick examination of the types of laws with which these latter Welsh Princes concerned themselves.[8] The largest number of Welsh acts[9] dealt with ownership of land. What is of note is that the Welsh acts of this period are specific in their terms rather than general. As well as private law a number of acts dealt specifically with terms agreed between Welsh Princes or between Welsh Princes and the English King. We may call these acts, treaties. A good example is the Treaty of Woodstock agreed between Owain ap Gruffudd, Llywelyn ap Gruffudd, and Henry III on 30 April 1247. The treaty allows for the cessation of hostilities, the recognition of the Welsh Princes' rights to land in North Wales, and the terms of homage to Henry III (which included an agreement to provide troops). An important provision in this treaty is the provision for dealing with land disputes. Under the treaty all parties agreed that the English King would be responsible for adjudicating, but that the dispute would be heard in Wales or the Marches, and would be decided according to Welsh law. Treaties agreed in Oxford (17 June 1258) and Montgomery (22 August 1260) provided for a further truce between Llywelyn and Henry III. Disputes as to any alleged breach of the treaties would be adjudicated upon by twelve trustworthy men. This is significant in terms of the fact that the Welsh system of law did not incorporate a form of trial by jury; this was an English method of dispute resolution. The Treaty of Aberconwy on the other hand, agreed between Llywelyn and Edward I on 9 November 1277, confirmed the agreement in the Treaty of Woodstock and also guaranteed the right for Welsh land disputes to be decided in Wales and according to Welsh law.

The output of Welsh laws in this period was in fact relatively low. Huw Pryce, in his earlier mentioned work, gives the example that even at his most prolific Llywelyn ap Gruffudd only averaged 5.5 acts per annum. Compare this to William the Lion of Scotland (1165–1214), who averaged 12 per year, or Henry II of England who averaged over 100 letters of a legal nature per year, let alone his other legal acts such as charters or treaties.[10] Few of the acts of the later Welsh princes were ground breaking in constitutional or public law terms. Some treaties were key in the struggle for jurisdiction between the Welsh and English Kings, but on the whole there were few acts and they mainly dealt with private land matters. In terms of the public law importance of this period the focus should not so much be on what was done, but the fact that Wales possessed the legal autonomy to do it.

[8] It should not be forgotten that the underpinning legal code, or at least the principles established in the legal code, of Hywel Dda continued to apply, albeit with some alterations.

[9] This should not be taken to imply a legislative Act as we know it today, but rather an action or order by a Monarch.

[10] The reasons for this, of course, may be myriad. The move to written records in this period may be a significant element, as could the different forms of administration developed at the English court.

The end of the Welsh Princes 1-12

In 1272 Edward I came to the English throne. On his return to England in 1274 he summoned the Prince of Wales, Llywelyn ap Gruffudd, on five occasions to do homage. Llywelyn unwisely failed to attend on each occasion. In 1276 Edward declared Llywelyn a rebel. Edward then began to reduce Welsh legal autonomy. He assumed the right to resolve land disputes between Welsh rulers according to English law; Llywelyn conversely sought to rely on the Treaty of Aberconwy, which guaranteed that Welsh land disputes would be decided by Welsh law. In the end Llywelyn's dispute would be moot as war broke out between England and Wales in 1282, before the dispute was resolved.

The war of 1282 was the last throw of the dice by a confederation of Welsh Princes. The resisting princes failed abysmally with the major player, Llywelyn ap Gruffudd, dying in a minor skirmish on 11 December 1282. He was the last Welsh Prince to hold the title 'Prince of Wales'. Edward quickly asserted his rule. The final stroke for Edward was to enact the Statute of Rhuddlan, otherwise known as the Statute of Wales, in 1284, which ushered a great many of the English common law's features into Wales. The two sets of laws becoming as close as they would until their complete union under Henry VIII, it is important to note that England and Wales did not at this point have a unified legal system. The Statute became governing law for Wales and brought in many English legal provisions, but at this time England and Wales had separate legal systems.

Whilst the Plantagenet Kings may have begun a more aggressive imposition of English law in Wales, it is only fair to observe that they remained sensitive to the client Welsh and Marcher Lord's wish to retain local justice. These wishes were observed to the extent that where in England a great deal of civil and criminal litigation could be begun locally but ultimately determined in Westminster or the Court of the King's Bench (that travelled with the King), in Wales all stages of such litigation were started and heard in Wales.

AFTER THE WELSH PRINCES

The law in Wales prior to the Plantagenet Kings of England was based on the laws 1-13
of Hywel Dda. Since the reign of Henry III Welsh law and Welsh legal autonomy was being chipped away. Under Edward I it became infiltrated (although not yet overrun) by English law. The Statute of Rhuddlan 1284 brought Wales directly under the governance of the English King, either directly or via a Marcher Lord.

The prerogative writs 1-14

A major development in public law, and one which still affects administrative law today, first arose around this time. Since the twelfth century the monarch had the power to issue writs, later known as the prerogative writs (that is to say issued at the prerogative of the monarch), which would require a branch of the state to act in a certain way or explain a certain decision. There were a huge number of writs that existed from this time until the twentieth century (indeed some still exist today). The four most important, in public law terms, were known, and would be known until the twentieth century, as:

- Certiorari
  To declare that the decision of a public body has no lawful force and, therefore, does not have any effect.

- Mandamus
  To compel a public body to act in a particular way, thus exercising its discretion or discharging its public law duty.

- Prohibition
  Similar in function to a quashing order, save that it applies to actions that the public body has indicated an intention to take, but has not yet taken.

- Habeas corpus
  To order the release or production of anyone unlawfully detained.

From the twelfth to the twentieth century these writs developed their individual procedural and remedial character. The writs exist today in the form of judicial review remedies (with the exception of habeas corpus which retains its own procedure).[11]

A person applying to the monarch for one of these writs would apply to the Court of the King's Bench, rather than to the King himself. Thus, the King's justices were to act as the check on the executive and lower level judicial arms of the state. Access to the prerogative writs, which form the basis of administrative law as we know it today, was restricted to Westminster and the Court of the King's Bench, which settled at Westminster during the fifteenth century.

1-15 The Council of Wales

The idea of a National Assembly is not a wholly new one. In fact the first National Assembly, of sorts, was established by Edward IV in 1471. That year he made his son, Edward, the Prince of Wales and established a Council of Wales.[12] Chiefly the Council ensured that disputes between the shires were resolved and that the cross-shire administrative systems functioned properly. Under the Tudors the

[11] The modern day nature of these public law remedies, the writ from which they originated and their procedures are discussed in greater detail later in this chapter and in chapter 5; see 1-32 and 5-47.

[12] Sometimes known as 'the Council in the Marches of Wales' or 'the Council of Wales and the Marches'.

Council would also gain a judicial role. It acted as administrative overseer for the lower courts and it also heard criminal cases and real and personal actions. At its peak, between 1610 and 1620 it heard around 1,200 cases per year. The council would remain the 'regional' authority for Wales after the Tudors took power. Importantly, it should be noted that the council was still answerable to the Monarch via the Privy Council. The Council would continue as the ruling body for Wales, until the Stuart era. In 1641 it lost its criminal jurisdiction (as did that of the Star Chamber in England) and in 1649 it was finally abolished.

Diminishing autonomy 1-16

The key tenets of Edward I's laws continued to apply until the sixteenth century. Whilst the English controlled legislative and executive authority, the judicial system was largely based in Wales and made its decisions based upon the pre-existing Welsh law and newly enacted English law. In public law terms, English common law now ruled. Criminal law was English law and access to the prerogative writs went with the Court of the King's Bench, not with the local Welsh courts. The Plantagenet legacy for Wales was the removal of autonomous rule. The Tudors would go one further.

THE LEGAL UNION OF ENGLAND AND WALES 1-17

The Acts of Union

In 1457 Henry Tudor was born in Pembroke castle. He was one-quarter Welsh and, after he defeated Richard III (the last Plantagenet King) at the battle of Bosworth Field on 22 August 1485, he became Henry VII of England. Henry VII was not the architect of the death blow to Welsh law; it was his son, Henry VIII. In the early sixteenth century there was growing discontent from the Englishmen (and some Welshmen) who ran the counties of Wales. The opinion largely held was that Welsh justice was ineffective, unenforced and easily corrupted. Widespread jury tampering was also alleged. Under pressure from land-owning families the Acts of Union[13] were brought into force. The Acts were ground breaking and imposed a unified system of law for all England and Wales. Welsh law was no longer to be practised in Wales, only that law that had been English law. It should not be forgotten that many in Wales campaigned for a unification of the law. They believed that by unifying both the legal and administrative systems with England they would acquire greater business opportunities and a greater opportunity to acquire lands, public offices, and access to the English Parliament. Counties, sheriffs, justices of the peace, coroners and constables were all to be features of the new unified administrative systems of

[13] Comprised of the Act for Law and Justice to be Ministered in Wales in like Form as it is in this Realm of 1535/6 and the Act for Certain Ordinances in the King's Dominion and Principality of Wales of 1542/3.

England and Wales created by Henry VIII. The introduction of sheriffs and justices of the peace certainly brought a more effective administration of judicial and executive power, which was largely viewed positively in Wales. However, whilst efficaciously an improvement, the legislative, executive and administrative systems were centralised by the Acts, thus diluting the legal autonomy of Wales. It would remain so until the beginning of the twenty-first century.

1-18 The Great Sessions

The second of the Acts of Union brought in a new judicial system that allowed for a separate judicial system in Wales, with separate justices of the peace (who dealt with minor criminal matters at the Quarter Sessions as well as numerous administrative and licensing duties), sheriffs, and Courts to serve the newly created shires in Wales. Wales retained its practice of having much litigation considered locally in newly created Courts, based on the model of session courts that had been established after the conquest by Edward I. From 1543 these Courts, known as the Great Sessions, began to hear cases in Wales.

The Sessions heard a multitude of types of cases, with a wide jurisdiction, including a public law jurisdiction (as we would use the term today) in the power to issue prerogative writs. By sitting in Wales they ensured local justice was provided. The high water mark for the sessions came after the abolition of the Council of Wales in 1649. With nowhere for the most serious criminal and civil cases to be heard, the sessions assumed the responsibility and acted as Wales' highest Court, a successor to the Council itself.

By the seventeenth century the tradition of Welsh cases involving the Crown being heard in Wales was beginning to be chipped away. This started when the Court of the King's Bench began issuing writs of certiorari to remove cases from the Great Sessions, to the King's Bench.[14] In 1723 the King's Bench, in *R* v *Athoe*,[15] ordered that the English assizes had jurisdiction to hear a criminal case that would previously have been heard by the Sessions in Wales. In that case the King's Bench issued a writ of certiorari to force a murder trial being heard in Wales to Hereford Assizes and the Justice of the Great Sessions acceded to the writ. In 1769 the case of *Lloyd* v *Jones*[16] established a precedent for Welsh civil cases to be heard by the English courts. As a result of these cases the separate judicial authority that Wales had enjoyed was eroded. Furthermore, the King's Bench in London established itself as a superior Court to the Great Sessions, rather than one of equal jurisdiction.

Finally, in 1830, Parliament acted to abolish the Great Sessions.[17] From that point onwards all of the most serious cases, including those cases we would now

[14] An early example of this is 'Sir John Carew's Case' in 1618 where the King's Bench issued a writ of certiorari to remove an indictment for riot from the Great Sessions.

[15] *Dominus R* v *Athoe Senior' er Junior'* 93 ER 694; (1722) 1 Str 553.

[16] (1769) 1 Dougl 213, n. 10.

[17] Which it did in the Law Terms Act 1830.

associate with public law challenges (save criminal cases, which continued to be dealt with before local Courts), were started and considered in London with judgment also given in London, although the hearings themselves were on occasion still heard in Wales. The reform removed the ability of Wales to keep its own judicial check on its public officials. It also brought Wales to its lowest form of political and judicial autonomy, with no legislative, executive or judicial authority of its own.

The low tide for Welsh legal autonomy 1-19

Having lost any legal, executive, or judicial autonomy Wales was, by the nineteenth century, simply a part of Great Britain, to the extent that the infamous 1888 edition of *Encyclopaedia Britannica* contained the entry 'For Wales – See England'. The position in 1830 remained at a constant for another fifty-one years until, in the first step of a renaissance, Parliament recognised the Welsh identity for the first time in a legislative guise. The Sunday Closing (Wales) Act 1881 was the first Act to make provision for Wales only. The Act represented the first step towards separate laws applicable in Wales only, albeit passed by a legislature in London. Soon after came the Welsh Intermediate Education Act 1889, which allowed Welsh local authorities to create intermediate and secondary schools. This represented an important step in specifically devolved powers for Wales and, interestingly, as a result of low fees and ready scholarships in Wales, did much to improve social mobility. The nineteenth and twentieth centuries were to see some recognition of a national Welsh identity, but only in a legislative guise, and wholly controlled by Westminster and Whitehall.

THE ESTABLISHMENT OF THE CURRENT JUDICIAL SYSTEM IN ENGLAND AND WALES 1-20

The nineteenth-century reforms in the judicial system would create a legal system for England and Wales that is much closer to the system today. An examination of how our current court system was created and operates will allow for a greater understanding of the place of public and administrative law in the legal system of England and Wales.

The present day domestic judicial system[18] in England and Wales can (broadly) be separated into three sections: the inferior courts, the tribunals, and the superior courts. The inferior courts can, in some circumstances at least, have their decisions reviewed by the Administrative Court[19] by way of judicial review (along with other public bodies).[20] No matter is deemed to be beyond the jurisdiction of a superior

[18] See Annex H for a diagram illustrating the appeal system in England and Wales.

[19] Although note the restriction where an appeal to another court may be an adequate alternative remedy and thus act as a bar to judicial review. See 5-9.

[20] See the discussion of the differences between inferior and superior courts in *R* v *Chancellor of St Edmundsbury and Ipswich Diocese, ex parte White* [1948] 1 KB 195.

court unless it is expressly shown to be so. As such they cannot be subject to judicial review. Conversely, nothing is within the jurisdiction of an inferior court unless it is expressly shown on the face of the proceedings that the particular matter is within jurisdiction of the court.[21] The tribunals are not courts and as such cannot technically be considered inferior or superior courts. The exception is the Upper Tribunal which is a superior court by virtue of s. 3(5) of the Tribunals, Courts and Enforcement Act 2007. As the tribunals may be subject to judicial review, they could be seen to fall within the same category as the inferior courts. The circumstances in which the Upper Tribunal may be subject to judicial review in the Administrative Court are discussed in chapter 5.[22]

The inferior courts

1-21 Magistrates' courts

Justices of the peace, the formal title for today's magistrates, have been an important figure in the English judicial system since the middle of the fourteenth century. They were first appointed in Wales in 1536 after the first of the Acts of Union. Since 1536 justices of the peace in Wales have dealt with minor offences and licensing matters. Historically they also possessed administrative functions such as controlling vagrancy and poor relief.

Today the justices of the peace sit in magistrates' courts and have jurisdiction in both civil and criminal matters. Their jurisdiction extends wherever they have common law or statutory powers, which includes:

- criminal matters, where it is the function of magistrates to conduct the trial of summary offences, that is to say minor offences, and of offences triable either way, that is to say offences that could be heard in Magistrates' Court or the Crown Court (the magistrates may refuse to deal with an either-way offence if it is too serious and the defendant may elect a Crown Court trial for either-way offences);
- youth courts, which are criminal courts where the defendants are aged 10 to 17;
- a licensing jurisdiction as an appellate court. The local authorities are the arbiters of applications for licences (for example, a licence to sell alcohol) but the magistrates may hear an appeal against the local authority's decision; and
- civil matters such as complaints (for example, applications for anti-social behaviour orders or to prevent nuisances).

Magistrates also have jurisdiction to consider some family law cases, but not in the magistrates' court. Since the creation of the 'single Family Court', which is

[21] R v *Chancellor of St Edmundsbury and Ipswich Diocese, ex parte White* [1948] 1 KB 195 at 205–6.

[22] See 5-64.

discussed later in the chapter, magistrates now deal with family law matters in the Family Court.

Magistrates' courts are presided over by a bench of two or three justices of the peace whilst others are presided over by a district judge sitting alone.

The County Court 1-22

In 1846 the County Court system as we know it today (more or less) was established across England and Wales by the County Courts Act 1846. It has been moulded into today's form by subsequent County Court Acts, the latest being the County Courts Act 1984, as well as the creation of the 'single County Court' by the Crime and Courts Act 2013.[23] The creation of the single County Court on 22 April 2014 acted to merge all 173 County Courts in England and Wales into one County Court for the whole of England and Wales. There are two business centres (which existed before the creation of the single County Court), the County Court Money Claims Centre in Salford and the County Court Business Centre in Northampton, where a number of types of County Court money claims must be lodged and where the administration of the claim will take place.[24] The old County Courts continue to act as hearing centres for the single County Court, and claims that are not reserved to the Salford and Northampton centres may be commenced and managed in any hearing centre,[25] but, importantly, there are no jurisdictional boundaries (in terms of geography).

The County Court deals with the vast majority of civil cases in England and Wales. Subject to upper monetary limits, the County Court has jurisdiction to entertain nearly all types of claims that may be the subject of civil proceedings in the High Court. Thus, within those limits, it may hear and determine any claim including (but not limited to):

- contract;
- tort;
- any claim for the payment of money recoverable by statute;
- any claim for the recovery of land;
- any of the classes of equity and probate proceedings; and
- claims expressly allocated to the County Court by statute.

County Court proceedings are predominantly dealt with by a judge sitting alone (although in some rare cases the claim is still considered by a judge and jury). The judges authorised to sit in the County Court include High Court judges, circuit

[23] See s. 17(1), which inserts s. A1 into the County Courts Act 1984.

[24] Claims for money alone, but subject to certain restrictions – see CPR PD 7A, para. 4A.1 and CPR PD 7C.

[25] CPR PD 7A, para. 2.4A(1).

judges, district judges and deputy judges.[26] The level of judge allocated depends on the value and/or complexity of the claim. There is also an internal appeal structure in the County Court, with decisions of district judges being capable of appeal to a circuit judge.[27]

1-23 The Family Court

On 22 April 2014, the 'single Family Court' was created.[28] Like the single County Court there is one Family Court for all England and Wales, with the old County Courts acting as hearing centres. Each area has a designated hearing centre acting as a 'single point of entry' where all Family Court proceedings must be lodged and managed. The hearings may take place at that centre or at other local centres.

The proceedings before the Family Court are expressly assigned to the Family Court by statute. A useful table, which outlines a number of relevant statutes, as well as the level of judge that will consider the case, can be found in Schedule 1 to the Family Court (Composition and Distribution of Business) Rules 2014. Essentially, the Family Court has jurisdiction to hear (amongst other matters) matrimonial cases, adoptions, residence and contact with children cases, proceedings for taking a child into care and child support cases.

The Family Court will determine which level of judge will hear the case.[29] This can include magistrates, district judges, circuit judges and High Court judges (sitting in the Family Court).[30] For those cases that were once dealt with in the High Court, but are now dealt with by a High Court judge sitting in the Family Court, the Family Court has all the powers of the High Court.[31]

1-24 Tribunals

The Tribunals grew up piece-meal over time to provide a means of review for the individual against administrative decisions of public bodies. The review jurisdiction of the tribunals was (and indeed is) far narrower than the judicial review jurisdiction of the High Court (formerly the prerogative writs). A tribunal is only able to review the decisions within its express frame of reference. Further, the test to be

[26] See s. 5 of the County Court Act 1984 for the long list of judges who may sit as judges in the County Court.

[27] CPR PD 52A, para. 3.5.

[28] See s. 17(3) of the Crime and Courts Act 2003, which inserts s. 31A into the Matrimonial and Family Proceedings Act 1984.

[29] The level of judge is allocated according to the Family Court (Composition and Distribution of Business) Rules 2014. Schedule 1 to the 2014 Rules provides a useful table outlining relevant proceedings and the level of judge to be assigned.

[30] See s. 31C of the Matrimonial and Family Proceedings Act 1984 for the list of judges authorised to sit in the Family Court.

[31] Section 31E(1)(a) of the Matrimonial and Family Proceedings Act 1984.

applied on review is not as restrictive as the judicial review test.[32] Each tribunal therefore has a specialised area of jurisdiction with different rules governing them. The current system incorporates a two-tier tribunals system. However, not all tribunals are within the new system, and those that are still, in some cases, retain individual rules. The modern day tribunals (First-tier Tribunal, Upper Tribunal, and those outside the two-tier structure) all sit in Wales as required.

First-tier Tribunal 1-25

The First-tier Tribunal is currently spilt into six chambers, organised as follows:[33]

1. the Social Entitlement Chamber;
2. the War Pensions and Armed Forces Compensation Chamber;
3. the Health, Education and Social Care Chamber;
4. the Tax Chamber;
5. the General Regulatory Chamber; and
6. the Immigration and Asylum Chamber.

Each chamber may also incorporate a number of specific tribunals that deal with reviews of the decisions of specific public bodies or even specific decisions from specific public bodies.[34] The tribunal sits with expert judges and other members (as required in the relevant tribunal or relevant case) in the field over which the tribunal has authority.

Upper Tribunal 1-26

The Upper Tribunal is the second tier in the independent two-tier system. It primarily has two functions in that it considers appeals on a point of law from the First-tier Tribunal[35] and it also exercises a limited judicial review jurisdiction.[36] Appeals from the First-tier Tribunal are allocated to one of four chambers in the Upper Tribunal:[37]

1. the Administrative Appeals Chamber;
2. the Tax and Chancery Chamber;

[32] See chapters 3 and 5.

[33] As outlined in article 2 of the First-tier Tribunal and Upper Tribunal (Chambers) Order 2008.

[34] For example, the Social Entitlement Chamber is made up of ten separate tribunals, one example of which is the First-tier Tribunal (Consumer Credit) which hears appeals that were previously heard by the Consumer Credit Appeals Tribunal under the Consumer Credit Act 1974.

[35] The right of appeal from the First-tier Tribunal can be found in s. 11(2) of the Tribunals, Courts and Enforcement Act 2007. There are some decisions which are excluded from the right of appeal: see s. 13(1) and (8) of the Tribunals, Courts and Enforcement Act 2007. It should be noted that appeals are on a point of law only. A facts based appeal is outside the scope of an appeal to the Upper Tribunal.

[36] For a discussion of the interplay between the Upper Tribunal and the Administrative Court, including when the Upper Tribunal may consider an application for judicial review and when it may be subject to judicial review, see 5-61.

[37] Article 6 of the First-tier Tribunal and Upper Tribunal (Chambers) Order 2008.

3. the Lands Chamber; and
4. the Immigration and Asylum Chamber.

A judge of the Upper Tribunal may be a full-time specialist judge or a deputy judge who may be appointed to sit on a less frequent basis. A number of judges from other jurisdictions are also authorised to sit as Upper Tribunal judges.[38]

1-27 Tribunals outside the two-tier system (including the Welsh tribunals)

There are some tribunals that fall outside the two-tier structure. The most well known of these is the employment tribunal, which has its own appellate tribunal, the Employment Appeals Tribunal. There are a number of tribunals that operate outside the two-tier system that only operate in Wales:

- Adjudication Panel for Wales;
- Agricultural Land Tribunal;
- Board of Medical Referees;
- Forestry Committees for Wales;
- Independent Review of Determinations Panels in Wales;
- Mental Health Review Tribunal for Wales;
- Registered Nursery Education Inspectors Appeal Tribunal;
- Registered School Inspectors Appeal Tribunal;
- Residential Property Tribunal for Wales;
- School Admission Appeal Panels for Wales;
- School Exclusion Appeal Panels for Wales;
- Special Educational Needs Tribunal for Wales;
- Traffic Penalty Tribunal (when conducting hearings in Wales);
- Valuation Tribunals in Wales;
- Welsh Language Tribunal.

These are the tribunals which were listed in the Administrative Justice and Tribunals Council (Listed Tribunals) (Wales) Order 2007[39] with alterations as a result of various reforms since 2010.[40] Each of these tribunals has specific rules and a specific appellate structure. Some provide for an appeal to the Upper Tribunal, some to the Administrative Court, and some have no right of appeal at all, leaving judicial review in the Administrative Court as the only method of reviewing the tribunal.

[38] Including Court of Appeal Judges, High Court Judges, and Circuit Judges.

[39] The 2007 Order was revoked on 19 August 2013 by the Public Bodies (Abolition of Administrative Justice and Tribunals Council) Order 2013, which abolished the Administrative Justice and Tribunals Council. Although the order was revoked, the tribunals remain.

[40] The altered list was compiled by Bangor Law School for the Cardiff Administrative Justice Workshop, held at the Millennium Stadium on 9 March 2015.

Superior courts

Crown Courts 1-28

The Crown Court was established by the Courts Act 1971 and replaced the Courts of assize and the Courts of quarter sessions. The Crown Court's jurisdiction extends to:

- all criminal proceedings on indictment.[41] This includes indictment only proceedings (the most serious crimes, all of which must be heard in the Crown Court) and some either-way offences, which the magistrates' court deems too serious to be dealt with in the magistrates' court or where the defendant elects a trial in the Crown Court;
- proceedings on the committal of a person for sentence, where the offence in the magistrates' court is so serious that the sentencing powers of the magistrates would not be sufficient;
- appeals from magistrates' courts, as well as some other bodies such as local authorities; and
- a limited civil jurisdiction, which is now concerned with the repair of highways and certain matters concerning firearms certificates.

The Crown Court sits with a judge,[42] who determines questions of law, and a jury, which determine questions of fact, in proceedings on indictment. On appeals, the Crown Court sits with a judge and one or two magistrates, who determine questions of both fact and law.

The Crown Court is a superior court, but in reality it is something of a hybrid between a superior and an inferior court. Where the Crown Court is dealing with a trial on indictment it is a superior court.[43] It could be considered to be an inferior court in all other circumstances.

High Court 1-29

In the 1870s the Judicature Acts 1873–5 fused a number of the courts, including the Queen's Bench,[44] which still dealt with all applications for one of the prerogative writs, into a new court of first instance known as the High Court. With effect from 1 October 1971, the divisions of the High Court were reorganised so that the

[41] Section 46(1) of the Senior Courts Act 1981. It would be wise to note at this point that from 1981 until 2009 the Senior Courts Act 1981 was known as the Supreme Courts Act 1981. The change came as a result of the creation of the Supreme Court in 2009, which is discussed below.

[42] The judge may be a High Court judge, a circuit judge or a deputy judge known as a recorder.

[43] Sections 1, 29(3) and 46(1) of the Senior Courts Act 1981. Although see 5-13 for a discussion of circumstances in which a trial on indictment may be challenged by way of judicial review.

[44] The title King's or Queen's Bench began changing depending on the sex of the Monarch during the reign of Queen Victoria.

High Court was divided into the Chancery Division, the Queen's Bench Division and the Family Division.[45]

The current High Court is still made up of these three divisions, now provided for by the Senior Courts Act 1981.[46] Since the 1981 Act, business has been assigned to each of the three divisions. The High Court retains the jurisdiction it had before the Senior Courts Act 1981,[47] but as that pre-1981 Act jurisdiction is not defined, it can be difficult to outline in full what areas of business the High Court considers and to which Division that work would be assigned. In general terms, the work of the three divisions includes (but is not limited to):[48]

- Queen's Bench Division
  1. all Administrative Court proceedings;
  2. contract, tort and libel proceedings (civil wrongs);
  3. all control order proceedings;
  4. all financial restrictions proceedings;
  5. all causes and matters involving the exercise of the admiralty jurisdiction of the High Court or its jurisdiction as a prize court; and
  6. all causes and matters entered in the commercial list.

- Chancery Division
  1. corporate and personal insolvency disputes;
  2. business, trade and industry disputes;
  3. the enforcement of mortgages;
  4. intellectual property matters, copyright and patents;
  5. disputes relating to trust property; and
  6. contentious probate (relating to wills and inheritance) actions.

- Family Division
  1. all family law proceedings involving the inherent jurisdiction of the High Court or international family law cases;[49] and
  2. probate business not assigned to the Chancery Division.

It should be noted that whilst the High Court is split into three divisions, the three divisions still constitute separate parts of one High Court.[50] When the High Court

[45] Administration of Justice Act 1970.

[46] Section 5(1) of the Senior Courts Act 1981.

[47] Section 19(2) of the Senior Courts Act 1981.

[48] As per Schedule 1 to the Senior Courts Act 1981.

[49] All other family law proceedings, which are based in statute, are now dealt with by the single Family Court (discussed earlier in the chapter).

[50] *Re Hastings (No. 3)* [1959] Ch 368.

sits it will sit with a single judge of the High Court (or a deputy judge[51]), although a court of not less than two High Court judges may sit as a Divisional Court.[52]

Court of Appeal 1-30

The Court of Appeal was created by the Supreme Court of Judicature Act 1873. Whilst the High Court became one court, fusing a number of the superior courts, the Court of Appeal became one Court by fusing the appellate courts. The current Court of Appeal consists of two divisions: the Criminal Division and the Civil Division. The Court of Appeal's work is allocated between the divisions by the Senior Courts Act 1981. The jurisdiction that the Court of Appeal enjoyed before the 1981 Act is also retained.[53]

- Civil Division
  The jurisdiction of the Civil Division is entirely appellate, hearing appeals from the County Court, High Court and Upper Tribunal. The Civil Division exercises the whole of the jurisdiction of the Court of Appeal, except such as is exercisable by the Criminal Division.[54]

- Criminal Division
  The Criminal Division's jurisdiction is mainly one of appeal. It includes all appeals specifically assigned to the Court of Appeal (Criminal Division) by statute[55] or rules of Court,[56] primarily (but not exclusively) the Criminal Appeal Act 1968, the Administration of Justice Act 1960 and the Senior Courts Act 1981. It does also deal with some first instance applications: for example, the Attorney General may refer a case to the Criminal Division for review if he considers that a sentence passed by the Crown Court has been unduly lenient. The Criminal Division exercises jurisdiction to order the issue of writs of *venire de novo* (ordering the trial of an offender where the court rules that his purported trial has been a nullity).

Cases in the Court of Appeal are heard by judges of the Court of Appeal (or other additional judges authorised to sit in the Court of Appeal).[57] The Court of Appeal generally sits with three judges considering a case. On occasion it sits with more than three judges. It may sit with two judges or a single judge, but there are some cases that require three or more judges.

[51] Senior Courts Act 1981, s.9.

[52] Senior Courts Act 1981, s.66.

[53] Senior Courts Act 1981, s. 15(2).

[54] Senior Courts Act 1981, s. 53(3).

[55] Senior Courts Act 1981, s. 53(2).

[56] Senior Courts Act 1981, s. 53(1). See, for example, devolution references assigned to the Court of Appeal (Criminal Division) discussed at 6-26.

[57] Senior Courts Act 1981, s. 9.

1-31 Supreme Court (formerly the House of Lords)

It is thought that the appellate jurisdiction of the High Court of Parliament arose as an extension of the forum of the King's Council.[58] In 1399 the House of Commons declared, by petition to the King, that they had no role in this jurisdiction, which belonged only to the King and the Lords. This was later confirmed by Henry IV.[59] This was notably before the Acts of Union and thus did not apply to Wales until after the first of those Acts in 1535/1536. Since this time the House of Lords (as the Court would become known) acted as the final appellate Court for England and Wales.

On 1 October 2009 the appellate jurisdiction was removed from the House of Lords and is now exercised by the Supreme Court of the United Kingdom.[60] The Supreme Court[61] now acts as the final appellate Court from the Court of Appeal (and on some occasions directly from the High Court). Such an appeal may be brought on a point of law or a point of fact, but the House of Lords and the Supreme Court have been traditionally reluctant to disturb the findings of fact made by the lower courts.[62] The Supreme Court also acts as a constitutional court to determine questions of competence in the devolution settlement.[63]

When the Supreme Court sits it must constitute an uneven number of at least three Supreme Court judges[64] (or another judge authorised to sit in the Supreme Court).[65]

In a policy decision that directly affects Welsh cases, the President of the Supreme Court, Lord Neuberger, has announced that where practicable a senior judge with knowledge of Wales will be invited to sit on cases dealing with Welsh issues. He also noted that whilst the Supreme Court has never sat outside London, he saw no reason why it could not, in an appropriate case, sit in Wales.[66]

58 *Halsbury's Laws of England* (5th edn) (2010), Courts and Tribunals, vol. 24, para. 640.

59 III Parliament Rolls 427 no. 79 (3 November 1399, 1 Henry IV).

60 Constitutional Reform Act 2005, s. 23(1).

61 The Supreme Court of England and Wales was what the Senior Courts were called before the Supreme Court of the United Kingdom was created in 2009. Readers may see reference to the Supreme Court in pre-2009 judgments or legislation. The pre-2009 Supreme Court was the Crown Court, High Court and Court of Appeal and their predecessors (as discussed above). They should not be confused with the Supreme Court as it exists today. The Crown Court, High Court and Court of Appeal are now known as the Senior Courts.

62 Constitutional Reform Act 2005, s. 40(2) and (5).

63 See 4-9 to 4-16.

64 Constitutional Reform Act 2005, s. 42(1).

65 Constitutional Reform Act 2005, s. 38(1).

66 Lord Neuberger speaking at the Legal Wales Conference at Bangor University on 10 October 2014.

MODERN DEVELOPMENT OF ADMINISTRATIVE LAW AND THE CROWN OFFICE/ADMINISTRATIVE COURT OFFICE

Modernisation of the prerogative writs 1-32

In 1933 the Hanworth Committee[67] recommended the first substantive changes to the long-standing *writ* system (discussed above) and the beginnings of a procedure akin to that used today. The Administration of Justice (Miscellaneous Provisions) Act 1938 replaced the prerogative writs (other than habeas corpus) with orders of the same name. However, the writs, now restyled as orders, still had their own separate procedures.

In 1976 the Law Commission produced a recommendation for wide-ranging reform of public law procedures in the *Report on Remedies in Administrative Law.*[68] In essence the Commission recommended that the orders could be unified under a single procedure, to be known as judicial review. These recommendations were implemented by an amendment to the Rules of the Supreme Court[69] ('RSC') and in January 1978 the new RSC Order 53 came into force – judicial review, in its contemporary form, was born, although it was not given statutory force until 1981 under s. 31 of the Senior Courts Act 1981. Following the creation of judicial review the procedure was continually streamlined to allow more effective access. RSC Order 53 continued to act as the governing procedure for applications for judicial review until the implementation of the Civil Procedure Rules 1998 ('CPR'), although not until eighteen months after the initial implementation of the CPR was provision made for judicial review.[70] On 2 October 2000, the same day as the Human Rights Act 1998 came into force, CPR Part 54 was brought into force and the current procedure was created.[71]

The Crown Office 1-33

In 1981 the then Lord Chief Justice, Lord Lane, handed down the *Practice Direction (Trials in London)*,[72] which provided for the allocation of administrative law claims, including judicial review (then under Rules of the Supreme Court Order 53) into a new High Court list known as the Crown Office List.[73] At this time the exercise of this jurisdiction was still confined to London.

[67] Formally known as *The Business of the Courts Committee: Interim Report*, Cmd 4265 (1933).

[68] Cmnd 6407 (1976).

[69] RSC (Amendment No. 3) 1977.

[70] See the Bowman Report later in this chapter for more detail.

[71] There have been changes between implementation and the current procedure. The current procedure is outlined in chapter 5.

[72] [1981] 1 WLR 1296.

[73] Incidentally, regular users of the modern day Administrative Court will note that case numbers begin with a 'CO' (e.g. CO/1234/2015). The CO used to identify the case as an Administrative Court case arises from the days when the Administrative Court Office was called the Crown Office.

When the Crown Office was established it was a small team that supported a small cadre of specialist public law judges. There were only five nominated judges in 1981. Case numbers in those days were few: in 1980 there were just 580 administrative law cases dealt with in the High Court.[74] However, the applications in the Crown Office List steadily increased to the point where they cast a heavy burden on judicial and administrative resources. The ever-increasing case load resulted in extreme delays. In 1992 the delays in hearing cases were exceeding two years.[75] The Law Commission expressly noted this problem in a 1994 report entitled *Administrative Law: Judicial and Statutory Appeals*,[76] which recommended increased numbers of judges able to hear cases in the Crown Office list. The report also noted that more widespread changes could be implemented as a part of Lord Woolf's Reforms to the Civil Justice System, or what we know today as the Civil Procedure Rules. The Law Commission's report is also one of the first to mention, albeit in passing, the possibility of a decentralised Crown Office List.[77]

1-34 The Administrative Court Office

The numbers of cases lodged with the Crown Office continued to rise and the system began to feel the strain. The committee, chaired by Sir Geoffrey Bowman, reported to the Lord Chancellor in March 2000 in the report *Review of the Crown Office List*[78] (commonly known as 'The Bowman Report'). The Bowman Report endorsed the continuing need for a specialised court dealing with administrative law cases. The report called for the Crown Office List to be renamed 'The Administrative Court' with a view to making it clear that administrative law cases were separated from other High Court work. On 20 July 2000 Lord Woolf, as Lord Chief Justice, handed down *Practice Direction (Administrative Court: Establishment)*.[79] The practice direction followed the recommendations of the Bowman Report and ordered the establishment of the new Administrative Court and Administrative Court Office. On 2 October 2000, CPR Part 54 was brought into force.[80] Alongside the implementation of the CPR Part 54 and the new code for judicial review, the Administrative Court was born.[81]

[74] Civil Justice Quarterly, *The Law Commission Report on judicial review* (1995) 14 CJQ, 97 at 98.

[75] Civil Justice Quarterly, *The Law Commission Report on judicial review* (1995) 14 CJQ, 97 at 98.

[76] Law Com. No. 226.

[77] Law Com. No. 226 at Appendix C, paras 4.1 and 4.2.

[78] LCD, 2000.

[79] [2000] 1 WLR 1654.

[80] Civil Procedure (Amendment No. 4) Rules (SI 2000 No. 2092).

[81] See chapter 2 for analysis of how the Administrative Court developed in Wales from the year 2000.

THE EUROPEAN ELEMENT 1-35

Whilst Parliament remains the sovereign law maker for England and Wales and the Supreme Court remains the highest legal authority in the UK, there are elements from Europe that have, since the mid-twentieth century, had an effect on the law of England and Wales. Those elements are European human rights law and European law. Both now form part of the UK constitution as they have been incorporated into UK law by the Human Rights Act 1998 and the European Communities Act 1972 respectively. Whole textbooks are dedicated to this subject. This section will be a general overview of those two elements.

European human rights law

Following the Second World War the international community committed to a programme of protecting the human rights of individuals from the State. A range of international human rights treaties followed, perhaps the most important of which for Europe was the Convention for the Protection of Human Rights and Fundamental Freedoms established in Rome 1950, otherwise known as the European Convention on Human Rights ('the ECHR'). In article 1 of the ECHR it requires the signatory states to secure to everyone within their jurisdiction the rights and freedoms that it goes on to define. The detail and effect of European human rights law on administrative law and the UK generally is discussed in greater detail in chapter 3.[82] The Convention was opened for signature on 4 November 1950 and was ratified and entered into force on 3 September 1953. The United Kingdom ratified the Convention on 8 March 1951 and was the first country to do so. 1-36

The ECHR also made provision for the establishment and operation of the European Court of Human Rights ('ECtHR') to ensure the implementation of the protected rights. From 1953 until 1966 allegations of breaches of the ECHR could only be brought against the UK to the ECtHR by other states. After 1966 the UK accepted that individuals could also petition the ECtHR for a judgment, provided that they had exhausted the appeals process in the domestic Courts.[83] Until 1994 the ECHR made provision for a two-tier structure to bring complaints against states alleged to have breached the terms of the ECHR. Under the two-tier structure a Commission would analyse the complaint and, if admissible, bring the case to the ECtHR on behalf of the applicant. The Commission stage has now been abolished and there is a single ECtHR which sits either as a Chamber of seven judges (which allows the ECtHR to sit as several chambers hearing several cases at once) or, for more important cases, a Grand Chamber of seventeen judges. A committee of three judges can decide cases that can be disposed of on the basis of the well-established case law of the Court and a single judge may declare cases

[82] At 3-25.

[83] Now enshrined in art. 34 of the ECHR.

inadmissible or strike them from the Court's list. The UK Supreme Court is still the highest Court in England and Wales to create binding precedent, but the judgments of the ECtHR are highly persuasive and are generally (but not always) followed by the domestic Courts.[84]

1-37 European Community and European Union law[85] ('European law')

In 1957 the European Economic Community ('EEC') was created when the Treaty Establishing the European Community[86] ('Treaty of Rome') was signed and entered into by the six original member states, of which the UK was not one. The UK joined the EEC on 1 January 1973, and membership of the EEC was confirmed in domestic law by the European Communities Act 1972.[87] Since 1973 the EEC has grown in both the number of member states and in power. In 1993 the EEC was renamed the European Community ('EC'),[88] and a larger European body, with powers outside the EC, was established called the European Union ('EU'). On 13 December 2007, the member states signed the Treaty of Lisbon.[89] The Treaty of Lisbon entered into force on 1 December 2009 and made sweeping changes to the constitution of the EU (and the EC, the EC being part of the EU) and increased the powers of the EU.

As a result of the UK's membership of the European Union an obligation arises, as with all member states, to 'take appropriate measures ... to ensure fulfilment of the obligations arising out of this treaty'.[90] The doctrine of supremacy of European law has developed since the Treaty of Rome. It is now established that the courts of member states are bound to give effect to directly effective European law even if it is incompatible with the national law of a state.[91] The UK Courts

[84] See the discussion of this principle in chapter 3 at 3-30.

[85] For a detailed discussion of the differences see H. Woolf et al., *De Smith's Judicial Review* (7th edn) (Sweet & Maxwell, 2013), p. 703. Further, for a short yet effective discussion of the history and constitution of the European Union see H. W. R. Wade and C. F. Forsyth, *Administrative Law* (10th edn) (Oxford University Press, 2009), pp. 161–7.

[86] The Treaty of Lisbon renames the Treaty Establishing the European Community (Treaty of Rome) as the Treaty on the Functioning of the European Union. It also amended and renumbered large parts of the Treaty.

[87] There was a UK referendum on continued membership of the EEC in 1975. The electorate voted 'Yes' by 67.2% to 32.8% to remain members of the EEC. It should be noted this was not a referendum on joining the EEC; the UK had already joined three years earlier.

[88] Treaty on European Union signed at Maastricht on 7 February 1992 ('Treaty of Maastricht') and taking effect on 1 November 1993.

[89] Treaty of Lisbon amending the Treaty on European Union and the Treaty establishing the European Community, signed at Lisbon, 13 December 2007.

[90] Article 10(5) of the Treaty on the Functioning of the European Union.

[91] *Internationale Handelsgesellschaft mbH* v *Einfuhr und Vorratsstelle für Getreide und Futtermittel* (Case 11/70) [1970] ECR 1125.

have accepted this requirement[92] and as a result where a UK Act of Parliament or other law is incompatible with European law it will not be given effect by English courts, which will give effect instead to the European law. The domestic courts are also required to interpret UK statutes in the light of any relevant European law.[93]

The Court of Justice of the European Union ('CJEU')[94] is the Court of the European Union, which determines all questions on European law. Unlike the ECtHR its effect is more than persuasive. In legal proceedings the UK courts must decide in accordance with principles laid down by the CJEU as to the effect of any of the Treaties or other European instrument.[95] References may be made to the CJEU to question whether the actions of a member state comply with community law by the national courts themselves,[96] other member states,[97] or the European Commission.[98] The CJEU has a judge appointed from each member state who sits for terms of six years, although these terms are renewable. Not all the judges need sit for every case. The CJEU has two tiers, the Court of First Instance and the CJEU itself. The Court of First Instance has a limited jurisdiction for more minor matters and a right of appeal exists to the CJEU itself. If a matter is not within the jurisdiction of the Court of First Instance then it will be heard by the CJEU. The CJEU (but not Court of First Instance) sits with an advocate general. After oral argument the advocate general will write an opinion advising the CJEU how to act. Although the CJEU need not follow the opinion of the advocate general, it does so more often than it does not.

THE ROAD TO DEVOLUTION 1-38

As the mid-twentieth century approached, the lack of a Welsh presence in the highest levels of Government was notable. The tide eventually turned. First, the Council of Wales returned in 1948 after a two-hundred-and-ninety-nine-year absence. The Council was not a shadow of its seventeenth-century predecessor. It

[92] *R* v *Secretary of State for Transport, ex parte Factortame Ltd (No. 2)* [1991] 1 AC 603 where the House of Lords accepted the judgment of the CJEU in *R* v *Secretary of State for Transport, ex parte Factortame Ltd* (C-213/89) [1991] 1 All ER 70 that when a reference has been made to the European Court, an English court may grant an injunction against the Crown or suspend the operation of an Act of Parliament despite the fact that it apparently had no power to do so under English law.

[93] *Marleasing SA* v *La Comercial Internacional de Alimentacion SA* [1990] ECR I-4135.

[94] The Court of Justice of the European Union is the term used by the CJEU. In English statutes, the CJEU is known as the 'European Court' (see s. 1(2) of and Sch. 1 Pt II to the European Communities Act 1972 and s. 5 of and Sch.1 to the Interpretation Act 1978. In other works the term 'European Court of Justice' or 'ECJ' is used. CJEU is used in this work to ensure that the CJEU is not confused with the European Court of Human Rights ('ECtHR').

[95] European Communities Act 1972, s. 3(1).

[96] See 7-27.

[97] Article 227 of the Treaty on the Functioning of the European Union.

[98] Article 226 of the Treaty on the Functioning of the European Union.

was an advisory body only and was not chaired by a cabinet member. The Council did, however, recommend a specific executive authority for Wales in the form of the Secretary of State for Wales along with a Welsh Office based in Cardiff. Both of these recommendations were enacted in 1964 giving Wales a cabinet minister. From 1964 onwards executive authority was passed to the Secretary of State in numerous fields, including housing, local government, roads, education, industry, and agriculture and fisheries. By 1979 the Secretary of State for Wales and the Welsh Office administered a budget of £1.5 billion and there were over forty quasi-autonomous non-governmental organisations ('quangos') in Wales. Executive powers that directly related to Wales were being exercised with the Welsh people in mind and with an administration in the Welsh Office, based partly in Wales. Legislation and judicial checks were still coming from London but executive and administrative powers were being decentralised.

Whilst various bills and reports proposed devolution throughout the early twentieth century,[99] momentum behind the measure first seriously grew in 1973 after the Kilbrandon Report[100] was published. The report, bar the two dissenters on the committee, recommended an elected Parliament in Scotland and a Welsh Assembly, with powers to govern domestic matters. The initial referendum on devolution was comprehensively defeated: just 20 per cent of voters backed a devolved government in Wales and every single county held an opposed majority.

The Conservative governments of the 1980s and 1990s increased Welsh executive powers by increasing the number of Welsh Office run quangos. By 1997 there were some eighty quangos, including a Welsh Economic Council (created in 1994), and the Secretary of State for Wales and the Welsh Office commanded a budget of £7 billion. Some have even argued that the executive power in Wales grew to the extent that the first National Assembly simply added much needed democratic weight to pre-existing devolved authority. Nonetheless, the Conservatives did not engage with proposals for a devolution settlement. The result was that a second referendum did not take place until 1997.

In 1997 a referendum was held and the measure passed, but only just, with 50.3 per cent of voters being in favour of devolution. The result of the positive referendum was the Government of Wales Act 1998 ('GOWA 1998').

THE GOVERNMENT OF WALES ACT 1998

1-39 Institutions and powers under the 1998 Act

The result of the affirmative vote in the referendum was the Government of Wales Act 1998 ('GOWA 1998'). This is perhaps understating matters. The actual result of the referendum was that for the first time since 1282 Wales was to have its own

[99] For example S. O. Davies, MP for Merthyr Tydfil brought a Parliament for Wales Bill before the House of Commons in 1955. It received little support.

[100] *Report of the Royal Commission on the Constitution*, Cmnd 5460 (1969–73).

national law makers and for the first time in history they were democratically elected national law makers. These powers came into force on 1 July 1999 and, via GOWA 1998, on that date the National Assembly for Wales of sixty members came into existence. GOWA 1998 gave the Assembly secondary legislation making powers, that is to say the executive powers that had previously been held by UK Government Ministers, primarily those of the Secretary of State for Wales. The Assembly was a single corporate body with both legislative and executive functions. It had a First Secretary and an executive to perform its administrative functions. The National Assembly for Wales (Transfer of Functions) Order 1999[101] formally transferred a huge number of statutory executive functions vested in UK Government Minsters to the Assembly. The full list of transferred functions can be found in Schedule 2 to the Order and represents some thirty pages of specific, pre-existing powers that would be transferred to the Assembly.

The Order, and other less encompassing Transfer of Functions Orders, transferred functions to the Assembly in the eighteen fields of competence (or areas), as listed in Schedule 2 to GOWA 1998:

1. Agriculture, forestry, fisheries and food
2. Ancient monuments and historic buildings
3. Culture (including museums, galleries and libraries)
4. Economic development
5. Education and training
6. The environment
7. Health and health services
8. Highways
9. Housing
10. Industry
11. Local government
12. Social services
13. Sport and recreation
14. Tourism
15. Town and country planning
16. Transport
17. Water and flood defence
18. The Welsh language.

Whilst the eighteen areas of competence did give a general overview of the competence of the Assembly's secondary legislative powers no entire area had actually been transferred. The individual powers arose out of individual provisions in primary legislation made by the UK Parliament. What the Assembly had was a collection of powers given to it piecemeal in a number of Acts and transfer of function orders.

[101] SI 1999 No. 672. The order itself is secondary legislation pursuant to s. 22(1) of GOWA 1998.

The sixty-member-strong legislature of the Assembly was responsible for debating and passing the secondary legislation over which it had competence. The Assembly did not control revenue-raising powers but it did have a budget of £8 billion to back its executive authority.

1-40 The case for change

In 1997 it was estimated that 40 per cent of the population were opposed to devolution; by 2007 this had dropped to 17 per cent.[102] It was also widely acknowledged that the Assembly's legislative powers under GOWA 1998 were limited and, due to the attempt to so specifically define the legislative competence of the Assembly, they were unnecessarily complex. What followed was the report of the Commission on the Powers and Electoral Arrangements of the National Assembly for Wales, chaired by Lord Richard QC. The Richard Commission, which carried out the review on behalf of the Welsh Assembly Government, found:

> [T]he most frequently cited cause for disappointment was the inability of the Assembly to fulfil its potential due to its limited powers.[103]

The Richard Commission's report was published in April 2004, recommending a move to a National Assembly with primary legislative powers. Following on from the Richard Commission, the Wales Office published a white paper entitled *Better Governance for Wales* in June 2005. It proposed increasing the National Assembly's powers in three respects:

1. giving the Assembly wider powers to make subordinate legislation;
2. allowing the United Kingdom Parliament to confer enhanced legislative powers on the Assembly in relation to specified matters in devolved fields; and
3. following a referendum, enabling the Assembly to make laws in all devolved fields without recourse to Parliament.

These proposals were adopted by Parliament, and implemented in the Government of Wales Act 2006 ('GOWA 2006').

[102] Institute of Welsh Affairs, *Devolution: A Decade On. IWA Response to the House of Commons Constitutional Affairs Committee Call for Evidence* (November 2007), para. 1.1.

[103] Report of the Richard Commission (Cardiff, 2004), p. 25.

THE GOVERNMENT OF WALES ACT 2006

The legislature (2007–11) 1-41

The Government of Wales Act 2006 retained a National Assembly for Wales as Wales' legislature.[104] By virtue of s. 93(1) of GOWA 2006 the Assembly was granted powers to make primary legislation. The enactments, to be known as Assembly Measures, were equivalent to Acts of Parliament. Section 94 of GOWA 2006 established that Assembly Measures were only lawful if they fell within the areas of competence defined in Schedule 5 to GOWA 2006. Upon the enactment of GOWA 2006 there were no items in Schedule 5 (save field thirteen which had regard to the Assembly itself); the intention being that the law-making function of the National Assembly would grow gradually and in specific areas in a piecemeal fashion. Schedule 5 would be added to either directly by an Act of the UK Parliament or the Assembly could apply to the UK Parliament to add to Schedule 5 by approving a Legislative Competence Order ('LCO').[105] Once an area of competence (called a 'matter') was listed in Schedule 5, the Assembly could then pass an Assembly Measure relating to that matter. This represented a marked advancement in legislative autonomy from GOWA 1998.

The legislature (2011–present) 1-42

There was one more step to be taken before the Welsh constitutional arrangement as it is known today was formed. Section 103(1) of GOWA 2006 contained a provision to allow for a referendum on whether the Assembly Act's provisions[106] should come into force. In essence an affirmative vote in any such referendum would expand powers the National Assembly had to make primary legislation. It is of some interest that, under the provisions of GOWA 2006, the referendum was the first referendum to have binding effect on the Government. All previous referendums were reflections of the will of the people, which the Government could then decide whether to act upon.

The case for fuller primary legislative powers was gaining momentum. Some commentators noted that Parliamentary time in the UK Parliament really only allowed for one Wales-only bill to be debated per session of Parliament.[107] Others noted that the process of making legislation for Wales in the UK Parliament did not allow for proper participation by the Welsh institutions due to the competing priorities of Parliament and the fact that last-minute changes to bills would not

[104] GOWA 2006, s. 1(1).

[105] These were Orders in Council, made in Council by Her Majesty having been approved by both Houses of Parliament and the Assembly.

[106] Which, according to s. 103(8) of GOWA 2006 means the provisions in ss. 107, 108, 110 and 115 of GOWA 2006.

[107] See K. Patchett, 'The Constitutional Architecture', in J. Osmond and B. Jones (eds), *Birth of Welsh Democracy: The First Term of the National Assembly for Wales* (Institute of Welsh Affairs, 2003), p. 15.

allow for proper consultation.[108] Further, some noted that the LCO system involved a great deal of scrutiny, both in the National Assembly and the UK Parliament, and that acquiring competence took up a great deal of time on non-contentious matters, let alone those matters over which Cardiff and Whitehall disagreed.[109]

On 3 March 2011 a referendum was held in Wales whereby 63.5 per cent of voters approved increasing the powers of the National Assembly for Wales by providing for the Assembly to have fuller powers to make primary legislation, known as Assembly Acts.[110] The new system was free of the cumbersome legislative competence system that so restricted the Assembly Measure system. Under the now redundant Schedule 5 to GOWA 2006 the Assembly's powers were very clearly defined and limited in each area of competence. The result of the referendum was to bring into force, as of 5 May 2011, Part 4 of GOWA 2006 and the current system under which the National Assembly passes legislation.

1-43 The powers of the National Assembly

The powers of the National Assembly are primary law-making powers whereby the National Assembly may make 'Acts of the Assembly'. In s. 108(1) of GOWA 2006, the fact that the Acts of the Assembly are primary legislation is expressly noted. This said, s. 108(2) of GOWA 2006 notes that the Act 'is not law' if it is outside the Assembly's competence. For detailed analysis of the legislative competence and law-making powers of the Assembly, attention should be drawn to chapter 4.[111] For the purposes of this introduction, it is sufficient to note that the Assembly may, issues of legislative competence aside, make Assembly Acts relating to the subjects under the twenty-one headings outlined in Part 1 of Schedule 7 to GOWA 2006:

1. Agriculture, forestry, animals, plants and rural development
2. Ancient monuments and historic buildings
3. Culture
4. Economic development
5. Education and training
6. Environment
7. Fire and rescue services and fire safety
8. Food
9. Health and health services
10. Highways and transport
11. Housing
12. Local government
13. National Assembly for Wales

[108] See R. Hazel, 'Multi-Level Governance', in Osmond and Jones (eds), *Birth of Welsh Democracy*.

[109] See T. Watkin, *The Legal History of Wales* (2nd edn) (University of Wales Press, 2012), pp. 202–6.

[110] GOWA 2006, s. 107(1).

[111] At 4-8.

14. Public administration
15. Social welfare
16. Sport and recreation
17. Taxation
18. Tourism
19. Town and country planning
20. Water and flood defence
21. Welsh language.

It is obviously early days in terms of primary legislation and we may have to wait a few years to be able to comment on the actual impact that the Acts of the Assembly are having. The potential impact of primary legislative powers is wide ranging and will likely have a great deal to do with how public and administrative law develops in Wales. Importantly, the Acts of the Assembly will also play a large part in determining the extent of the gap between Welsh and English law.

Executive and administrative functions 1-44

GOWA 2006 formally created a separate executive in the Welsh Assembly Government.[112] The Welsh Assembly Government is now formally known as the Welsh Government.[113] The National Assembly having acquired primary law-making powers, the secondary legislative powers passed to the Welsh Ministers.[114] The day-to-day exercise of executive functions is also carried out by the Welsh Ministers,[115] who number a maximum of twelve (including any deputy ministers),[116] headed and appointed by the First Minister with the approval of the Queen. The functions of the Welsh Government are discussed to a greater extent in chapter 4 at 4-20.

GOWA 2006 contains provision for a body corporate known as the National Assembly for Wales Commission,[117] which, as a corporate body, may enter into contracts and own property for the Assembly, as provided for in Schedule 2 to GOWA 2006. The Commission ensures that the Assembly is provided with the property, staff and services required for the Assembly's purposes.[118]

112 GOWA 2006, s. 45(1).

113 Wales Act 2014, s. 4(1).

114 GOWA 2006, s. 22 and Schs 2 and 3.

115 GOWA 2006, s. 48(1).

116 GOWA 2006, s. 51(1).

117 GOWA 2006, s. 27(1).

118 GOWA 2006, s. 27(5).

1-45 CONCLUSION

This chapter started with the aim of discovering the context within which the current legislative, executive and judicial systems of Wales appear in the grand scheme of history. Wherever Welsh law heads in the twenty-first century it will be new but, in some ways, familiar ground. The Welsh legal system has existed in a variety of guises over hundreds of years and the manner of challenge to public bodies has changed with it. Some of these changes resulted in greater legal autonomy; some resulted in greater ties with England and the United Kingdom. The rest of this work can now properly consider the current legal and procedural provisions for administrative law in Wales and how judicial checks have been devolved alongside legislative and executive powers.

Chapter 2

The Administrative Court in Wales: Creation and Jurisdiction

INTRODUCTION 2-1

This chapter will analyse the creation of the Administrative Court in Wales and its geographical jurisdiction. The chapter may be read with the historical introduction to this work in mind but it has not been included in that chapter for good reason. First, the creation of the Administrative Court in Wales requires greater analysis than an introductory chapter would allow. It is a landmark moment in terms of decentralising judicial checks and advancing the principles of devolution. Secondly, the debate over the proper jurisdiction of the Administrative Court in Wales is an ongoing and detailed one that needs to take into account the legislative, executive and judicial views on the subject, all of which differ slightly. The reader should be in a position to properly analyse when a claim may be brought in the Administrative Court in Wales, be that from the practitioner or litigant's practical point of view ('where can I lodge my claim?') or from the academic analysis in terms of the wider debate on decentralisation and devolution.

CREATING THE ADMINISTRATIVE COURT IN WALES

The first Administrative Court in Wales: 1999–2009 2-2

Before devolution, and indeed since the abolition of the Great Sessions in 1830, judicial checks on public bodies in Wales had always been heard in London. After the affirmative result in the referendum in 1997 and the enactment of the Government of Wales Act 1998 it was soon acknowledged by executive and judiciary alike that it was essential that legal challenges to decisions of the new Welsh institutions and other public bodies in Wales should be brought, heard and decided in Wales.

On 30 June 1999 the then Lord Chief Justice, Lord Bingham, issued the *Practice* 2-3
Direction (Supreme Court: Devolution),[1] which allowed certain Welsh cases to be heard in Wales. Lord Bingham had previously commented on:

[1] [1999] 1 WLR 1592.

> The need for the Principality of Wales to have its own indigenous institutions operating locally and meeting the needs of citizens there.[2]

The practice direction was designed to meet that need. Paragraphs 14.1–14.4 of the practice direction outlined the provisions for hearing judicial review claims in Wales:

> [F]acilities will be available for applications for judicial review to be lodged at … Cardiff … if the relief sought or the grounds of the application involve either or both of the following:
> (1) a devolution issue arising out of the Government of Wales Act 1998;
> (2) an issue concerning the Welsh Assembly, the Welsh executive, or any Welsh public body (including a Welsh local authority) even if it does not involve a devolution issue.
> Such applications may continue be lodged at the Crown Office in London, if the applicant prefers to do that.[3]

When, on 2 October 2000 the new Part 54 of the Civil Procedure Rules was enacted,[4] and the current judicial review procedure was brought into force, the practice direction to Part 54 incorporated Lord Bingham's practice direction in CPR PD 54, para. 3.1.[5]

Between the implementation of the Administrative Court in Wales version one in 1999 and the implementation of the Administrative Court in Wales, version two in 2009 (which is discussed later in this chapter), a fair number[6] of applications for judicial review were heard in the Administrative Court in Wales. They included cases against the National Assembly for Wales, the Welsh Ministers[7] and local authorities. They covered a wide range of issues including a challenge to a sea fisheries order (the South Wales Sea Fisheries District (Variation) Order 2001, which set out the expenses that would be payable by the councils making up the South Wales Sea Fisheries Committee) on the grounds that the order was unlawful in that it required the councils to pay fixed amounts rather than make proportionate contributions,[8] and the fate of Shambo, the Hindu Temple bull,

[2] From a speech by Lord Bingham when opening the Mercantile Court in Cardiff in May 2000. Quoted in *Strengthening the Administrative Court in Wales*, October 2006, a joint paper by Public Law Wales and the Standing Committee on Legal Wales, para. 15.

[3] [1999] 1 WLR 1592, para. 14.2.

[4] Civil Procedure (Amendment No. 4) Rules (SI 2000 No. 2092).

[5] This paragraph was removed from the Civil Procedure Rules when practice direction 54D was implemented in 2009, as will be discussed later in the chapter.

[6] The exact number is unknown.

[7] This is not to say that the Welsh Ministers existed as a body since 1999. See chapter 4 for public bodies in Wales.

[8] *R (South Wales Sea Fisheries Committee)* v *National Assembly for Wales* [2002] RVR 134.

which decided whether an order requiring destruction of a Hindu temple bull with tuberculosis was compatible with article 9 of the European Convention on Human Rights 1950.[9]

Despite the apparent success of the first Administrative Court in Wales, the working practices were perhaps not all they could be. Whilst a number of hearings took place in the Civil Justice Centre in Cardiff and other court centres in Wales, the practice direction allowing judicial review claims to be lodged in Cardiff stopped exactly there. The claim was lodged in Cardiff but then immediately sent to the Administrative Court Office in London where the claim file was kept, where all correspondence was forwarded, where the Administrative Court Office staff and lawyers were solely based and where the claim was entirely managed. In effect the Cardiff Office was nothing more than a post box. 2-4

The working practices of the first Administrative Court in Wales were, in terms of the autonomy and development of Welsh institutions, a significant advancement. This was, after all, the first occasion on which the Administrative Court had sat regularly outside London. That said, those practices did not go far enough for many. The legal profession in Wales, by means of a joint paper by Public Law Wales and the Standing Committee on Legal Wales, summarised the concern that the Administrative Court in Wales was not being used to its full potential:

> [A]lthough the operation, to date, of the Administrative Court in Wales has been a great success, it has so far failed to achieve its full potential. It is not yet fully preeminent as the forum for ... testing the legality of administrative action on the part of devolved and local government in Wales. Many cases suitable for hearing in Wales continue to be heard in London.[10]

Whilst the provisions of CPR PD 54, para. 3.1 were welcomed in Wales, having made possible a hearing in Wales for challenges to the decisions of Welsh public bodies, there were democratic and constitutional issues that concerned many. The main concerns on these issues can be summarised as:

- Access to justice
  The procedural provisions were defendant dependant. Whilst a Welsh claimant could challenge a decision of a Welsh public body locally, they could not challenge the decision of a UK public body locally. As a result Welsh claimants were denied easy access to justice against the decisions of the UK Government.

- Uncertainty of venue
  Whilst the provisions allowed for hearings to take place in Wales there was no presumption in place that such claims would take place in Wales. On a

[9] *R (Swami Suryananda)* v *Welsh Ministers* [2007] EWHC 1736. The Court of Appeal also sat in Cardiff to hear the appeal, see [2007] EWCA Civ 893.

[10] *Strengthening the Administrative Court in Wales*, para. 5.

number of occasions Welsh cases were still heard in London. This represented a constitutional issue as devolved decisions could still be challenged in London. It also represented a practical concern for claimants. If a defendant wanted a hearing in London (as may happen where the defendant's counsel were based in London) then the claimant may have been wary of objecting to the request for fears of exposure to costs liability if the objection was unsuccessful.

- Less effective administrative support
  As the cases were administratively managed by the Administrative Court Office in London, Welsh practitioners were denied an as readily accessible service as practitioners in London had (who could simply and easily attend the offices in the Royal Courts of Justice). Further, as the judges' lists in Wales were not managed by the Administrative Court Office in London, but by Welsh Court Offices, there was less certainty and flexibility in arranging hearings before judges in Wales.

The UK Government was alive to these concerns. In October 2005 the Department of Constitutional Affairs (the predecessor to the Ministry of Justice) published a consultation paper called *Focusing Judicial Resources Appropriately: The Right Judge for the Right Case*. The paper considered the reallocation of the judiciary to appropriately manage Court business. The report expressly considered the fact that Cardiff should be allocated appropriate judicial resources based not just on workload but on the fact that it is a capital city.[11] The judiciary also took notice of these concerns and established a working group to address them. That group produced the *Justice Outside London* report.

2-5 The *Justice Outside London* report

The 2007 working group report *Justice Outside London* was chaired by Lord Justice of Appeal and then vice-president of the Queen's Bench Division, Sir Anthony May. The working group was not specifically convened to consider the Administrative Court in Wales. In fact it was asked, in April 2006, by the civil sub-committee of the judicial executive board, to consider and make recommendations about arrangements for judges to hear cases out of London. The report recommended that fully operational offices of the Administrative Court should be established in Cardiff, Birmingham, Manchester and Leeds and that its judges should regularly sit to hear Administrative Court cases in those centres. The main basis for the recommendation to decentralise the Administrative Court was summarised as follows:

[11] See *Focusing Judicial Resources Appropriately: The Right Judge for the Right Case* (October 2005), para. 78.

> The essential point is proper access to justice is not achieved if those in the regions can only bring judicial review and other claims in the Administrative Court in London.[12]

As well as advancing access to justice, the report gave special attention to the case for devolved justice in Wales based on constitutional considerations, concluding that:

> [D]ecisions in relation to Wales are made in Wales by the Assembly or by the ministers of the Welsh Assembly Government and a judicial review of such decisions should be heard in Wales.[13]

As well as constitutional and access to justice arguments the report detailed a number of express considerations in favour of a dedicated Administrative Court and Administrative Court Office in Wales:

- Express mention was made of the increasing divergence in applicable public law statutes and statutory instruments.[14]
- It was noted that s. 22 of the Welsh Language Act 1993 entitles those who desire to do so to speak in the Welsh language in any legal proceedings in Wales. Hearing cases in England denied those who wish to speak in Welsh the opportunity of doing so.[15]
- Whilst there were geographical problems for claimants in North Wales lodging claims in Cardiff, the constitutional principle supported a decentralised Administrative Court for all of Wales. Hearings could be arranged in North Wales to counter the geographical problem.[16]

The idea of decentralised Administrative Courts was not unanimously sup- 2-6
ported. Judges and staff from within the Administrative Court Office in London raised concerns over the deployment of the judiciary and the effective cases management of this complex area of work if the cases were not centralised.[17] The legal profession highlighted concerns over the available quantity and quality of the decentralised judiciary as well as the fears that claimants would be able to 'forum

[12] *Justice Outside London* (2007), para. 51.

[13] *Justice Outside London* (2007), para. 60.

[14] *Justice Outside London* (2007), para. 59.

[15] *Justice Outside London* (2007), para. 62.

[16] *Justice Outside London* (2007), para. 66.

[17] *Justice Outside London* (2007), Appendix L.

shop' and thus choose the venue that would be more likely to be favourable in terms of waiting times and decisions.[18]

The working group concluded that the arguments in favour of decentralisation outweighed those against it and recommended a new, decentralised Administrative Court and Administrative Court Office in Wales, with a strong recommendation that Welsh Administrative Court cases should be heard in Wales:

> [W]e accept and adopt the argument that there should be a strong expectation that Welsh cases are heard in Wales. We recommend that rules of court or a practice direction should provide that Administrative Court cases within the present paragraph 3.1 of the Part 54 practice direction (or a suitably modified version of it) should normally be issued in Cardiff. If they are not, they should normally be transferred to Cardiff administratively upon issue.[19]

The remainder of this chapter will discuss the current practical and jurisdictional arrangements for the Administrative Court in Wales and the extent to which the principle of a decentralised Administrative Court in Wales, within the terms envisaged in *Justice Outside London*, actually exists.

THE CURRENT ARRANGEMENT FOR THE ADMINISTRATIVE COURT IN WALES

2-7 Establishment and statistics

After the *Justice Outside London* report Her Majesty's Court Service,[20] agreed that the proposals in the report should be implemented. A project board was established and steps were taken to establish Administrative Court Offices in Cardiff, Birmingham, Leeds and Manchester. Sir Anthony May's vision became a reality on 21 April 2009.[21] The Administrative Court in Wales has been hearing Administrative Court cases in Wales and the Administrative Court Office in Wales, the office that supports the Court, has been handling the administrative aspect of those claims since that date.

[18] See S. Nason, 'Regionalisation of the Administrative Court and the Tribunalisation of Judicial Review' [2009] PL 440 at 442, S. Nason et al., 'Regionalisation of the Administrative Court and Access to Justice' [2010] JR 220 at paras 3–8, and S. Nason and M. Sunkin, 'The Regionalisation of Judicial Review: Constitutional Authority, Access to Justice and Specialisation of Legal Services in Public Law' (2013) 76(2) MLR 223 at 229. The research of Sarah Nason et al. also goes on to suggest that these concerns have been largely overcome.

[19] *Justice Outside London*, para. 65.

[20] The predecessor to Her Majesty's Courts and Tribunals Service.

[21] Having been implemented in conjunction with the coming into force of CPR PD 54D.

There has been a steady, year on year, rise in the number of cases that the Administrative Court Office in Wales has dealt with (see Annex F for statistics on the Administrative Court in Wales). The number of claims, it must be conceded, is comparatively low. For example, when compared to the most prolific regional Administrative Court, Birmingham, the numbers pale in comparison, with Birmingham issuing 722 claims in 2012 to Cardiff's 187. One possible explanation may be that the variation can be put down to population size. In 2012 it is estimated that Wales had a population of 3,074,100[22] whereas the Midlands had an estimated population of 10,210,300,[23] creating an obviously smaller pool of potential claimants in Wales. Nonetheless, the availability of the Administrative Court Office in Wales does appear to be increasing the number of claims brought in Wales. Between 2009 and 2013, in non-immigration judicial reviews, there was a 20 per cent increase in claims brought by solicitors in Wales, a 15 per cent increase in claims brought by litigants in person, and a 14 per cent increase in claims against Welsh local authorities.[24] Thus, the availability of local administration and local hearings appears to be providing greater local access to justice. 2-8

The *Justice Outside London* report did expressly observe that claim numbers were likely to be smaller in Wales.[25] Further, the number of claims dealt with is going up year on year, although it should be noted that large numbers do come from the Western Circuit.[26] Whilst the statistics give an appreciation of the access to justice based need for decentralised Administrative Courts it should be noted that the report firmly concluded that it was access to justice *and* constitutional reasons that justified and, indeed, required an Administrative Court in Wales.

Judges of the Administrative Court in Wales 2-9

Under the current judicial arrangement, cases in the Administrative Court in Wales are heard by both High Court and deputy High Court judges.[27] Both the High Court and deputy High Court judges predominantly sit in Cardiff Civil Justice Centre. However, it is important to note that the Administrative Court in Wales is an Administrative Court *for Wales*, not just Cardiff. As such the judges also sit in court centres all over Wales. At the time of writing the Administrative Court in Wales has sat in Caernarfon, Carmarthen, Cardiff, Mold, Newport, Port Talbot, Rhyl, Swansea, Welshpool and Wrexham.

Overall judicial responsibility for the Administrative Court in Wales is assumed by the Queen's Bench liaison judge for Wales (who is also the liaison judge for the

[22] *Annual Mid-year Population Estimates, 2011 and 2012* (Office for National Statistics, 8 August 2013).

[23] *Annual Mid-year Population Estimates, 2011 and 2012* (Office for National Statistics, 8 August 2013).

[24] Nason and Sunkin, 'The Regionalisation of Judicial Review' (2013) 76(2) MLR 223 at 235.

[25] *Justice Outside London*, para. 90.

[26] See a discussion of this later in the chapter.

[27] Those judges being authorised to sit as High Court judges under s. 9 of the Senior Courts Act 1981.

Midlands and the Western Circuit).[28] From 21 April 2009 to 31 December 2012 the liaison judge was Mr Justice Beatson (as he then was). Between 1 January 2013 and 31 December 2015 the liaison judge was Mr Justice Hickinbottom. The liaison judge from 2016 is Mr Justice Lewis. The liaison judge sits in Wales once every legal term for a period of typically two to three weeks but does sometimes sit in Wales outside those periods when necessary. A visiting High Court judge also sits once a term for a period of two to three weeks, the result being that every legal term the Administrative Court in Wales has four to six weeks of dedicated High Court judge time.[29] There is no specific time set aside for Divisional Court[30] sittings but Divisional Courts are arranged on an *ad hoc* basis as required.

The deputy High Court judges[31] who sit in Wales are local judges who sit as judges in other jurisdictions for the majority of the time. When the Administrative Court in Wales in its current form opened on 21 April 2009 the local judges authorised to sit were HHJ Bidder QC, HHJ Curran QC, HHJ Farmer QC, HHJ Jarman QC, HHJ Seys Llewellyn QC and HHJ Vosper QC. The list of local judges has changed a little since then. The number has been added to with HHJ Keyser QC and Upper Tribunal Judge Grubb being authorised to sit. HHJ Cooke QC also sat briefly before leaving his post in Cardiff to sit in the Central Criminal Court in London. Sadly, on 9 April 2011 HHJ Farmer passed away whilst in office.[32] The deputy High Court judges are not allocated dedicated Administrative Court weeks like the High Court judges. As they sit in Wales permanently, cases are listed before them on an *ad hoc* basis to fit around their civil, criminal and upper tribunal lists. As a final point of practice, practitioners and litigants should note that when deputy judges sit they sit 'as a Judge of the High Court', to use the language of the Senior Courts Act 1981. As such, in court both High Court and Deputy High Court Judges are addressed with the title 'My Lord/ My Lady'.

[28] There are two liaison judges in total. The other judge has charge of the Northern and North Western circuits.

[29] It should be noted that since 5 November 2012 this time has been shared with sittings required in the Bristol hearing centre. See later in the chapter for analysis on this point.

[30] Two or more judges sitting together pursuant to s. 66 of the Senior Courts Act 1981.

[31] Technically, the circuit judges who sit in the High Court sit 'as a Judge of the High Court' under s. 9(1) of the Senior Courts Act 1981, rather than as Deputy High Court Judges. The term 'deputy' in this work is used to ensure that the difference is easily identified.

[32] The author would like to note the incredible contribution Michael Farmer made to the advancement of administrative law, use of the Welsh language in the justice system, and indeed law generally in Wales. Michael Farmer mainly sat in North Wales and his tireless work advancing the profile of justice in North Wales is sadly missed.

Staff of the Administrative Court Office in Wales 2-10

The Administrative Court Office in Wales has existed since the implementation of the present arrangements for the Administrative Court in Wales, which is to say since 21 April 2009. The office[33] is based in Cardiff Civil Justice Centre.[34] It has a small staff of four persons with three distinct roles.

- The Administrative Court Office lawyer
  There is a single ACO lawyer attached to the Administrative Court Office in Wales who must be a qualified solicitor or barrister. The ACO lawyer acts as the principal legal adviser for the office. The role in itself is three fold. First, the ACO lawyer provides advice on practice and procedure in the Administrative Court to whoever requires it; be they judges, court staff, practitioners, or litigants. Secondly, the ACO lawyer provides legal research and updates for the judges of the Administrative Court. Thirdly, the ACO lawyer has limited judicial powers to ensure that cases in the Administrative Court in Wales are managed properly.[35]

- The Administrative Court Office manager
  The Administrative Court Office in Wales has an office manager who in practice has other management responsibilities within Cardiff Civil Justice Centre. The ACO manager is the line manager for the ACO caseworkers and is ultimately responsible for the actions of the caseworkers. The manager also works with the ACO lawyer on local policy issues for the office, such as the ACO Wales listing policy.[36] Finally, the ACO manager is the complaints officer for the Administrative Court Office in Wales.

- The Administrative Court Office caseworkers
  The Administrative Court Office in Wales has two dedicated caseworkers. The caseworkers handle the day-to-day running of the ACO from the start of the process to the finish. Between them they are the front line for telephone, email and postal queries, they accept and register new claims over the counter and by post, they ensure that the cases are properly managed by requesting missing or late documents from the parties and by referring problematic issues to the ACO lawyer, they list any hearings and they are responsible for producing court orders and obtaining the transcripts of proceedings.

[33] Which, for judicial review purposes, is also the Upper Tribunal (Immigration and Asylum Chamber) Office for Wales and the Planning Court Office for Wales since 1 November 2013.

[34] See Annex C for contact details.

[35] For more details see 5-36.

[36] The policy can be found at Annex B.

THE JURISDICTION OF THE ADMINISTRATIVE COURT IN WALES

2-11 The legislative background

The legislative landscape for where a judicial review (as well as the statutory appeals and applications considered in the Administrative Court) can be lodged and ultimately heard are contained within CPR PD 54D. The considerations that a party lodging a judicial review must have in mind when assessing an appropriate venue (and also the considerations for a judge considering transfer) are listed at para. 5.2 of that practice direction. They are worth setting out in full:

> 5.2
> The general expectation is that proceedings will be administered and determined in the region with which the claimant has the closest connection, subject to the following considerations as applicable –
> (1) any reason expressed by any party for preferring a particular venue;
> (2) the region in which the defendant, or any relevant office or department of the defendant, is based;
> (3) the region in which the claimant's legal representatives are based;
> (4) the ease and cost of travel to a hearing;
> (5) the availability and suitability of alternative means of attending a hearing (for example, by videolink);
> (6) the extent and nature of media interest in the proceedings in any particular locality;
> (7) the time within which it is appropriate for the proceedings to be determined;
> (8) whether it is desirable to administer or determine the claim in another region in the light of the volume of claims issued at, and the capacity, resources and workload of, the court at which it is issued;
> (9) whether the claim raises issues sufficiently similar to those in another outstanding claim to make it desirable that it should be determined together with, or immediately following, that other claim; and
> (10) whether the claim raises devolution issues and for that reason whether it should more appropriately be determined in London or Cardiff.

Whilst there are these ten considerations, including one on devolution, the practice direction gives priority to the location of the claimant, thus underpinning the conclusions of *Justice Outside London* that access to justice should be improved by decentralisation, whilst not putting the constitutional arguments of *Justice Outside London* on the same level. A further important point should be highlighted. Paragraph 5.2 lists only considerations; it is clear following CPR PD 54D, para. 2.1 that the claimant may lodge a claim in any Administrative Court Office. Whilst the claim may be transferred on the application of a party or by judicial intervention, there is no mandatory requirement to abide by these considerations.

A practitioner wishing to lodge Administrative Court proceedings in the Administrative Court Office in Wales should also be aware of the list of exceptions to the principle that the claimant may choose their venue. If the case is one that falls within the class of cases outlined in the list of exceptions then the case is automatically transferred to the Administrative Court Office in London.[37] The list of exceptions can be found at CPR PD 54D, para. 3.1: 2-12

> 3.1
> The excepted classes of claim … are –
> (1) proceedings to which Part 76 or Part 79 applies, and for the avoidance of doubt –
> (a) proceedings relating to control orders (within the meaning of Part 76);
> (b) financial restrictions proceedings (within the meaning of Part 79);
> (c) proceedings relating to terrorism or alleged terrorists (where that is a relevant feature of the claim); and
> (d) proceedings in which a special advocate is or is to be instructed;
> (2) proceedings to which RSC Order 115 applies;
> (3) proceedings under the Proceeds of Crime Act 2002;
> (4) appeals to the Administrative Court under the Extradition Act 2003;
> (5) proceedings which must be heard by a Divisional Court; and
> (6) proceedings relating to the discipline of solicitors.

To clarify, CPR PD 5D, para. 3.1(5) does not suggest that Divisional Courts cannot be convened by judicial order to hear cases in Wales. In fact they are often convened to consider some of the more high profile cases. CPR PD 54D, para. 3.1(6) requires that those cases where a Divisional Court is required by statute to consider the claim be transferred to London.

Finally, it should be noted that urgent applications[38] may be dealt with by the Administrative Court in Wales,[39] but only within the office hours of 10 a.m. to 4 p.m. Outside these hours, if the application cannot wait, the application must be made to the out-of-hours duty judge in London.[40] 2-13

Before concluding an examination of the jurisdiction of the Administrative Court in Wales, a note on historical status is worth considering. The practice direction mirrors the King's Bench decisions of the eighteenth century in that public law matters that arise out of Welsh authorities' decisions can be decided upon by a Court in England.[41] On the face of it the decentralised Administrative Court in Wales, whilst representing greater legal autonomy in public law litigation than in the nineteenth and twentieth centuries, is not as close to autonomous as perhaps it

[37] CPR PD 54D, para. 3.2.

[38] See 5-31 to 5-34.

[39] CPR PD 54D, para. 4.1.

[40] CPR PD 54D, para. 4.2.

[41] See 1-18 for details of these cases.

once was. That, anyway, is the impression given from an analysis of the legislative provisions behind jurisdiction. The picture is not quite that clear when judicial interpretation of these provisions is considered.

2-14 Judicial interpretation and guidance

Whilst the legislative perspective establishes a presumption that a judicial review will be considered in accordance with a claimant's location, if we examine the judicial perspective a slightly different pattern emerges. In 2006 the Court of Appeal (Civil Division) gave judgment in the case of *R (Condron)* v *The National Assembly for Wales*.[42] This was the first occasion upon which the issue of the venue of Administrative Court hearings involving the devolved government was considered by a Court. In that claim all the hearings, in the Administrative Court and Court of Appeal, took place in London, a fact that Richards LJ took a dim view of:

> There are procedures in place to enable Welsh judicial review cases and similar statutory challenges to be heard in the Administrative Court in Wales … In my view the present case cried out to be heard in Wales both at first instance and on appeal, and it is a matter of considerable regret that efforts were not made to have it listed for hearing accordingly. Practitioners and listing officers alike need to be alert to this issue.[43]

Only the next year the Administrative Court was required to consider the issue of venue in *R (Deepdock)* v *The Welsh Ministers*.[44] This claim was brought after the National Assembly had given planning permission for the building of a marina at Gallows Point, Beaumaris, Anglesey. The Welsh Ministers subsequently gave the developer permission to deposit materials on the seabed, which was necessary for the construction works to proceed. The claimants, who were mussel farmers, fearing that those deposits would harm the marine environment, brought a judicial review of the Welsh Ministers' decision to permit the deposit of materials in the sea. With the dicta of Richards LJ no doubt in mind, the point on venue was considered prior to the actual determination of the claim and HHJ Hickinbottom (as a Judge of the High Court), as he then was, went further than the Court in *Condron*:

> The devolution settlement as a matter of principle transfers political accountability to the organs of devolved government in Wales; and, where a decision of such a body is challenged, the devolved administration is directly accountable through the Courts. The location of the relevant arm of government is in any event a factor that must be taken into account in considering the appropriate

[42] [2007] 2 P&CR 4. See 3-15, for an examination of the facts and the administrative law impact of this case.

[43] [2007] 2 P&CR 4 at 68 (para. 110 of Richards LJ's judgment).

[44] [2007] EWHC 3347 (Admin).

> venue for proceedings ... [W]ith the increased impetus given to devolved government by the Government of Wales Act 2006 and with increasing powers actually being devolved to the National Assembly for Wales, there is in my view a deepening imperative that challenges to any devolved decisions are (like the decisions themselves) dealt with in Wales ... [S]uch cases should be heard in Wales unless there are good reasons for their being heard elsewhere.[45]

It appears, therefore, that *Deepdock* sets a precedent that, as well as the presumption that the claimant will lodge a claim in the Administrative Court Office to which they have the closest connection, there is also a presumption that devolved bodies in Wales will be answerable for their decisions to the Administrative Court in Wales.

There have been post-decentralisation decisions that confirm *Deepdock*. The issue of venue reared its head within nine days of the opening of the decentralised Administrative Court in Wales, and in a serendipitous occurrence the claimant was the same Mrs Condron that gave rise to the first *Condron* case referred to above. In *R (Condron)* v *Merthyr Tydfil County Borough Council*[46] the claimant sought permission to challenge four planning permissions granted by Caerphilly County Borough Council and Merthyr County Borough Council. The planning permissions were granted for the Cwmbargoed disposal point, a facility in Merthyr Tydfil, to extend and refurbish an existing coal preparation plant, to provide a water storage tank and coal haulage vehicle workshop, and to extend and refurbish ancillary facilities, including office accommodation, staff welfare facilities and a visitor training centre. Mrs Condron requested that her claim be considered in London rather than Wales as, to quote her advocate:

> She considers that she will not have a fair trial. Opencast coal mining in Wales is highly contentious and the Claimant is concerned that any regional court may not be impartial.[47]

This argument is not dissimilar to that accepted by the King's Bench Division in *R* v *Athoe*[48] in the eighteenth century when it removed the autonomous jurisdiction from the Great Sessions and commented unfavourably on the chances of Justice being done in Wales. In the twenty-first century Beatson J's judgment came to a very different conclusion and wholly rejected the idea that local interest led to bias. Instead he supported the idea of a judicial presumption that Welsh public law cases be heard in Wales:

> The submission that cases should be heard at a location remote from the places and events with which they are concerned is to my mind an extraordinary

[45] [2007] EWHC 3347 (Admin) at para. 20.

[46] [2009] EWHC 1621 (Admin).

[47] [2009] EWHC 1621 (Admin), para. 57.

[48] (1723) Strange 553. See 1-18 for further discussion.

> one … in a case involving a Welsh public authority … there may be justification for a more robust approach. In those cases the court may be more proactive in initiating the transfer. The Practice Direction implements the *Justice Outside London* report. That states in paragraph 65 that there is a 'strong expectation' for Welsh judicial review cases against the decisions of devolved institutions and of Welsh local and public authorities will be heard in Wales, and if issued elsewhere transferred to Wales, absent good reason.[49]

The spirit of the *Condron* cases and *Deepdock* was also observed in *Jones* v *The Director of Public Prosecutions*[50] where the Court found itself in a similar position to that in the first *Condron* case. On that occasion an appeal by way of case stated from Caernarfon Crown Court had been lodged in the Administrative Court in Manchester. The point on proper venue was made by Wyn Williams J, who stated: '[A] hearing in Wales would have been desirable given the obvious local interest in the outcome of the case.'[51]

2-15 A number of the judiciary have made extra-judicial comments that support the judicial idea of a presumption that claims against Welsh public bodies should be heard in Wales. Sir David Lloyd Jones (Lord Justice Lloyd Jones) has commented:

> An essential change was that the [Administrative] court was now administered by a team based at the Cardiff Civil Justice Centre, as opposed to the Royal Courts of Justice in London. The new arrangements have the advantage of enabling the Court to operate more efficiently and to provide a speedier service. There is a robust judicial policy of transfer which is intended to ensure that Welsh cases will normally be heard in Wales and at the most appropriate court centre in Wales.[52]

When he was liaison Judge for Wales, Sir Jack Beatson (Mr Justice Beatson, as he then was) made similar points to Sir David Lloyd Jones when speaking to the legal profession in Wales:

> The May report [a reference to the *Justice Outside London* Report] … recognised that there is a strong constitutional reason for an Administrative Court in Wales, as well as providing access to justice.[53]

The appetite within the judiciary to keep Welsh work in Wales has been commented upon in lectures organised by the Administrative Court Office. At the 1st Administrative Court Office for Wales Lecture, given by Sir Gary Hickinbottom

[49] *R (Condron)* v *Merthyr Tydfil County Borough Council* [2009] EWHC 1621 (Admin) at para. 61.

[50] [2012] RTR 3.

[51] [2012] RTR 3 at 43 (para. 75 of Wyn Williams J's judgment).

[52] D. Lloyd Jones, 'Law in a Small Nation: Wales and England in a Shared Jurisdiction', Lord Williams of Mostyn Memorial Lecture 2013, 4 July 2013, The Hall, Grey's Inn.

[53] J. Beatson, The Administrative Court Event: North Wales, 24 March 2011, Mold Law Courts.

(Mr Justice Hickinbottom) on 20 February 2014, the liaison Judge commented (with reference to planning law judicial reviews):

> [The judiciary] are transferring out of London planning cases which clearly have a connection to a particular circuit. Welsh cases are transferred to the Administrative Court Office in Cardiff, to be managed here and heard wherever appropriate in Wales ... You might think that it is quite difficult for parties to say that a claim involving a site in Cardiff, where the Claimant is a South Wales company and the Defendant is a Welsh local authority should be heard in London. But it happens, and happens frequently. The usual reasons are two-fold. First, it is said that there is a greater chance of getting a planning judge in London. But that simply is not so; a planning case will get an appropriate planning judge in or out of London. Second, it is said that solicitors and Counsel from London have been instructed. That is fine. Privately paying parties are entitled to instruct legal representatives of their choice; but, if they choose lawyers who are required to travel, that is a very weak factor in the balancing exercise required on determining where a case should be managed and listed.
>
> It is also said, in an increasing number of cases, that interest and emotions are running so high that it would be dangerous to have a local hearing; the hearing should be in London because it will be more difficult for protesters to get to London. This argument too is usually unimpressive. Nobody in these cases has ever disrupted my court – and, if they were to attempt to do so, the court has adequate weapons at its disposal to prevent it. But, in my experience, proper respect is usually maintained; and it is important that local people with a real interest in these issues are enabled to attend the court which hears them if possible ...
>
> We have advantages over London, and over the regions in England, in that we understand the country and its legal needs, and we have a real dialogue with practitioners here that enables us, I hope, to provide a different and thus better service for those who use the Administrative Court in Wales.[54]

This strong message was echoed by Milwyn Jarman (HHJ Jarman QC) in the 2nd Administrative Court Office Lecture:

> Any claim started in Cardiff will normally be heard in Wales, and although claims from Wales may be started in another Administrative Court, for example London, the general expectation is that proceedings will be administered and determined where the claimant has the closest connection, subject to a number of considerations set out in the relevant practice direction 54D. Most cases where the claimant has the closest connection to Wales are now issued in Cardiff. Those

[54] G. Hickinbottom, 'The Administrative Court in Wales: Evolution or Revolution', The 1st Administrative Court Office for Wales Lecture, 20 February 2014, Law Society Wales Offices paras 9, 10, and 14.

> that are not are usually transferred. However, for whatever reason, some are not and the lesson must be that if the parties wish their cases to be dealt with and heard in Wales then the claim should be issued in Cardiff.[55]

What we observe from the judiciary, both formally in case law and informally through extra-judicial comments, is what appears to be a drive to go beyond the terms of the current practice direction, CPR PD 54D, which prioritises access to justice and the choice of venue for the claimant. The judiciary appear to seek a system closer to that envisaged in *Justice Outside London* which places the constitutional importance of Welsh cases being heard in Wales on a par with, if not above the principle of claimant choice.

2-16 The minded to transfer System

Following on from the judicial impetus, as of early 2013 the Administrative Court Office has operated a 'minded to transfer' system. The aim of the system is to identify Administrative Court cases lodged in a particular Administrative Court Office that should, perhaps, more appropriately be heard on a different circuit and to take steps to transfer them to that circuit. The system involves Administrative Court staff checking a list of cases issued in any Administrative Court Office. Any case that appears to be more suitable for a different office to the one it was lodged in, based on the considerations in CPR PD 54D (for example, where the claimant and/or defendant is based on that circuit), is referred to one of the liaison Judges. If the liaison Judge agrees they will make an order that the Judge is minded to transfer the claim to the relevant Administrative Court Office. The parties will be given a set number of days to make representations. The order will contain provision, in the form of an 'unless order', whereby the claim will automatically be transferred without further order if the parties do not make representations. If any of the parties do make representations then the case will be referred back to the liaison Judge to consider ultimately whether the case should be transferred.

The minded to transfer system appears to represent the latest judicial initiative to ensure that Welsh cases (as well as regional cases in England) are heard in local hearing centres and administered in local Administrative Court Offices.

2-17 The views of Welsh public bodies

The Welsh public bodies, especially the national authorities, are also keen to uphold the spirit of the precedent set by Richards LJ in *Condron*. Public figures have spoken frequently on the issue of the decentralised Administrative Court and their support for the idea that cases with a Welsh connection should be heard in Wales. This ideological stance is often followed up in practice by a policy of applying to transfer any

[55] M. Jarman, 'Administrative Court in Wales: Challenges and Opportunities', The 2nd Administrative Court Office for Wales Lecture, 19 November 2014, Swansea University para. 16.

'Welsh cases' not lodged in the Administrative Court Office in Wales to that office. This stance has been commented upon from the top of Welsh Government. When addressing the Cardiff Law School on 7 May 2009, Carwyn Jones AM commented:

> The increasing divergence of the law in relation to England and the law in relation to Wales, and the bilingual character of the legislation produced by both the Welsh Assembly Government and the National Assembly for Wales, has also given impetus to the need for institutions of justice managed locally, which are responsive to the needs of Wales and are familiar with the law as it applies to Wales ... [S]ince 2000 there has been a growing expectation that administrative cases relating to Wales should also be heard in Wales. In that respect it has for some time been the practice of the Assembly Government in response to judicial review applications to apply for a direction that the case be heard in Wales.[56]

This practice was encouraged by John Griffiths AM, when he was Counsel General for Wales:

> There appears to be a presumption that Administrative Court cases from Wales should be heard in Wales ... [and] for some time the Welsh Assembly Government have applied for transfer of Welsh cases.[57]

The view of the Counsel General was mirrored by the Welsh Government generally, as outlined by Jeff Godfrey, the director of legal services for the Welsh Government:

> Legal challenges to decisions taken in Wales by the Welsh Assembly Government and by the wider public sector, on the basis of policies formulated in Wales, and increasingly on the basis of legislation framed in Wales, and having regard to local circumstances, requires the operation of a fully functioning court office. There is a need now to deliver on the expectations that judicial review cases commenced in Wales will be heard in Wales ... Arrangements are also needed to strengthen and support a presumption that cases falling within paragraph 3.1 of the CPR Part 54 Practice Direction which are commenced in the Administrative Court at the Royal Courts of Justice should be transferred to Wales for hearing.[58]

The frequency with which the executive in Wales comments on its support for a decentralised Administrative Court in Wales highlights the importance that the Welsh authorities put in a Welsh system of judicial checks. It is clear that they regard

[56] C. Jones, 'Getting the Devolution Dividend: Legal Wales in the next ten years', 7 May 2009, Cardiff Law School Public Lecture Series.

[57] J. Griffiths, The Administrative Court Event: North Wales, 24 March 2011, Mold Law Courts.

[58] Welsh Assembly Government Representations to the Working Party chaired by Lord Justice May, 25 October 2006, available at Appendix F to the *Justice Outside London* report (2007), para. 6.1.

further decentralisation of the Administrative Court as a supportive point to their calls for further devolution.

2-18 THE WESTERN CIRCUIT

When *Justice Outside London* made its recommendation for decentralised Administrative Courts a notable absence from the provision was an Administrative Court Office for the western circuit (that is to say, the south west of England). All other circuits were provided for, but the western circuit was not. The report explained why:

> The Presiding Judge of the Western Circuit (Owen J) did not feel able to make a strong case for having Administrative Court cases administered in Bristol. Bristol is an important commercial centre with a strong concentration of the legal professions. But it is not, we believe, a population centre comparable with the four cities for which we do make this recommendation. Travel from Bristol to London or Birmingham is as good as congestion will allow – though no better than travel from Birmingham to London.[59]

What the report did not comment on is that, in fact, travel times from Bristol to Cardiff are shorter than either Bristol to London or Bristol to Birmingham. It is a stark, and originally unanticipated, fact that the presumption in CPR PD 54D, para. 5.2 that claimants lodge claims in the centre closest to them requires most south west based claimants to lodge in Cardiff. Practitioners and litigants have made use of this locality since the opening of the Administrative Court Office in Wales and it was observed that, by 2013, a large number of the claims lodged in the Administrative Court Office in Wales originated from the Western Circuit.[60]

The question for HMCTS and the judiciary was how best to continue the aims of *Justice Outside London* and maintain access to justice for the western circuit in the light of this local interest. Two key factors in this consideration were the facts that western circuit case numbers would still not warrant a dedicated Administrative Court Office and that, since the set up of the four decentralised offices, the UK had suffered from a global recession, meaning that set-up funds available would be minimal.

The answer from HMCTS and the judiciary was that the Administrative Court Office in Wales would, being the closest geographically, operate as the Administrative Court Office for the Western Circuit as well as for Wales. All documentation and communication would be dealt with by the Administrative

[59] *Justice Outside London* (2007), para. 30.

[60] Sarah Nason suggests that in non-immigration judicial reviews, Western Circuit claims make up 42% of the ACO Wales caseload. See Nason and Sunkin, 'The Regionalisation of Judicial Review' (2013) 76(2) MLR 223 at 238.

Court Office in Wales. There would be no dedicated Administrative Court staff on the Western Circuit. Any hearings, however, would take place on the Western Circuit, principally at Bristol Civil Justice Centre. Despite lodging the claim in Wales, hearings could be conducted on a different circuit, as long as a judicial order is made pursuant to CPR PD 54D, para. 5.4 allowing the claim to be heard outside Wales. Such an order is often made by judges when considering permission to apply for judicial review but it is also a delegated power under CPR 54.1A and as such the Administrative Court Office lawyer for Wales may also make such an order.[61]

The Bristol hearing centre (as it became known) was opened on 5 November 2012 by the President of the Queen's Bench Division, Sir John Thomas (as he then was). Since then Western Circuit claims have been frequently heard in Bristol. The operation of the hearing centre in terms of judiciary is very similar to that in Wales. The liaison judge sits there once a term, as does one other High Court judge. There is also a locally based cadre of deputy High Court judges. The deputy judges on the western circuit are HHJ Blair QC, HHJ Cotter QC, and HHJ Denyer QC.

CONCLUSION 2-19

What appears to have developed is a presumption that cases involving Welsh public authorities will be considered in Wales. Further, following the case law, the courts and the parties seem largely proactive in their encouragement of the presumption. Since the creation of the National Assembly and the Welsh Government both legislative and executive powers have been transferred to Wales. It was perhaps inevitable that judicial checks were to follow. It is certainly arguable that cases that directly affect the devolved institutions are considered in Wales. For example, *R (Brynmawr Foundation School Governors)* v *The Welsh Ministers*[62] in which the Administrative Court was required to determine the extent to which the Welsh Government could delegate its powers to Welsh local authorities, was lodged, managed and determined in Wales. This fact, and indeed this chapter, establishes that any judicial check on the powers of the Welsh Ministers and other Welsh public bodies should take place in Wales. Such a system allows greater access to justice as local persons may more easily attend and watch justice in action. It also serves a constitutional principle; that principle being that a decentralised, devolved body's decisions are subject to judicial check by a decentralised (although not yet devolved) Administrative Court. Nonetheless, administrative law in Wales now finds itself in a position akin to that experienced during the eighteenth and nineteenth centuries when the Great Sessions had authority to consider Welsh public law matters but so did the King's Bench in London. The difference is that there is now a drive by both the Welsh executive and the judiciary that there should be a presumption that Welsh matters be considered in Wales.

[61] See 5-36 for details.

[62] [2011] EWHC 519 (Admin).

A question arises out of this established presumption – To what end? As observed above, it is the view of the Welsh executive and the judiciary that decentralisation of these public law claims allows greater access to justice as well as, in Wales, serving a constitutional purpose. This may not, however, be the end. The devolution settlement in Wales continues to evolve. As part of that the jurisdiction of the Administrative Court in Wales also continues to evolve. It is not beyond the realms of possibility that as more powers come to Wales from Westminster, so version three of the Administrative Court in Wales may develop. If greater autonomy for Wales is the goal then a fully decentralised system of checks and balances must also be developed. When it becomes an accepted principle that any legal business that involves Welsh institutions is conducted in Wales this may also be seen as a stage in the transition towards a separate legal jurisdiction for Wales. To date no policy initiative on this point has come forward and it is not clear whether at this stage one is warranted, but it appears logical that the next step in decentralisation (and perhaps devolution) for the Administrative Court in Wales is to remove the possibility of judicial checks in the Administrative Court outside Wales. The minded to transfer system, as outlined earlier in the chapter, could evolve into a mandatory transfer system whereby challenges to the decisions of Welsh public bodies (using Lord Bingham's model as to what a Welsh public body is) are to be automatically transferred to the Administrative Court Office in Wales if they are lodged elsewhere. Such a system would preserve the access to justice provisions of CPR PRD 54D whilst strengthening constitutional autonomy for Wales. If devolution is truly a process not an event then it must follow that decentralisation is too.

Chapter 3

Administrative Law

INTRODUCTION 3-1

Public law is the law that grants public bodies their powers to act on behalf of the public and governs how the public body may act.[1] Administrative law is the law in accordance with which the public body must exercise its public law powers. Public administration is the playing of the game and administrative law is the rules of the game.

If administrative law is the rules of the game then there must be an umpire. This is the Administrative Court. The Administrative Court is part of the Queen's Bench Division of the High Court. It hears most applications for judicial review and also some statutory appeals and applications. It is by way of the judicial review procedure[2] that an individual, company or organisation[3] may challenge the act or omission of a public body and ensure that the public body is meeting its obligations in complying with the law.

A public law claim brought in the Administrative Court must be a challenge to the decision of a public body. The Administrative Court will not consider private law disputes. The nature of public bodies is discussed in greater detail in chapter 4. In *O'Reilly* v *Mackman*[4] Lord Denning MR commented:

> In modern times we have come to recognise two separate fields of law: one of private law, the other of public law. Private law regulates the affairs of subjects as between themselves. Public law regulates the affairs of subjects vis-à-vis public authorities. For centuries there were special remedies available in public law. They were the prerogative writs of certiorari, mandamus and prohibition … they were taken in the name of the sovereign against a public authority which had failed to perform its duty to the public at large or had performed it wrongly. Any subject could complain to the sovereign: and then the King's courts, at their discretion, would give him leave to issue such one of the prerogative writs as was appropriate to meet his case.[5]

[1] See 4-2 for a discussion of the differences between public and private law.

[2] See chapter 5.

[3] Judicial review and its associated procedures are available to all but the reader should be aware of the common bars to judicial review discussed at 5-8.

[4] [1983] 2 AC 237.

[5] [1983] 2 AC 237 at 255.

When considering administrative law in Wales it is important to keep in mind that the law in Wales, be it public or private law, is, and has been since the sixteenth century,[6] the law of England and Wales, not just Wales. Law made by the UK Parliament that only affects England is part of the law of England and Wales, law made by the National Assembly for Wales is part of the law of England and Wales; even a byelaw that affects only a single street is part of the law of England and Wales. This book considers the administrative law of England and Wales as it affects Wales and the concept of public and administrative law in Wales. At the outset it should be recognised that law governing both administrative law itself and its procedures are virtually identical in England and in Wales. The everyday practices, whilst largely similar, do have some differences. Where a differing practice has established itself for Wales then this will be expressly noted. Administrative law in Wales is a quickly developing area in terms of the effect administrative law is having on the decisions and decision-making processes of public bodies in Wales, but it must not be forgotten that the fundamental rules behind administrative law in Wales and the Administrative Court in Wales do not differ from England.

3-2 OVERVIEW

When a public body[7] makes any decision it must abide by certain rules, the nature of which will be discussed in this chapter. The public body is also bound by these same rules if it fails to act where it should, thereby failing to perform its duties by omission.

At the outset it is important to note that in administrative law the public body must consider the facts and apply the relevant law to those facts. Generally speaking the decision of the public body will not be subject to judicial review by the Administrative Court if the decision made is subject to criticism based on the merits of the decision. It is often said that in an application for judicial review the Administrative Court sits in a supervisory jurisdiction, as opposed to an appellate jurisdiction.[8] As such the decision of the public body will only be vitiated on the grounds that the decision is wrong in law. The one exception to this is where 'the public body, consciously or unconsciously, [is] acting perversely'[9] in which case the Administrative Court may intervene on fact-based grounds. This may involve

[6] See 1-17.

[7] See chapter 4 for the definition of a public body and a discussion of the various public bodies in Wales.

[8] The appellate jurisdiction generally has a less restrictive test that reconsiders both the evidence given in the lower court or tribunal and the legal decisions made. Whether the review takes place by way of rehearing or by considering the witness statements presented in the lower court depends on the court or tribunal, as does the test on which the court will overturn the decision of the lower court or tribunal. Appeals in the Administrative Court are discussed in chapter 6.

[9] *R* v *Hillingdon London Borough Council, ex parte Puhlhofer* [1986] AC 484 at 518.

a material mistake of fact or a lack of any supporting evidence, but it should be noted that the courts have been slow to uphold errors based on such circumstances as such challenges often appear to stray into the realm of a merits-based decision. This principle was summarised in *R* v *Independent Television Commission, ex parte TSW Broadcasting Ltd*[10] where Lord Templeman stated:

> The courts have invented the remedies of judicial review not to provide an appeal machinery but to ensure that the decision maker does not exceed or abuse his powers ... Judicial review does not issue merely because a decision-maker has made a mistake.[11]

In *E* v *Secretary of State for the Home Department*[12] Carnwarth LJ stated that the error of fact must also be uncontroversial in the sense that only one view of the facts is possible. There are relatively few administrative law cases that quash a decision on the grounds of material mistake of fact. One example is *Hollis* v *Secretary of State for the Environment.*[13] This planning law case involved an application for permission to build a residential development in Woking. The planning inspector's report stated that the appeal site had never been green belt land, but unbeknown to the inspector the land had in fact been proposed green belt land in 1959, although the proposal was never actually determined. Glidewell J held that there was a real likelihood that the Secretary of State might have come to a different decision had the inspector's error not been made and quashed the grant of planning permission. The lesson then for the litigant before embarking on a judicial review is that judicial review will generally not be appropriate if you disagree with the decision maker on the assessment of the facts. You must show an error of law, or that the decision is perverse.

To understand how to apply administrative law, the process of decision making must be examined. When making any decision a public body must consider the facts of the case and make their decision by applying the rules relevant to that area of public law. The areas of law that come under the broad heading of public law are numerous. They can include (but are not limited to) immigration and asylum, housing, criminal, planning, extradition, family, education, local government, child support and social security. They would also include the twenty-one areas which form the headings under which the subjects in relation to which the National Assembly for Wales has competence to legislate are listed.[14] As well as considering the decision with reference to the relevant area of public law, the public body must also, in tandem, consider whether the decision complies with the principles of administrative law. The example in Figure 3.1 relates to housing law.

10 [1996] EMLR 291.

11 [1996] EMLR 291 at 304–6.

12 [2004] QB 1044 at 1071.

13 [1984] 47 P&CR 351.

14 See 1-43.

Figure 3.1 The decision-making process in administrative law

Decision-making process	Housing law example
FACT OF THE CASE	Individual requests the local authority provide him with accommodation as he is homeless
APPLICATION TO THE RELEVANT AREA OF PUBLIC LAW	The local authority considers whether it is required to provide accommodation by considering the terms of the Housing Act 1996
CONSIDERATION OF ADMINISTRATIVE LAW PRINCIPLES	Is the decision on provision of accommodation: 1) unlawful 2) unreasonable 3) procedurally improper 4) a breach of human rights?

When presented with a homeless person requesting accommodation a local authority must consider the request by applying the Housing Act 1996. This includes the terms of the statute itself, associated secondary legislation, and also central and local government policies. The local authority must also consider the principles of administrative law, that is to say it must decide in a manner which is lawful, reasonable, procedurally proper, and human rights compliant. Greater examination will be given to these principles later in the chapter. For the purposes of this introductory example it should be observed that simply because the local authority justifies its position with reference to the statutory scheme under the Housing Act 1996, does not mean that the decision is not vulnerable on administrative law grounds. For example, the local authority may apply a local policy that is held to be an unreasonable policy, thus vitiating the decision.

As mentioned, in broad terms the public body must ensure that it acts in a way that is:

- lawful;
- reasonable;
- procedurally proper; and
- human rights compliant.

The first three of these are long-standing, established public law grounds, as identified by Lord Diplock in *Council of Civil Service Unions* v *Minister for the Civil Service*[15] (which is sometimes known as the *GCHQ Case*). The latter is a more recent addition from the Human Rights Act 1998. The lines between these doctrines (as well as the sub-categories within doctrines) will blur as some grounds for challenge will appear to fit into various boxes. This is an inevitability of public law challenges as it is not unfeasible for a decision to be both (say) unlawful and unreasonable. The key then is that a public law ground of challenge can be based on many categories, but it must, at a minimum, be one. Bearing in mind the potential for cross over, the four key doctrines are worth examining in some detail.

UNLAWFULNESS 3-3

This doctrine is also known as the doctrine of *Ultra Vires* and is sometimes referred to as the public body acting 'outside its jurisdiction'.[16] Unlawfulness can be described in a number of ways. The short version is summarised by Lord Diplock in *The GCHQ Case*:[17]

> By 'illegality' as a ground for judicial review I mean that the decision-maker must understand correctly the law that regulates his decision-making power and must give effect to it.

The slightly longer version is summarised by Lord Pearce in *Anisminic Ltd* v *Foreign Compensation Commission (No. 2)*[18] (it is useful when reading the sections below to substitute the phrase 'public body' for the word 'tribunal'; the principles are the same but *Anisminic* dealt specifically with tribunals):

> [T]ribunals must ... confine themselves within the powers specially committed to them on a true construction of the relevant Acts of Parliament. It would lead to an absurd situation if a tribunal, having been given a circumscribed area of inquiry ... were entitled of its own motion to extend that area by

[15] [1985] AC 374.

[16] In this context jurisdiction refers to then remit of the public body, rather than a geographical jurisdiction. Historically there was some debate as to the differing legal positions of a public body acting outside its jurisdiction and a public body acting unlawfully in some other way. The two positions were comprehensively fused in *Anisminic* [1969] 2 AC 147 and the functional reality can now simply be termed 'unlawfulness'. The distinction will technically exist and the constitutional lawyer should probably be aware of that fact – see H. Woolf et al., *De Smith's Judicial Review* (7th edn) (Sweet & Maxwell, 2013), p. 196 or H. W. R. Wade and C. F. Forsyth, *Administrative Law* (10th edn) (Oxford University Press, 2009), pp. 30–3.

[17] [1985] AC 374 at 410.

[18] [1969] 2 AC 147.

> misconstruing the limits of its mandate to inquire and decide as set out in the Act of Parliament.[19]

and

> Lack of jurisdiction may arise in various ways. There may be an absence of those formalities or things which are conditions precedent to the tribunal having any jurisdiction to embark on an inquiry. Or the tribunal may at the end make an order that it has no jurisdiction to make. Or in the intervening stage, while engaged on a proper inquiry, the tribunal may depart from the rules of natural justice; or it may ask itself the wrong questions; or it may take into account matters which it was not directed to take into account. Thereby it would step outside its jurisdiction. It would turn its inquiry into something not directed by Parliament and fail to make the inquiry which Parliament did direct. Any of these things would cause its purported decision to be a nullity.[20]

These principles of unlawfulness have been the basis on which unlawfulness has been adjudged ever since. The principles have been confirmed in a string of more modern cases such as *O'Reilly* v *Mackman*,[21] *R* v *Hull University Visitor, ex parte Page*[22] and *Boddington* v *British Transport Police*.[23] As such we can break the category 'unlawfulness' down into further sub-categories. For its actions to be lawful a public body must:

- understand and act within the terms of the powers it possesses;
- only take into account matters that are relevant to its decision;
- act in accordance with any public duties; and
- adhere to the rules of natural justice.

[19] [1969] 2 AC 147 at 194.

[20] [1969] 2 AC 147 at 195.

[21] [1983] 2 AC 237, HL.

[22] [1993] AC 682, HL.

[23] [1999] 2 AC 143, HL.

A public body must act within its powers 3-4

The powers of any public body will generally be granted by legislation, be it primary[24] or secondary legislation,[25] although on occasion the power derives from common law sources such as the royal prerogative,[26] or inherent powers such as under the Ram doctrine.[27] A public body may not act outside the powers that it possesses. It is common sense that a public body must also understand the law that it is applying, or the questions that it must consider, in making a decision to come to a proper conclusion. If the public body fails in this regard and acts outside its powers then the decision is unlawful. Thus, by this principle, the public body is compelled to comply with two of the fundamental principles of the rule of law:[28] (1) that the law is prescribed, understandable, and available to individuals; and (2) that the law may not be used arbitrarily in the exercise of state power.

The law makers for Wales (primarily, but not exclusively, the UK Parliament, the UK Government, the National Assembly for Wales, and the Welsh Ministers) cannot legislate for every scenario and, as such, the legislation often requires interpretation by the courts. This will usually involve an analysis of the statutory background, previous case law based precedents, and then application to the facts of the case. Consideration can range from interpretation on a narrow scale of a specific point, to interpretation on a wider, more subjective scale; it depends on how much

[24] Defining 'primary legislation' can be complex. Acts of the UK Parliament and the National Assembly for Wales can be considered primary legislation. Section 21(1) of the Human Rights Act 1998 gives a definition for the purposes of the 1998 Act which includes, but is not limited to, Acts and Orders in Council made in exercise of Her Majesty's royal prerogative. For a discussion of the nature of primary and secondary legislation see A. McHarg, 'What is delegated legislation?' [2006] PL 539–61.

[25] Defined under s. 21(1) of the Interpretation Act 1978 as 'Orders in Council, orders, rules, regulations, schemes, warrants, byelaws and other instruments made or to be made under any Act'. Generally, secondary legislation (otherwise known as 'subordinate legislation') is legislation enacted by a public body, which possesses the power to enact legislation by virtue of a power granted by primary legislation. For further discussion see McHarg, 'What is delegated legislation?' [2006] PL 539–61.

[26] The prerogative powers are an exhaustive but non-defined list of common law powers possessed by the Crown, now exercised by ministers. They are powers that appertain only to the Crown, not to its citizens. Examples are the power to make treaties or recognise foreign governments.

[27] The inherent powers of public bodies are seldom relied upon by the authorities themselves and this generally covers actions incidental to their actions or obligations. The ram doctrine (also seldom relied upon) is named after Sir Granville Ram, the First Parliamentary Counsel who set out the doctrine in a memorandum dated 2 November 1945. It holds that a minister of the Crown may exercise any powers that the Crown may exercise, except in so far as the minister is precluded from doing so (as opposed to only being able to act where express power exists).

[28] The concept of the rule of law has been discussed by academics and jurists for hundreds of years and there is no single definition. Generally speaking, the rule of law provides that everything must be done according to law, everyone is subject to the law and the law must protect from tyranny. For further discussion on the principle of the rule of law see T. Bingham, 'The Rule of Law' (2007) 66(1) CLJ 67 or M. Arden, 'The changing judicial role: human rights, Community law and the intention of Parliament' (2008) 67(3) CLJ 487–507.

discretion the source of the power gives the decision maker. On occasion statutes will allow the decision maker to act 'as he thinks fit' or 'as appropriate'. Where the decision maker has complete discretion the Administrative Court may still act in its supervisory role, but will consider whether the decision can be 'reasonably and objectively justified by relevant facts'[29] and we begin to stray into the principle of 'unreasonableness'. An example of this spectrum can be found in s. 5(3) of the Housing (Wales) Measure 2011:

> The Welsh Ministers must not make a decision under subsection (2)(b) [to reject a local housing authority's application for a direction suspending the right to buy] unless they have considered –
> (a) any statement that the authority is required to prepare under section 87(2) of the Local Government Act 2003, and
> (b) any other information which the Welsh Ministers consider relevant.

Brief observation of the above tells us that s. 5(3)(a) can be narrowly interpreted: either the Welsh Ministers have or have not considered s. 87(2) of the Local Government Act 2003 (although if they have given it proper consideration is another matter). However, s. 5(3)(b) is an example of the other end of the spectrum as 'any other information which the Welsh Ministers consider relevant' is a potentially infinite category within the subjective, yet judicially reviewable, opinion of the Welsh Ministers.

An example of this point in Welsh administrative law can be found in the case of *R (Long)* v *Welsh Ministers*.[30] In that case the claimant challenged the decision of the Welsh Ministers to exercise their power, under s. 58(2)(d) of the Local Government (Wales) Act 1994, to repeal s. 28 of the Abergavenny Improvement Act 1854, which required the local authority to hold a livestock market within the town of Abergavenny. The 1994 Act empowered the Welsh Ministers to repeal any local statutory provision that appeared to have become spent, obsolete or unnecessary, or to have been substantially superseded by any enactment. Nicola Davies J determined that the Welsh Ministers had lawfully used their power under the 1994 Act. The requirement under s. 28 of the 1854 Act was obsolete as it required the livestock market to be held within the boundaries of Abergavenny as they were in the nineteenth century. A location which was suitable and/or convenient in the nineteenth century was not or might not be so today. Further, there was power under the Food Act 1984 that allowed the local authority to choose a site appropriate for the twenty-first century. Therefore, the decision of the Welsh Ministers that s. 28 of the 1854 Act had been 'substantially superseded' properly reflected the powers provided by the 1994 Act. Furthermore, s. 28 of the 1854 Act was 'unnecessary' as Abergavenny was the only place in Wales where such a prescriptive regime

[29] *Office of Fair Trading* v *IBA Health Ltd* [2004] All ER 1103 at para. 45.

[30] [2012] EWHC 3131 (Admin).

existed. It permitted a consistency of approach throughout Wales and allowed the local authority to make its own planning and development decisions.

The failure of a public body to make an order or perform an act which it is empowered to do, but has discretion over whether to do it or not, is also subject to unlawfulness principles. The Administrative Court, in such a case, will consider whether the decision maker has taken into account the proper considerations in refusing to exercise their discretion,[31] as discussed below.

Considering relevant matters 3-5

When making any decision a public body must only take into account matters that are relevant to its decision. Thus it must consider relevant matters and ignore irrelevant matters. The different classes of relevant considerations were summarised by Simon Brown LJ in *R* v *Somerset County Council, ex parte Fewings*:[32]

> First, those clearly (whether expressly or impliedly) identified by the statute as considerations to which regard must be had. Second, those clearly identified by the statute as considerations to which regard must not be had. Third, those to which the decision-maker may have regard if in his judgment and discretion he thinks it right to do so.[33]

What matters are relevant and irrelevant are to be considered on a case-by-case basis. The primary considerations will always be those considerations stipulated in the source of the power (usually the statute or statutory instrument)[34] itself and, as such, decision makers should carefully consider the source of their powers before exercising them.

As well as statutory considerations there will likely be numerous non-statutory, case-specific considerations (as per Simon Brown LJ's third class of consideration). As these are discretionary considerations that are subject to judicial review, a party may thus argue that a consideration deemed to be relevant by the public body is in fact not relevant, or vice versa.

A good, Welsh example of the relevant considerations principle can be found in *Trail Riders Fellowship* v *Powys County Council*,[35] which involved a challenge to the decision of the council to make two traffic regulation orders that would prohibit motor vehicular use of two byways. Cranston J held that the council had properly considered the relevant considerations for making such an order as required under the relevant statute, the Road Traffic Regulation Act 1984. However, the council

[31] *Padfield* v *Minister for Agriculture, Fisheries and Food* [1968] AC 997.

[32] [1995] 1 WLR 1037.

[33] [1995] 1 WLR 1037 at 1049.

[34] Any document by which secondary legislative power is exercised is known as a statutory instrument – see ss. 1 and 1A of the Statutory Instruments Act 1946.

[35] [2013] EWHC 3144 (Admin).

officer's report which recommended making the orders also included a note that the council were still defending separate appeals which challenged the failure of the council to keep the byways in good repair. The officer suggested that "any decision that goes against the proposal of this report will put that defence in jeopardy". Cranston J determined that whilst the council should not be barred from knowing about the appeal proceedings, the unfortunate language used meant it was possible that the council were influenced by the improper consideration that making the orders would benefit the council's position in the appeal or not doing so would jeopardise it. As the decision was potentially based on an improper consideration the orders were quashed.

Whilst relevant considerations must be assessed on a case-by-case basis there are some recurring themes in the field worthy of specific mention.

3-6 Public policy

If a public body has a particular policy on an area then it should take that into account as a relevant consideration. It is not, per se, unlawful for a public body not to act in accordance with its policy. The policy should, however, be considered and the decision maker should explain why the policy has not been followed in the event that it has not.[36] This is a topic that raises its head frequently, especially in planning law cases as there are numerous policies in place both at the national and local levels.

There was debate as to the approach that the court will take when it comes to interpretation of policy.[37] This debate appeared to be settled and the courts today generally approach the question of interpretation of a policy by not relying on the interpretation of those who prepared the policy, but rather to give the policy its ordinary meaning. To quote Sedley LJ: 'What a policy means is what it says'.[38] The most recent formulation of the principle can be found in *Tesco Stores Ltd* v *Dundee City Council*[39] where Lord Reed held:

> [P]olicy statements should be interpreted objectively in accordance with the language used, read as always in its proper context … That is not to say that such statements should be construed as if they were statutory or contractual provisions … As has often been observed, development plans are full of broad statements of policy, many of which may be mutually irreconcilable, so that in a particular case one must give way to another. In addition, many of the provisions of development plans are framed in language whose application to a given set of

[36] There are numerous authorities on this point. For examples see: *R (Munjaz)* v *Mersey Care NHS Trust* [2006] 2 AC 148; *Argos Ltd* v *Office Fair Trading* [2006] UKCLR 1135; *Royal Mail Group Plc* v *The Postal Services Commission* [2007] ACD 81.

[37] For the now disapproved of approach see *R (Springhall)* v *Richmond on Thames LBC* [2006] BLGR 419.

[38] *First Secretary of State* v *Sainsbury's Supermarkets Ltd* [2005] NPC 60 at para. 16.

[39] [2012] PTSR 983.

> facts requires the exercise of judgment. Such matters fall within the jurisdiction of planning authorities, and their exercise of their judgment can only be challenged on the ground that it is irrational or perverse … Nevertheless, planning authorities do not live in the world of Humpty Dumpty: they cannot make the development plan mean whatever they would like it to mean.[40]

Lord Reed's judgment suggests that whilst the general principle of objectively reading a policy remains, a good deal of respect should be given to the public body's interpretation of context and the net result of competing policies.

Resources 3-7

A public body may, subject to the doctrine of reasonableness, consider its resources when making a decision. A public authority will have finite resources and many competing demands and this is relevant when the decision in question relates to a discretionary power. It may be that a public authority, whilst accepting that a particular action is desirable, chooses to channel funds elsewhere. However, if the decision in question relates to an 'absolute duty', such as under s. 23(1) of the Children Act 1989 which establishes a duty for a local authority looking after a child to provide accommodation while he is in the authority's care, then the public authority must comply with the duty irrespective of its resources.[41]

Act in accordance with public duties 3-8

If a public body does not act in accordance with its duties then it is acting unlawfully. Legislation places a great number of duties on public bodies, which they must act upon accordingly. These duties generally fall within four categories, one of specific (in a sense) application, and three of wide-ranging application.

Statutory duties 3-9

There are numerous statutes and statutory instruments that place specific duties on public bodies. To list them all would be virtually impossible and so we may take an example.

> Section 192(2) Housing Act 1996 requires a local authority to provide accommodation for any person who is homeless and a priority need for accommodation.[42]

These statutory duties are often narrowly drafted with a specific intent, in this case to ensure that all local authorities provide homelessness accommodation. The key

[40] [2012] PTSR 983, per Lord Reed JSC at paras 18 and 19.

[41] *R (G)* v *Barnett LBC* [2004] 2 AC 208.

[42] Subject to multiple caveats in Part VII of the Housing Act 1996. The example, nonetheless, is a useful illustrative tool and one that frequently arises in the Administrative Court.

question for the Administrative Court will be to ask: (1) whether the statutory duty exists; and (2) whether the public body complied with it.

In a Welsh context an example can be found in *Western Power Distribution Investments Ltd* v *Cardiff County Council*.[43] The claimant landowner challenged the decision of the council to designate land in the Nant Fawr Corridor in Cardiff as a local nature reserve. The claimant noted that whilst the council had considered the terms of s. 21 of the National Parks and Access to the Countryside Act 1949, which governed designation of local nature reserves, all of the relevant land was held by the council pursuant to s. 164 of the Public Health Act 1875, which imposed a statutory trust over the land in favour of the public for use as public walks and pleasure grounds. It was the claimant's contention that the council had not properly considered that those two statutory provisions were in conflict as both asserted their own goal was to be the council's primary consideration. Ouseley J held that there was no reason to hold that, generally, dual designations were inevitably unlawful. However, in this case the council had made it clear that it intended to manage the lands conforming with its duties under the 1949 Act, so that nature conservation had priority. It had attempted to resolve the incompatibility with s. 164 by pointing out that public access would continue. Nonetheless, as the management plan did not restrict access in the interests of the recreational enjoyment of nature conservation, but in the interests of nature conservation as a value in its own right, those measures were not compatible with the duty held under s. 164 of the 1875 Act. The designation was therefore unlawful.

3-10 Duties under s. 149 of the Equality Act 2010

A relatively recent, yet increasingly important duty, is the public sector equality duty in s. 149 of the Equality Act 2010. The relevant provisions are below:

> **149 Public sector equality duty**
>
> (1) A public authority must, in the exercise of its functions, have due regard to the need to –
>
> (a) eliminate discrimination, harassment, victimisation and any other conduct that is prohibited by or under this Act;
>
> (b) advance equality of opportunity between persons who share a relevant protected characteristic and persons who do not share it;
>
> (c) foster good relations between persons who share a relevant protected characteristic and persons who do not share it.
>
> (2) A person who is not a public authority but who exercises public functions must, in the exercise of those functions, have due regard to the matters mentioned in subsection (1).
>
> (3) Having due regard to the need to advance equality of opportunity between persons who share a relevant protected characteristic and persons who do not share it involves having due regard, in particular, to the need to –

[43] [2011] NPC 25.

(a) remove or minimise disadvantages suffered by persons who share a relevant protected characteristic that are connected to that characteristic;
(b) take steps to meet the needs of persons who share a relevant protected characteristic that are different from the needs of persons who do not share it;
(c) encourage persons who share a relevant protected characteristic to participate in public life or in any other activity in which participation by such persons is disproportionately low.

(4) The steps involved in meeting the needs of disabled persons that are different from the needs of persons who are not disabled include, in particular, steps to take account of disabled persons' disabilities.

(5) Having due regard to the need to foster good relations between persons who share a relevant protected characteristic and persons who do not share it involves having due regard, in particular, to the need to –
(a) tackle prejudice, and
(b) promote understanding.

(6) Compliance with the duties in this section may involve treating some persons more favourably than others; but that is not to be taken as permitting conduct that would otherwise be prohibited by or under this Act.

(7) The relevant protected characteristics are –
- age;
- disability;
- gender reassignment;
- pregnancy and maternity;
- race;
- religion or belief;
- sex;
- sexual orientation.

It is important to highlight the words used in s. 149(1): 'A public authority *must*, in the exercise of its functions, *have due regard*' (emphasis added). As such the public authority must have regard to this duty in every decision it makes, even if it is simply to acknowledge the duty and declare that it does not apply (assuming it does not). Failure to have regard to the duty is unlawful. The manner in which a local authority should approach the duty was summarised by Aikens LJ in *R (Brown)* v *Work and Pensions Secretary*,[44] who outlined the following principles:

1. Decision makers must be aware of the duty to have due regard to the goals specified in the 2010 Act.
2. The duty must be consciously fulfilled before and at the time that a particular policy or decision is being considered.

[44] [2009] PTSR 1506, paras 90–5.

3. The duty must be exercised in substance, with rigour and with an open mind.
4. The duty cannot be delegated.
5. The duty is continuing.
6. It is good practice for such decision makers to keep an adequate record showing the consideration given to such a duty.

An illustrative example is *R (Griffiths)* v *Secretary of State for Justice*,[45] where the claimant challenged the apparent failure of the Secretary of State for Justice to make adequate provision for approved premises to accommodate women released from prison on licence. The claimant, who was imprisoned for attempted murder, spoke Welsh as her first language and lived in North Wales. She noted that there were no approved premises in Wales, which she contended discriminated against her on grounds of sex (there were such approved premises for men) and on the grounds of race (with no premises in Wales she was unable to speak Welsh at the approved premises she would have to attend whilst released on licence in England). Cranston J held that the Secretary of State's approved premises provision did not directly or indirectly discriminate against the claimant. However, he did consider that the various reports on approved premises did not adequately address whether more could be done to advance equality for women and Welsh speakers. As such, the Secretary of State had not properly considered the public sector equality duty and he would have to reconsider his decision on approved premises with the duty in mind.

In Wales, relevant public bodies[46] are also subject to further PSED requirements by virtue of the Equality Act 2010 (Statutory Duties) (Wales) Regulations 2011. Regulation 3(1) of the 2011 Regulations requires authorities to publish objectives, which are referred to as 'equality objectives', which must be designed so as to enable the authority to better perform the general duty. As such, as well as the general PSED, Welsh authorities must also comply with their own stated equality objectives. Otherwise the authority may have failed to properly consider its own policy, and fall foul of the principle of unlawfulness.[47]

3-11 Duties under the European Convention on Human Rights 1950 ('ECHR')[48]

It is important to note that there is a general duty on all public bodies to act in a way that is compatible with the ECHR.[49] Further, all domestic legislation should be interpreted, as far as possible, to bring it into line with the ECHR.[50] The decisions

[45] [2013] EWHC 4077 (Admin).

[46] As defined in Part 2 of Schedule 19 to the Equality Act 2010. The Schedule includes most of the bodies expressly considered in chapter 4 of this work, but it should be checked to be sure.

[47] See 3-6 for a discussion of this principle with regard to the importance of public policy.

[48] This duty will be considered to a greater extent later in this chapter.

[49] Human Rights Act 1998, s. 6(1).

[50] Human Rights Act 1998, s. 3(1).

of the European Court of Human Rights must be taken into account by domestic courts in effecting that interpretation.[51] A failure on the part of the public body to act in an ECHR-compliant way will be unlawful.

Duties under European Community and European Union law[52] ('European law') 3-12

Where a public body is making a decision in an area in which there is national law and European law the public body is under a duty to ensure that it implements its decision in accordance with both sets of law. This stems out of an obligation on all member states to 'take appropriate measures ... to ensure fulfilment of the obligations arising out of this treaty'.[53] It is now established that the courts of member states are bound to give effect to European law even if it is incompatible with the national law of a state.[54] UK courts have accepted this requirement[55] and, as a result, where a UK Act of Parliament or other law is incompatible with European law it will not be given effect by the domestic courts, which will give effect instead to European law.[56] The domestic courts are also required to interpret UK statutes in the light of any relevant European law.[57]

A common example of this dual consideration can be found in planning and environmental law. A local authority must consider whether a development requires an environmental impact assessment ('EIA') before granting planning permission. The local authority will consider whether an EIA is necessary according to the statutory scheme in accordance with reg. 3(2) of the Town and Country Planning (Environmental Impact Assessment) (England and Wales) Regulations 1999. However, the public body (and the courts) will also be under a duty to consider European law on the area, in this case under Directive 85/337/EEC.

A Welsh example of the direct effect that European law can have is to be found in the case of *R (TA Gwillim & Sons)* v *Welsh Ministers.*[58] The claimant firm bred cows and ewes from a 116-hectare site. The firm had entered into a lease for 451 hectares of additional land in order to expand production. However, its plans were frustrated by restrictions and uncertainties arising out of agri-environmental

[51] Human Rights Act 1998, s. 2(1).

[52] For a discussion of the differences see *De Smith's Judicial Review*, p. 703.

[53] Article 10(5) of the Treaty on the Functioning of the European Union (Treaty of Rome).

[54] *Internationale Handelsgesellschaft mbH* v *Einfuhr und Vorratsstelle für Getreide und Futtermittel* (Case 11/70) [1970] ECR 1125.

[55] *R* v *Secretary of State for Transport, ex parte Factortame Ltd (No. 2)* [1991] 1 All ER 70 where the House of Lords accepted the judgment of the CJEU in *R* v *Secretary of State for Transport, ex parte Factortame Ltd* (C-213/89) [1991] 1 All ER 70 that when a reference has been made to the CJEU, a domestic court may grant an injunction against the Crown or suspend the operation of an Act of Parliament despite the fact that it apparently had no power to do so under domestic law.

[56] See, for example, *R* v *Minister for Agriculture, Fisheries, and Food, ex parte FEDESA* [1988] 3 CMLR 661, HC.

[57] *Marleasing SA* v *La Comercial Internacional de Alimentacion SA* [1990] ECR I-4135.

[58] [2009] NPC 136 for the Administrative Court Decision and [2011] 1 WLR 966 for the affirming Court of Appeal decision.

commitments affecting the land. That led to the decision not to renew the lease. The firm applied to the Welsh Government for a single farm payment, which is a payment granted to the farmers under EU subsidies. European law (Regulation 1782/2003) provided the framework for when national governments must provide payments to support farmers and art. 40 of the Regulation outlined an alternative method of calculation of the quantum when the farmer is experiencing hardship. Under the 2003 Regulation the payment was calculated considering the numbers of livestock per hectare. As the calculation base line was in that period when the firm had leased more land but had not yet had the chance to increase livestock numbers the firm was entitled to a lower payment under the 2003 Regulations unless the hardship provisions applied, which would allow the calculation base line to be taken from an earlier date. The Welsh Government had determined the hardship provisions in art. 40 did not apply as the firm could not show that a dip or reduction in production had taken place, only that the land area had increased, and as such any payment should be calculated in accordance with a base line calculation arising from the short period when the firm had leased the extra 451 hectares. However, both HHJ Jarman QC (sitting as a Judge of the High Court) and the Court of Appeal held that art. 40 did not necessarily require a dip or reduction to establish hardship. Production could also be adversely affected where agri-environmental commitments prevented or restricted an increase in production. It was, therefore, appropriate, under the hardship provisions, to consider the earlier period when an increase in land area had not yet taken place.

3-13 Natural justice

Natural justice is often described as having two pillars. The first pillar is the principle that a decision of a public body is only valid in law if it was a legitimate decision that does not display fraud, dishonesty, malice or personal self-interest. These terms are sometimes summarised as being decisions made in bad faith, or being subject to bias. The second pillar is that a decision maker must ensure that the decision-making process is approached fairly[59] with each side having the opportunity to be heard and properly put their case. This second principle is sometimes referred to by the Latin *audi alteram partem* ('hear the other side').

3-14 Bad faith

What can amount to bad faith can be any number of activities. The term is seldom defined in case law, the closest is perhaps the much-quoted comment of Harman LJ in *Ridge* v *Baldwin*:[60] 'natural justice, which after all is only fair play in action'.[61]

[59] See later in the chapter for the procedural unfairness outside the terms of natural justice. In practical terms, given the wider application of the post-*GCHQ Case* doctrine of procedural unfairness, natural justice based procedural unfairness is diminishing as a ground relied on by parties to proceedings.

[60] [1963] 1 QB 539.

[61] [1963] 1 QB 539 at 578.

It appears to be something easier to identify on a case-by-case basis than it is to define. A few examples are:

- A local authority was deemed to be acting fraudulently by acquiring land ostensibly to widen a street when in fact the true purpose was to resell it at a profit.[62]
- A local authority was deemed to be acting dishonestly where licensing decisions were being used to increase public funds.[63]
- A local authority was deemed to be acting with malice where it ceased advertising in newspapers controlled by the *Times Newspaper* on the grounds that said newspapers had written articles critical of its counsellors.[64]

Bias 3-15

What can amount to bias, however, does have an established test, as confirmed by Lord Hope in *Porter* v *Magill*.[65] There are two types of bias that the courts will consider in administrative law: actual bias and apparent bias.

- Actual bias
  If a decision maker shows himself to actually be biased then he should disqualify himself from the decision-making process, otherwise the decision will be held to be made unlawfully.[66] This is a subjective test that rarely raises its head in the Administrative Court as these days it has largely been overtaken by the test of apparent bias.

- Apparent bias
  The decision of a public body will be deemed to be unlawful in the event that 'the fair-minded and informed observer, having considered the facts, would conclude that there was a real possibility that the tribunal was biased'.[67] It is this objective test that public bodies must consider when making any decision.
  In the context of a Welsh example the case of *R (Condron)* v *National Assembly for Wales*[68] is an example of the debate as to bias. A planning

[62] *Gard* v *Commissioners of Sewers for the City of London* [1885] 28 ChD 486.

[63] *R* v *Birmingham Licensing Planning Committee, ex parte Kennedy* [1972] 2 QB 140.

[64] *R* v *Derbyshire County Council, ex parte The Times Supplement Ltd* [1991] 3 Admin LR 241.

[65] [2001] UKHL 67.

[66] *R* v *Gough* [1993] AC 646 at 661G. See also *Laker Airways Inc* v *FLS Aerospace Ltd* [2000] 1 WLR 113 at 117H, where it was said that 'actual bias will of course always disqualify a person from sitting in judgment'.

[67] This quote comes from Court of Appeal (Civil Division) case of *Director General of Fair Trading* v *Proprietary Association of Great Britain* [2001] 1 WLR 700 (CA) at para. 85, and was adopted by Lord Hope in *Porter* v *Magill* [2001] UKHL 67 at para. 103.

[68] [2006] Env LR 35.

application for open-cast mining on a large site in South Wales was 'called in' for determination by the National Assembly, whereby the National Assembly exercised its right to make the decision on whether to grant planning permission rather than allowing the local authority to make the decision. In the planning inspector's report, he recommended that planning permission be granted subject to conditions. The Assembly delegated the final decision to a planning decision committee, chaired by Carwyn Jones AM, the Minister for Environment, Planning and Countryside in the Welsh Assembly Government[69] (as he then was). The question of apparent bias arose out of a remark allegedly made by Carwyn Jones to a member of a local protest group. She alleged that, before the committee had met, he had said that he was 'going to go with the Inspector's Report', which the committee duly did. In the Administrative Court, Lindsay J determined that there was unacceptable possible predetermination; as such the decision was unlawful on the grounds of apparent bias.[70] The Court of Appeal overturned the decision of Lindsay J. The Court ruled that whilst predetermination can amount to bias, the full context must be explored. They considered the inspector's report, the 'unusually prolonged' meeting of the committee, and the detailed consideration given by them. As such it was determined that Carwyn Jones' comment was simply a throwaway comment that could actually be read to mean: 'On all I have read and all I know at the moment, but subject to further argument, I am going with the Inspector'. There was, therefore, no apparent bias.

3-16 Both sides must be heard (*audi alteram partem*)

A fair procedure will not have taken place unless both parties to a dispute have a fair opportunity to put their case and be heard. This is a centuries-old doctrine that has its roots in natural justice principles, but goes a little further than bias or bad faith. The principle has been invoked to declare decisions to be unlawful where parties were not given the opportunity to address the decision maker.[71] Similarly, it has been invoked where the court made a decision based on a document that had not been disclosed to the other party.[72]

A relatively recent example of the principle being invoked can be found in the Supreme Court decision of *Al-Rawi* v *Security Service*.[73] The issue had arisen in a civil claim for damages where the claimants alleged that the UK security services

[69] Although under the Government of Wales Act 1998 there was technically no Welsh Assembly Government and the title was unofficial. See 1-39, 1-42 and 4-20 for further discussion.

[70] See *R (Condron)* v *National Assembly for Wales* [2005] EWHC 3007 (Admin).

[71] For example, *Abraham* v *Jutsun* [1963] 1 WLR 658, where the Court of Appeal held that the Divisional Court had unfairly ordered a solicitor to pay costs personally because he had taken a bad point but they gave him no opportunity to meet the complaint.

[72] For example, *B* v *W* [1979] 1 WLR 1041, where the court relied on a speech from a House of Lords debate without informing the parties.

[73] [2012] 1 AC 531.

had been complicit in their detention and ill-treatment by foreign authorities at various locations, including Guantanamo Bay. The security services indicated that they were in possession of material that they wished the court to consider as part of their defence but were obliged to withhold from disclosure on national security grounds. The defendants proposed the adoption of a closed material procedure where the documentation would not be disclosed to the claimants but to independent special advocates who would protect the claimants' interests. The court found that there was no common law power to adopt a closed material procedure in an ordinary civil claim for damages. Unlike the statutory public interest immunity procedure, a closed material procedure involved a departure from the principles of open and natural justice and such a change could only be made by Parliament. Thus the defendants were not entitled to rely on the documentation without a change in legislation.

UNREASONABLENESS

A definition of unreasonableness in administrative law terms can be found in Lord Diplock's judgment in the *GCHQ Case*:[74] 3-17

> By 'irrationality' I mean what can by now be succinctly referred to as '*Wednesbury* unreasonableness' (*Associated Provincial Picture Houses Ltd. v. Wednesbury Corporation* [1948] 1 K.B. 223). It applies to a decision which is so outrageous in its defiance of logic or of accepted moral standards that no sensible person who had applied his mind to the question to be decided could have arrived at it.

The case of *Associated Provincial Picture Houses Ltd* v *Wednesbury Corporation*[75] established the ground rules for what may be deemed unreasonable in administrative law terms, which it must be noted is a higher standard than what would be deemed unreasonable by dictionary definition. It is for this reason that this higher standard is referred to as *Wednesbury unreasonableness*. In *Wednesbury* Lord Greene MR stated that the courts would only interfere with the decision of a public body on the ground that the decision was unreasonable if the decision was 'so unreasonable that no reasonable authority could ever have come to it'.[76] As such Lord Greene MR sought to convey the point that judges would not lightly interfere with the merits-based decisions of public bodies. There is some doubt as to whether the test of unreasonableness still exists in this extreme formulation. The courts have, since the advent of the twenty-first century, begun to shift their perspective and a

[74] [1985] AC 374 at 410.

[75] [1948] 1 KB 223.

[76] [1948] 1 KB 223 at 229–30.

common phrase now used is whether the decision is 'within the range of reasonable responses',[77] which would appear to slightly lower the bar.

The *Wednesbury* test, whether or not it has been diluted, is not prescriptive in its application. In general, however, for a decision to be vitiated by unreasonableness it will fall into one of three categories:

- an unreasonable process;
- a lack of proportionality; or
- a breach of a legitimate expectation.

These categories are worthy of specific consideration.

3-18 Unreasonable process

Consideration of this category has its roots in the consideration of the decision-making process which the decision maker has adopted. It shares similarity with the unlawfulness category of relevant considerations. It does go slightly further as, whilst confined to the overall principle of unreasonableness, the court may consider the weight applied to those relevant considerations by the decision maker, rather than simply considering whether relevant considerations were or were not considered. This supervisory consideration was summarised by Silber J in *R (BT3G Ltd)* v *Secretary of State for Trade and Industry*:[78]

> The balancing and weighing of *relevant* considerations is primarily a matter for the public authority and not the Courts. Courts, have, however, been willing to strike down as unreasonable decisions where manifestly excessive or manifestly inadequate weight has been accorded to a relevant consideration.[79]

It is a high hurdle to cross and the use of the word 'manifestly' should be noted. Excessive or inadequate weight is not necessarily unreasonable in administrative law terms. It is well established that failures must be manifest and that due deference will be afforded to the decision maker when assigning weight to considerations. This is a principle that applies across all areas of public law, although is particularly underlined in planning law, as the dictum of Lord Hoffmann in *Tesco Stores Ltd* v *Secretary of State for the Environment*[80] establishes:

[77] See, for example, the judgment of Dyson LJ in *R (Razgar)* v *Secretary of State for the Home Department (No. 2)* [2003] Imm AR 529 at paras 40 and 41.

[78] [2001] Eu LR 325.

[79] [2001] Eu LR 325 at para. 187.

[80] [1995] 1 WLR 759.

> The law has always made a clear distinction between the question of whether something is a material consideration and the weight which it should be given. The former is a question of law and the latter is a question of planning judgment, which is entirely a matter for the planning authority. Provided that the planning authority has regard to all material considerations, it is at liberty (provided that it does not lapse into Wednesbury irrationality) to give them whatever weight the planning authority thinks fit or no weight at all.[81]

Numerous applications for judicial review citing excessive or inadequate weight are made, particularly in the field of planning law. For example, in *Brecon Beacons National Park Authority* v *National Assembly for Wales*[82] the applicant National Park authority applied to quash the decision of the National Assembly, by its planning inspector, to grant third party planning permission to build an anaerobic digester plant. The applicant alleged (amongst other points) that the inspector had given inadequate consideration to the relevant considerations as to whether the development was subsidiary: namely the cost of the plant, the quantity of electricity generated and the income generated in relation to other farm income. Ouseley J held that these issues were not ignored in a way that made the decision legally objectionable. The principal points, in relation to subsidiarity, namely source of input and location of outputs, were dealt with explicitly and adequately reasoned. The other purported considerations were deemed minor and as such the other facets of subsidiarity did not require specific comment, even if they were material considerations.

It should also be noted that the unreasonable process category also covers those irrational decisions that go beyond a failure in the balancing act and that, quite simply, ostensibly lack logical reasoning. It is common sense that if improper weight to a factor can be unreasonable, then a complete failure to properly approach the relevant considerations may also be unreasonable.

Proportionality 3-19

When making a decision a public authority must ensure that it is proportionate, that is to say that it must not have a disproportionately oppressive or onerous result for a member of the public. Laws LJ summarised this in *R (Khatun)* v *Newham LBC*:[83]

> Clearly a public body may choose to deploy powers it enjoys under statute in so draconian a fashion that the hardship suffered by affected individuals in consequence will justify the court in condemning the exercise as irrational or perverse.[84]

[81] [1995] 1 WLR 759 at 780.

[82] [2010] EWHC 3780 (Admin).

[83] [2005] QB 37.

[84] [2005] QB 37 at para. 41.

What is disproportionately oppressive or onerous will be case specific, but some examples (many of which are encompassed in statutory or European law duties today) are:

- Planning conditions which required a developer to construct buildings to local authority standards and to take tenants from the local authority's waiting list were deemed disproportionate.[85]
- Prison Rules that allowed a prison Governor to censor correspondence between a prisoner and his solicitor, and thus potentially prevent litigation against the prison, were held to be oppressive.[86]

For illustration of this principle in a Welsh case see *R (National Association of Memorial Masons)* v *Cardiff City Council*.[87] A local authority policy had resulted in a refusal to recognise a new scheme for accreditation of stonemasons working in municipal cemeteries. It was noted by Blake J that the refusal, which denied competent accredited masons access to the market for work, could be disproportionate without careful evidence-based assessment and appraisal of the new scheme. However, on that occasion the local authority had properly considered the evidence (the decision was instead quashed on the grounds of apparent bias).

A disproportionately long delay can be as much of a problem for a potential claimant as a disproportionate decision. As such an unreasonable delay in making a decision or taking an action can also be a ground for challenge. In *R (FH)* v *Secretary of State for the Home Department*,[88] Collins J summarised the principles behind this ground:

> [6] … there is an implicit obligation on the defendant to decide the applications within a reasonable time …
> [8] … what is reasonable will depend on the circumstances. It is not possible for the court to say that a particular period of time should be the limit of what is reasonable …
> [11] … [Delay] can only be regarded as unlawful if it fails the *Wednesbury* test and is shown to result from actions or inactions which can be regarded as irrational … What may be regarded as undesirable or a failure to reach the best standards is not unlawful. Resources can be taken into account in considering whether a decision has been made within a reasonable time, but (assuming the threshold has been crossed) the defendant must produce some material to show that the manner in which he has decided to deal with the relevant claims and the resources put into the exercise are reasonable. That does not mean that the

85 *R* v *Hillingdon LBC, ex parte Royco Homes Ltd* [1974] QB 720.

86 *R* v *Secretary of State for the Home Department, ex parte Leech (No. 2)* [1994] QB 198.

87 [2011] ACD 77.

88 [2007] EWHC 1571 (Admin).

> court should determine for itself whether a different and perhaps better approach might have existed. That is not the court's function. But the court can and must consider whether what has produced the delay has resulted from a rational system. If unacceptable delays have resulted, they cannot be excused by a claim that sufficient resources were not available. But in deciding whether the delays are unacceptable, the court must recognise that resources are not infinite and that it is for the defendant and not for the court to determine how those resources should be applied to fund the various matters for which he is responsible.

It is important to note the point that whether a time period is considered to be unreasonable is assessed on a case-by-case basis[89] and a time period that is unreasonable in one case may not be unreasonable in another. A myriad of factors may play a part, such as resources, the nature of the public body's administrative systems, the conduct of the claimant, or any other relevant factor.

It should also be noted that the concept of proportionality exists, and indeed to a stronger degree, in European law. The Court of Justice of the European Union ('CJEU') applies a more detailed test of proportionality and, as such, following on from the duty of public bodies to abide by European law discussed earlier in this chapter, when a public body has a duty to comply with European law, it must ensure it does so proportionately and to the European law standard. The CJEU will consider the decision in two stages:

1. whether the means employed to achieve the aim correspond to the importance of the aim (the suitability test); and
2. whether they are necessary for its achievement (the necessity test).

This test follows on from one of the fundamental principles outlined in article 5 of the Treaty of Rome, which requires that 'the individual should not have his freedom of action limited beyond the degree necessary for the general interest'.[90]

The test of proportionality also applies to those human rights classified under the ECHR as qualified rights. These will be discussed later.[91]

Legitimate expectation 3-20

Where a public body affords a potential claimant a legitimate expectation that it will act in a particular way, the public body will have acted unreasonably if it does

[89] Delay in making a decision is frequently raised in immigration cases. See, for example, *R (Tecle)* v *Secretary of State for the Home Department* [2013] EWHC 3823 (Admin) where Lewis J held that there had been unlawful delay on the part of the Home Office in dealing with an application for indefinite leave which had not been considered after two-and-a-half years.

[90] *Internationale Handelsgesellschaft mbH* v *Einfuhr- und Vorratsstelle fur Getreide und Futtermittel* (11/70) [1970] ECR 1125.

[91] See the discussion on human rights as a principle of administrative law later in this chapter.

not conform to the legitimate expectation. A legitimate expectation will arise in two ways, which were outlined by Lord Diplock in the *GCHQ Case*:[92]

> [T]he decision must have consequences which affect some person ... by depriving him of some benefit or advantage which either (i) he had in the past been permitted by the decision-maker to enjoy and which he can legitimately expect to be permitted to continue to do until there has been communicated to him some rational grounds for withdrawing it on which he has been given an opportunity to comment; or (ii) he has received assurance from the decision-maker will not be withdrawn without giving him first an opportunity of advancing reasons for contending that they should not be withdrawn.[93]

Lord Diplock's dictum establishes that a legitimate expectation can arise in two ways:

1. through an express promise to act in a particular way; or
2. through an established practice (sometimes referred to as an implied promise).

The *GCHQ Case* was an established practice legitimate expectation case and it is a good illustration of that principle. In the *GCHQ Case* the House of Lords considered that civil servants held a legitimate expectation that they would be consulted before their trade union membership was revoked as consultation had taken place in the past when conditions of service had been substantially altered.

For a legitimate expectation to exist, a representation must be made and it must be 'clear, unambiguous and devoid of relevant qualification'.[94] This is a higher hurdle than many anticipate. See, for example, *R* v *Shropshire County Council, ex parte Jones*[95] in which Carnwath J (as he then was) held that a student who had been informed that he had 'a very good chance' of receiving a grant did not hold a legitimate expectation (although the decision was quashed on other grounds). The principles of legitimate expectation, and the relevant tests to apply, were outlined by Stuart-Smith J in *R (Alansi)* v *Newham London Borough Council*:[96]

> (1) Where a person asserts a legitimate expectation to enforce what amounts to a substantive right based on a promise or assurance by a public authority, the authority's statement must be clear, unambiguous and devoid of relevant qualification. (2) Where a public authority has made statements to an individual that are said to give rise to a legitimate expectation, the court should ascertain the meaning which the authority's statements would reasonably convey

92 [1985] AC 374.

93 [1985] AC 374 at 408–9.

94 *R* v *Inland Revenue Commissioners, ex parte MFK Underwriting Agents Ltd* [1990] 1 WLR 1545 at 1570.

95 [1997] 9 Admin LR 625.

96 [2014] PTSR 948.

> to that person in the light of all the background knowledge which he or she had in the situation in which he or she was at the time that the statements were made. (3) Where a person is relying on a promise or representation by a public authority as giving rise to a substantive right, the court will not be limited to a Wednesbury irrationality test but will be required to consider whether the public authority has struck the correct balance between the public interest and the interests of the person relying on the promise or representation. (4) The test to be applied is whether frustrating the claimant's expectation is so unfair that to take a new and different course will amount to an abuse of power. Once the expectation has been established, the court must weigh the requirements of fairness against any overriding interest relied on for the change of policy. Both procedural and substantive unfairness may be taken into account when applying this test. (5) Reliance and detriment are not essential prerequisites to a finding of unlawful abuse of power but their presence (or absence) may be taken into account in deciding where the balance of fairness lies and whether the authority has acted unlawfully. (6) The court should give due weight to the proper role of public authorities as agents of change and as being responsible for the adoption and implementation of policies that are in the public interest even though they may conflict with the interest of private individuals, including those to whom assurances have been given.[97]

An example of a legitimate expectation can be found in *R* v *Devon County Council, ex parte Baker*[98] in which a letter promising 'the fullest possible consultation' before closing a care home required the local authority to abide by that representation.

A legitimate expectation can be established by a representation to an individual or a group (as it was in *Baker*). Further, the representation must be made by someone with the authority to make it. The representation will not be binding on the public body if the person making the representation knew, or ought to have known, that they had no power to make a binding representation.[99] A legitimate expectation is also not valid if adhering to the promise would require the public authority to act contrary to statute.[100]

PROCEDURAL IMPROPRIETY 3-21

Procedural impropriety (sometime called procedural unfairness) is summarised by Lord Diplock in the *GCHQ Case*:

[97] [2014] PTSR 948 at 962–3.

[98] [1995] 1 All ER 73.

[99] *South Buckinghamshire District Council* v *Flanagan* [2002] 1 WLR 2601.

[100] See *R (Albert Court Residents' Association)* v *Westminster City Council* [2012] PTSR 604 at paras 34 and 35. Confirmed in *R (Jackley)* v *Secretary of State for Justice* [2015] EWHC 342 (Admin) at paras 42 and 43.

> I have described the third head as 'procedural impropriety' ... This is because susceptibility to judicial review under this head covers also failure by an administrative tribunal to observe procedural rules that are expressly laid down in the legislative instrument by which its jurisdiction is conferred, even where such failure does not involve any denial of natural justice.[101]

Procedural impropriety can be found in a number of ways, but essentially this doctrine requires public bodies to act in a way that is both fair and in accordance with established procedures. The majority of mandatory procedures are outlined in statute or statutory instrument. They are so numerous that they cannot be covered in this work[102] but a public authority should be aware that a failure to follow a statutory procedure may find its decision, which should have been arrived at in accordance with the said procedure, quashed by the Administrative Court on the grounds of procedural impropriety.

Whilst the vast majority of procedures are outlined in legislation the courts have been willing to infer supplementary procedures to ensure that procedures are fair. This was expressly observed by Lord Bridge in *Lloyd* v *McMahon*:[103]

> [W]hen a statute has conferred on any body the power to make decisions affecting individuals, the courts will not only require the procedure prescribed by the statute to be followed, but will readily imply so much and no more to be introduced by way of additional procedural safeguards as will ensure the attainment of fairness.[104]

There are a few specific examples that should be given greater examination.

3-22 Fettering discretion

A public body that has been entrusted with a discretionary power to make a decision must not disable that power by adoption and application of an overly rigid policy. By failing to properly consider exercising the discretion the public body acts improperly by fettering its discretion. This rule is outlined by Lord Reid in *British Oxygen Co Ltd* v *Minister of Technology*:[105]

> The general rule is that anyone who has to exercise a statutory discretion must not 'shut his ears to an application' ... I do not think there is any great difference

[101] [1985] AC 374 at 410.

[102] Examples would include the planning law procedure in the Town and Country Planning (Development Management Procedure) (Wales) Order 2012 and the criminal law procedure in the Criminal Procedure Rules 2015.

[103] [1987] AC 625.

[104] [1987] AC 625 at 702–3.

[105] [1971] AC 610.

> between a policy and a rule. There may be cases where an officer or authority ought to listen to a substantial argument reasonably presented urging a change of policy. What the authority must not do is to refuse to listen at all. But a Ministry or large authority may have had to deal already with a multitude of similar applications and then they will almost certainly have evolved a policy so precise that it could well be called a rule. There can be no objection to that, provided the authority is always willing to listen to anyone with something new to say – of course I do not mean to say that there need be an oral hearing.[106]

Reasons 3-23

A duty to give reasons can arise either expressly or impliedly from statute. For example the First-tier Tribunal and the Upper Tribunal are required by their procedural rules to give reasons for their decisions.[107] Where a duty to give reasons arises out of statute, the decision maker must give reasons or the decision is procedurally improper (and unlawful).

Where no statutory requirement exists, there is no general common law requirement for a public body to give reasons for an administrative decision.[108] The question of whether reasons are required under common law will depend on the circumstances of the case. Some examples of decisions on this point are given below:

- When refusing to review a mandatory life sentence, the Secretary of State must inform prisoners who are serving mandatory life sentences how long a term was recommended for them by the judiciary before their sentences would be reviewed.[109]
- A decision by the Health Committee of the General Medical Council about a doctor's fitness to practise must be supported by reasons.[110]
- No reasons were required from the Solicitor General when deciding not to institute contempt proceedings against newspaper editors.[111]

Whilst there is no general common law requirement to give reasons for decisions, the requirement to give reasons is no longer an exceptional one.[112] The Court

[106] [1971] AC 610 at 625.

[107] See, for example, rr. 22, 30 and 40 of the Tribunal Procedure (Upper Tribunal) Rules 2008.

[108] As confirmed by Lord Clyde in *Stefan* v *General Medical Council (No. 1)* [1999] 1 WLR 1293 at 1300.

[109] *R* v *Secretary of State for the Home Department, ex parte Doody* [1994] 1 AC 531.

[110] *Stefan* v *General Medical Council (No. 1)* [1999] 1 WLR 1293.

[111] *R* v *Solicitor General, ex parte Taylor and Taylor* [1996] 1 FCR 206.

[112] As was expressly noted as far back as 1994 in *R* v *Higher Education Funding Council, ex parte Institute of Dental Surgery* [1994] 1 WLR 242 at 257.

of Appeal in *R (Hassan)* v *Secretary of State for Trade and Industry*[113] was careful to confirm that there is no common law rule requiring reasons to be given. Nonetheless, the Court noted that the situations in which reasons were required, either by statute or under common law, were so numerous and varied that the situations in which reasons were not required could now be seen to be exceptional:

> There is a trend towards an increased recognition of the duty upon decision-makers of many kinds to give reasons. But the trend is proceeding on a case by case basis and the law does not at present recognise a general duty to give reasons for administrative decisions. There are exceptions to this for individuals and classes of individuals, and there may be a trend for the exceptions to become the norm and the cases where reasons are not required may appear to be exceptions.[114]

There is force behind the assertion that for a decision to be procedurally fair the decision must be explained; otherwise it cannot be shown that the decision is lawful and reasonable. As such, public bodies should think very carefully before refusing to give reasons for a decision.

There is a long-established rule that where the duty to give reasons arises, the reasons must be 'not only be intelligible, but … deal with the substantial points that have been raised'.[115] The principle was fleshed out somewhat by Lord Brown in *South Buckinghamshire DC* v *Porter (No. 2)*:[116]

> The reasons for a decision must be intelligible and they must be adequate. They must enable the reader to understand why the matter was decided as it was and what conclusions were reached on the 'principal important controversial issues', disclosing how any issue of law or fact was resolved. Reasons can be briefly stated, the degree of particularity required depending entirely on the nature of the issues falling for decision. The reasoning must not give rise to a substantial doubt as to whether the decision-maker erred in law, for example by misunderstanding some relevant policy or some other important matter or by failing to reach a rational decision on relevant grounds. But such adverse inference will not readily be drawn. The reasons need refer only to the main issues in the dispute, not to every material consideration … Decision letters must be read in a straightforward manner, recognising that they are addressed to parties well aware of the issues involved and the arguments advanced. A reasons challenge will only succeed if the party aggrieved can satisfy the court that he has

[113] [2009] 3 All ER 539.

[114] [2009] 3 All ER 539 at para. 19.

[115] *Re Poyser and Mills' Arbitration* [1964] 2 QB 467 at 478.

[116] [2004] 1 WLR 1953.

genuinely been substantially prejudiced by the failure to provide an adequately reasoned decision.[117]

Lord Brown's principles on reasons can be summarised as a five-point list of considerations for those formulating reasons:

1. reasons must enable the reader to understand why the matter was decided as it was and what conclusions were reached on the principal issues;
2. reasons can be brief, the level of detail required depending entirely on the nature of the issues falling for decision;
3. reasons need refer only to the main issues in the dispute, not to every material consideration;
4. reasons must be read in a straightforward manner, recognising that they are addressed to parties who are aware of the issues involved; and
5. a reasons challenge will only succeed if the party aggrieved can satisfy the court that he has genuinely been substantially prejudiced by the failure to provide an adequately reasoned decision.

Consultation 3-24

There is no general duty for a public body to consult before taking any decisions.[118] If a public body had to consult on all decisions the machinery of government would grind to a halt. This said, if a duty arises, or if a public body decides to consult despite the lack of a duty,[119] it must adhere to the principles of a lawful consultation.

The duty will arise in one of three ways:

1. through statute, whereby the statute requires a public body to consult before exercising a specific power;
2. where an established practice of consultation has developed, therefore creating a legitimate expectation;[120] and

[117] [2004] 1 WLR 1953 at para. 36.

[118] *R (BAPIO Action Ltd)* v *Secretary of State for the Home Department* [2008] ACD 7 at paras 41–7. Confirmed in *R (Moseley)* v *Haringey London Borough Council* [2014] 1 WLR 3947 at para. 35.

[119] See *R* v *North and East Devon Health Authority, ex parte Coughlan* [2001] QB 213 at para. 108: '[W]hether or not consultation … is a legal requirement, if it is embarked upon it must be carried out properly.'

[120] As outlined by Law LJ in *R (Nadarajah)* v *Secretary of State for the Home Department* [2005] EWCA Civ 1363 at para. 68. The principles of legitimate expectation are discussed earlier in the chapter.

3. where a general duty of fairness requires the public body to consult before withdrawing a benefit enjoyed by a person or group.[121]

The nature of a public authority's duty to consult (and, in particular, the relationship between that duty and public law fairness) has been considered and confirmed in two more recent, illumining cases, namely by the Divisional Court in the proceedings concerning consultation on the resting place of remains of Richard III in *R (Plantagenet Alliance Ltd)* v *Secretary of State for Justice*[122] and by the Supreme Court in proceedings concerning a council tax reduction scheme in *R (Moseley)* v *Haringey London Borough Council.*[123] These cases emphasise and confirm that there is no general common law duty to consult, but there may be duty to consult in the aforementioned circumstances.

Where a duty to consult does arise the courts have established a procedural code for proper consultation. The general principles applicable to consultation by public bodies were outlined by Lord Woolf in *R* v *North and East Devon Health Authority, ex parte Coughlan,*[124] which, when supported by subsequent cases,[125] can be distilled into four principles that a public body must adhere to for proper consultation to have occurred:

1. the proposals must be set out clearly and accompanied by enough information to enable those being consulted upon to engage in the process and give an informed view. Sufficient information to enable an intelligible response requires the consultee to know not just what the proposal is, but also the factors likely to be of substantial importance to the decision, or the basis upon which the decision was likely to be taken. Where criteria and their precise role were expressly stated, a fair and lawful consultation may prevent departure from the criteria and their stated significance unless there was further consultation enabling representations to be made on that changed basis;[126]
2. the consultation should be undertaken when the proposals are in their formative stage;
3. sufficient time to respond to the consultation must be given; and

[121] As outlined by Longmore LJ in *R (LH)* v *Shropshire Council* [2014] PTSR 1052 at para. 21 and before that by Simon Brown LJ in *R* v *Devon County Council, ex parte Baker* [1995] 1 All ER 73 at 90–1.

[122] [2014] EWHC 1662 (Admin) at paras 83–98.

[123] [2014] 1 WLR 3947 at paras 23–8 and 34–41.

[124] [2001] QB 213. The principles were first discussed in *R* v *Brent LBC, ex parte Gunning* (1985) 84 LGR 168.

[125] Modern examples include *R (Committee of Care North East Newcastle)* v *Newcastle City Council* [2012] EWHC 2655 (Admin) (flawed consultation on closing care homes) and *R (JM)* v *Isle of Wight Council* [2012] Eq LR 34 (flawed consultation on eligibility criteria for access to adult social care).

[126] See *Devon County Council* v *Secretary of State for Communities and Local Government* [2011] BLGR 64.

4. the decision maker must approach the process with an open mind and be prepared to change course if necessary. This is not to say that the decision maker cannot have an opinion in advance of the decision and it is not to say that the decision maker must act in accordance with the responses to consultation. The decision maker must properly consider the relevant considerations and be prepared to change the pre-held opinion if necessary.[127]

In *Moseley* the Supreme Court noted that the degree of specificity with which the public body should conduct its consultation exercise will depend on the identity of those who contend they should be consulted. The more likely the complainant is to be actually affected by the decision, the more detail and enquiry will be needed in the consultation.[128] Further, particularly when statute does not limit the subject of the requisite consultation to the preferred option, fairness may require that interested persons be consulted not only upon the public body's preferred option but also upon arguable yet discarded alternative options, or at least passing reference should be made to the arguable yet discarded alternative options.[129]

A Welsh example of a consultation case can be found in the case of *R (Thomas)* v *Hywel Dda University Health Board*.[130] The claimant, who lived in Cardigan, challenged the decision of the defendant local health board ('the LHB') to cease provision of in-patient beds at Cardigan Hospital on the single ground that the defendant failed to consult on the proposed change. The LHB's board referred to plans to construct a new facility and to its general strategy, including allowing more people to receive care at home. It also stated that no beds would be lost to the county, as they would be provided through alternative means. The LHB had a statutory duty to consult, either directly or through representatives, under s. 183(1) of the National Health Service (Wales) Act 2006, on changes to health services in the area. The LHB concluded that the closure of a small number of beds on a site that was clinically and environmentally unsuitable for patients and their re-provision elsewhere did not constitute a substantial service change. A substantial service change was required under the Welsh Ministers' guidance on the 2006 Act before the changes should generally be the subject of formal consultation. Furthermore, the 2006 Act required the LHB to consult with the local community health council ('CHC'), which it had done, and the CHC had not formally raised any objections with the Welsh Ministers. In his judgment, Hickinbottom J reviewed the authorities on consultation (as discussed above). He concluded that the statutory context was important in determining the circumstances in which statutory consultation was required. It was a material factor that the CHC had a statutory role in respect of the public interest and a power to refer to the Welsh Ministers a failure by the LHB to consult it about a proposed service change. The statutory scheme had that

[127] See the section on bias above, especially *R (Condron)* v *National Assembly for Wales* [2007] BLGR 87.

[128] [2014] 1 WLR 3947 at para. 26.

[129] [2014] 1 WLR 3947 at paras 27–8.

[130] [2014] EWHC 4044 (Admin).

check and balance inherent in it. As such, the LHB would be entitled to take a robust view about consulting the wider public and, in this case, was entitled not to consult further. The LHB had been entitled to find that the closure of the in-patient facilities was not a substantial service change within the terms of the guidance, considering the factual background. As there was no requirement to consult under the statutory regime there was no scope to read in any additional common law obligation to consult, unless the duty of procedural fairness required it. There was no foundation to suggest there was a legitimate expectation or any breach of the common law duty of fairness.

3-25 HUMAN RIGHTS

On 2 October 2000 the European Convention on Human Rights 1950 ('ECHR') was (for the most part) incorporated into the law of England and Wales by s. 6(1) of the Human Rights Act 1998.[131] Since that date, where a public body has failed to act in accordance with the ECHR it has acted unlawfully. In pure administrative law terms, breach of a relevant right forms part of the doctrine of unlawfulness. However, it has become such a widely used ground, with such a large amount of case law emanating from it, that human rights compliance is now seen as a fourth administrative law ground on top of those identified by Lord Diplock in the *GCHQ Case*.[132] The reason for this is based in the treatment of human rights cases by the courts. A number of judgments have established that when considering whether there has been a breach of human rights the court will apply a 'high intensity review',[133] a more stringent test than under the other three principles of administrative law. The higher test was summarised by Beatson LJ in *R (A)* v *Chief Constable of Kent*:[134]

> [W]here the question before a court concerns whether a decision interferes with a right under the ECHR and, if so, whether it is proportionate and therefore justified, it is necessary for the court to conduct a high-intensity review of the decision. The court must make its own assessment of the factors considered by the decision-maker. The need to do this involves considering the appropriate weight to give them and thus the relative weight accorded to the interests and considerations by the decision-maker. The scope of review thus goes further than the traditional grounds of judicial review.[135]

[131] Brought into force by article 2 of the Human Rights Act 1998 (Commencement No. 2) Order 2000 (SI 2000 No. 1851).

[132] [1985] AC 374.

[133] *R (A)* v *Chief Constable of Kent* [2013] EWCA Civ 1706.

[134] *R (A)* v *Chief Constable of Kent* [2013] EWCA Civ 1706.

[135] *R (A)* v *Chief Constable of Kent* [2013] EWCA Civ 1706 at para. 36.

In *Huang* v *Secretary of State for the Home* Department,[136] perhaps the leading judgment on this point, Lord Bingham stated that 'although the Convention calls for a more exacting standard of review, it remains the case that the judge is not the primary decision-maker'.[137] In essence, the court must make a value judgment, but there is no shift to a merits review.[138]

When considering whether there has been a potential breach of human rights there are, whilst keeping the above principles in mind, three questions to ask:[139]

1. Does a right set out in an article apply (or as the law terms it, is it 'engaged')?
2. Has there been a breach of the right?
3. Can the interference be justified by a limitation or qualification?

The first question principally asks whether the right applies. It may be that on the facts of the case the right simply does not apply. The second question asks whether, if the right is engaged, it has as a matter of fact been breached. Finally, the third question applies to limited and qualified rights only (discussed below) and asks, if the engaged right has been breached, whether the breach can be lawfully justified.

The rights established under the ECHR can be separated into three types of rights: absolute rights, qualified rights and limited rights.

Absolute rights 3-26

An absolute right is unqualified. No matter what the circumstances, every human being possesses them.

The absolute rights are:

- Article 2(1) – The right to life
  This said, article 2(2) does make an exception where the taking of a life is necessary for the lawful purposes of self-defence, to prevent unlawful escape, or to prevent insurrection. It is generally, nonetheless, considered to be an absolute right.

- Article 3 – Freedom from torture and inhuman or degrading treatment or punishment

136 [2007] 2 AC 167.

137 [2007] 2 AC 167 at para. 13.

138 [2007] 2 AC 167 at para. 13. Also see *R (Daly)* v *Secretary of State for the Home Department* [2001] 2 AC 532.

139 For an examination of these principles in the context of the competence of the National Assembly to make Assembly Acts, see the case of *Re Recovery of Medical Costs for Asbestos Diseases (Wales) Bill* [2015] AC 1016, which is discussed at 4-12. In essence, if the proposed Act breaches human rights law as discussed in this section, then the National Assembly does not have competence to make the Act by virtue of s. 108(6) of GOWA 2006.

- Article 4(1) – Freedom from slavery and servitude
- Article 7 – Freedom from punishment without lawful authority.

If a public body is shown to breach an absolute right then there is no defence, no test of proportionality; the public body will be shown to have acted unlawfully. Thus, as is popularly reported, even a suspected terrorist must be afforded his right to life and freedom from torture, even to the point where he cannot be removed from the UK on national security grounds if removal would breach an absolute right. This point was illustrated in *Chahal* v *United Kingdom* (22414/93).[140] The UK authorities wished to deport the claimant on national security grounds as he was suspected of being a member of the International Sikh Youth Federation and was suspected to have been involved in conspiracies to murder moderate Sikhs and the Indian Prime Minister. However, there was substantial evidence of serious human rights abuses by the Indian authorities and evidence that the claimant had been tortured by Indian authorities before escaping to the UK. The ECtHR held that article 3 absolutely prohibited torture or inhumane or degrading treatment, regardless of the circumstances of the case. As such the main consideration for the UK authorities was not national security but the possibility of the ill-treatment of the claimant in India if he was deported. Therefore deportation would violate article 3 and was not lawful.

3-27 Limited rights

A limited right is one that is subject to qualification within the ECHR itself. As such the public body need not act in accordance with the right if the ECHR provides for a situation in which the public body need not do so.

The limited rights, with their exceptions, are:

- Article 4(2) – Freedom from forced or compulsory labour
  Under article 4(3) forced or compulsory labour does not include any work required in the ordinary course of detention or punishment, any service of a military character, any service exacted in case of an emergency or any work or service that forms part of normal civic obligations.

- Article 5 – The right to liberty and security
  The exceptions to article 5 are applicable only in accordance with a procedure established by law and in the following circumstances:

  a. the lawful detention of a person after conviction by a competent court;

140 (1997) 23 EHRR 413.

b. the lawful arrest or detention of a person for non-compliance with the lawful order of a court or in order to secure the fulfilment of any obligation prescribed by law;

c. the lawful arrest or detention of a person effected for the purpose of bringing him before the competent legal authority on reasonable suspicion of having committed an offence or when it is reasonably considered necessary to prevent his committing an offence or fleeing after having done so;

d. the detention of a minor by lawful order for the purpose of educational supervision or his lawful detention for the purpose of bringing him before the competent legal authority;

e. the lawful detention of persons for the prevention of the spreading of infectious diseases, of persons of unsound mind, alcoholics or drug addicts or vagrants;

f. the lawful arrest or detention of a person to prevent his unauthorised entry into the country or of a person against whom action is being taken with a view to deportation or extradition.

- Article 6(1) – The right to a fair and public hearing
  This right is limited in that it only applies to the determination of civil rights and obligations and criminal charges. In terms of criminal charges, the duty applies early on in the criminal process, the right applying from 'the official notification given to an individual by the competent authority of an allegation that he has committed a criminal offence'.[141] What can be considered to be a 'civil right and obligation' is far less specific. As noted in *James* v *United Kingdom*:[142]

> Article 6(1) extends only to 'contestations' (disputes) over (civil) 'rights and obligations' which can be said, at least on arguable grounds, to be recognised under domestic law: it does not in itself guarantee any particular content for (civil) 'rights and obligations' in the substantive law of the Contracting States.[143]

The ECtHR has, therefore, held that there is a potentially inexhaustible list of scenarios in which civil rights and obligations may exist. The important point is that there must be a dispute over the nature of the right and the right must exist in UK law. It should be noted that right in this context means any lawfully guaranteed right not just human rights. A few specific decisions of

[141] As noted in *Eckle* v *Federal Republic of Germany* (1983) 5 EHRR 1 at para. 73.

[142] (1986) 8 EHRR 123.

[143] (1986) 8 EHRR 123 at 157–8.

the ECtHR on whether a civil right or obligation may exist help to illustrate the diffuse nature of this definition:

- Immigration- and asylum-based decisions as to whether a person unlawfully present in a country may remain in the country were held *not* to be decisions affecting civil rights and obligations.[144]
- The administrative decision-making process concerning the objection of a third party to the grant of planning permission, provided that third party's civil rights were affected, was held to be determinative of civil rights and obligations.[145]
- A decision to remove a solicitor's right to practise as a solicitor could be a determination of civil rights and obligations, although other disciplinary proceedings, such as a mere reprimand, would not trigger any article 6 issue.[146]

Article 6(1) incorporates a number of subsidiary rights including a right to a fair and public hearing within a reasonable time by an independent and impartial tribunal established by law.

Article 6(3) also provides further subsidiary rights in criminal law:

a. to be informed promptly, in a language which he understands and in detail, of the nature and cause of the accusation against him;

b. to have adequate time and facilities for the preparation of his defence;

c. to defend himself in person or through legal assistance of his own choosing or, if he has not sufficient means to pay for legal assistance, to be given it free when the interests of justice so require;

d. to examine or have examined witnesses against him and to obtain the attendance and examination of witnesses on his behalf under the same conditions as witnesses against him;

e. to have the free assistance of an interpreter if he cannot understand or speak the language used in court.

- Article 12 – The right to marry and found a family
  Article 12 is limited in two ways. First, those marrying must be of the nationally determined marriageable age. Secondly, the marriage must be according

[144] *Maaouia* v *France* (39652/98) (2001) 33 EHRR 42.

[145] *R (Friends Provident Life & Pensions Ltd)* v *Secretary of State for Transport, Local Government and the Regions* [2001] EWHC Admin 820.

[146] *R (Thompson)* v *Law Society* [2004] 1 WLR 2522.

to the national laws governing the exercise of this right. This limitation is fairly narrow in its effect. In essence, as long as the marriage complies with the UK's procedural requirements and those being married are over 16 years old then everyone has the right to marry in the UK. The ECtHR has acted to declare that the procedural restrictions must serve some legitimate state purpose. To this end, separate UK legislation that banned prisoners and transsexuals marrying were held to be unlawful.[147]

- Article 2 of the First Protocol – The right to education
  This right is on the border of being an absolute right, but it is limited in that public authorities are not required to supply education of a particular type,[148] although the State shall respect the right of parents to ensure such education and teaching in conformity with their own religious and philosophical convictions.

Qualified rights 3-28

A qualified right is subject to principles of qualification, which will be examined later in this section. First, an examination of the qualified rights:

- Article 8 – The right to a private and family life
  The right to a private and family life is perhaps the most often pleaded right in the Administrative Court. This is presumably because it is so widely encompassing, as the ECtHR itself identified in *Pretty* v *the United Kingdom*:[149]

  > [T]he concept of 'private life' is a broad term not susceptible to exhaustive definition. It covers the physical and psychological integrity of a person. It can sometimes embrace aspects of an individual's physical and social identity. Elements such as, for example, gender identification, name and sexual orientation and sexual life fall within the personal sphere protected by Article 8. Article 8 also protects a right to personal development, and the right to establish and develop relationships with other human beings and the outside world. Though no previous case has established as such any right to self-determination as being

[147] See *Hamer* v *United Kingdom* (1982) 4 EHRR 139 at paras 70–4 and *Goodwin* v *United Kingdom* (2002) 35 EHRR 18 at para. 103 respectively.

[148] See, for example, *Ali* v *United Kingdom* (2011) 53 EHRR 12 where the ECtHR held that where a child suspected of arson on school grounds was suspended pending a criminal investigation the right to education was not automatically breached. The right guaranteed access to education. It did not guarantee a right of access to a particular institution, nor did it exclude disciplinary measures such as expulsion or temporary exclusion. Any breach of the right on exclusion grounds would be assessed on a case-by-case basis considering whether a fair balance had been struck between the exclusion and the justification for it.

[149] (2002) 35 EHRR 1.

> contained in Article 8 of the Convention, the Court considers that the notion of personal autonomy is an important principle underlying the interpretation of its guarantees.[150]

The non-exhaustive list of what may be an article 8 right is long. Some examples are business relationships,[151] freedom from noise pollution,[152] and a prohibition from covert surveillance ('bugging') of a police cell.[153]

- Article 9 – Freedom of thought, conscience, and religion
  There is no strict definition as to what is protected as 'thought, conscience, and religion'. In *Campbell and Cosans* v *United Kingdom*[154] the ECtHR held that it must be beyond mere opinion or ideas, but instead:

  > Denotes views that attain a certain level of cogency, seriousness, cohesion and importance … are worthy of respect in a 'democratic society' and are not incompatible with human dignity; in addition, they must not conflict with [a] fundamental right.[155]

  The ECtHR and the UK domestic courts have interpreted this right broadly. Past examples of views that have been held to be protected by article 9 are: anti-corporal punishment,[156] secularism,[157] and a belief in anthropogenic causes in climate change.[158]

- Article 10 – Freedom of expression
  This right includes the freedom to hold opinions and to receive and impart information and ideas without interference by public authority. The right even goes as far as to protect speech that shocks, offends, or disturbs.[159]

  Article 10(2) provides for the extent of the limitation to this freedom which 'may be subject to such formalities, conditions, restrictions or penalties as are prescribed by law and are necessary in a democratic society'. As previously mentioned, the essence of this test will be examined below,

150 (2002) 35 EHRR 1 at para. 61.
151 *Niemietz* v *Germany* (1993) 16 EHRR 97.
152 *Hatton* v *United Kingdom* (2002) 34 EHRR 1.
153 *Wood* v *United Kingdom* [2004] Po LR 326.
154 (1982) 4 EHRR 293.
155 (1982) 4 EHRR 293 at para. 36.
156 (1982) 4 EHRR 293 at para. 36.
157 *Lautsi* v *Italy* (2012) 54 EHRR 3 at para. 58.
158 *Grainger plc* v *Nicholson* [2010] 2 All ER 253.
159 *Lingens* v *Austria* (1986) 8 EHRR 407.

but it is important to note that the qualification exists only in the following scenarios:[160]

a. in the interests of national security, territorial integrity or public safety;
b. for the prevention of disorder or crime;
c. for the protection of health or morals;
d. for the protection of the reputation or rights of others;
e. for preventing the disclosure of information received in confidence; or
f. for maintaining the authority and impartiality of the judiciary.

- Article 11 – Freedom of assembly and association
  Under article 11(1) everyone has the right to freedom of peaceful assembly and to freedom of association with others. This extends as far as the state being obliged to protect the right from interference from other individuals (such as counter-protestors).[161]

  Article 11(2) expressly excludes the armed forces, the police, and the administration of the State from this freedom.

- Article 14 – Freedom from discrimination
  Article 14 deserves special mention in that it sits outside the other right-establishing articles. It establishes that the enjoyment of the rights and freedoms *set forth in the Convention* shall be secured without discrimination on any ground such as sex, race, colour, language, religion, political or other opinion, national or social origin, association with a national minority, property, birth or other status. At first glance it appears that this article provides for a general freedom from discrimination. However, the freedom extends only as far as providing that public bodies may not discriminate in how they secure the other rights established by the ECHR.

  Article 14 does, however, still include an element of qualification as per the qualified rights mentioned above. The manner in which the domestic courts will approach violations of article 14 is described by Lord Nicholls in *R (Carson)* v *Secretary of State for Work and Pensions*:[162]

> Article 14 does not apply unless the alleged discrimination is in connection with a Convention right and on a ground stated in article 14. If this prerequisite is satisfied, the essential question for the court is whether the alleged discrimination, that is, the difference in treatment of which complaint is made, can withstand scrutiny. Sometimes the answer to this question will be plain. There may be such an obvious,

[160] Save where that state is dealing with the licensing of broadcasting, which is expressly preserved in article 10(1).

[161] *Plattform 'Ärzte für das Leben'* v *Austria* (1991) 13 EHRR 204.

[162] [2006] 1 AC 173.

> relevant difference between the claimant and those with whom he seeks to compare himself that their situations cannot be regarded as analogous. Sometimes, where the position is not so clear, a different approach is called for. Then the court's scrutiny may best be directed at considering whether the differentiation has a legitimate aim and whether the means chosen to achieve the aim is appropriate and not disproportionate in its adverse impact.[163]

It is an important article in that it ensures that the ECHR is to apply to everyone, no matter what their background, subject to the qualification principles. For the provisions establishing general freedom from discrimination in the UK, attention should be drawn to the Equality Act 2010[164] and not the ECHR.

- Article 1 of the First Protocol – The right to enjoyment of possessions
Under Article 1 of the First Protocol everyone is entitled to peaceful enjoyment of his possessions. No one shall be deprived of his possessions except in the public interest and subject to the conditions provided for by law. The law of England and Wales has steered clear of a definition as to what can be deemed property, leaving the definition wide. In *National Provincial Bank Ltd* v *Ainsworth*[165] Lord Wilberforce stated:

> Before a right or an interest can be admitted into the category of property, or of a right affecting property, it must be definable, identifiable by third parties, capable in its nature of assumption by third parties, and have some degree of permanence or stability.[166]

Whilst this may seem a wide-ranging right, the qualification has, in the majority of situations, justified the breach. For example, the compulsory transfer of freehold property can be lawful as long as it pursues a legitimate social objective.[167]

- Article 3 of the First Protocol – The right to free elections
This article imposes an obligation on the State to hold free elections at regular intervals by way of a secret ballot, under conditions that will ensure the free expression of the opinion of the people in the choice of the government and legislature. The right does not extend to the right to vote or stand for election as long the obligation is substantively complied with.

163 [2006] 1 AC 173 at para. 3.

164 See 3-10 for a discussion of the public sector equality duty.

165 [1965] AC 1175.

166 [1965] AC 1175 at 1247–8.

167 See, for example, *James* v *United Kingdom* (1986) 8 EHRR 123.

The qualification principles 3-29

A qualified right, that is to say any of the rights listed as qualified rights above, are applicable unless an exception is established in line with three principles (all three must be present to form an exception). Those principles are somewhat, but not precisely,[168] uniformed and can be described thus:

1. the limitation must be prescribed by law;
2. the limitation must secure a legitimate aim under the article; and
3. the limitation must be necessary (or proportionate).

Challenges on points one and two are relatively rare. If a limitation is not prescribed by domestic law other administrative law grounds will usually provide a remedy. The existence of a legitimate aim is a fairly broad category that does not receive much attention from the courts, especially when you consider the scope for challenge in the third category.[169]

The term 'necessary' is interpreted narrowly in the ECtHR, with the emphasis on maintaining the right over allowing the exception. The position is summarised by the ECtHR in *The Sunday Times* v *United Kingdom*:[170]

> [W]hilst the adjective 'necessary' … is not synonymous with 'indispensable', neither has it the flexibility of such expressions as 'admissible', 'ordinary', 'useful', 'reasonable' or 'desirable' and that it implies the existence of a 'pressing social need'.[171]

The ECtHR expanded its explanation of necessity in *Dudgeon* v *United Kingdom*:[172]

> The notion of 'necessity' is linked to that of a 'democratic society' … [A] restriction on a Convention right cannot be regarded as 'necessary in a democratic

[168] It should be noted that different qualified rights use different terminology to define the qualification principles. The three-stage test proposed here is a good guideline to the principles generally considered by the ECtHR and the domestic courts when interpreting the ECHR but it must be noted that the different words used to describe the principles in different articles allows for a nuanced approach in relation to the differing terminology. For a detailed analysis of the interpretation, see J. Beatson, et al., *Human Rights: Judicial Protection in the United Kingdom* (Sweet & Maxwell, 2008), paras 2-173–2-220.

[169] For a detailed analysis of the concept of lawfulness and legitimate aim in this context, see Beatson et al., *Human Rights*, paras 2-149–2-172.

[170] (1979–80) 2 EHRR 245.

[171] (1979–80) 2 EHRR 245 at para. 59. See also *Handyside* v *United Kingdom* (1979–80) 1 EHRR 737 at 754 for a virtually identical quote.

[172] (1982) 4 EHRR 149.

> society' (two hallmarks of which are tolerance and broadmindedness) unless, amongst other things, it is proportionate to the legitimate aim pursued.[173]

From the jurisprudence of the ECtHR it can be observed that when considering the qualification principle of necessity the public body may only oust the right where the act is:

1. required by some pressing social need;[174] and
2. proportionate to the legitimate aim pursued.[175]

The proportionality test forms part of the ECHR as a democratic principle. Human rights are to be enjoyed by all, but it is recognised that on occasion the State must interfere with those rights to properly run the country. Where the State is required to interfere with human rights the interference must be limited as much as possible. Thus the principle of human rights takes precedence whilst giving way to practicality only where necessary.

3-30 The European Court of Human Rights

In chapter 1, it was noted that the domestic courts are not the only courts that have an effect on the law of England and Wales. When interpreting human rights the domestic courts are required to 'take into account'[176] the decisions of the European Court of Human Rights ('ECtHR'). The ECtHR does not give binding authority that the domestic courts must follow; rather it gives guidance that should be taken into account. In *R (Hicks)* v *Commissioner of Police of the Metropolis*,[177] Maurice Kay LJ summarised the principles that the domestic courts will apply when considering the judgments of the ECtHR:

> (1) It is the duty of the national courts to enforce domestically enacted Convention rights. (2) The European Court of Human Rights is the court that, ultimately, must interpret the meaning of the Convention. (3) The UK courts will be bound to follow an interpretation of a provision of the Convention if given by the Grand Chamber as authoritative, unless it is apparent that it has misunderstood or overlooked some significant feature of English law or practice which, properly explained, would lead to that interpretation being reviewed by

[173] (1982) 4 EHRR 149 at para. 53.

[174] In *Dudgeon* (1982) 4 EHRR 149, there was held to be no pressing social need for the UK Government to criminalise homosexuality in Northern Ireland.

[175] In *Dudgeon* (1982) 4 EHRR 149, the aim of protecting those who regarded homosexuality as immoral from offence was not sufficient to impose the excessive burden of penal sanctions on conduct between consenting adults.

[176] Human Rights Act 1998, s. 2(1).

[177] [2014] 1 WLR 2152.

> the European Court of Human Rights when its interpretation was being applied to English circumstances. (4) The same principle and qualification applies to a 'clear and constant' line of decisions of the European Court of Human Rights other than one of the Grand Chamber. (5) Convention rights have to be given effect in the light of the domestic law which implements in detail the 'high level' rights set out in the Convention. (6) Where there are 'mixed messages' in the existing Strasbourg case law, a 'real judicial choice' will have to be made about the scope and application of the relevant provision of the Convention.[178]

As may be clear from this dictum, in practice it is extremely rare for the domestic courts not to follow where the ECtHR has led.

CONCLUSION 3-31

In broad terms, to comply with the requirements of administrative law the public body must ensure that it acts in a way that is: lawful, reasonable, procedurally proper, and human rights compliant. The public body must also be aware of the various sub-categories to which these doctrines extend. Establishing whether a breach of these requirements exists is to be assessed on a case-by-case basis, but one may consider that when attempting to establish a breach of administrative law principles, the hurdle is a high one. This high hurdle reflects the balancing act that the judiciary must undertake. On the one hand public bodies must be given the respect they deserve as the democratically appointed decision makers and must not be subject to constant judicial interference on minor technical points. Failure to observe this risks an inappropriately strong judiciary as well as a less effective executive, and thus a breakdown in the separation of powers. One the other hand, the executive must not be allowed to act without an appropriate check on their powers to ensure that public law powers are used lawfully. A lack of administrative law risks an inappropriately strong executive that has the potential to abuse its powers. In summation, administrative law maintains good governance and democratic principles.

[178] [2014] 1 WLR 2152 at para. 80.

Public Law Defendants in Wales

INTRODUCTION

This chapter will, in two parts, explore the nature of public bodies, and thus the nature of the bodies subject to the principles of administrative law. The first part will consider the principles establishing the nature of public bodies. The second part will provide a brief overview of the public bodies in Wales and the manner in which their decisions may be challenged. As such, this chapter will explore the creation, development and the source of powers of the Welsh governmental institutions, both national and local. These institutions, as well as the UK-wide institutions (some of which will also briefly be discussed), make the public law decisions that are subject to challenges in the Administrative Court in Wales. The Welsh authorities comprise a significant legislative, executive and bureaucratic system. There are, at the time of writing, 1,264 local authority councillors in Wales and 60 Members of the National Assembly for Wales (up to 12 of whom are Welsh Ministers). In 2010/11 the Welsh Government spent £8.6 billion, more than half of its £15.8 billion budget, on local government services.[1] In 2014 the Williams Commission estimated that there were 935 public bodies in Wales,[2] but even it précised that estimate by calling it 'conservative' and noting that there is no clear definition of a public body, let alone a Welsh public body.[3]

A number of public bodies make decisions that affect persons in Wales which are not mentioned in this chapter: for example, prisons or the courts and tribunals of England and Wales.[4] This chapter will not attempt a discussion of all public bodies whose decisions affect Wales. There are so many that it would be impractical to list and discuss them all.

[1] Figures provided by the Welsh Local Government Association.

[2] *Report of the Commission on Public Service Governance and Delivery* ('Report of the Williams Commission'), para. 1.30.

[3] *Report of the Commission on Public Service Governance and Delivery* ('Report of the Williams Commission'), paras 1.28–1.30.

[4] As discussed at 1-20.

PUBLIC BODIES – DEFENDANTS IN ADMINISTRATIVE COURT CASES

4-2 Principles for establishing public law defendants

A public law claim brought in the Administrative Court must be a challenge to the decision of a public body. The Administrative Court will not consider private law disputes. In *O'Reilly* v *Mackman*,[5] Lord Denning MR commented:

> In modern times we have come to recognise two separate fields of law: one of private law, the other of public law. Private law regulates the affairs of subjects as between themselves. Public law regulates the affairs of subjects vis-à-vis public authorities. For centuries there were special remedies available in public law. They were the prerogative writs of certiorari, mandamus and prohibition … they were taken in the name of the sovereign against a public authority which had failed to perform its duty to the public at large or had performed it wrongly. Any subject could complain to the sovereign: and then the King's courts, at their discretion, would give him leave to issue such one of the prerogative writs as was appropriate to meet his case.[6]

The definition of a public body is wide and designed to be as all encompassing as possible. In *R* v *Panel on Takeovers and Mergers, ex parte Datafin plc*,[7] Sir John Donaldson MR defined the limits of judicial review with regards to public body decisions:

> In all the reports it is possible to find enumerations of factors giving rise to the jurisdiction, but it is a fatal error to regard the presence of all those factors as essential or as being exclusive of other factors. Possibly the only essential elements are what can be described as a public element, which can take many different forms.[8]

The non-defined, broad nature was well summarised by Jurgens and Van Ommeren, who commented: 'the distinction between public and private law [is] a multifunctional and context-dependant distinction'.[9] This broad definition of a public body decision maker is generally supported in legislation such as s. 6(3) of the Human Rights Act 1998: 'Any person certain of whose functions are functions of a public nature', and Civil Procedure Rule 54.1(2)(a)(ii), which refers to 'public functions'. The key consideration is that it is the nature of the function which is determinative

[5] [1983] 2 AC 237.

[6] [1983] 2 AC 237 at 255.

[7] [1987] QB 815.

[8] [1987] QB 815 at 838.

[9] G. Jurgens and J. Van Ommeren, 'The public–private divide in English and Dutch law: a multifunctional and context-dependant divide' (2012) 71(1) CLJ 172–99.

rather than the nature of the body that is performing the function.[10] A commonly relied upon test is described as the 'But For' test. Pursuant to the *But For* test, power will be public if exercised pursuant to the carrying out of a function in circumstances where, in the absence of a non-governmental body to perform the function, the government itself would almost invariably carry out the function. See, for instance, *R* v *Disciplinary Committee of the Jockey Club, ex parte Aga Khan*[11] when the court concluded that the Jockey Club was not a public body:

> The club nominates three members of the Horserace Betting Levy Board, but this is to represent the disparate private interests of the racing industry, which enjoys the benefit of the levy. There is nothing to suggest that, if the Jockey Club had not voluntarily assumed the regulation of racing, the government would feel obliged or inclined to set up a statutory body for the purpose.[12]

In more recent cases the courts have adopted a case-specific, factor-based approach. Factors have included 'the extent to which in carrying out the relevant function the body is publicly funded, or is exercising statutory powers, or is taking the place of central government or local authorities, or is providing a public service'.[13]

In essence a public body can be defined as a body that exercises powers that display a 'public element'. This has included, but is not confined to, central government departments, local authorities, the inferior courts and tribunals,[14] quasi-autonomous non-governmental organisations (quangos), and private bodies that exercise public functions, thus including those scenarios where a public body has out-sourced its public functions. The jurisdiction of the court to hold that a private body is exercising a public function is certainly the least clear-cut when considering possible public law defendants. A common modern example is where the Secretary of State for Justice has delegated the power to manage a prison to a private company. In such situations the private company is subject to judicial review where it is exercising public functions in relation to its running of the prison.

A public body, defined as such because it can exercise public law powers, that is acting in a private law capacity (for example, entering into a contract of employment) is not subject to the control of administrative law and the Administrative

[10] *YL* v *Birmingham City Council* [2008] 1 AC 95 at para. 148.

[11] [1993] 1 WLR 909.

[12] [1993] 1 WLR 909 at 932.

[13] *Aston Cantlow and Wilmcote with Billesley Parochial Church Council* v *Wallbank* [2004] 1 AC 546 at para. 12, endorsed in *YL* v *Birmingham City Council* [2008] 1 AC 95 at paras 64 and 65.

[14] That is to say all courts and tribunals save the Supreme Court, the Court of Appeal and the High Court. The Upper Tribunal and the Crown Court are subject to judicial review, but only in certain scenarios. See *R (Cart)* v *Upper Tribunal* [2012] 1 AC 663 and s. 28(2)(a) of the Senior Courts Act 1981 respectively. A discussion of the court and tribunals system in England and Wales can be found at 1-20.

Court.[15] Instead, any dispute should be directed to the relevant civil court or tribunal.

4-3 Examples of public law defendants

As discussed above, the definition of a public body is a broad one. The following are some examples of borderline cases, where the court has held the decision maker to be a public body or a body exercising a public function:

- the Panel on Takeovers and Mergers;[16]
- the Advertising Standards Authority;[17]
- the managers of a privately owned psychiatric hospital;[18] and
- a community interest company funded by central government.[19]

Some examples of borderline cases where the court has held that the decision maker is not a public body are:

- organisations regulating sports;[20]
- the Medical Defence Union;[21]
- 'pub watch' schemes (in which publicans cooperate through an unincorporated association to bar customers banned from one licensed premises from all others in the scheme).[22]

It should be noted that the fact that these bodies were held not to be exercising public functions in these cases does not mean that they could not acquire public functions in different scenarios, and, indeed, vice versa.

Although an Act of the UK Parliament is, considering the earlier definition, technically an act by a public body, Parliament is sovereign and as such Acts of Parliament cannot be challenged in the courts.[23] The extent to which this principle applies to the National Assembly for Wales is discussed later in this chapter.

[15] See *R* v *East Berkshire Health Authority, ex parte Walsh* [1985] QB 152.

[16] *R* v *Panel on Takeovers and Mergers, ex parte Datafin plc* [1987] QB 815.

[17] *R v Advertising Standards Authority Ltd, ex parte Insurance Services plc* [1990] COD 42.

[18] *R (A)* v *Partnerships in Care Ltd* [2002] 1 WLR 2610.

[19] *R (Jenkins) v Marsh Farm Community Development Trust* [2011] EWHC 1097 (Admin).

[20] *R* v *Disciplinary Committee of the Jockey Club, ex parte Aga Khan* [1993] 1 WLR 909.

[21] *R (Moreton)* v *Medical Defence Union Ltd* [2006] ACD 102.

[22] *R (Boyle)* v *Haverhill Pub Watch* [2009] EWHC 2441 (Admin).

[23] See *R (Jackson)* v *Attorney General* [2006] 1 AC 262 for modern confirmation of this long-standing principle.

Practical observations 4-4

A final, practical observation is that a private person should not be named as a defendant in Administrative Court proceedings, even where a private individual is the sole decision maker on behalf of the public body. The person is acting on behalf of the public body and thus the public body is the named defendant. An example would be where a planning officer makes a planning decision on behalf of a local planning authority. The defendant would not be *Mr A. N. Officer*, it would be *Local Authority X*.

Having discussed what makes a public body, this chapter can analyse the most common public body defendants for the purposes of the Administrative Court in Wales.

UNITED KINGDOM GOVERNMENT 4-5

The United Kingdom Government is the executive for the United Kingdom and is accountable to the UK Parliament. The UK Government is formally headed by the Queen. The functions of the monarch are practically administered by Government departments of state led by Secretaries of State or ministers, subordinate departments or sub-departments (such as the HMRC Board or the Land Registry), and quangos, which are responsible for particular advisory, regulatory or promotional functions, such as the Equality and Human Rights Commission. There are also semi-autonomous public corporations responsible for public services, for example the British Broadcasting Corporation (the BBC).

A list of potential UK Government public law defendants (although by no means an exhaustive list) can be found in Annex 2 to CPR 66, which contains the list of Government bodies and their representative legal department as noted under the Crown Proceedings Act 1947. The annex is reproduced at Annex D of this work.

As these UK Government bodies exercise public functions, the exercise of these functions is subject to the principles of administrative law, and thus may be checked by way of judicial review or one of the similar procedures as outlined in chapter 6. Importantly, despite the fact that the main offices of the UK Government departments are largely situated in London, Administrative Court proceedings against the UK Government may be brought in the Administrative Court in Wales.[24]

[24] See chapter 2 for a discussion of the reasons for this, which largely lie in principles of access to justice, formulated under CPR PD 54D.

4-6 THE NATIONAL ASSEMBLY FOR WALES

The creation of the National Assembly under the Government of Wales Act 1998 ('GOWA 1998') and its developing role under the Government of Wales Act 2006 ('GOWA 2006') is discussed in chapter 1.[25] This section in this chapter will consider the powers and competence of the Assembly and its status as a potential public law defendant.

4-7 Powers of the National Assembly

Whilst the UK Parliament remains the sovereign Parliament for the UK,[26] the powers of the National Assembly are primary law-making powers whereby the National Assembly may make 'Acts of the Assembly'. In s. 108(1) of GOWA 2006, the fact that the Acts of the Assembly are primary legislation is expressly noted:

> An Act of the Assembly may make any provision that could be made by an Act of Parliament.

This said, s. 108(2) of GOWA 2006 notes that the Act is not law if it is outside the Assembly's competence. Any subject that is listed in Schedule 7 to GOWA 2006 is automatically within the competence of the National Assembly and the National Assembly may make Acts of the Assembly relating to that subject, unless Schedule 7 notes that there is an exception.[27] The current twenty-one headings outlined in Part 1 of Schedule 7 to GOWA 2006, under which the devolved subjects are to be found, are:

1. Agriculture, forestry, animals, plants and rural development
2. Ancient monuments and historic buildings
3. Culture
4. Economic development
5. Education and training
6. Environment
7. Fire and rescue services and fire safety
8. Food
9. Health and health services
10. Highways and transport
11. Housing

[25] See 1-39.

[26] As expressly noted in s. 107(5) of GOWA 2006.

[27] For example, under Sch. 7, Pt 2, para. 5 to GOWA 2006 all legislation relating to 'Education, vocational, social and physical training and the careers service. Promotion of advancement and application of knowledge' in Wales is now made by the Assembly, except any legislation dealing with research councils.

12. Local government
13. National Assembly for Wales
14. Public administration
15. Social welfare
16. Sport and recreation
17. Taxation
18. Tourism
19. Town and country planning
20. Water and flood defence
21. Welsh language.

Notable absences from the declared areas of competence, certainly from the perspective of lawyers, are policing and criminal justice as well as the judiciary and legal system.

By virtue of s. 108 of GOWA 2006, even if the legislation passed by the National Assembly relates to one of the subjects in question, it will still fall outside the Assembly's legislative competence if:

- it falls within a specific exception in Part 1 of Schedule 7 to GOWA 2006;[28]
- it extends otherwise than to England and Wales;[29]
- it applies other than in relation to Wales;[30]
- it is incompatible with European Law;[31]
- it is incompatible with the European Convention on Human Rights 1950;[32]
- it removes, modifies, or imposes a pre-commencement function of a UK Government minister without consent. A pre-commencement function means a function which is exercisable by a minister before the day on which the Assembly Act provisions come into force;[33]
- it modifies one of a number of Acts of Parliament (which principally relate to UK constitutional issues, UK civil emergencies, and the use of UK data) listed in GOWA 2006, Sch. 7, Pt 2, para. 2[34] unless there is an exception listed;

[28] GOWA 2006, s. 108(4)(a).
[29] GOWA 2006, s. 108(6)(b).
[30] GOWA 2006, s. 108(4)(b).
[31] GOWA 2006, s. 108(6)(c).
[32] GOWA 2006, s. 108(6)(c).
[33] GOWA 2006, s. 108(6)(a) and Sch. 7, Pt 2, para. 1.
[34] Namely, European Communities Act 1972, Data Protection Act 1998, Human Rights Act 1998, Civil Contingencies Act 2004, Re-Use of Public Sector Information Regulations 2005 and GOWA 1998, ss. 145, 145A and 146A(1).

- it falls within one of the other general restrictions in GOWA 2006, Sch. 7, Pt 2, paras 3 and 4 (relating to borrowed sums and auditors); and
- it modifies the provisions of GOWA 2006 (save for those provisions that are expressly subject to modification).[35]

The Assembly has legislative competence to enforce a provision that falls within competence or if it is incidental to or consequential upon a provision that falls within competence.[36] A fairly common example is ensuring compliance with a provision by making it a criminal offence not to comply. Criminal law is not listed as a devolved subject, but the provision would be within competence as the criminal provisions are used to enforce the devolved provision.[37] It is important to note that this principle only applies to competence in line with Part 1 of Schedule 7 to GOWA 2006 (as noted in bullet point 1 above). The general restrictions in s. 108(6) of GOWA 2006 (as noted in the bullet points above except bullet point 1) would still apply to the enforcement provisions.

The list of areas of competence in Schedule 7 may be added to or subtracted from under s. 109(1) of GOWA 2006, where the Monarch amends it by way of an Order in Council. Before an Order in Council can be made it must, by virtue of s. 109(4) of GOWA 2006, be approved by both Houses of the UK Parliament and approved by a resolution of the Welsh Assembly. Alternatively, of course, an Act of Parliament could amend GOWA 2006, the UK Parliament being sovereign.

4-8 Legislative competence of the National Assembly

The memorandum of understanding between the UK Government and the National Assembly states:

> The United Kingdom Government retains authority to legislate on any issue, whether devolved or not. It is ultimately for Parliament to decide what use to make of that power. However, the UK Government will proceed in accordance with the convention that the UK Parliament would not normally legislate with regard to devolved matters except with the agreement of the devolved legislature. The devolved administrations will be responsible for seeking such agreement as may be required for this purpose on an approach from the UK Government.[38]

The UK Parliament remains sovereign but there is a convention that the UK Parliament (as far as primary legislation is concerned) and the UK Government

[35] GOWA 2006, s. 108(6)(a) and Sch. 7, Pt 2, para. 5.

[36] GOWA 2006, s. 108(5).

[37] A good illustrative example of this is discussed in *R (Petsafe Ltd)* v *Welsh Ministers* [2011] Eu LR 270.

[38] See the summary in Ministry of Justice, *Devolution Guidance Note No. 9*.

(as far as secondary legislation is concerned) will not legislate in the areas where the Assembly and the Welsh Government have competence, unless the Assembly has agreed to the proposed legislation. In practice this process may result in some complex negotiations between the Welsh Government, the Welsh Office, and the relevant Whitehall department, with the Welsh Government asserting that it has competence and with the UK Government asserting that the point in question is not within competence.

A particularly pertinent section of GOWA 2006 when it comes to interpreting legislative competence is s. 154:

> **154 Interpretation of legislation**
> (1) This section applies to –
> (a) ...
> (b) any provision of an Act of the Assembly, or a Bill for such an Act, which could be read in such a way as to be outside the Assembly's legislative competence, and
> (c) any provision of subordinate legislation made, or purporting to be made, under an ... Act of the Assembly which could be read in such a way as to be outside the powers under which it was, or purported to be, made.
> (2) The provision is to be read as narrowly as is required for it to be within competence or within the powers, if such a reading is possible, and is to have effect accordingly.
> (3) In subsection (1)(c) 'made' includes confirmed or approved.

A further provision of particular relevance to defining legislative competence is s. 108(7) of GOWA 2006, which states:

> [T]he question whether a provision of an Act of the Assembly relates to one or more of the subjects listed in Part 1 of Schedule 7 (or falls within any of the exceptions specified in that Part of that Schedule) is to be determined by reference to the purpose of the provision, having regard (among other things) to its effect in all the circumstances.

These sections ensure that where there is any debate as to the competence of any Act of the Assembly or subordinate legislation made pursuant to an Act of the Assembly, the provision shall be read 'narrowly' and with reference to the purpose of the provision. This may perhaps be considered a statutory manner of giving the National Assembly and the Welsh Ministers the benefit of the doubt when it comes to interpretation. They are important provisions when disputes arise. They are even more important in terms of constitutional significance. The UK Parliament recognises the National Assembly is a democratic body that speaks for Wales and as such the democratically approved provisions of the Assembly should not be interfered with unless absolutely necessary.

4-9 Defining legislative competence – references to the Supreme Court

The Government of Wales Act 2006 includes a method of judicial challenge to Assembly Acts on the grounds that the terms of the devolution settlement have been breached. The mechanism is contained in s. 112 of GOWA 2006. Under s. 112(1) of GOWA 2006 the Counsel General or the UK Attorney General may challenge a bill passed by the National Assembly on the grounds that it is not within the Assembly's legislative competence. Where such a challenge is raised it is determined by the Supreme Court. These cases give further guidance on how legislative competence is to be determined.

4-10 *Re: Local Government Byelaws (Wales) Bill 2012*[39]

In the first such reference, *Re: Local Government Byelaws (Wales) Bill 2012*,[40] the Supreme Court concluded that the Local Government Byelaws (Wales) Bill, in particular sections 6 and 9, which were intended to remove the need for the confirmation of byelaws by the Welsh Ministers or by the Secretary of State for Wales, was within the legislative competence of the National Assembly. In one of the two judgments of the Court, Lord Hope JSC highlighted that whilst constitutional statutes (to the extent that such a term exists), such as GOWA 2006, are of great importance, they must be interpreted in the same way as any other statute:[41]

> Reference was made in the course of the argument in the present case to the fact that the 2006 Act was a constitutional enactment. It was, of course, an Act of great constitutional significance, and its significance has been enhanced by the coming into operation of Schedule 7. But I do not think that this description, in itself, can be taken to be a guide to its interpretation. The rules which the court must apply in order to give effect to it are those laid down by the statute, and the statute must be interpreted like any other statute.[42]

[39] [2013] 1 AC 792.

[40] [2013] 1 AC 792.

[41] In her address to the Welsh Government Legal Services Conference on 9 October 2013 Dame Mary Arden (Lady Justice Arden) compared the devolution settlement to the federal system of governance practised in other countries of both civil and common law. She argued that as the constitutional arrangement that is the devolution settlement does not have an established jurisprudence the judiciary should draw on the experience of the federal systems. The term she used to describe the devolution settlement in these circumstances was 'in fact federalism'. The comments of Arden LJ in *R (Horvarth)* v *Secretary of State for the Environment, Food and Rural Affairs* [2007] Eu LR 770, particularly paras 51–75, expand upon this point. In relation to the 'quasi-federal' character of the UK, see V. Bogdanor, *Devolution in the United Kingdom* (Oxford University Press, 2001), p. 291; R. Masterman and J. Murkins, 'Skirting supremacy and subordination: the constitutional authority of the United Kingdom Supreme Court' [2013] PL 800–20; M. Laffin and A. Thomas, 'The United Kingdom: Federalism in Denial?' *Publius*, 29/3 (1999), 89–107.

[42] [2013] 1 AC 792 at para. 80.

This should not be misconstrued to think that the constitutional nature of the statute is not relevant to the interpretation of such statutes, but rather that it is a mistake to think that a statute's purpose is only relevant when interpreting constitutional statues.[43] Lord Hope JSC went on[44] to endorse what is sometimes called a 'pith and substance approach'. This is to say that it is the substance of the provisions, not their incidental consequences, that are of importance. As such, by virtue of s. 154(2) of GOWA 2006 (as discussed at §4-8), the Bill was to be read as narrowly as was required to bring it within the Assembly's legislative competence. With regards to the byelaws case, Lord Hope highlighted that the key question for the court when considering the issue of whether a provision was within competence was whether the offending provision, in this case the removal of the Secretary of State's power to confirm certain Welsh byelaws, was incidental to, or consequential on, any other provision contained in the Bill. This was an expressly defined exception to the issue of competence as outlined in GOWA 2006, Sch. 7, Pt 3, para. 6(1)(b). Lord Hope determined:

> The words 'incidental to, or consequential on, any other provision contained in the Act of the Assembly' make it clear that the interpretative exercise to which it points is one of comparison. How significant is the removal of the pre-commencement function, when it is seen in the context of the Act as a whole? If the removal has an end and purpose of its own, that will be one thing. It will be outside competence. If its purpose or effect is merely subsidiary to something else in the Act, and its consequence when it is put into effect can be seen to be minor or unimportant in the context of the Act as a whole, that will be another. It can then be regarded as merely incidental to, or consequential on, the purpose that the Bill seeks to achieve.[45]

The Attorney General had argued that it was outside the legislative competence of the National Assembly as the Bill would remove the power of the Secretary of State for Wales to confirm byelaws. The Supreme Court held that the Bill was intended to remove the need for confirmation by any public body of any byelaw made under the enactments contained in the Schedule to the Bill. As that was the primary purpose of the Bill, the removal of the Secretary of State's confirmatory powers would be incidental to that primary purpose. Thus, the Bill was within the Assembly's competence.

[43] See the discussion of this point in S. J. Dimelow, 'The interpretation of "constitutional" statutes' (2013) 129 LQR 498–503.

[44] [2013] 1 AC 792 at paras 78–84.

[45] [2013] 1 AC 792 at para. 83.

4-11 *Re: Agricultural Sector (Wales) Bill*[46]

The second reference to the Supreme Court gave further, more wide-ranging guidance, on how the court would approach the issue of determining legislative competence and defining the devolved subjects. The Agricultural Sector (Wales) Bill sought to reintroduce in Wales legislation in respect of agricultural wages. Such legislation had previously been contained in the Agricultural Wages Act 1948, which had been repealed by the Enterprise and Regulatory Reform Act 2013, enacted by the UK Parliament. The Bill proposed to establish a regime in Wales setting minimum terms and conditions of employment for agricultural workers. The Attorney General contended that such provisions related to employment matters and were therefore outside the competence of the Assembly as employment was not a subject under a heading in Schedule 7 to GOWA 2006. The Assembly considered it did have competence to enact the Bill as it had competence to make legislation which related to agriculture, horticulture, forestry, fisheries and fishing, animal health and welfare, plant health, plant varieties and seeds, and rural development, all of which are subjects under the first heading in Schedule 7 to GOWA 2006.

This dispute required the court to consider how it would determine the definitions of the subjects in Schedule 7 to GOWA 2006. The question in this case was how the term 'agriculture' was to be defined and whether it could encompass the broad definition contended by the Assembly. Lord Thomas CJ and Lord Reed JSC, in a joint judgment, stated:

> This is not however a case in which the court has to turn to a dictionary in order to find out the meaning of an unfamiliar word. The problem is to decide what Parliament meant by the subject of 'Agriculture' in this specific context: in particular, in the context of the other subjects listed in the schedule. Each is intended to designate a subject matter which is the object of legislative activity. In this context, it is clear to us that agriculture cannot be intended to refer solely to the cultivation of the soil or the rearing of livestock, but should be understood in a broader sense as designating the industry or economic activity of agriculture in all its aspects, including the business and other constituent elements of that industry, as it is to that broader subject matter that legislative activity is directed.[47]

The Court, therefore, determined that, when considering how the devolved subjects were to be defined, a dictionary definition was not to be applied, but rather the relevant consideration was the intention of Parliament in enacting GOWA 2006 in the manner it had. The court also stated that it did not find ministerial statements, correspondence between the UK Government and the Welsh Government,

[46] [2014] 1 WLR 2622.

[47] [2014] 1 WLR 2622 at para. 49.

or the distribution of powers under previous phases of devolution[48] to be of assistance in determining the intentions of Parliament.[49]

The court, having determined that agriculture was to be given a broad definition, went on to consider the relevance of any effect on employment, a non-devolved subject. Lord Thomas and Lord Reed stated:

> [T]he scheme of the conferred powers model adopted for Welsh devolution, as embodied in the 2006 Act, is to limit the legislative powers of the Assembly in relation to subjects listed in Schedule 7 by reference to the express exceptions and limitations contained in the Act, rather than via some dividing up of the subjects in Schedule 7 along lines not prescribed in the legislation. Under section 108(4) and (7), the Assembly has legislative competence if the Bill relates to one of the subjects listed in Part 1 of Schedule 7, provided it is not within one of the exceptions. In most cases, an exception will resolve the issue. Where however there is no exception, as in the present case, the legislative competence is to be determined in the manner set out in section 108. Provided that the Bill fairly and realistically satisfies the test set out in section 108(4) and (7) and is not within an exception, it does not matter whether in principle it might also be capable of being classified as relating to a subject which has not been devolved.

The Supreme Court, therefore, determined that the key indicators as to what may be considered to be within legislative competence were the terms of GOWA 2006 itself. Where the subject area is not sufficiently defined, then the intention of Parliament is to be used to define the subject. Where the Bill does not fall within an exception it is within competence, irrespective of the effect on non-devolved subjects.

It is of note that in both of the references discussed above, the court has given a broad definition to the devolved subjects and a narrow approach in determination of those provisions that may fall outside legislative competence. This follows the statutory requirements in ss. 108 and 154 of GOWA 2006 discussed earlier in the chapter and follows the principle that an elected legislature's decisions should not be subject to interference unless absolutely necessary.

Re: Recovery of Medical Costs for Asbestos Diseases (Wales) Bill[50] 4-12

This reference, made by the Counsel General for Wales, raised for determination the question of whether the Recovery of Medical Costs for Asbestos Diseases (Wales) Bill was within legislative competence. The Bill, and specifically section 2, sought to impose liability on persons by whom or on whose behalf compensation payments are made to or in respect of victims of asbestos-related diseases to pay charges in respect of National Health Service services provided to the victims as a

[48] See 1-38, for a discussion of the phases of devolution in Wales.

[49] [2014] 1 WLR 2622 at paras 35–9.

[50] [2015] AC 1016.

result of the diseases. Section 14 of the Bill further required insurers to cover the charges where an insurance policy would cover a compensation payment. Two questions were referred to the court. First, whether the Bill fell within s. 108(4) and (5) of GOWA 2006 (see 4-7 above), which in turn depended on whether it related to 'Organisation and funding of national health service' in GOWA 2006, Sch. 7, Pt 1, para. 9 or was incidental or consequential to that provision, which would bring it within competence. Secondly, whether it was outside the Assembly's competence by virtue of s. 108(6) on the ground that it is incompatible with the right to property under article 1 of the First Protocol to the European Convention on Human Rights.

As to the first question, Lord Mance JSC (for the majority[51]) held that the key question was whether GOWA 2006 provided legislative competence for the imposition of liabilities on compensators and insurers. On this point, Lord Mance held:

> The expression 'organisation and funding of national health service' could not have been conceived with a view to covering what would amount in reality to rewriting the law of tort and breach of statutory duty by imposing on third persons (the compensators), having no other direct connection in law with the NHS, liability towards the Welsh Ministers to meet costs of NHS services provided to sufferers from asbestos-related diseases towards whom such third persons decide to make a compensation payment for liability which may or may not exist or have been established or admitted.[52]

As such, the Court held that Parliament cannot have intended paragraph 9 to permit the raising of money in any way, even if the only purpose for which the moneys raised would be used was on the Welsh NHS. The nature of any charges permissible under paragraph 9 would have to be more directly connected with the service provided and its funding. Further, s. 108(5) of GOWA 2006 was not directed to or wide enough to cover what amounted to a separate scheme for the provision of financial recourse against third party insurers by the compensators who are primarily affected by the scheme introduced. Thus, s. 14 of the Bill was incapable of being regarded as incidental or consequential to s. 2. As such, the wide interpretation of competence brought about by *Re: Local Government Byelaws (Wales) Bill 2012*[53] and *Re: Agricultural Sector (Wales) Bill*[54] has been somewhat checked by the judgment of Lord Mance and the requirement that there be some direct

[51] A minority judgment was given by Lord Thomas of Cwmgiedd CJ, with whom Baroness Hale of Richmond DPSC agreed. The minority judgment cannot be said to be law, and it agreed that the Bill was outside competence, but it does provide a different interpretation of the provisions discussed in this case and gives a wider interpretation to the competence of the Assembly. Lord Thomas' judgment can be found from para. 71 onwards.

[52] [2015] AC 1016 at 1032 (para. 27 of the judgment).

[53] [2013] 1 AC 792.

[54] [2014] 1 WLR 2622.

connection between effect of the power created and the provision that is asserted to give competence to the power.

As to the question of a breach of the right to property, Lord Mance held that the effect of the Bill was to impose on compensators, in the first instance, and their insurers, in the second instance, burdens which had not previously existed. Thus, the right was engaged as the Bill would deprive both employers and their insurers of their previous legal freedom from exposure to the relevant charges and of their possessions in the form of the assets they would have to use to discharge the new liabilities imposed by the Bill. Nonetheless, whilst the Bill would no doubt have been proportionate if introduced in relation to future exposure to asbestos and future insurance contracts, rewriting historically incurred obligations to impose it in relation to future Welsh NHS costs would be different. Special justification was necessary, but none was shown. Therefore the Bill was not proportionate, breached the ECHR, and thus fell outside legislative competence.

Reference to the Supreme Court – procedure 4-13

As well as the discussion of the judgments of the Supreme Court defining competence, a practical guide to making references to the Supreme Court is within the ambit of this work. This section will, therefore, discuss the procedure for making a reference to the Supreme Court under s. 112(1) of GOWA 2006, which can primarily be found in GOWA 2006, the Supreme Court Rules 2009, Practice Direction 10 – Devolution Jurisdiction ('Practice Direction 10') of the Supreme Court Rules 2009, and in the judgment of Lord Hope JSC in *Re: Local Government Byelaws (Wales) Bill 2012*.[55]

When and how to challenge a Bill 4-14

The power to challenge an Assembly Bill arises out of s. 112(1) of GOWA 2006, which allows the Counsel General or the Attorney General to refer the question whether a Bill, or any provision of a Bill, would be within the Assembly's legislative competence to the Supreme Court. The Counsel General or the Attorney General may make a reference in relation to a Bill at any time during the period of four weeks beginning with the passing of the Bill or any subsequent approval of the Bill in accordance with provision included in the standing orders.[56] If the four weeks expires a reference may not be made and this time period cannot be extended. If the Counsel General or Attorney General has notified the Clerk of the Assembly that no reference is to be made then that party may not then make a reference, even if they change their mind within the four-week period (unless the Bill has subsequently been reconsidered and approved).[57] If, within the four-week period discussed above, either the Counsel General or the Attorney General informs

[55] [2013] 1 AC 792 at paras 88–95.

[56] GOWA 2006, s. 112(2).

[57] GOWA 2006, s.112(3).

the Clerk that they intend to submit a reference then, by virtue of s. 115(2) of GOWA 2006 , the Clerk may not request Royal Assent for the Bill. The Bill cannot, therefore, pass into law until the Supreme Court has determined the reference.

4-15 The reference procedure

The reference procedure is outlined in r. 41 of the Supreme Court Rules 2009:

> **Devolution jurisdiction**
>
> **41.—**
>
> (1) Appeals or references under the Court's devolution jurisdiction shall in general be dealt with in accordance with these Rules but the Court shall give special directions as and when necessary …
>
> (2) A reference made by the relevant officer[58] is made by filing the reference and by serving a copy on any other relevant officer who is not already a party and who has a potential interest in the proceedings.
>
> (3) A reference must state the question or issue to be decided by the Court.
>
> (4) The Registrar [of the Supreme Court] shall give notice of the question or issue to the appropriate relevant officer where that officer is not already a party to any proceedings.

Proceedings on a reference are proceedings *sui generis*, that is to say of its own kind or of a unique character. In this situation, it is a case issued without a respondent (hence the title 'Re: Bill X'). The reference is served on any other relevant officer in his capacity as a relevant officer, not as a respondent. The relevant officer will become a respondent if, and only if, they notify the Registrar that they wish to participate in line with the procedure in Practice Direction 10 (see below). Lord Hope noted in *Re: Local Government Byelaws (Wales) Bill 2012*[59] that in the case of a reference by the Attorney General, the Counsel General had a potential interest in the proceedings, so the reference should be served on the Counsel General. There is no requirement for the reference to be served on the National Assembly; although paragraph 10.2.6 of Practice Direction 10 states that it must be notified. Notification, also, should be given to the Clerk of the Assembly.

Under paragraph 10.2.2 of Practice Direction 10 the reference should state:

1. the question to be determined by the Supreme Court; and
2. whether it applies to the whole Bill or to a provision of it.

Further, the reference shall have annexed to it a copy of the Bill to which it relates.

Any relevant officer (other than the one making the reference) who wishes to participate in the proceedings shall within seven days of service of the reference on

[58] Rule 3(2) of the Supreme Court Rules 2009 defines the expression 'relevant officer' in relation to devolution proceedings relating to Wales as the Attorney General and the Counsel General.

[59] [2013] 1 AC 792 at para. 90.

him notify the Registrar of the Supreme Court and the other parties.[60] Any relevant officer who gives notice automatically becomes a respondent to the proceedings.

It should be noted that the procedure set out in Practice Direction 10 does not require any particular form for use in reference proceedings. There is no requirement to use Form 1, which is designed for use in appeals to the Supreme Court. As such, the relevant officer making the reference may adopt whatever style and layout is thought to be most appropriate in the circumstances. In a covering document, to which the reference and any accompanying documents should be attached, the Registrar of the Supreme Court must be provided with the following information for administrative purposes:

1. the names, addresses and contact details of the party making the reference and his legal representatives;
2. the same details of any relevant officer on whom the reference has been served; and
3. the same details of any person who has been notified.

The relevant officer making the reference shall, within fourteen days of filing the reference, file a case with respect to the question referred,[61] that is to say the grounds which seek to persuade the Supreme Court to determine the question in their favour. The referring relevant officer's case should include a copy of any statement made in relation to the Bill in accordance with the relevant statute and any relevant extracts from the official report of proceedings in the Assembly. Any other relevant officer who is participating in the proceedings shall file a case with respect to the question referred within fourteen days of notifying the Registrar that they wish to participate.[62]

Determining the reference 4-16

The Supreme Court will list a hearing and hear representations from the parties. It will then give a judgment determining whether the Bill is within the legislative competence of the Assembly. If the Bill is within competence then the Clerk may submit the Bill for Royal Assent; if it is not within competence then the Clerk may not and the Bill must be dropped or amended to come within competence.[63] An amended Bill, if approved by the Assembly, may be the subject of a further reference.

[60] Practice Direction 10, para. 10.2.3.

[61] Practice Direction 10, para. 10.2.4.

[62] Practice Direction 10, para. 10.2.5.

[63] GOWA 2006, s. 115(3).

4-17 Challenging Bills passed by the Assembly – intervention by the Secretary of State

Whilst the National Assembly may make any Act within its competence, the Secretary of State for Wales retains a power by which they are able to ensure the UK Government's interests are not adversely affected by such Acts. Under s. 114(2) of GOWA 2006, the Secretary of State may make an order prohibiting the Clerk of the Assembly from submitting a Bill passed by the National Assembly for Royal Assent.

The Secretary of State may only make such an order where he has reasonable grounds to believe that the Bill contains provisions which:[64]

> (a) would have an adverse effect on any matter which is not listed under any of the [devolved] headings in Part 1 of Schedule 7 [to GOWA 2006] (or falls within any of the exceptions specified in that Part of that Schedule);[[65]]
> (b) might have a serious adverse impact on water resources in England, water supply in England or the quality of water in England;
> (c) would have an adverse effect on the operation of the law as it applies in England; or
> (d) would be incompatible with any international obligation or the interests of defence or national security.

The Secretary of State may make such an order at any time during the period of four weeks beginning with the passing of the Bill, any period of four weeks beginning with any subsequent approval of the Bill in accordance with the standing orders, or, if a reference is made in relation to the Bill under s. 112 of GOWA 2006, the period of four weeks beginning with the reference being decided by the Supreme Court.[66] It should also be noted that once the Secretary of State has informed that Clerk that he or she does not intend to intervene, then he or she may not then change his or her mind and make an order, even within the relevant four-week period.[67] Finally, when making the order, the Secretary of State must ensure the order identifies the Bill and the provisions in question and state the reasons for making the order.[68]

There is a check on the Secretary of State's power, as outlined in s. 114(8) of GOWA 2006. A statutory instrument containing an order under s. 114 is subject to annulment in pursuance of a resolution of either House of Parliament.

[64] GOWA 2006, s.114(1).

[65] It should be highlighted that this ground is not that there was no competence, but that the Bill would have an adverse effect on a matter with which it does not deal directly, but which is outside legislative competence.

[66] GOWA 2006, s. 114(4).

[67] GOWA 2006, s. 114(5).

[68] GOWA 2006, s. 114(3).

This is a potentially important, arguably democratically damaging, provision. Under s. 114, the provisions made by the elected Assembly, which are within their competence, may be blocked by a single minister of the UK Government. To date the Secretary of State has not exercised this power.

Judicial review of Acts of the Assembly 4-18

There is a specific statutory application that can be made under Schedule 9 to GOWA 2006 where a participant in civil or criminal proceedings wishes to raise a devolution issue or challenge the competence of an Assembly Act as part of those proceedings. That application is discussed in chapter 6.[69]

The question of whether or not an Act of the Assembly may be subject to judicial review has never specifically come before the courts. For guidance it is appropriate to consider the decision of the Supreme Court in *AXA General Insurance Ltd* v *Lord Advocate*[70] ('The *AXA* case'). In fact in *Re: Local Government Byelaws (Wales) Bill 2012*, Lord Hope JSC suggested that whilst the relevant statutes for Scotland (to which the *AXA* case applied), Wales, and Northern Ireland were subtly different, the principles established in the *AXA* case could apply to all three devolution settlements.[71] The *AXA* case concerned judicial review of an Act of the Scottish Parliament. Despite the fact that it is not a case relating to Wales, it is ground breaking in devolution terms, so much so that both the Counsel General for Wales and First Counsel to the Welsh Government appeared as interveners. With regards to the Scottish Parliament, Lord Hope stated:

> [I]n principle Acts of the Scottish Parliament are amenable to the supervisory jurisdiction of the Court.[72]

However:

> Acts of the Scottish Parliament are not subject to judicial review at common law on the grounds of irrationality, unreasonableness or arbitrariness. This is not needed, as there is already a statutory limit on the Parliament's legislative competence if a provision is incompatible with any of the Convention rights … But it would also be quite wrong for the judges to substitute their views on these issues for the considered judgment of a democratically elected legislature unless authorised to do so, as in the case of the Convention rights, by the constitutional framework laid down by the United Kingdom Parliament.[73]

[69] See 6-22.

[70] [2012] 1 AC 868.

[71] [2013] 1 AC 792 at para. 81.

[72] [2013] 1 AC 792, para. 47.

[73] [2013] 1 AC 792, para. 52.

Lord Reed JSC also commented:

> Parliament did not legislate in a vacuum: it legislated for a liberal democracy founded on particular constitutional principles and traditions. That being so, Parliament cannot be taken to have intended to establish a body which was free to abrogate fundamental rights or to violate the rule of law.[74]

It appears that these principles would apply equally to GOWA 2006. Therefore, in principle an Act of the Assembly can be subject to judicial review, but only on the grounds that the Act abrogated fundamental rights or violated the rule of law. This is an extremely high test which, within itself, and within our constitutional democracy, suggests that it will never be passed.

Two further practical points should be noted relating to any such proceedings. First, by virtue of s. 41(1) of GOWA 2006, any legal proceedings by or against the Assembly are to be instituted by or against the Assembly Commission on behalf of the Assembly. Thus, the defendant in any judicial review challenging an Act of the Assembly would be the Assembly Commission.[75] Further, by virtue of ss. 41(3) and (5) of GOWA 2006, in any proceedings against the Assembly the court must not grant an interim or final mandatory, prohibiting or quashing order or an injunction, but may instead make a declaration. Thus, if a judicial review of an Act of the Assembly were to be successful, the court could only declare that the Act abrogated fundamental rights or violated the rule of law; it would be for the Assembly to take into account the court's guidance and correct the provision. This follows the principle across the UK that legislation made by a democratically elected legislature should not be quashed by unelected judges.[76]

4-19 Judicial review of Assembly Members, the Assembly Commission and Officers of the Assembly

The question as to the extent to which judicial review is available against Assembly Members, the Assembly Commission and Officers of the Assembly is more complex. The question has not come before the court in England and Wales. As such, an analogous case must be considered. *Whaley* v *Lord Watson of Invergowrie*[77] was a case heard by the Scottish Court of Session. In that case the petitioner (claimant) sought an order preventing a member of the Scottish Parliament ('MSP') from promoting and introducing a Bill to outlaw fox hunting with dogs on the grounds

[74] [2013] 1 AC 792, para. 153.

[75] See 1-44.

[76] In *R* v *Parliamentary Commissioner for Standards, ex parte Al-Fayed* [1998] 1 WLR 669, Lord Woolf MR endorsed the phrase of Sedley J (as he then was) who referred to this as 'a mutuality of respect between two constitutional sovereignties'. See the commentary on declarations of incompatibility at 5-33 for a further discussion of this principle.

[77] 2000 SC 340.

that the MSP had received legal, administrative and other assistance from a pressure group, which breached the rules relating to MSP's interests. The Court of Session considered the extent to which proceedings could be brought against an MSP. Lord Rodger stated:

> [W]here a competent interim remedy is sought against a member, the correct approach will be to apply the law in the usual way and to have regard to all the relevant factors in deciding where the balance of convenience lies.[78]

This point was also made by Lord Prosser:

> [T]he Courts are in no way deprived of their primary function, of identifying wrongs or threatened wrongs.[79]

The reduced grounds of judicial review outlined in *AXA*[80] apply in relation to the challenging Acts of the Scottish Parliament, and thus Acts of the Assembly. However, *AXA* was a case that dealt specifically with the jurisdiction of the courts in relation to the legislative powers of a devolved legislature. Further, *AXA* directly referred to the judgment in *Whaley* but did not comment on the power of the courts in relation to the powers of MSPs or corporate bodies and officers associated with the legislature. As such, judicial review would appear to be available according to the general principles of administrative law, outlined in chapter 3, against MSPs, and thus Assembly Members ('AMs'). Following this principle it is submitted that general grounds would also be available against the Assembly Commission and Officers of the Assembly (providing they were conducting a public function).

Whilst general grounds are available to bring a challenge against AMs, the Commission and Officers, GOWA 2006 contains a provision limiting the relief available. Under ss. 41(4) and (5) of GOWA 2006, in legal proceedings against any AM, the Presiding Officer or Deputy Presiding Officer, any member of the staff of the Assembly, or the Assembly Commission, the court must not grant an interim or final mandatory, prohibiting or quashing order or an injunction, if the effect of doing so would be to give any relief against the Assembly which could not have been given in proceedings against the Assembly. The limits of this power were also discussed in *Whaley*, which considered s. 40 of the Scotland Act 1998, the equivalent of s. 41 of GOWA 2006 in Scotland, and an order for interdict, the equivalent of a prohibiting order in Scotland. Lord Rodger stated:

> Subsection (3) provides that the court is not to grant various forms of relief, including interdict, in proceedings against the Parliament. So, for example, the court could not grant an interdict against the Parliament considering a Bill,

78 2000 SC at 350.

79 2000 SC at 357.

80 [2013] 1 AC 792.

> even if it would not be within the legislative competence of the Parliament. That protection for the Parliament could easily be rendered worthless if, for instance, it were possible for interdict to be pronounced, on the same basis, against the Presiding Officer granting the necessary certificate of legislative competence—which would have the effect that the Bill could not be introduced and hence could not be considered by the Parliament. Subsection (4) outlaws such stratagems.[81]

Thus, when considering whether the restriction under s. 41 of GOWA 2006 applies in a particular case, it is the function being challenged that should be considered. If the function is one that impacts upon the legislative process, thus challenging the legislative process 'by the back door' then the restriction in s. 41 will apply. Otherwise, the protection of s. 41 is not available.

It should be noted that by virtue of s. 41(2) of GOWA 2006 any legal proceedings by or against the Presiding Officer, Deputy Presiding Officer or a member of the staff of the Assembly are to be instituted by or against the Assembly Commission on behalf of the Assembly. Thus, in any judicial review the defendant would be the Assembly Commission.

The interesting final question on this subject is whether a decision of the Attorney General or Counsel General to refer a Bill to the Supreme Court under s. 112 of GOWA 2006, or a decision of the Secretary of State for Wales to block a Bill under s. 114 of the GOWA 2006, or a failure to refer or block a Bill, may be subject to judicial review. There is no judicial authority on this point. All three are executive officers and thus represent a public office susceptible to judicial review. As the decision or failure is not a matter of passing primary legislation under a constitutional settlement, it is submitted that the decision would be one that would be made subject to general administrative law principles, as opposed to the higher test outlined above in *AXA*.[82]

4-20 THE WELSH GOVERNMENT AND THE WELSH MINISTERS

As discussed in chapter 1, GOWA 2006 established the Welsh Assembly Government. The Welsh Assembly Government is now formally known as the

[81] 2000 SC 340 at 350.

[82] An argument that could, perhaps, reduce the availability of judicial review in relation to the Secretary of State's decision to block under s. 114 of GOWA 2006, lies in the power of Parliament to set any statutory instrument aside under s. 114(8). It may be arguable that the Parliamentary check should oust the judicial. It is submitted that such a check should not be fatal to judicial review. It cannot be an adequate alternative remedy as it is not an option available to any person. Further, as Parliament is sovereign, it could technically set aside any statutory instrument, and thus this remedy is actually available for all statutory instruments.

Welsh Government.[83] The Welsh Government is the executive branch of the devolved political system in Wales. The Welsh Government comprises the First Minister, other Welsh Ministers, Deputy Welsh Ministers, and the Counsel General to the Welsh Government. The First Minister, with the approval of the Monarch, appoints the Welsh Ministers and Deputy Ministers from the National Assembly Members. GOWA 2006 limits the number of Ministers and Deputy Ministers to twelve, excluding the First Minister and Counsel General, who, while a member of the Government is not a Welsh Minister.[84] Just as the UK Government is accountable to the UK Parliament, the Welsh Government is accountable to the National Assembly.

Powers of the Welsh Government 4-21

The executive powers of the Welsh Government can largely be divided into three parts:

- the development and implementation of policy;
- the exercise of a range of devolved functions; and
- the making of subordinate legislation.

Primary legislation, be it passed by the National Assembly or the UK Parliament, will often introduce general powers and objectives, the fine detail and proper implementation of which will require the use of subordinate legislation (the power to make such legislation being conferred by the relevant primary legislation). In Wales, under the devolved headings discussed earlier in the chapter,[85] the relevant primary legislation will usually confer on the Welsh Ministers the power to make the subordinate legislation, although sometimes the subordinate power is delegated straight to another body, such as a local authority or a quango. Subordinate legislation that is within the power of a minister in the UK Government may, under s. 58(1) of GOWA 2006,[86] be transferred to the Welsh Ministers to exercise in Wales by virtue of an Order in Council by the Monarch.[87] On 25 May 2007,[88] those functions previously transferred to the National Assembly for Wales by Order

[83] Wales Act 2014, s. 4(1).

[84] GOWA 2006, s. 51(1).

[85] See 4-7.

[86] Which is supplemented by Sch. 3 to GOWA 2006.

[87] The Order in Council is contained in a statutory instrument that has been approved by the UK Parliament and the Welsh Ministers before final Royal Assent: GOWA 2006, s. 58(4). See, for example, Welsh Ministers (Transfer of Functions) Order 2008.

[88] This being the date the provisions came into force under s. 161(5) of GOWA 2006, in turn being the date that the first First Minister of the Welsh Assembly Government was appointed after the 2007 election.

in Council under s. 22 of the GOWA 1998[89] (the most wide-ranging of which being the National Assembly for Wales (Transfer of Functions) Order 1999) and any functions specifically conferred on the National Assembly by enactments made subsequent to the passing of GOWA 1998, were transferred to the Welsh Ministers pursuant to GOWA 2006, s. 162(1) and Sch. 11, para. 30. This is a key point to look out for as a number of pre-2007 UK Parliament Acts and Statutory Instruments refer to the power of the National Assembly when in fact the power now lies with the Welsh Ministers.

4-22 Challenging decisions of the Welsh Government

A large number of functions (including the development of guidance and policy) is vested in the Welsh Government. As a public body all of these decisions may be subject to judicial review (or similar procedures) in the Administrative Court. The types of decision of the Welsh Government that come before the Administrative Court in Wales can, broadly, be split into three categories:

- functions directly delegated to the Welsh Ministers by primary legislation;
- confirming the decisions of local authorities or other delegated bodies; and
- subordinate legislation.

4-23 Functions directly delegated to the Welsh Ministers by primary legislation

There are a range of functions delegated directly to the Welsh Ministers by primary legislation: for example, determining the size of the landfill allowances allocated to waste disposal authorities in Wales, as discussed in *R (Newport City Council)* v *Welsh Ministers.*[90] Sometimes these functions are then further delegated by the Welsh Ministers: for example, decisions on planning matters are often further delegated to a planning inspector.

4-24 Confirming the decisions of local authorities or other delegated bodies

In fact this category could form part of the first category, as considering and confirming the decisions of other bodies will be a function delegated by legislation. In some circumstances the Welsh Ministers will exercise this power of their own volition or as part of a duty to do so. In other circumstances this consideration will be more in the form of an appeal.

An example of this power can be found where the Welsh Ministers are obliged, in some circumstances, to confirm the decisions of local authorities on the provision of primary education, such as a local authority's proposals to change the way in which primary education was delivered in the area. This duty was discussed in *R (Roberts)* v *Welsh Ministers.*[91] In that case it was proposed that two English-medium

[89] See 1-39 for a discussion of the functions of the National Assembly under GOWA 1998.

[90] [2010] Env LR 27.

[91] [2011] EWHC 3416 (Admin).

primary schools should be closed and replaced by a single English-medium school and a Welsh-medium primary school. Wyn Williams J determined that the decision was a lawful one, the Welsh Ministers having (for the most part) properly considered, interpreted and implemented their own guidance on when closure of a school was appropriate. Where the Ministers had erred, a fresh decision would have come to the same conclusion and so the decision was upheld.

A more common example can be found in the numerous planning law appeals considered by the Welsh Ministers, which then go on to be considered in the Administrative Court on judicial review or some other procedure, such as an application to quash the decision under s. 288 of the Town and Country Planning Act 1990.

Subordinate legislation 4-25

Subordinate legislation made by the Welsh Ministers may also be the subject of judicial review. A number of challenges to subordinate legislation made by the Welsh Ministers have been considered by the Administrative Court in Wales. One example of such a challenge is *R (Petsafe Ltd)* v *Welsh Ministers*,[92] where the claimants, a manufacturer and distributor of pet products and an association representing electronic collar manufacturers, unsuccessfully challenged the Animal Welfare (Electronic Collars) (Wales) Regulations 2010 which prohibited, in Wales, the use on cats and dogs of any electronic collar designed to administer an electric shock. Beatson J (as he then was) rejected the claimants' arguments that the regulations were incompatible with European Union law and article 1 of Protocol 1 to the European Convention on Human Rights 1950 (the right to property), as well as arguments as to the *Wednesbury* unreasonableness of the regulations.

Practice point – the Welsh Ministers as defendant 4-26

A final point of practice arises out of ss. 57(1) and (4) of GOWA 2006, which state that all functions conferred on the Welsh Government are conferred or imposed on the Welsh Ministers by that name. Further, any act or omission of any of the Welsh Ministers is to be treated as an act or omission of, or in relation to, each of them. As a result, any decision of the Welsh Government, an individual Welsh Minister or Deputy Minister or a delegated person such as a planning inspector must be brought against 'the Welsh Ministers', the Ministers possessing the decision-making authority.

[92] [2011] Eu LR 270.

LOCAL GOVERNMENT

4-27 The basis of local government in Wales

Local government in Wales can be defined as the administration of powers and duties conferred on a corporate body of locally elected councillors.[93] In Wales there are twenty-two unitary authorities (otherwise known as local authorities).[94] They come in the form of City Councils, County Councils and County Borough Councils.[95] The local authorities are creatures of statute, their powers being wholly conferred by either the UK Parliament, the National Assembly, the relevant Secretary of State, or the Welsh Ministers. As well as delegating powers, the UK or Welsh Government can (to consider the range of powers with a broad brush) make regulations prescribing the procedures to be adopted in making decisions, they can act in default where performance is unsatisfactory[96] or 'call in' certain decisions so the UK or Welsh Government may take the decision rather than the local authority. The UK or Welsh Government can also confirm byelaws, issue guidance, consider appeals against local authority decisions, and will often act as adjudicator in disputes between local authorities or between local authorities and individuals.

It should be noted that the decisions of the UK or Welsh Government may be the subject of judicial review by local authorities, thus representing a check on central power. An example of such a challenge can be found in *R (Vale of Glamorgan Council)* v *The Lord Chancellor*,[97] where the local authority challenged the decision of the Lord Chancellor to close Barry Magistrates' Court. In that case the Vale of Glamorgan Council submitted that whilst the Lord Chancellor had consulted on the closure he had failed to consult on alternative ways of achieving efficiency savings. It was also submitted that he had given too much weight to the desirability of ensuring maximum utilisation of the Magistrates' Court at Cardiff. Finally, the Council alleged that the Lord Chancellor had failed to consider economic consequences to the public purse including the fact that Barry had been designated as a strategic regeneration area. The Divisional Court held that there was no obligation in law for the Lord Chancellor to consult on all the possible alternative ways in which a specific objective might arguably be capable of being achieved. The court further held that the Lord Chancellor was entitled to give weight to the desirabil-

[93] Local Government Act 1972, s. 21.

[94] It seems likely that, within the next few years, this number will be reduced to twelve, eleven or ten as a result of the recommendations of the Williams Commission: *Public Service Governance and Delivery* (2014).

[95] Section 20 of and Sch. 4 to the Local Government Act 1972, as amended by the Local Government (Wales) Act 1994.

[96] As happened with the Isle of Anglesey County Council when, between March 2011 and May 2013, the Welsh Government assumed all executive functions. See 'Anglesey council to be taken over, says Carl Sargeant', 16 March 2011, BBC Online; and 'Anglesey council: Ministers hand control back to councillors', 23 May 2013, BBC Online.

[97] [2011] EWHC 1532 (Admin).

ity of maximising the use of the Cardiff Court and that the Lord Chancellor had properly assessed that there would be no real adverse economic impact following the closure of the court in Barry. This example is a good one as it highlights the often competing demands of central and local government. The local authority was clearly concerned for local access to justice and the local economy, whereas central government was considering the efficient administration of the UK justice system and what economic savings could be made.

Local authority powers 4-28

The source of local authorities' powers arises from numerous statutes, but the majority of the said powers emerge from the Local Government Act 1972, Local Government Act 1974, the Local Government Finance Act 1988 and the Local Government Act 2000. There is no definitive list as to the areas of responsibility enjoyed by the local authorities, but they certainly include: education, social services, welfare, homelessness and housing, town and country planning, public health, sanitation, roads, public transport, licensing, and care of children. Some areas are solely the responsibility of the local authority and some are apportioned between local and national government. The powers broadly separate into two sets: executive functions and the power to make byelaws.

Executive functions 4-29

The local authorities in Wales are primarily executive bodies rather than legislative ones as they simply implement and enforce the provisions and objectives of primary legislation. The House of Lords defined a local authority's functions widely to include:

> [A]ll the duties and powers of a local authority; the sum total of the activities Parliament has entrusted to it. Those activities are its functions. Accordingly a local authority can do anything which is calculated to facilitate or is conducive or incidental to the local authority's function.[98]

The functions range from specific functions, such as the provision of services, to preparing strategic plans for the local authority's area, which they are obliged to do by the UK or Welsh Government or by primary legislation in a number of areas, such as housing strategies and planning strategies.

In practice the local authority's functions are the responsibility of the local authority's executive committee.[99] This is due to s. 13 of the Local Government Act 2000, which states that the executive committee automatically has responsibility

[98] *Hazell* v *Hammersmith and Fulham London Borough Council* [1992] 2 AC 1 at 29.

[99] Local Government Act 2000, s. 11(3) and (8) define the executive committee as a councillor of the authority elected as leader of the executive by the local authority and no less than two but no more than ten councillors appointed to the executive by the leader or the authority.

for all executive functions, unless the enacting legislation reserves the function to the full local authority or another body. Alternatively, the Welsh Ministers may make regulations that reserve the matter to themselves, the full local authority or another body. Further, the powers of the full local authority or its executive committee may be further delegated to a committee, a sub-committee, an officer of the authority, or another local authority[100] (although for the purposes of a legal challenge to the decision the local authority itself remains the principal decision maker). For example, local authorities often delegate consideration of applications for planning permission to sub-committees or officers.

The provisions under which local authorities may enter into executive arrangements by forming an executive committee, thus allowing them to properly perform their executive functions, are outlined in Part II of the Local Government Act 2000. Before such executive arrangements may be made they must be drawn up in accordance with s. 25 of the Local Government Act 2000,[101] which requires consultation with the local government electors and other interested parties,[102] and then submission to the Welsh Ministers,[103] who may make directions on the proposal before it is enacted.[104] When operating any executive arrangements or functions the local authority must have regard to any guidance given on the subject by the Welsh Ministers.[105]

4-30 Byelaws

The local authorities do possess some secondary legislative powers. Under s. 235(1) of the Local Government Act 1972 the local authority may make byelaws, that is to say specific secondary legislation that only applies to the local authority area, 'for the good rule and government of the whole or any … principal area … and for the prevention and suppression of nuisances therein'. Section 235(1) is the general byelaw-making power but a number of other statutes also contain a specific power to make byelaws. For a byelaw to be confirmed as well as it being voted for by the councillors of the local authority it must be confirmed by the relevant Secretary of State.[106] Where the functions of the Secretary of State have been transferred to the National Assembly for Wales or the Welsh Ministers then the Welsh Ministers

[100] Local Government Act 1972, s. 101(1).

[101] Sections 26 and 27 of the Local Government Act 2000 outline the procedure for those occasions where the proposals would require a referendum. Further, s. 48(6) stipulates that the act of confirming the executive arrangements may not be undertaken by the executive committee; it must be the full local authority.

[102] Local Government Act 2000, s. 25(2).

[103] Local Government Act 2000, s. 25(1)(b).

[104] Local Government Act 2000, s. 25(6)(a).

[105] Local Government Act 2000, s. 38(1).

[106] Local Government Act 1972, s. 235(2).

will consider and, if appropriate, confirm the byelaw.[107] All byelaws must be made available for inspection and be published in a local newspaper one month before confirmation.[108]

As a result of s. 6 of the Local Government Byelaws (Wales) Act 2012, if the enactment containing the power to make the relevant byelaw is listed in Part 1 of Schedule 1 to the 2012 Act, no confirmation by the Welsh Ministers will be required. The local authority will still have to comply with the publication requirements set out in ss. 6 and 8 of the 2012 Act before the byelaw can be confirmed by the local authority.

Challenging decisions of a local authority 4-31

As every decision, executive or legislative, made by a local authority in Wales is a decision of a public body, every decision is subject to the principles of administrative law. Therefore, those decisions may be subject to the scrutiny of the Administrative Court.[109] Judicial review will be available to challenge the impugned decision, but any potential litigant should be aware of the great number of statutory appeals that are available from local authority decisions. A litigant should, therefore, be aware of the principle of judicial review that requires all reasonable remedies (including applications and appeals) to be exhausted before judicial review becomes available. The statute or statutory instrument which grants the local authority the specific power will often also include provision for how that decision may be challenged. An often exercised example can be found in the field of planning law, which allows a, potentially, five-tier system of consideration.[110] The system includes judicial checks, which completely bypass judicial review:

- Stage 1 – Local authority decision on planning permission under s. 58(1)(b) of the Town and Country Planning Act 1990;
- Stage 2 – The local authority's decision may be appealed to the Welsh Ministers under s. 78 of the Town and Country Planning Act 1990. In practice the Welsh Ministers will often appoint a planning inspector to consider the appeal;
- Stage 3 – The Welsh Minister's decision may be quashed by the Administrative Court on an application under s. 288 of the Town and Country Planning Act 1990;[111]

[107] Local Government Byelaws (Wales) Act 2012, s. 7(11). Although, note the exception in s. 7(11)(a) which allows the applicable primary legislation to specify an alternate confirming authority.

[108] Local Government Act 1972, ss. 236(4) and (5).

[109] For a discussion of use of judicial review against local authorities in England and Wales before decentralisation of the Administrative Court see M. Sunkin, 'Mapping the use of judicial review to challenge local authorities in England and Wales' [2007] PL 545–67.

[110] Ignoring the potential for a sixth tier, were one of the European Courts to become involved.

[111] See 6-3 for a discussion of the procedure.

- Stage 4 – The decision of the Administrative Court may be appealed to the Court of Appeal (Civil Division) under s. 16(1) of the Senior Courts Act 1981; and
- Stage 5 – The decision of the Court of Appeal (Civil Division) may be appealed to the Supreme Court under s. 40(2) of the Constitutional Reform Act 2005.

The test to be applied by the relevant adjudicator becomes progressively stricter in this system, and at judicial stages the permission of the court is needed, but nonetheless, there is a potentially five-tier domestic system. A litigant must, therefore, ensure they have properly analysed the statutory landscape for an appeal system before embarking upon judicial review. The Administrative Court in Wales has considered a number of these statutory appeals and applications, some of which follow the five-tier structure outlined above, but others do not. An application to quash a planning decision under s. 288 of the Town and Country Planning Act 1990 is by far the most common example. Further examples are as follows:

- applications to quash a designated map modification order (to designate a footpath) under the Wildlife and Countryside Act 1981, Sch. 15, para. 12;[112]
- applications to quash a compulsory purchase order (whereby a landowner is forced to sell their land) under s. 23(1) of the Acquisition of Land Act 1981;[113]
- appeals on a question of law arising out of a decision under the Council Tax (Alteration of Lists and Appeals) Regulations 1993 by a Valuation Tribunal (which considers liability for council tax), the said appeal being to the High Court (in the case of the tribunal in Wales only) under reg. 32(1) of those regulations;[114]

[112] For example, see *Devine* v *Welsh Ministers* [2011] EWHC 358 (Admin) (Administrative Court), [2011] EWCA Civ 1328 (Court of Appeal (Civil Division)), which considered whether a planning inspector's fact finding and reasons for making a designated map modification order were reasonable.

[113] For example, see *Boland* v *Welsh Ministers* [2011] EWHC 629 (Admin). Beatson J (as he then was) considered whether the choice of land, as opposed to other plots, to be acquired for the purposes of building a school was reasonable and the lawfulness of the form of the notices indicating the intention to apply for a compulsory purchase order. The judge held that the notices were lawful and the planning inspector's decision that the land was suitable was proper and thus the choice was reasonable.

[114] For example, see *Daniels* v *Monmouth School* [2009] EWHC 2720 (Admin) where HHJ Bidder QC (sitting as a High Court Judge) determined that a tribunal acted unlawfully where it found that a school did not comprise a single hereditament but, for the purposes of valuation, combined all the individual composite hereditaments rather than applying the regulations to them individually.

- applications to quash a traffic regulation order (whereby a local authority may restrict vehicular access to a highway) under the Road Traffic Regulation Act 1984, Sch. 9, paras 34–37.[115]

The lesson to be learnt, when considering challenging the decision of a local authority on administrative law grounds, is that redress will generally be available, but a thorough examination of the statutory provisions for an alternative remedy should be conducted before opting for judicial review.

OTHER WELSH PUBLIC BODY DEFENDANTS 4-32

As noted at the beginning of this chapter, the number of potential public body defendants in Wales cannot be calculated and this work will not attempt a complete list. This said, the following bodies are bodies that have made decisions that have, in the past, been subject to the scrutiny of the Administrative Court.

Ombudsmen 4-33

There is an important procedure for challenging administrative decisions in Wales outside the Administrative Court. The Public Services Ombudsman (Wales) Act 2005 created an integrated ombudsman service for Wales which merged the three separate offices of Welsh Administration Ombudsman, Health Service Commissioner for Wales, and the Welsh Local Government Ombudsman. The Public Services Ombudsman for Wales ('PSOW') is an important resource for Wales. A complaint to the PSOW against maladministration by a public body in Wales has several advantages for a potential Administrative Court litigant. A complaint to the ombudsman is cheaper than court proceedings (complaint to the PSOW is free) and the decisions of the PSOW are subject to administrative law principles and thus to judicial review, meaning that judicial review may still be an option after the ombudsman's decision. It should be noted that the PSOW's remit extends to the select public bodies as outlined in Schedule 3 to the 2005 Act, which may be amended by the Welsh Ministers under s. 28(2) of the 2005 Act.

The PSOW may investigate the following:

[115] For example, see *Trail Riders Fellowship* v *Powys County Council* [2013] EWHC 3144 (Admin), where Cranston J determined that the local authority had proper regard to the relevant legal tests for making a traffic regulation order, but the decision was vitiated by the wording of an officer's report which meant it could not be ruled out that members of the committee were influenced in their decision to make the orders on the improper consideration that doing so would benefit the local authority's position in other court proceedings.

- general complaints about maladministration by the Schedule 3 public bodies in Wales;[116]
- service failure and failure to provide a service by the Schedule 3 public bodies in Wales;[117]
- complaints about clinical care and treatment in the NHS, as well as the exercise of professional judgment in connection with health and social care generally;[118] and
- complaints that local government members have failed to comply with their code of conduct.[119]

Maladministration is a flexible concept that has not been defined in legislation but has been given a wide definition by the courts. In *R* v *Local Commissioner for Administration for the North and East Area of England, ex parte Bradford City Council*,[120] Lord Denning applied such a wide definition:

> It will cover 'bias, neglect, inattention, delay, incompetence, ineptitude, perversity, turpitude, arbitrariness and so on.' It 'would be a long and interesting list,' clearly open-ended, covering the *manner* in which a decision is reached or discretion is exercised; but excluding the *merits* of the decision itself or of the discretion itself. [Italic emphasis in the original judgment][121]

Where the complaint is against a public authority which is not listed in Schedule 3 to GOWA 2006, and thus falls outside the remit of the PSOW, there are other UK ombudsmen who may have jurisdiction to consider the complaint. Examples of other ombudsmen are as follows:

- Parliamentary and Health Service Ombudsman;
- Local Government Ombudsman;
- Financial Ombudsman Service;
- European Ombudsman;
- Legal Ombudsman;
- Property Ombudsman;

[116] Public Services Ombudsman (Wales) Act 2005, s. 7(1)(a).

[117] Public Services Ombudsman (Wales) Act 2005, s. 7(1)(b) and (c).

[118] Public Services Ombudsman (Wales) Act 2005, s. 11(2).

[119] This type of investigation is actually conducted pursuant to ss. 68–74 of the Local Government Act 2000 but the investigation procedure is still conducted by the ombudsman and is fairly similar to that under the 2005 Act. Under this type of investigation procedure the ombudsman may refer the local government member to the Adjudication Panel for Wales (Chapter IV of the Local Government Act 2000), who may take disciplinary measures.

[120] [1979] QB 287.

[121] [1979] QB 287 at 311.

- Housing Ombudsman;
- Prisons and Probation Ombudsman;
- Energy Services Ombudsman; and
- Telecommunications Ombudsman.

In *R (British Bankers Association)* v *Financial Services Authority*,[122] Ouseley J set out a complainant's options following the determination of the Financial Services Ombudsman, which broadly applies to all the ombudsmen:

> If the Complainant notifies the Ombudsman that he accepts the reasoned written determination, it is binding on both parties and is final. Otherwise he is treated as having rejected it, and can pursue a claim by other means or by judicial review of the Ombudsman's decision.[123]

The extent to which the ombudsman's decisions are subject to judicial review was considered in *R.* v *Commissioner for Administration, ex parte Turpin*,[124] where Collins J confirmed that the Ombudsman's decisions are reviewable on administrative law grounds:

> It seems to me that if it is clear that the Ombudsman in reaching a decision has misdirected himself as a matter of law, or has failed to have regard to a relevant consideration, or has had regard to an irrelevant consideration, or has given reasons which are so defective that they indicate that his decision is bad in law, then the court can and should intervene. The court will be careful to ensure that it does so only if such errors are clear but, as it seems to me, there is nothing in the legislation to exclude the court's usual power to consider whether a discretion, however widely conferred, has been exercised in accordance with law. In addition, if the Ombudsman has conducted his investigation, or as in this case his investigation as to whether there should be an investigation, in a manner which is unfair, again the court is entitled to intervene if satisfied that there has been a risk of prejudice.[125]

The work of an ombudsman has, therefore, been accepted by the Administrative Court as exercising a public function, and thus the decision of an ombudsman may be subject to judicial review. There is rarely a right of appeal from a decision of the ombudsman and, as such, judicial review is generally the only means of redress. A litigant should, however, be wary of the few exceptions. In Wales an example of such an exception is the power of the Public Services Ombudsman for Wales, under ss. 68–74 of the Local Government Act 2000, to investigate complaints that

[122] [2011] Bus LR 1531.

[123] [2011] Bus LR at 1537 (para. 24 of the judgment).

[124] [2001] ACD 90.

[125] [2001] ACD 90 at para. 36.

local councillors have failed to comply with their code of conduct, and refer the councillor to the Adjudication Panel for Wales for a determination.

4-34 Natural Resources Wales

As of 1 April 2013 the Welsh Ministers ordered[126] that Natural Resources Wales assume the substantive functions of the Environment Agency, Forestry Commission Wales and Countryside Council for Wales, in Wales. Natural Resources Wales is a corporate body with over 2,000 staff and an operating budget of £177 million. It also manages 7 per cent of the land in Wales.[127] The purpose of the body is to ensure that the environment and natural resources of Wales are sustainably maintained, sustainably enhanced and sustainably used.[128] The body is also the principal adviser to the Welsh Government on environmental matters.[129]

The Natural Resources Body for Wales (Establishment) Order 2012 (as amended) outlines the duties of the body to further its purpose. This broadly covers the following duties:

- to further nature conservation and enhance natural beauty and amenity;[130]
- to have regard to actual or possible ecological changes;[131]
- to promote the provision and improvement of access to, and enjoyment of, the countryside and open spaces, open-air recreation and the study, understanding and enjoyment of the natural environment;[132]
- to have regard to the desirability of protecting and conserving buildings, structures, sites and objects of archaeological, architectural, engineering or historic interest. Also, the desirability of maintaining the availability to the public of any facility for visiting or inspecting any such building, structure, site or object; and[133]
- to have regard to the health and social well-being of individuals and communities and the economic well-being of individuals, businesses and communities.[134]

[126] By virtue of art. 3(1) of the Natural Resources Body for Wales (Establishment) Order 2012 and the provisions of the Natural Resources Body for Wales (Functions) Order 2013.

[127] Figures provided by the Natural Resources Wales website.

[128] Natural Resources Body for Wales (Establishment) Order 2012, art.4(1).

[129] Natural Resources Body for Wales (Establishment) Order 2012, art. 10.

[130] Natural Resources Body for Wales (Establishment) Order 2012, art. 5A(1).

[131] Natural Resources Body for Wales (Establishment) Order 2012, art. 5B(1).

[132] Natural Resources Body for Wales (Establishment) Order 2012, art. 5C(1).

[133] Natural Resources Body for Wales (Establishment) Order 2012, art. 5D(1).

[134] Natural Resources Body for Wales (Establishment) Order 2012, art. 5E(1).

In furthering these duties a number of powers are conferred on Natural Resources Wales from a number of statutes and statutory instruments. As is the case with local authorities, these powers tend to be either an executive function or the power to make a byelaw. An example is the power under s. 46(1) of the Forestry Act 1967 to make byelaws, relating to any land which is under the control of the body for the preservation of any trees or timber on the land, for prohibiting or regulating any act or thing tending to injury or disfigurement of the land or its amenities, and for regulating the reasonable use of the land by the public for the purposes of exercise and recreation.

As Natural Resources Wales is a public body the manner in which it exercises its functions are subject to judicial review on administrative law grounds. As with local authority powers, any potential litigator should be aware of any potential appeal or review that may offer a reasonable alternative or make any judicial review academic. Such an appeal or review will usually be found in the statute or statutory instrument that grants the power. To continue the example of byelaws under s. 46 of the Forestry Act 1967, under subsection (4C), a draft of any statutory instrument containing such byelaws must be laid before the National Assembly.

National Park Authorities in Wales 4-35

Since the enactment of the National Parks and Access to the Countryside Act 1949 there have been national parks in Wales (as well as England and Scotland). Under the current provisions of the 1949 Act, land is deemed a national park by the order of Natural Resources Wales,[135] after consultation with the local authorities[136] within whose area the national park would fall and after the proposed order is confirmed by the Welsh Ministers.

The body responsible for management of these parks has varied since the parks were created. On 23 November 1995, by virtue of art. 3 of the National Park Authorities (Wales) Order 1995, the current system of management was implemented. The 1995 Order created the national park authorities in Wales. The current national park authorities for Wales, as established by art. 4 of and Schedule 1 to the 1995 Order are:

- Brecon Beacons National Park Authority;
- Pembrokeshire Coast National Park Authority; and
- Snowdonia National Park Authority.[137]

[135] Section 5(3) of the National Parks and Access to the Countryside Act 1949. Whilst s. 5(3) itself refers to Natural England and the relevant Secretary of State, not Natural Resources Wales and the Welsh Ministers, it is taken to refer to Natural Resources Wales and the Welsh Ministers by virtue of s. 4A(1) and 4A(2) of the 1949 Act. This provision applies across the entire Act.

[136] Ibid, s. 7(1).

[137] See the national parks websites for maps of the areas for each national park and its corresponding authority.

It is the purpose of the national park authorities to conserve and enhance the natural beauty, wildlife and cultural heritage of the national parks and promote opportunities for the understanding and enjoyment of the parks by the public.[138] The authorities must also seek to foster the economic and social well-being of local communities within the national park.[139] Any public body, including the relevant national park authority itself, exercising a public function within a national park must have regard to these purposes.[140] As is the case with local authorities, the powers of the national park authorities tend to be either an executive function or the power to make a byelaw. Some examples of the powers include the following:

- a general power to do anything which is calculated to facilitate, or is conducive or incidental to the accomplishment of the purposes of the authority or the carrying out of any functions conferred on it by virtue of any other enactment;[141]
- the power to prepare and publish a national park management plan, which formulates policy for the management of the park and for the carrying out of functions in relation to that park;[142]
- all functions under the Planning Acts[143] (including considering applications for planning permission) as the sole local planning authority for the area of the national park.[144]

As the national park authorities are public bodies, the manner in which they exercise their functions is subject to judicial review on administrative law grounds. As with local authority powers, any potential litigator should be aware of any potential appeal or review that may offer a reasonable alternative or make any judicial review academic. Such an appeal or review will usually be found in the statute or statutory instrument that grants the power.

An example of a judicial review against a national park authority can be found in *R. (Usk Valley Conservation Group)* v *Brecon Beacons National Park Authority*.[145] The Defendant National Park Authority had granted planning permission to relocate a camping facility. The Authority considered that the site owner had breached the terms of the permission by exceeding the number of caravans permitted on the site

[138] National Parks and Access to the Countryside Act 1949, s. 5(1).

[139] National Parks and Access to the Countryside Act 1949, s. 11A(1).

[140] National Parks and Access to the Countryside Act 1949, s. 11A(2).

[141] Environment Act 1995, s. 65(5).

[142] Environment Act 1995, s. 66(1).

[143] The 'Planning Acts' is defined in s. 336 of the Town and Country Planning Act 1990 as: Town and Country Planning Act 1990, the Planning (Listed Buildings and Conservation Areas) Act 1990, the Planning (Hazardous Substances) Act 1990 and the Planning (Consequential Provisions) Act 1990.

[144] Town and Country Planning Act 1990, s. 4A(2).

[145] [2010] 2 P&CR 14.

and their duration of use and storage. The Authority decided to bring enforcement action against the owner, rather than discontinuance action (the latter would allow compensation for the site owner). Ouseley J determined that the planning permission did not include caravans and as such was not lawful. The consequence was that the permission for caravans, as the parties had agreed it should be interpreted, could not lawfully be granted on the application. Further, the Authority had not properly considered the environmental impact of the development. Furthermore, a local planning authority (as the National Park Authority was in this case) was entitled to take into account in reaching a planning decision that one course of action but not another would lead to the payment of compensation, and to choose the one which avoided that payment. However, in this case, there was no evidential basis for the valuation of compensation the authority considered would be payable. Thus, the Authority's decision was flawed because of its reliance on an irrelevant consideration, namely the unsustainable valuation.

CONCLUSION

At present, Wales has acquired greater legislative and executive autonomy than at any time since that of the Welsh Princes. Wales is now subject to two primary legislative assemblies – the UK Parliament and the National Assembly – two national executive governments in the UK Government and the Welsh Government, as well as a host of local and other public bodies. Convention dictates that where the National Assembly does have competence to make primary legislation, the UK Parliament will not make law for Wales in that area. 4-36

As it stands Wales has a 'quasi-autonomous' legislature. It can make primary legislation where the subject is set out under a heading in Schedule 7 to GOWA 2006, but it is 'quasi-autonomous' because the legislative competence of the National Assembly is conferred by the grant of the UK Parliament. Parliament could, in theory, revoke GOWA 2006 and thus dissolve the National Assembly. This may be unlikely in practice, but it is constitutionally possible.

Wales has its own executive, separate from the National Assembly, Parliament, and the UK Government. Until 1 July 1999, when the National Assembly came into being with executive powers,[146] and save for the powers of the Secretary of State for Wales, an office which only came into existence in 1964, Wales had not controlled its own executive since the dissolution of the Council of Wales in 1649, arguably even since the Statute of Rhuddlan in 1282. The existence of separate legislative and executive bodies in Wales represents a number of constitutionally important steps. In democratic terms, it might be considered a step in the right direction. A separation of legislative and executive powers exists in a clearer form than was ever anticipated by GOWA 1998. It also represents a step towards a legally autonomous Wales. Whilst not completely autonomous Wales now has a National

[146] See 1-39.

Assembly that can legislate on the majority of domestic matters and an executive in the Welsh Government that possesses the secondary powers and administrative machinery to make and enforce the law. Again, this level of autonomy was not anticipated in GOWA 1998.

Finally, as this chapter has explored, the public bodies of Wales are subject to judicial checks. Primarily, with some exceptions, this is through the Administrative Court in Wales. The geographical jurisdiction of the Administrative Court in Wales is explored in detail in chapter 2 of this work. For the purposes of this section it is appropriate simply to note that the justice system is not a devolved area and so the Administrative Court in Wales still forms part of Her Majesty's Courts and Tribunals in England and Wales. This said, whilst justice is not yet devolved, the devolved public bodies (as well as UK public bodies) can still be held to account at the request of the people of Wales by the Court in Wales.

Chapter 5

Judicial Review

INTRODUCTION

This chapter will explore the practice and procedure behind judicial review, one of the more often utilised methods[1] of challenge when it is considered that a public body has breached the principles of administrative law. Judicial review can only be initiated in the Administrative Court, save for in certain circumstances where the Upper Tribunal has jurisdiction (discussed later in the chapter). To begin a case in the Administrative Court a claimant must first deal with the Administrative Court Office ('ACO'), a part of Her Majesty's Courts and Tribunals Service ('HMCTS'), which in turn is an executive agency of the Ministry of Justice ('MOJ'). There are ACOs in Wales (in Cardiff), Birmingham, Leeds, Manchester, and in the Royal Courts of Justice in London.[2] This chapter will focus on procedure in the ACO in Wales but it should be recognised that only the informal procedures will differ. The rules and practice directions governing the work of the Administrative Court and the ACOs are largely identical in England and Wales. 5-1

ESTABLISHING THE PARTIES

The parties 5-2

The claimant

The claimant in judicial review proceedings can be any individual (sometimes referred to as a 'natural person') or incorporated company (also known as a corporation). Both natural persons and corporations are considered to be a single 'legal personality' and thus may bring proceedings or have proceedings brought against them in their own name.[3] Whilst partnerships do not have legal personality, they have long been able to bring proceedings in the name of the partnership.[4] Generally, unincorporated associations have been held to lack standing as they do not have legal personality. In some cases permission to apply for judicial review has been refused for this reason.[5] However, on a number of occasions claims have proceeded

[1] See chapter 6 for the other methods.

[2] See chapter 2 for a discussion of the origins of the out-of-London ACOs.

[3] Legal personality is established for incorporated companies by virtue of s. 16(2) of the Companies Act 2006.

[4] See *Sadler* v *Whiteman* [1910] 1 KB 868 at 889.

[5] See *R* v *Darlington BC, ex parte Association of Darlington Taxi Owners* [1994] COD 424.

with unincorporated associations as claimants.[6] These cases did not expressly give the unincorporated association legal standing; rather the Court simply did not comment on the issue of standing. The safer route for the unincorporated association that wishes to bring proceedings is to lodge the proceedings under the name of one or more individuals to bring the claim on behalf of the association[7] or to form a private limited company, thereby acquiring legal personality. In the latter case the Court will be wary of allowing an unincorporated association to change status to a corporation simply to attempt to avoid adverse costs orders.[8] Public bodies can also be claimants in judicial review proceedings. The Attorney General has a common law power to bring proceedings on behalf of the Crown. Local authorities may bring proceedings by virtue of s. 222 of the Local Government Act 1972.

5-3 The defendant

The defendants in judicial review proceedings are always public bodies, the nature of which has been fully discussed in chapter 4. Administrative Court claims are not brought against individuals,[9] even if there is a single decision maker in the public body. For example, if Mr A. N. Inspector makes a decision as a planning inspector to refuse planning permission, then the defendant in the case would not be Mr Inspector, it would be *The Welsh Ministers* as the planning inspector made the decision on behalf of the Welsh Ministers. It is the public body that is answerable for the decision, not the individual who made the decision on the public body's behalf. Further, it is the highest office that is challenged. As such where the decision is made by the UK government it is the relevant Secretary of State who is the defendant. Therefore, even if the decision challenged is that of a junior civil servant working in the Home Office, the defendant would still be the Secretary of State for the Home Department. In Wales, any decision from the Welsh Government is subject to the scrutiny of the Administrative Court and, by virtue of s. 45(2) of the Government of Wales Act 2006, the defendant is always simply stated as *The Welsh Ministers*. With local government, the local authority itself is the highest office and so the defendant would be, for example, Flintshire County Council. Where the

[6] In Wales, one such example is *R (Usk Valley Conservation Group)* v *Brecon Beacons National Park Authority* [2010] 2 P&CR 14. See *De Smith's Judicial Review*, para. 2-012 for a number of examples.

[7] Any costs order would stand against the claimant(s) in the claim and so said claimant(s) need to be wary and secure some agreement with the association as to the apportionment of any costs. Alternatively, the claimants may act as representatives for the group under CPR 19.6(1). Any orders would be binding on all members of the group, but would only be enforceable against the claimant, unless the court gives permission to enforce against the other representatives under CPR 19.6(4)(b).

[8] See *R* v *Leicestershire CC, ex parte Blackfordby and Boothorpe Action Group Ltd* [2001] Env LR 2 at paras 34–8.

[9] There are exceptions. Most of these exceptional cases will not be heard in Wales as they are matters reserved to the Administrative Court in London by virtue of CPR PD 54D, para. 3.1. In fact the only Administrative Court matter that can be brought in Wales against an individual is an application for committal for contempt under CPR Part 81.

decision maker is an inferior court or tribunal it is the court or tribunal that must be the defendant.[10]

Interested parties 5-4

In a number of judicial review claims it may be that there are interested parties. An interested party is defined as any person (and, like claimants, this may include corporations or partnerships), other than the claimant or defendant, who is directly affected by the claim.[11] An example of an interested party, in planning law claims, would be where a claimant challenges the decision of a defendant local authority to grant planning permission to a third party. The third party would have a direct interest, and thus must be an interested party. Interested parties must be named on the claim form and thus they must be served with claim papers under CPR 54.7(b).[12]

Interveners 5-5

Judicial reviews are public proceedings and as such the court retains a power to hear from any person, whether they are a party to proceedings or not. Any persons can apply, under CPR 54.17(1), to make representations or file evidence in judicial review proceedings. Potential interveners should be aware that any application must be made promptly[13] and that there are discrete costs considerations.[14]

Case titles 5-6

Like the majority of civil proceedings, every statutory appeal and application that the Administrative Court in Wales will consider will be a dispute between the parties. As such the case title will reflect this:

Claimant/Appellant X -v- Defendant/Respondent Y

In judicial review proceedings the case title differs to reflect the fact that judicial review is the modern version of a historical procedure whereby Her Majesty's Judiciary, on her behalf, act as the supervisors of the executive power. Technically,

[10] When considering whether to apply for judicial review of the decision of a county court a claimant should be aware that the court will apply the second-tier appeals criteria, to the case, as suggested in *R (Cart)* v *The Upper Tribunal* [2012] 1 AC 663 at paras 57 and 94. As such, permission to apply for judicial review is unlikely to be granted unless the claimant can establish an important point of principle affecting large numbers of similar claims or some other compelling reasons. This principle is discussed with reference to judicial review of the Upper Tribunal at 5-64.

[11] CPR 54.1(2)(f).

[12] CPR PD 54A, para. 5.1.

[13] CPR 54.17(2).

[14] Discussed at 7-17.

a judicial review is brought by the Crown, on the application of the claimant, to check powers are being properly exercised. The case title also reflects this:

The Queen (on the application of Claimant X) -v- Defendant Y

or

R (on the application of Claimant X) -v- Defendant Y

or

R (Claimant X) -v- Defendant Y.

This is not to say that the Crown will in any way practically involve itself in the claim on behalf of the claimant; it is a constitutional title only.

The form of the case title is stipulated in *Practice Direction (Administrative Court: Establishment)* [2000] 1 WLR 1654. Before the implementation of this practice direction the case title used the Latin and the title looked like this: '*R* v *Defendant Y, ex parte Claimant X*'. All pre-2000 judicial reviews will have this case title.

PRE-ACTION CONSIDERATIONS

5-7 The provisions

Modern judicial review is a creature of statute. The authority for the High Court to conduct judicial review proceedings is contained in s. 31(1) of the Senior Courts Act 1981. However, for the substantive procedural landscape s. 31 simply refers the reader to the rules of the court. The relevant rules of court, a 'must read' for anyone conducting judicial review proceedings, can be found in Part 54 of the Civil Procedure Rules.[15] Before instigating judicial review proceedings there are some considerations to which attention must be given.

5-8 Bars to judicial review

There are situations in which judicial review will not be appropriate and, even if a public body does appear to have made a decision contrary to the principles of administrative law then the claimant should, nonetheless, not instigate judicial review proceedings.

[15] An unedited copy of Part 54 can be found at Annex A to this work.

Adequate alternative remedy 5-9

Judicial review is often said to be a remedy of last resort.[16] If there are other methods of challenge available to the claimant, and that method of challenge provides an adequate remedy, the alternative remedy should be exhausted before applying for judicial review. This is a long-standing principle in judicial review. In *R* v *Epping and Harlow General Commissioners, ex parte Goldstraw*,[17] Sir John Donaldson, MR commented:

> [I]t is a cardinal principle that, save in the most exceptional circumstances, that [the judicial review] jurisdiction will not be exercised where other remedies were available and have not been used.[18]

The alternative remedy can come in any guise. Frequently pleaded options by defendants include internal complaints procedures, statutory appeals or a complaint to an ombudsman.[19]

When considering whether the alternative remedy would be adequate the court will consider a number of factors. In *R* v *Huntingdon District Council, ex parte Cowan*,[20] Glidewell J (as he then was) said:

> Where there is an alternative remedy available but judicial review is sought, then in my judgment the court should always ask itself whether the remedy that is sought in the court, or the alternative remedy which is available to the applicant by way of appeal, is the most effective and convenient, in other words, which of them will prove to be the most effective and convenient in all the circumstances, not merely for the applicant, but in the public interest.[21]

The relevant considerations were also discussed by Simon Brown LJ in *R* v *Falmouth and Truro Port HA, ex parte South West Water Ltd*:[22]

> If the applicant has a statutory right of appeal, permission should only exceptionally be given … The judge should, however, have regard to all relevant circumstances which typically will include … the comparative speed, expense

[16] See *Kay* v *Lambeth London Borough Council* [2006] 2 AC 465 at 492 and more recently in *R (Gifford)* v *Governor of Bure Prison* [2014] EWHC 911 (Admin) at para. 37.

[17] [1983] 3 All ER 257.

[18] [1983] 3 All ER at 262. Confirmed in *R* v *Birmingham City Council, ex parte Ferrero Ltd* [1993] 1 All ER 530 and *R (Willford)* v *Financial Services Authority* [2013] EWCA Civ 677.

[19] Ombudsmen as public law defendants are further discussed in chapter 4 at 4-33. For a discussion of when a referral to an ombudsman may be an adequate alternative remedy, see *R* v *Lambeth London Borough Council, ex parte Crookes* (1997) 29 HLR 28 at 38–9 or *R (Umo)* v *Commissioner for Local Administration in England* [2004] ELR 265 at para. 17.

[20] [1984] 1 WLR 501.

[21] [1984] 1 WLR at 507.

[22] [2001] QB 445.

> and finality of the alternative processes, the need and scope for fact finding, the desirability of an authoritative ruling on any point of law arising, and (perhaps) the apparent strength of the applicant's substantive challenge.[23]

5-10 Lack of standing (or *locus standi*)

A person may not bring an application for judicial review in the Administrative Court unless they have a sufficient interest in the claim. This is one of the statutory principles behind judicial review enshrined in s. 31(3) of the Senior Courts Act 1981. The issue of standing will generally be determined when considering permission[24] but it is a general, jurisdictional point that may be raised and determined at any stage. When the issue of standing is not obvious and forms part of the legal and factual context of the case then it would be more appropriate to deal with the issue as part of the substantive judicial review.[25]

In *Inland Revenue Commissioners* v *National Federation of Self-Employed and Small Businesses Ltd*,[26] the House of Lords sought to give guidance on the sufficient interest test:

> The courts ... have always reserved the right to be satisfied that the applicant had some genuine *locus standi* to appear before it ... For all cases the test is expressed as one of sufficient interest in the matter to which the application relates. As to this I would state two negative propositions. First, it does not remove the whole – and vitally important – question of *locus standi* into the realm of pure discretion. The matter is one for decision, a mixed decision of fact and law, which the court must decide on legal principles. Secondly, the fact that the same words are used to cover all the forms of remedy allowed by the rule does not mean that the test is the same in all cases ... a rule of common sense [applies], reflecting the different character of the relief asked for.[27]

Whilst this definition does establish that the test is not a discretionary one (that is to say, the parties and/or the court cannot agree that a case should continue even where the claimant does not appear to have standing[28]), the definition is quick to establish that sufficient interest is a case-specific question.

A fairly clear-cut example is the position of the claimant who is aggrieved by the decision. Those whom a decision directly and adversely affects will seldom (if

[23] [2001] QB 445 at 473.

[24] The permission requirement is discussed later in this chapter at 5-38.

[25] See *Inland Revenue Commissioners* v *National Federation of Self-Employed and Small Businesses Ltd* [1982] AC 617 at 630.

[26] [1982] AC 617.

[27] [1982] AC 617 at 630–1.

[28] This principle has been confirmed in a number of other cases, for example in *R* v *Secretary of State for Social Services, ex parte Child Poverty Action Group* [1990] 2 QB 540 at 556.

ever) be refused relief for lack of standing.[29] Claimants have also been considered to have sufficient standing where the claim is brought in the public interest. It may be thought that all decisions of public bodies are of public interest, and as such the test for public interest standing falls on the true interest of the claimant. This was well summarised in *R (Kides)* v *South Cambridgeshire District Council*:[30]

> [T]here is an important distinction to be drawn between, on the one hand, a person who brings proceedings having no real or genuine interest in obtaining the relief sought [who will not have sufficient standing], and on the other hand a person who, whilst legitimately and perhaps passionately interested in obtaining the relief sought, relies as grounds for seeking that relief on matters in which he has no personal interest.[31]

As such a claimant who claims to have sufficient interest on the grounds of public interest must be prepared to establish that they have a genuine public interest. A good example can be found in *R (Howard League for Penal Reform)* v *Secretary of State for the Home Department (No. 2)*[32] where the Howard League was held to have a public interest in the treatment of under-eighteen-year-olds in young offenders institutions.

The defendant is not a public body 5-11

Judicial review is only available against public bodies, not private individuals or companies acting as a private body. What constitutes a public body has been discussed in chapter 4.

The claim is academic 5-12

Where a claim is purely academic, that is to say that 'there is no longer a *lis* to be decided which will directly affect the rights and obligations of the parties',[33] it will generally not be appropriate to bring judicial review proceedings. Only in exceptional circumstances where two conditions are satisfied will the court proceed to determine an academic issue. These conditions, as outlined by Silber J in *R (Zoolife International Ltd)* v *The Secretary of State for Environment, Food and Rural Affairs*,[34] are:

1. a large number of similar cases exist or are anticipated, or at least other similar cases exist or are anticipated; and
2. the decision in the academic case will not be fact-sensitive.

[29] *R* v *Secretary of State for Social Services, ex parte Child Poverty Action Group* [1990] 2 QB 540 at 625.

[30] [2003] 1 P&CR 19.

[31] [2003] 1 P&CR 19 at 132.

[32] [2003] 1 FLR 484.

[33] *R* v *Secretary of State for the Home Department, ex parte Salem* [1999] 1 AC 450.

[34] [2008] ACD 44 at para. 36.

5-13 The claim challenges a decision of one of the Superior Courts

The Superior Courts[35] are the High Court, the Court of Appeal and the Supreme Court. No matter is deemed to be beyond the jurisdiction of a Superior Court unless it is expressly shown to be so. As such they cannot be subject to judicial review.

Where the Crown Court is dealing with a trial on indictment it is a Superior Court and its actions are not subject to judicial review.[36] Otherwise, its functions are subject to judicial review. In *R* v *Manchester Crown Court, ex parte DPP*[37] the question of whether a matter relates to a trial on indictment was considered by the House of Lords. It was considered that the appropriate question to ask was 'Is the decision sought to be reviewed one arising in the issue between the Crown and the defendant formulated by the indictment (including the costs of such issue)?'[38] For example, an order restricting the reporting of a trial on indictment by preventing a defendant's name being published does not relate to the trial and thus may be subject to judicial review.[39] The above said, in *R (M)* v *Kingston Crown Court*,[40] the Divisional Court held that judicial review of an order arising out of a trial on indictment was possible where the order was made in circumstances where the defect was so severe that it deprived the court below of jurisdiction to make it. It is submitted that only in exceptional cases will this loophole make judicial review suitable. In *M* the trial judge had used a provision under the Mental Health Act 1983 to allow evidence to be collected from the defendant. However, such an order was manifestly not the purpose of the provision and the order was quashed.

The Upper Tribunal is also a Superior Court. The circumstances in which the Upper Tribunal is subject to judicial review are discussed later in this chapter.[41]

Once a claimant is satisfied that they may apply for judicial review then the parties are encouraged to negotiate with a view to avoiding said proceedings. This is where the pre-action protocol is so valuable.

5-14 The pre-action protocol

Before making an application for judicial review the potential claimant should follow the judicial review pre-action protocol. Failure to do so may result in costs sanctions being applied. The pre-action process is easy to overlook but should be utilised by any effective potential litigator. The process may allow for issues to be narrowed or even for proceedings to be avoided altogether.

[35] See the discussion of the differences between inferior and superior courts in *R* v *Chancellor of St Edmundsbury and Ipswich Diocese, ex parte White* [1948] 1 KB 195. Also see 1-20.

[36] Sections 1, 29(3) and 46(1) of the Senior Courts Act 1981.

[37] [1993] 1 WLR 1524.

[38] [1993] 1 WLR 1524 at 1530.

[39] See *R (Y)* v *Aylesbury Crown Court* [2012] Crim LR 893.

[40] [2015] 1 Cr App R 3 at para. 32.

[41] At 5-64.

The protocol expressly notes in its introduction that 'it does not affect the time limit specified by Rule 54.5(1) of the Civil Procedure Rules'.[42] As such a party considering applying for judicial review should act quickly. The protocol does note that it will not be appropriate in urgent cases (e.g. where there is an urgent need for an interim order to compel a public body to act) and it may not be appropriate in cases where one of the shorter time limits applies. In those cases, the parties should still attempt to comply with the protocol but the court will not apply costs sanctions where the court is satisfied that it was not possible to comply because of the shorter time limits.

Stage one of the pre-action process requires the parties to consider whether a method of alternative dispute resolution ('ADR') would be more appropriate. The methods of ADR are numerous; the protocol itself expressly mentions the following potential methods:

- discussion and negotiation;
- referral to the ombudsman (ombudsmen are not able to look into a complaint once court action has been commenced);
- early neutral evaluation by an independent third party (e.g. a lawyer experienced in the field of administrative law).
- mediation – a form of facilitated negotiation assisted by an independent neutral party.

Stage two is to send the defendant a pre-action letter. The letter should be made out in the specific format outlined in Annex A to the protocol.[43] The letter is designed to identify the points of dispute at an early stage with a view to resolution. The letter should contain the date and details of the act or omission being challenged and a clear summary of the facts on which the claim is based. It should also contain the details of any relevant information that the claimant is seeking and an explanation of why it is considered relevant.

The defendant should normally be given fourteen days to respond to the pre-action letter and they must do so in the format outlined in Annex B to the protocol. Where necessary the defendant may request that the claimant allow them additional time to respond. The temptation for the litigious claimant here is to refuse and state that they have complied with the protocol. It is submitted that this attitude is to be avoided. The pre-action protocol process is a useful tool as the defendant may well concede the claim at the pre-action stage, thus avoiding the costs and time of the judicial review process entirely. It may well be that, even if a claim is not conceded, the defendant's response highlights points not considered by the claimant and thus will help to narrow and focus the issues to be brought to the court, again saving time and costs.

[42] See below for details on time limits.

[43] The current protocol can be found on the Ministry of Justice website.

5-15 Forms

The parties should be aware of a number of forms. These forms can all be downloaded from the Ministry of Justice Website (www.justice.gov.uk) or copies can be provided by the Administrative Court Office in Wales at Cardiff Civil Justice Centre.

At this point it should also be noted that the Administrative Court Office in Wales is subject to s. 22 of the Welsh Language Act 1993 and as such must provide a bilingual service. Bilingual versions of the forms are available and a party is entitled to lodge their claim papers entirely in English, entirely in Welsh, or in both languages.

HMCTS Wales, of which the Administrative Court Office in Wales is a part, has a dedicated translation unit and as such the office is able to obtain for itself a translation of any Welsh documentation to allow staff and judges who do not speak Welsh to deal with the claim. Translations can, if necessary, be obtained on an urgent basis to deal with urgent applications. Similarly, Cardiff Civil Justice Centre has staff members who can speak Welsh and can translate for telephone or face-to-face contact between court users and Administrative Court Office staff.

Parties should note that there is no right to translated papers under the Welsh Language Act 1993, the Ministry of Justice's Welsh Language Scheme, or the Civil Procedure Rules. As such, if a party lodges papers in a language that the other party cannot read, unless a judicial order is made requiring translated or bilingual documents, it will be the responsibility of the receiving party to obtain a translation for themselves. The public body itself may have a Welsh Language Scheme, which may well place it under a duty to furnish such translations. The public body itself will be able to provide a copy of its own Welsh Language Scheme.

5-16 Disclosure

In an application for judicial review there is no rule covering disclosure of specific documents between parties, either before or during the proceedings, because disclosure should be unnecessary. The parties have a duty of candour to disclose all evidence to dispose of the case fairly.[44] The public body often makes all the relevant information public in any event. The Divisional Court in *R (Al-Sweady)* v *Secretary of State for Defence*[45] recognised that the position may be different in human rights cases because such cases tend to be very fact specific and any judgment on the proportionality of a public authority's interference with a protected right is likely to call for a careful and accurate evaluation of the facts.

Whilst disclosure is not normally appropriate in judicial review proceedings, the claimant may request an order for specific disclosure under CPR 31.12(1)

[44] See the discussion of this principle in *R (Al-Sweady)* v *Secretary of State for Defence* [2010] HRLR 2 at 18.

[45] [2010] HRLR 2.

requiring the public body to disclose known, specific documents or documents of a certain class or type as specified in the order. An order for specific disclosure will be made only where it is necessary to determine the case fairly and to clarify some inaccuracy or inadequacy in the available evidence disclosed under the duty of candour.[46]An application under CPR 31.12(1) is made in accordance with the interim applications procedure.[47]

Time limits 5-17

The general time limit for bringing a claim for judicial review can be found in CPR 54.5:

> 54.5 (1) The claim form must be filed –
> (a) promptly; and
> (b) in any event not later than 3 months after the grounds to make the claim first arose.

The provision in CPR 54.5(1)(a) is important. Judicial review is designed to be an expeditious process; as such any potential claimant must act promptly. It must not be presumed that just because the claim has been lodged within the three-month time limit in CPR 54.5(1)(b) that the claim will be deemed to be within time.[48] Claimants who have not acted promptly have been held to be out of time for lodging their papers, despite the fact that they lodged them within the three-month time limit.[49] When considering whether a claim is within time a claimant should also be aware of three important points:

- the time limit may not be extended by agreement between the parties;
- the time limit begins to run from the date the decision to be challenged was made; and
- there are three exceptions to the general time limit rule.

These points are discussed below.

[46] As discussed in *R* v *Secretary of State for Foreign and Commonwealth Affairs, ex parte World Development Movement Ltd* [1995] 1 WLR 386 at 396–7.

[47] See 5-31.

[48] The extent to which the promptness complies with EU law doctrine on certainty has been questioned but not fully resolved. Practitioners should approach the time limit question considering the promptness rule to be a lawful rule, but for a discussion of the EU principles in this context see *De Smith's Judicial Review*, para. 16-054.

[49] See, for example, *R* v *Cotswold District Council, ex parte Barrington Parish Council* [1998] 75 P&CR 515.

5-18 The time limit may not be extended by agreement between the parties

The provision in CPR 54.5(2) that the parties may not extend the time for lodging the claim is a reference to the general power in CPR 2.11 which allows the parties to extend time limits by written agreement. If the parties wish to extend the time limit they must obtain an order from the court extending the time limit.

5-19 The time limit begins to run from the date the decision to be challenged was made

There is a tendency amongst litigants and practitioners to believe that the 'clock starts to run' when they are served with the decision or they discover that the decision has been made. In fact, the time limit is to be calculated from the date the decision was made, irrespective of the knowledge of the claimant. In *R* v *Department of Transport, ex parte Presvac Engineering*[50] the Court of Appeal upheld this view and indicated that the date of knowledge was a matter relevant to the issue of extending time, not the date from which the time limit should be calculated.

5-20 Three exceptions to the general time limit rule in CPR 54.5(1)

- *Planning Law Judicial Reviews*
  By virtue of CPR 54.5(5), where the application for judicial review relates to a decision made by the Secretary of State, Welsh Ministers, or local planning authority under the planning Acts,[51] the claim form must be filed not later than six weeks after the grounds to make the claim first arose.

- *Public Contract Judicial Reviews*
  By virtue of CPR 54.5(6), where the application for judicial review relates to a decision under the Public Contracts Regulations 2015, which govern the procedure by which public bodies may outsource public services, the claim form must be filed within the time specified by reg. 92(2) of those Regulations, which is currently thirty days from the date when the claimant first knew or ought to have known that grounds for starting the proceedings had arisen.[52]

[50] [1992] 4 Admin LR 121.

[51] 'The planning Acts' has the same meaning as in s. 336 of the Town and Country Planning Act 1990, which defines 'the planning Acts' as the Town and Country Planning Act 1990, the Planning (Listed Buildings and Conservation Areas) Act 1990, the Planning (Hazardous Substances) Act 1990 and the Planning (Consequential Provisions) Act 1990.

[52] Note that this time limit begins to run from the date of knowledge, in contrast to the general rule where the relevant date is the decision date itself.

- *Judicial Review of the Upper Tribunal*
  By virtue of CPR 54.7A(3), where the defendant is the Upper Tribunal, papers must be filed no later than sixteen days after the date on which notice of the Upper Tribunal's decision was sent to the applicant.[53]

Where the claim papers have not been lodged in accordance with the relevant time limit as outlined above, it is not necessarily fatal to the claim and the ACO in Wales will still accept the papers and issue the claim. CPR 3.1(2)(a) allows the Court to 'extend or shorten the time for compliance with any rule, practice direction or court order (even if an application for extension is made after the time for compliance has expired)'. Where the claim is lodged out of time the claimant should apply for an extension of time to file the claim. This can be done by way of an interim application[54] but the simplest way to do it is to make the application, including the reasons for the delay, in Part 8 of the claim form, which deals with 'other applications'. The judge considering permission to apply for judicial review will then also consider the application for an extension of time at that point.

Where the court determines that there has been 'undue delay', whether the claimant has applied to extend time or not, the court may refuse permission to apply for judicial review.[55]

REPRESENTATION, FUNDING AND ADVICE 5-21

When it comes to representation and advice for Administrative Court Proceedings there are a number of avenues open to a party. A party may opt to conduct the litigation themselves, thus acting as a litigant in person. There are guides for litigants acting in person in court proceedings which can be found on the Ministry of Justice website. This said, Administrative Court proceedings are fairly complex, and legal advice and representation is advisable if possible.

Legal representation and funding 5-22

A number of solicitors firms in both Wales and England conduct public and administrative law litigation. Further, a number of barristers in both Wales and England will give advice without referral by a solicitor, acting on a direct access basis. Details of these legal professionals can be found on the Law Society and Bar Council[56] websites respectively.

[53] Again note the difference from the general rule: here the time limit is calculated from the date the decision was sent, not the date it was made.

[54] See the section on interim applications below, 5-31.

[55] Section 31(6)(a) of the Senior Courts Act 1981.

[56] The Bar Council website in turn refers to the Bar Directory and the Direct Access Portal.

There are, in essence, three ways that funding can be arranged for legal representation:

- fee paid representation;
- legal aid or representation orders; and
- pro-bono representation (i.e. free legal representation – to enquire about this service see an advice agency such as Law Works Cymru or the Bar Pro Bono Unit).

5-23 Fee paid representation

Legal representatives will act for a party that will pay their fees directly. Fee paid representation is generally conducted at an agreed hourly rate or by agreeing a fixed fee in advance. Alternatively, some legal representatives will act for a party under a conditional fee agreement ('CFA'). CFAs are commonly known as 'no win, no fee' agreements. The individual firm or barrister will be able to confirm the basis on which they will act.

5-24 Legal aid

The individual firm or barrister will be able to confirm whether they can work on a legal aid basis and whether a particular claimant will be entitled to apply for legal aid. The specific eligibility criteria change and a legal representative will be able to give advice on the current criteria. The following is an overview of the system.

There are three types of legal aid:

- legal help, which can be used to give limited, initial advice and assistance;
- investigative representation, which can be used to investigate a potential claim in greater depth than that under legal help; and
- full representation, which can be used to issue and conduct judicial review proceedings.

To obtain full representation, and thus engage the legal representative to conduct the judicial review proceedings, the claimant will be required to pass two eligibility tests:

- *Financial eligibility*

  The Legal Aid Agency will assess the claimant's disposable income and capital in accordance with the Civil Legal Aid (Financial Resources and Payment for Services) Regulations 2013. If the claimant's income and/or capital amount to more than the set sum then legal aid will not be available.

- *Merits criteria*

  The Legal Aid Agency will consider the merits of the proposed claim in accordance with the set criteria in the Civil Legal Aid (Merits Criteria)

Regulations 2013. If the Legal Aid Agency considers that the proposed claim lacks the requisite merit then legal aid will not be available.

Representation orders (criminal proceedings) 5-25

Funding for legal representation in criminal cases in the Administrative Court is also potentially available. Judicial review proceedings are not incidental to lower court proceedings and thus any representation order granted in the lower court will not cover judicial review proceedings.[57] The power for the court to grant a representation order in criminal cases arises out of ss. 16 and 19 of the Legal Aid, Sentencing and Punishment of Offenders Act 2012. Judicial review is not specified as a criminal matter in s. 14(a)–(g) of the 2012 Act or under the Criminal Legal Aid (General) Regulations 2013 and specific reference is not made to judicial review in the Criminal Legal Aid (Determinations by a Court and Choice of Representative) Regulations 2013. Thus, a representation order may not be granted by the Administrative Court itself, although legal aid may be available from the Legal Aid Agency.

Under reg. 7(1) of the Criminal Legal Aid (Determinations by a Court and Choice of Representative) Regulations 2013 the Administrative Court may grant a representation order in appeals by way of case stated. The court can also grant a representation order in committal proceedings.[58] In the High Court there are no financial eligibility criteria and, by virtue of reg. 21(b) of the Criminal Legal Aid (General) Regulations 2013, the interests of justice test is automatically passed. The representation order can be obtained by sending the relevant criminal legal aid application form (available on the Legal Aid Agency website) to the Administrative Court Office. To claim costs granted under a representation order made by the court the legal representative must fill out a Crown Office Billing Form and then send it to the Senior Courts Costs Office[59] together with a copy of the representation order.

[57] Regulation 20(2)(a) of the Criminal Legal Aid (General) Regulations 2013.

[58] Confirmed in *King's Lynn and West Norfolk BC* v *Bunning* [2015] 1 WLR 531.

[59] For contact details, see Annex C. For example forms, see *The White Book 2016*, vol. 1, p. 1635.

5-26 Representation at a hearing

The claimant is entitled to appear in person[60] or to be represented by a barrister or a solicitor with higher rights of audience.[61] The public body defendant will tend to be represented by a legally qualified person.

5-27 Advice agencies and assistance

A number of advice agencies can provide advice and assistance to litigants in person. Examples are:

- the Personal Support Unit (based in Cardiff Civil Justice Centre), which does not give legal advice but staff will assist by taking notes and discussing the workings of the court process;
- Law Works Cymru, based in Cardiff, helps to coordinate pro bono (that is to say, free legal advice) provision throughout Wales; and
- the Citizens Advice Bureau, which provides advice on a wide range of issues at drop-in centres, by telephone and online.

5-28 McKenzie friends

A claimant may have the assistance of a non-legally qualified person, known as a 'McKenzie Friend'.[62] Guidance on McKenzie Friends was given in *Practice Note (Sen Cts: McKenzie Friends: Civil and Family Courts)*,[63] which established that a McKenzie Friend may:

1. provide moral support for litigants;
2. take notes;
3. help with case papers; and
4. quietly give advice on any aspect of the conduct of the case.

[60] Legal Services Act 2007, Sch. 3, para. 1(6). Note CPR 39.6(2), which requires an individual acting in person for a limited company to provide the court with a statement that they have been authorised to do so by the board of directors or managing director (as well as further information listed in CPR PD 39A, para. 5.2) and to obtain the permission of the court to act. Provided this is done and the court does not believe there is some reason why the individual should not act then the court will generally grant permission – CPR PD 39A, para. 5.3.

[61] Legal Services Act 2007, s. 20 and Sch. 4, para. 1. All qualified barristers have higher rights of audience granted by the Bar Council. A solicitor must have a higher courts advocacy qualification granted by the Law Society (i.e. higher courts advocacy qualification under the Higher Rights of Audience Regulations 2000).

[62] The right to which was established in *McKenzie* v *McKenzie* [1970] 3 WLR 472.

[63] [2010] 1 WLR 1881.

They may not:

1. act as the litigant's agent in relation to the proceedings;
2. manage litigants' cases outside court, for example by signing court documents; or
3. address the court, make oral submissions or examine witnesses.

A litigant who wishes to exercise this right should inform the judge as soon as possible, indicating who the McKenzie Friend will be. The proposed McKenzie Friend should produce a short curriculum vitae or other statement setting out relevant experience, confirming that he or she has no interest in the case and understands the McKenzie Friend's role and the duty of confidentiality. The assistance of a McKenzie Friend is a right, but it may be circumscribed if the court believes there is good reason to do so.

AN OVERVIEW OF THE JUDICIAL REVIEW PROCEDURE 5-29

The procedural landscape for judicial review proceedings is entirely contained within Part 54 of the Civil Procedure Rules. It is essentially a two-stage process. First the claimant must obtain permission (sometimes referred to as 'leave') to apply for judicial review from the court.[64] If permission is granted by the court then the second stage is the substantive hearing itself. It should be noted that, unlike a number of other civil and criminal proceedings, the judicial review process does not incorporate a case management conference. The process expects the parties to liaise with each other and the Administrative Court Office to ensure that the claim is ready for the court. An open dialogue between the parties and the staff of the Administrative Court Office is essential to the smooth running of the case.

This chapter will go on to examine each stage of the judicial review process, but Figure 5.1 may be used as a guide to the judicial review process from start to finish and readers may wish to refer back to the diagram for the overall picture.

LODGING THE CLAIM[65] 5-30

Once the claim papers have been prepared they must be lodged at the Administrative Court Office with the appropriate fee or fee remission form.[66] The Administrative Court Office in Wales can be found in Cardiff Civil Justice Centre.[67]

[64] Section 31(3) of the Senior Courts Act 1981 and CPR 54.4.

[65] See Annex E for a tick box table outlining the minimum documentation required by the Administrative Court Office.

[66] See the Ministry of Justice website for the relevant fees.

[67] See Annex C for contact details and opening times.

Figure 5.1 Judicial review process chart

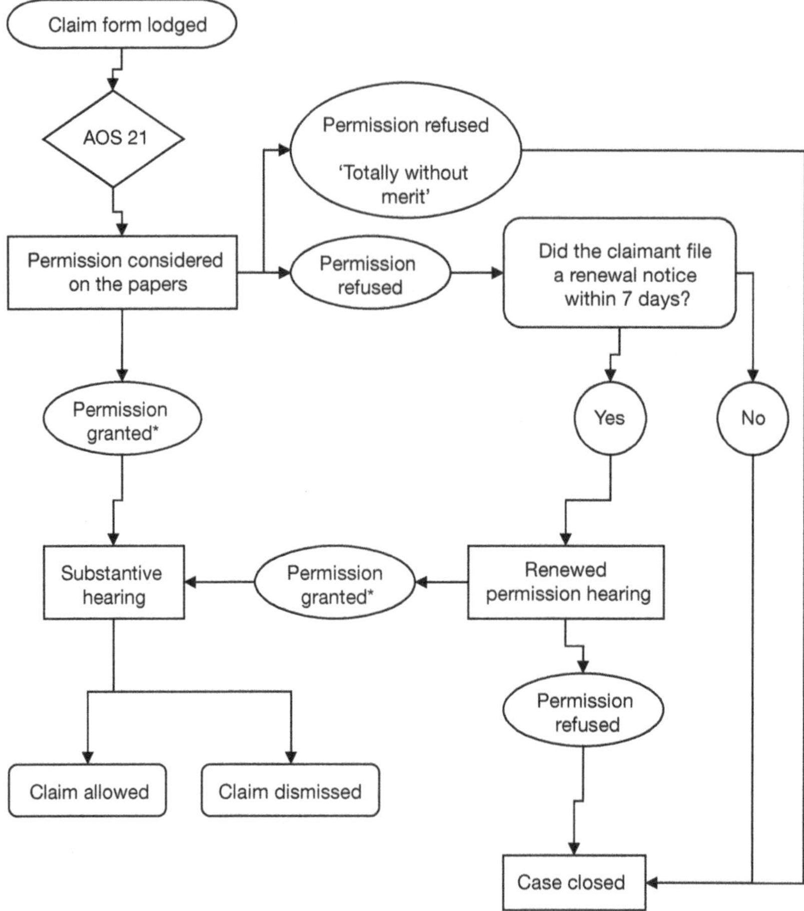

* The defendant has thirty-five days in which to file detailed grounds of defence and any evidence.

The claimant is required to apply for permission to apply for judicial review in the claim form.[68] The judicial review claim form automatically includes this application in Part 4 of the claim form. The claimant must also specify the judicial review remedies sought;[69] again, there is space for this in the claim form at Part 7.

By virtue of CPR PD 54A, paras 5.6 and 5.7, when lodging the claim papers, the claim form must include or be accompanied by:

[68] Senior Courts Act 1981, s. 31(3); CPR 54.4; and CPR 54.6(1)(b). See below for more detailed discussion of the application for permission.

[69] CPR 54.6(1)(c). See CPR 54.2 and 54.3 for a list of the judicial review remedies, or see 5-47.

5.6[70]

(1) a detailed statement of the claimant's grounds for bringing the claim for judicial review;
(2) a statement of the facts relied on;
(3) any application to extend the time limit for filing the claim form;
(4 any application for directions.

5.7

(1) any written evidence in support of the claim or application to extend time;
(2) a copy of any order that the claimant seeks to have quashed;
(3) where the claim for judicial review relates to a decision of a court or tribunal, an approved copy of the reasons for reaching that decision;
(4) copies of any documents on which the claimant proposes to rely;
(5) copies of any relevant statutory material; and
(6) a list of essential documents for advance reading by the court (with page references to the passages relied on).

If the claim raises a 'devolution issue' then that must be raised in the claim form when it is lodged[71] and the claim papers must outline why it is said that a devolution issue exists. The definition of a devolution issue can be found in the Government of Wales Act 2006, Sch. 9, para. 1:[72]

> (a) a question whether an Assembly Measure or Act of the Assembly, or any provision of an Assembly Measure or Act of the Assembly, is within the Assembly's legislative competence;
> (b) a question whether any function … is exercisable by the Welsh Ministers, the First Minister or the Counsel General;
> (c) a question whether the purported or proposed exercise of a function by the Welsh Ministers, the First Minister or the Counsel General is, or would be, within the powers of the Welsh Ministers, the First Minister or the Counsel General …;
> (d) a question whether there has been any failure to comply with a duty imposed on the Welsh Ministers, the First Minister or the Counsel General …; or
> (e) a question of whether a failure to act by the Welsh Ministers, the First Minister or the Counsel General is incompatible with any of the Convention rights.

[70] There is space for these details in the claim form but it is permissible to simply note 'see attached' on the claim form and then provide more extensive details in separate documentation as part of the court bundle.

[71] CPR PD 54A, para. 5.4.

[72] CPR PD 54A, para. 5.5.

All of the papers that the claimant submits when lodging the claim must be arranged in a paginated and indexed bundle, as required under CPR PD 54A, para. 5.9. This is an important practical provision. It allows a judge to read the papers and easily cross reference the documents. It also allows the parties easily to refer the judge to documents in court. CPR PD 54A, para. 5.9 also requires the claimant to provide two copies of the said bundle for use by the court (a master copy for the ACO and a copy bundle for the judge to use in court). A further copy must also be provided for each defendant and interested party,[73] which will be sealed by the ACO and returned to the claimant to serve on those parties.[74] The claimant must serve the papers with a sealed copy of the claim form on all parties within seven days of lodging the claim.[75] Local Authorities should be served at their main offices. Whilst not a requirement, it is of assistance to stipulate that papers should be directed to the authority's legal department. All central Government Departments should be served on the office as stipulated under the Crown Proceedings Act 1947.[76]

Once the claimant has served the papers on the defendant(s) and any interested parties the claimant must confirm this with the Administrative Court Office by filing a certificate of service (form N215) within twenty-one days of service of the claim form.[77] If, after twenty-eight days of lodging the claim form, the Administrative Court Office has not received a certificate of service or an acknowledgement of service from the defendant, then the case will be closed.

INTERIM, URGENT AND PRE-ACTION APPLICATIONS

5-31 When is interim relief appropriate?

The claim form will state the remedy required if the claimant is ultimately successful in the substantive judicial review. However, it may be that the claimant will require an interim remedy whilst the case is pending. Common examples are:

- an interim prohibiting order or injunction, staying the action the defendant plans to take (e.g. to prevent removal from the UK);
- an interim mandatory order requiring the defendant to act in a certain way (e.g. to provide the claimant with accommodation).

[73] By virtue of CPR PD 54A, para. 5.1, where the defendant public body is a court or tribunal then the other parties to the proceedings in the lower court or tribunal must be an interested party in the judicial review proceedings.

[74] CPR PD 54A, para. 6.1.

[75] CPR 54.7.

[76] CPR PD 54A, para. 6.2(b). A copy of the list of addresses can be found at Annex D.

[77] CPR 6.17(2)(a). Also see chapter 4 and Annex D for service addresses.

When considering whether to grant an interim order the judge will consider the test outlined in *R (Medical Justice)* v *Secretary of State for the Home Department*,[78] which states that 'the principles governing the grant of interim relief in judicial review proceedings are those contained in the well known decision of *American Cyanamid Company* v *Ethicon Limited [1975] AC 396*, but modified as appropriate to public law cases'.[79] In brief, the claimant must establish:

1. that there is a real prospect of succeeding at trial, that is to say more than a fanciful prospect of success; and
2. that the balance of convenience lies in granting the interim order.

In *R (Medical Justice)* v *Secretary of State for the Home Department*,[80] Cranston J stated that there is a strong public interest in permitting a public authority's decision to continue when, by hypothesis, it is acting in the public interest.

The required interim relief can be applied for at any stage of proceedings. The general procedure outlined in CPR Part 23 applies to interim applications but the process will differ depending on whether the application is made before the claim is lodged, when the claim is lodged, or after the claim is lodged.

Procedure for pre-action applications for interim relief 5-32

The terms of CPR Part 23, as modified by CPR Part 25, apply to pre-action applications in the Administrative Court. The court may only grant a pre-action order where the matter is urgent or it is otherwise necessary to do so in the interests of justice.[81] It is submitted that the claimant, not just the court, should carefully consider whether the matter is, in actual fact, urgent. If the order is not urgently required then it may be applied for at the time of lodging the claim papers.

To make an application for a pre-action order the claimant is required to do the following:

- the application must be made in accordance with CPR Part 23, which requires an application notice to be lodged;[82]
- the application must be accompanied by the requisite fee;[83]

[78] [2010] ACD 70.

[79] [2010] ACD 70 at para. 6.

[80] [2010] ACD 70 at para. 6.

[81] CPR 25.2(2)(b). The general application notice N244 is commonly used because it includes all the requirements of an application notice listed in CPR PD 23A, para. 2.1.

[82] CPR 23.3(1).

[83] See the Ministry of Justice website for the relevant fees.

- the application notice must be supported by evidence showing that the order is required;[84]
- it is good practice to include a draft order which the court is asked to approve;
- the general rule is that a copy of the application, evidence and draft order should be sent to the proposed defendants and interested parties to give them notice that the application is being made.[85] Where the application has been made without giving notice to the other parties then the evidence supporting the application should explain why the application has been made without giving notice[86] (the most common reason is the extreme urgency of the application);
- the application notice should specify whether the application should be considered without a hearing (that is to say by a judge considering the papers alone) or whether an oral hearing is required.

The ACO lawyer may make directions (see the section on powers of the ACO lawyer below) detailing how the application will be dealt with and giving a time limit for the other parties to respond. If the order is required urgently this stage may be bypassed and the papers will be sent to a judge to consider the application itself. Where the application requires an oral hearing then the ACO will list the hearing as soon as possible and without taking into account the availability of the advocates.[87] Such hearings are usually short hearings of thirty minutes to one hour in length.

By virtue of CPR 25.2(3), where the court does grant a pre-action order then it will also give directions requiring a claim to be commenced.

5-33 Interim relief when lodging the claim

The simplest and most common time to apply for interim relief is to do so at the same time as lodging the claim papers. Such an application can be made simply by making the application in section 8 of the claim form. As with the statement of facts and grounds, the substance of the application can be contained in an appended document to which section 8 of the claim form refers. The application for interim relief will then be considered by the judge on the papers at the same time as the application for permission to apply for judicial review. The advantage for all parties is that this process reduces paperwork, reduces court time, and does not require an additional fee.

In certain circumstances it will not be appropriate for the claimant to allow the procedure outlined by CPR Part 54 to take its natural course. The circumstances

[84] CPR 25.3(2).

[85] CPR 23.4(1).

[86] CPR 25.3(3).

[87] See Annex B: the ACO Wales Listing Policy.

will require urgent consideration of the application for permission to apply for judicial review and/or any interim relief. These situations will be those where some irreversible action will take place if the court does not act to prevent it, or where an expedited judicial review is required due to the circumstances in which the claimants finds themselves.

The procedure for requesting urgent consideration of an application lodged at the same time as the claim papers can be found in *Practice Statement (Administrative Court: Listing and Urgent Cases)*.[88] In essence, where the claimant requests urgent consideration of permission and/or interim relief the practice statement requires the following action:[89]

- the Administrative Court Office in Wales will have a judge available to consider any urgent application received between 10 am and 4 pm, Monday to Friday;[90]
- where a claimant makes an application for the permission application to be considered urgently and/or seeks an interim injunction, they must complete a prescribed form (form N463) which states: (a) the need for urgency; (b) the timescale sought for the consideration of the permission application; and (c) the date by which the substantive hearing should take place. Where an interim injunction is sought, a claimant must, in addition, provide a draft order and the grounds for the injunction;
- the claimant should serve (by fax and post) the claim form and the urgent application form, any draft order, and any grounds, on the defendant and interested parties, advising them of the application and that they may make representations;
- a judge or the ACO lawyer will consider the application within the time requested and may make such orders as considered appropriate; and
- in the event that an urgent application must be made outside the sitting hours of the Administrative Court in Wales and the application cannot wait until the sitting hours recommence, then the claimant must make the application to the out of hours High Court Judge by telephoning 020 7947 6000.[91]

When handing down the practice statement, Scott Baker J stated: 'Advocates must comply with this guidance; and where a manifestly inappropriate application is made, consideration will be given to a wasted costs order'.[92] When he was President of the Queen's Bench Division, Sir John Thomas expanded upon this,

[88] [2002] 1 WLR 810.

[89] These are not the exact terms of the practice statement; rather they have been modified to best explain the process in the Administrative Court in Wales.

[90] Public holidays are not included. See CPR PD 2A, para. 2.1.

[91] As required by CPR PD 54D, para. 4.2.

[92] [2002] 1 WLR 810 at 811.

and indeed took the point further. In *R (Hamid)* v *Secretary of State for the Home Department*[93] he noted that where urgent applications were made improperly (in this case the claimant's solicitor had delayed making the urgent application until the last minute and had not disclosed the full facts of the case in an attempt to use the urgent process to prevent his client's removal from the UK) then the court may summon the claimant or the firm's partner to court to explain their actions and would consider referring the partner to the Solicitors Regulation Authority.[94] As such practitioners and litigants in person ought to be careful to only use the urgent applications procedure when it is necessary.

5-34 Requesting interim relief after the claim has been lodged

Where a claim has already been lodged but it subsequently becomes clear that an interim order is required then CPR part 23, as modified by CPR part 25, once again applies. As such reference should be made to the pre-action procedure outlined above, save that the pre-action conditions of urgency or necessity (pursuant to CPR 25.2(2)(b)) do not apply.

5-35 Reconsideration if interim relief is refused

Where an application for an interim order has been refused without a hearing (that is to say that the judge made the order considering the papers alone) then a party may request that decision be reconsidered.[95] Such reconsideration is requested by lodging an application notice, with the requisite fee, which must be served on all parties.[96] If an application is made for reconsideration after refusal on the papers then that reconsideration must take place at an oral hearing in court. The ACO will list the hearing as soon as possible and without taking into account the availability of the advocates.[97] Such hearings are usually short hearings of thirty minutes to one hour in length. Finally, it should be noted that the Court of Appeal in *R (MD (Afghanistan))* v *Secretary of State for the Home Department*[98] stated that this was not an optional procedure. A claimant who wishes to challenge a refusal on the papers must apply for reconsideration in the Administrative Court before they can appeal the refusal to the Court of Appeal. If there has been no oral renewal to a High Court judge, the judge of the Court of Appeal may well refuse permission

93 [2013] CP Rep 6.

94 Which the court did in a subsequent case: see C. Baksi, 'High Court refers firm to SRA after contempt ruling', 9 August 2013, *Law Society Gazette*. There have also been a number of other '*Hamid* Courts' since the original case of *Hamid*. See *R (Butt)* v *Secretary of State for the Home Department* [2014] EWHC 264 (Admin).

95 *R (MD (Afghanistan)* v *Secretary of State for the Home Department* [2012] 1 WLR 2422.

96 See the Ministry of Justice website for fees and forms.

97 See the ACO Wales Listing Policy in Annex B.

98 [2012] 1 WLR 2422 at para. 21.

to appeal the paper refusal of interim relief on the ground that the appropriate procedure has not been followed.

Administrative Court Office lawyer powers 5-36

Whilst the majority of orders made in Administrative Court proceedings will be made by a judge, the parties should be aware that certain case management orders can be made by Administrative Court Office lawyers, providing they are a qualified barrister or solicitor. The power for the ACO lawyer to make such orders can be found in CPR 54.1A.[99] The specific powers that the ACO lawyer may use are delegated by the President of the Queen's Bench Division[100] and, to date, include:

- extending or abridging time for filing documents;
- making orders giving directions;
- adding or removing parties from the claim;
- varying a judge's order for directions by consent;
- considering applications for abridgement of time for acknowledgement of service;
- determining applications for an extension of time in which to file a renewal notice;
- ordering a claim issued in Cardiff to be heard in Bristol or elsewhere on the Western Circuit where the ACO lawyer is satisfied that the claim would have been issued on the Western Circuit if an ACO existed on the Western Circuit;[101]
- transferring a case to the Upper Tribunal (Immigration Asylum Chamber); and
- approving consent orders (including orders to quash and costs).

If a party is not content with an order of the ACO lawyer then CPR 54.1A(5) provides that the party may request that the order is reviewed by a High Court judge. Such a review may take place on the papers or by way of an oral hearing in court.[102] The choice of how the review takes place is the choice of the party requesting the review. The request for a review must be made by filing the request

[99] The Civil Procedure Rule Committee has power to make rules providing for the exercise of the jurisdiction of any court by officers or other staff of the court (Civil Procedure Act 1997, Sch. 1, para. 2).

[100] CPR 54.1A(1).

[101] It is via this procedure that a large number of Western Circuit based cases are heard on the Western circuit, albeit the administration is based in Wales.

[102] CPR 54.1A(5) and (6).

in writing (a letter or application notice may be used) within seven days of the date on which the party was served with the ACO lawyer's order.[103]

THE ACKNOWLEDGEMENT OF SERVICE

5-37 Any person served with the claim form who wishes to take part[104] in the application for permission to apply for judicial review must file and serve an acknowledgement of service.[105] The acknowledgement of service must be filed at the ACO[106] within twenty-one days of the claim papers being served[107] and then served on all other parties no later than seven days thereafter. It should be noted that the parties cannot agree between themselves to extend this deadline,[108] it can only be extended by an order of the Court under CPR 3.1(2)(a).

The acknowledgement of service must:

1. set out the summary grounds for contesting the claim, if the party does contest.[109] As with the claim form, the summary grounds of defence may be part of the acknowledgement of service, or it may be included in an attached separate document;

2. if intending to contest the application for permission on the basis that it is highly likely that the outcome for the claimant would not have been substantially different if the conduct complained of had not occurred, set out a summary of the grounds for doing so;[110] and

3. state the name and address of any person the party believes to be an interested party.[111]

Evidence may be filed with the acknowledgement of service but it is not required.

When lodging the acknowledgement of service the party may also request further directions from the court.[112] The most common applications made at this

[103] CPR 54.1A(7).

[104] Filing an acknowledgement of service is probably wise for any defendant and any interested party, but it is not mandatory.

[105] CPR 54.8(2). See the Ministry of Justice website for forms and fees.

[106] The same provisions on address and manner of service apply to filing an acknowledgement of service as apply to the claim papers. See 5-15, 5-30 and Annex D.

[107] CPR 54.8(2)(a).

[108] CPR 54.8(3).

[109] CPR 54.8(4)(a)(i). Note the difference from the standard form acknowledgement of service in other Part 7 and Part 8 civil claims where there is no requirement to set out the defendant's grounds at such an early stage.

[110] CPR 54.8(4)(a)(ia).

[111] CPR 54.8(4)(a)(ii).

[112] CPR 54.8(4)(b).

stage are for the party's costs of preparing the acknowledgement of service[113] and for the discharge of any previously made injunctions.

If a party fails to file an acknowledgement of service within the twenty-one-day time limit then this will have three effects on the claim:

1. the papers will be sent to a judge to consider permission to apply for judicial review without waiting for that party to respond;[114]
2. in the event that permission falls to be considered at an oral hearing (see below) the party may not take part in that hearing without the permission of the Court;[115] and
3. the judge considering any substantive application for judicial review may consider this failure when considering costs.[116]

As soon as an acknowledgement of service has been filed by each party to the claim, or upon the expiry of the twenty-one-day time limit, the papers will be sent to a judge who will consider whether to grant permission to apply for judicial review by considering the papers alone.[117]

It should be noted that the judicial review procedure does not allow for the claimant to respond to the acknowledgement of service during the paper application process. As such the Administrative Court Office does not delay consideration of permission on the basis that the claimant may wish to reply to the acknowledgement of service. Any replies that are received before a case is sent to a judge to consider permission are added to the file but it is a matter for the judge as to whether the judge is content to consider the reply.

PERMISSION TO APPLY FOR JUDICIAL REVIEW

As noted in the overview earlier in the chapter, the claimant must obtain permis- 5-38
sion to apply for judicial review before substantively applying for judicial review. Permission is, potentially, a two-stage process: first, the paper application; secondly, the oral application.

113 See 7-8 to 7-16 on costs for notes on what to include in said application.

114 The norm is that this will only take a few days; it is not uncommon for consideration to take place only a day after the expiry of the twenty-one-day time limit. Ultimately it depends on judicial availability.

115 CPR 54.9(1)(a).

116 CPR 54.9(2).

117 The ACO in Wales has relatively good turnaround times. In 2014, the average turnaround time for consideration of paper permission by a judge was fifty days from the date the claim was lodged. (Statistics provided by the Administrative Court Office in Wales.)

5-39 The paper application

In the paper application process the claim papers (comprising the papers lodged by the claimant and any acknowledgement of service with appended grounds and evidence) are sent to a High Court judge who has been authorised to sit in the Administrative Court.[118] The judge will then consider the papers and determine whether to grant permission to apply for judicial review.

The judge may refuse permission if there is a bar to judicial review.[119] Otherwise the judge will consider whether the grounds put forward by the claimant are 'arguable' and therefore deserving of substantive consideration. The test to apply is not formally defined in either the Senior Courts Act 1981 or the Civil Procedure Rules, but a number of cases have supported the idea that the test is that of whether the case is arguable. In *R (FZ)* v *London Borough of Croydon*[120] the Court of Appeal defined the test as one where 'there is a realistic prospect or arguable case'.[121] In *Sharma* v *Brown-Antoine*,[122] Lord Bingham stated that a realistic prospect of bringing an arguable case must be established:

> The ordinary rule now is that the court will refuse leave to claim judicial review unless satisfied that there is an arguable ground for judicial review having a realistic prospect of success and not subject to a discretionary bar such as delay or an alternative remedy.[123]

A good summary of the test was given by Lord Donaldson MR in *R* v *Secretary of State for the Home Department, ex parte Begum*:[124]

> [A] judge who is confronted with an application for leave to apply for judicial review should grant it if he is clear that there is a point fit for further investigation on a full inter parties basis with all such evidence as is necessary on the facts and all such argument as is necessary on the law. If he is satisfied that there is no arguable case he should dismiss it. But there is an intermediate category of cases in which the judge, on looking at the papers which support the application, can very reasonably come to the conclusion that he really does not know whether there is or is not an arguable case, either because the facts are not clear or because he has not received sufficient assistance with the law to enable him

[118] This includes non-High Court judges who have been authorised by the Lord Chief Justice to sit as High Court judges under s. 9 of the Senior Courts Act 1981. For ease of reference this book refers simply to High Court judges.

[119] See the section on common bars to judicial review and time limits above at 5-8 to 5-13.

[120] [2011] EWCA Civ 59.

[121] [2011] EWCA Civ 59 at para. 6.

[122] [2007] 1 WLR 780.

[123] [2007] 1 WLR 780 at 787.

[124] [1990] COD 107.

> to be satisfied as to precisely what the relevant law is ... In those circumstances, where he is in doubt, the right course, in my view, is always to invite the putative respondent to attend and to make representation as to whether leave should or should not be granted.[125]

Even if a case is thought to be arguable, the judge must refuse permission if it is considered that the outcome for the applicant would not have been substantially different if the conduct complained of had not occurred.[126] The judge may disregard that requirement if it is appropriate to do so for reasons of exceptional public interest.[127] The judge may consider this point of their own volition and must do so if the defendant requests it.[128]

As a result of the broad discretion afforded to the judge considering permission there is no limit to the terms of the decision that they make. The following are the most common orders made by judges considering permission to apply for judicial review:

1. *Permission granted*
   The judge has determined that there is an arguable case and that the case will proceed to a substantive hearing of the application for judicial review. It should be noted that once permission has been granted then a defendant may not apply to set aside the grant of permission.[129]

2. *Permission refused*
   The judge has determined that none of the grounds advanced by the claimant are arguable and as such the claim should not proceed to a substantive hearing.[130] When a judge refuses permission on the papers they are required to give reasons for doing so (which usually form part of the order refusing permission).[131] The claimant should also be aware of the power of the judge to order they pay the costs of preparing an acknowledgement of service at this stage.[132]

[125] [1990] COD 107 at 108.

[126] Senior Courts Act 1981, s. 31(3F).

[127] Senior Courts Act 1981, s. 31(3E).

[128] Senior Courts Act 1981, s. 31(3C).

[129] CPR 54.13. This said, the court does retain its inherent jurisdiction to set aside orders but this is a rare course of action generally taken only where some procedural error has taken place, such as the defendant never having been served with the papers. The courts have been quick to discourage applications to set aside, even in the case of procedural error (*R* v *Secretary of State for the Home Department, ex parte Chinoy* [1992] 4 Admin LR 457).

[130] However, see the section on renewed oral permission hearings as a means of progressing the claim.

[131] CPR 54.12(2).

[132] See the section on costs in 7-15.

3. *Permission granted in part*
   The judge has determined that some of the grounds advanced by the claimant are arguable and as such those grounds will proceed to a substantive hearing of the application for judicial review. The other grounds have been refused permission.

4. *Permission adjourned to an oral hearing on notice*
   The judge has made no determination on the application for permission. Instead the application for permission will be considered in court with the claimant, and any other parties who wish to, making representations to the court. The judge may also adjourn into court to consider the question of whether to refuse permission on the grounds that it is highly likely that the outcome for the claimant would not have been substantially different if the conduct complained of had not occurred and whether there are reasons of exceptional public interest which make it nevertheless appropriate to grant permission.[133] The hearing will take a similar form to that of a renewed permission hearing (see below).

5. *Permission adjourned to a 'rolled up hearing'*
   The judge has made no determination on the application for permission. Instead the application for permission will be considered in court at the same time as the substantive application for judicial review. The parties should effectively treat this order as one adjourning the case to substantive hearing with the relevant rules on substantive applications applying, but it should not be forgotten that at the substantive hearing the judge may still refuse permission.

   This is a relatively unusual order and its use is often discouraged by judges. Whilst there is no definitive guidance on when such an order should be made, and thus no bar to a judge making such an order in any circumstances, the order is generally reserved for two occasions:

   a. when the judge does not have the requisite information to grant or refuse permission but due to the obvious need for an expedited decision it is desirable to deal with the substantive hearing straight away if permission is granted;[134]

   b. where there appears to be an arguable case but there may be a bar to judicial review, about which the judge would like to hear from the parties (such as delay in lodging the claim).

[133] CPR 54.11A.

[134] This should not be taken to suggest that the judge at the rolled up hearing will consider permission then the substantive hearing one after another formulaically. The judge is more likely to consider both points together and give a single judgment encompassing both points. The manner in which the hearing is dealt with is in the discretion of the judge.

Where a rolled up hearing is ordered the claimant will be asked by the ACO to sign an undertaking to pay the fee for the substantive application for judicial review,[135] which would then become payable in the event that the judge grants permission at the rolled up hearing.

6. *The application for permission is to be resubmitted*
The judge has made no determination on the application for permission. Instead the judge will request the parties to perform some act (such as file additional documents or representations) that the judge requires before proceeding to determine the application for permission. Once the act has been performed, or when the time limit for doing so has expired, the papers will be resubmitted to the judge to consider permission on the papers.

Broadly, if a claim is not ended by the parties before permission is considered, the permission application will end in one of two ways: permission being granted or permission being refused. If permission is granted, the parties will then prepare for a substantive hearing. If permission is refused the claimant should first consider whether, having considered the judge's reasons for refusing permission on the papers, they wish to take any further action. If they do not then after seven days the ACO will close the case and the court will take no further action (any injunctions or costs orders made will continue to have effect unless the court has ordered otherwise). If, having considered the reasons, the claimant wishes to continue to contest the matter they may not appeal, but they may request that the application for permission to apply for judicial review be reconsidered at an oral hearing.[136] There is one caveat to this. If the judge considers that the application for permission is 'totally without merit' then they may declare so in the order. The term 'totally without merit' has been defined broadly, rather than narrowly, as applying to a case that is bound to fail, not one that is necessarily abusive or vexatious.[137] By virtue of CPR 54.12(7), where a case is certified as 'totally without merit' this has the effect of removing the right to a renewed oral hearing, albeit appeal rights do then apply (see the section on appeals at 7-28).

Reconsideration at a renewed oral hearing 5-40

When the ACO serves an order refusing permission to apply for judicial review on the papers it will also include a renewal notice. If the claimant wishes to have their application for permission to apply for judicial review reconsidered at an oral hearing they should complete and send this form[138] back to the ACO within seven

[135] See the Ministry of Justice website for forms and fees.

[136] CPR 54.12(3).

[137] *R (Grace)* v *Secretary of State for the Home Department* [2014] 1 WLR 3432.

[138] Unusually the CPR does not require this form to be filed; in fact any notice that the claimant wishes to renew will suffice. Use of the form is, however, good practice and will prevent confusion.

days[139] of the date upon which it is served.[140] It is also good practice to send a copy to any party that filed an acknowledgement of service.

Upon receipt of the renewal notice the ACO caseworkers will proceed to list a renewed oral hearing in line with the ACO Wales listing policy.[141] The hearing cannot, without judicial order, take place without all parties being given at least two days' notice of the hearing.[142] The ACO will send notice to all parties of the date of the hearing. Hearings can be arranged all over Wales and parties are encouraged to request a venue if this makes matters easier or if the claim has strong local interest. To date the Administrative Court in Wales has held hearings in Caernarfon, Cardiff, Carmarthen, Mold, Newport, Port Talbot, Rhyl, Swansea, Welshpool and Wrexham.

The renewed hearing will take place in open court before a High Court judge. As the only consideration at the hearing is whether the case is arguable, it is expected that the hearing will be short, with the parties succinctly making their case. The standard time estimate for a permission hearing is one hour and so, if more time is required, the parties should ensure the ACO is informed as far in advance as possible. It is rare that permission hearings will be allocated a time estimate over two hours in length.

The claimant may represent themselves or be represented by a suitably qualified barrister or solicitor.[143] The defendant and/or any other party may attend and make representations (provided they filed an acknowledgement of service) but they are not obliged to do so.[144]

There is no definitive guideline on how the hearing will operate; it is generally a matter for the judge to determine. Sometimes the hearing will take a less formal stance with the parties effectively entering into discussions with the judge. Often the judge will ask questions of one or more parties in the middle of submissions to assist or clarify certain aspects. Generally, the hearing will follow a formal, set pattern:

1. the claimant will speak first, setting out his grounds and why he contends they are arguable;
2. the defendant will speak second, setting out why the grounds are not arguable;
3. any interested parties will speak third as necessary to support or contest anything said; and

[139] CPR 54.12(4).

[140] It should be noted that the date of service is not necessarily the date it was received by the claimant. Service is calculated as the second business day after the date the ACO sent the order (CPR 6.14).

[141] See Annex B for a copy of the policy.

[142] CPR 54.12(5).

[143] See the discussion on representations in the substantive hearing section later in this chapter for full details. The provisions are identical for all hearings in the Administrative Court.

[144] CPR PD 54A, para. 8.5.

4. the judge will give a short judgment either granting or refusing permission to apply for judicial review.

The test for granting permission is identical to the one applied by the judge considering permission to appeal on the papers (see above).

In the event that permission is refused at the renewed hearing then the claim has ended in the Administrative Court. In the event that the judge does give permission then the case will be adjourned to the substantive hearing.

THE SUBSTANTIVE JUDICIAL REVIEW

Documents and directions – from permission to the substantive hearing 5-41

Where a judge grants permission to apply for judicial review, either on the papers or after a renewed hearing, then the claim is (unless it is a rolled up hearing) adjourned to allow the parties, in conjunction with the ACO, to prepare the claim for the substantive judicial review hearing. When granting permission a judge will often give directions, as they may do under CPR 54.10(1), which may include a stay of proceedings[145] (that is to say no action will be taken on a case pending a specified event),[146] that the substantive hearing is to be heard by a Divisional Court (a court with two or more judges[147]), and/or directions on what the parties must do to prepare for the substantive hearing and within what timescale they must do it. Judicial directions will supersede any standard directions;[148] otherwise the following standard directions apply:

- The claimant must pay the required fee to continue the application for judicial review.[149] Failure to do so within seven days of permission being granted will result in the ACO sending the claimant a notice requiring payment within a set time frame (normally seven more days). Further failure will result in the claim being struck out without further order.[150]
- Any party who wishes to contest or support the claim must file and serve any detailed grounds and any written evidence within thirty-five days of permission being granted.[151]

[145] CPR 54.10(2)(a).

[146] For example, a claim may be stayed pending a decision in a different claim that raises the same point of law.

[147] See CPR 54.10(2)(b) and s. 66 of the Senior Courts Act 1981.

[148] CPR 3.1(2).

[149] See the Ministry of Justice website for the relevant fees.

[150] CPR 3.7(1)(d), (2), (3) and (4).

[151] CPR 54.14(1).

- If the claimant wishes to file further evidence or rely on further grounds then they must have the permission of the court to do so.[152] This provision requires the claimant to make an application (in line with the interim applications procedure above) where further documents or grounds not lodged with the claim papers are relied on. This rule also applies to other parties who are filing such documents outside the thirty-five-day time limit in CPR 54.14(1). The application may be dealt with in advance of the substantive hearing or at the hearing itself. The decision on when the application should be dealt with is ultimately a judicial one, but the parties should indicate a preference when lodging the application.
- The claimant must file and serve a skeleton argument no less than twenty-one **working** days[153] before the substantive hearing (see below for the contents of the skeleton argument).[154]
- The defendant and any other party wishing to make representations at the substantive hearing must file and serve a skeleton argument no less than fourteen **working** days before the substantive hearing. The skeleton argument must also contain the details outlined in CPR PD 54A, para. 15.3, although if the defendant agrees with the claimant on a point raised in the skeleton that may simply be noted without repeating in full (e.g. 'The defendant accepts the chronology outlined by the claimant in the claimant's skeleton argument').
- The claimant must file a paginated and indexed bundle of all relevant documents required for the hearing of the judicial review when filing the skeleton argument[155] (twenty-one working days before the hearing unless judicial order allows for a different time period). The bundle must also include those documents required by the defendant and any other party who is to make representations at the hearing.[156] The parties should be liaising as far before the substantive hearing as possible to agree what is required in the agreed bundle.

5-42 Contents of the skeleton argument

The skeleton argument must include, by virtue of CPR PD 54A, para. 15.3, the following:

[152] CPR 54.15 and CPR 54.16(2) respectively.

[153] Note the use of working days, not clear days as is the normal presumption in the CPR as per CPR 2.8(3). Working days is not defined in the CPR but is generally considered to be any day that the ACO is open. It is a quirk of the CPR that if the judge, when granting permission, expressly orders the skeleton argument to be filed twenty-one days before the substantive hearing, then it must be provided twenty-one calendar days before, not working days. This is because CPR 2.8(3) applies to all judicial orders and the judicial order will supersede the terms of CPR PD 54A.

[154] CPR PD 54A, para. 15.1.

[155] CPR PD 54A, para. 16.1.

[156] CPR PD 54A, para. 16.2.

1. a time estimate for the complete hearing, including delivery of judgment;
2. a list of issues (that is to say a succinct statement as to the grounds relied on);
3. a list of the legal points to be taken (together with any relevant authorities with page references to the passages relied on);
4. a chronology of events (with page references to the bundle of documents);
5. a list of essential documents for the advance reading of the court (with page references to the passages relied on) and a time estimate for that reading; and
6. a list of persons referred to.

The skeleton argument is the one official court document that may be lodged by email.[157]

Listing the substantive hearing 5-43

The hearing is listed in accordance with the procedure outlined in the ACO Wales listing policy (see Annex B), although the procedure may be modified by judicial order. Once a case has been listed the ACO will send all parties a listing notice informing them of the hearing date. Listing notices do not contain the start time for the hearing or the judge considering the case as this may be changed up until the day before the hearing. The start time and judge may be checked the day before the hearing after 2 pm on the court hearings section of the Ministry of Justice website.

Format of the substantive hearing 5-44

The general rule is that a hearing is to be in public[158] and thus any member of the public may attend and observe the hearing. However, a hearing, or any part of it, may be in private, thus excluding members of the public, if a judge makes such an order. The judge may do so if one of seven conditions exists:[159]

1. publicity would defeat the object of the hearing;
2. it involves matters relating to national security;
3. it involves confidential information (including information relating to personal financial matters) and publicity would damage that confidentiality;
4. a private hearing is necessary to protect the interests of any child or protected party;

[157] See Annex C for the ACO's contact details.

[158] CPR 39.2(1).

[159] CPR 39.2(3).

5. it is a hearing of an application made without notice and it would be unjust to any respondent for there to be a public hearing;
6. it involves uncontentious matters arising in the administration of trusts or in the administration of a deceased person's estate; or
7. the court considers a private hearing to be necessary, in the interests of justice.

The court may also order that the identity of any party or witness must not be disclosed if it considers non-disclosure necessary in order to protect the interests of that party or witness.[160]

The hearing of the claim normally takes place before a single judge in open court. An order may be made directing that the claim be heard by a Divisional Court of two judges. On rare occasions a three-judge court is formed, but this is generally reserved for matters of national importance. The time estimate for the hearing will vary from case to case and will ultimately be decided either by the judge granting permission or the ACO lawyer, with the assistance of the parties. Rarely will substantive hearings be allocated less than half a day. It is also rare for hearings to last more than two days. The majority will be allocated one day.

The format of the substantive hearing is entirely within the discretion of the judge. Generally, the hearing will follow a formal, set pattern:

1. the claimant will speak first, setting out their grounds;
2. the defendant will speak second, setting out the grounds of defence;
3. any interested parties will speak third as necessary to support or contest anything said; and
4. the claimant will have a right to reply to the other parties' submissions.

The substantive hearing will take place, generally, by examination of witness statements and written evidence without allowing oral evidence to be given in court and without allowing cross-examination of witnesses. This reflects the fact that judicial review is a consideration of the legality of a decision, not a reconsideration of the facts of a case. This said, the Administrative Court retains an inherent power to hear from witnesses and if necessary the court may do so.[161] It is emphasised that this course of action is rarely taken.

If all parties agree, the substantive consideration may take place without a hearing, the judge deciding the matter on the papers. This provision, outlined in CPR 54.18, is available, but is in practice rarely used.

[160] CPR 39.2(4).

[161] See the comments of Munby J (as he then was) in *R (PG)* v *London Borough of Ealing* [2002] ACD 48 at paras 20 and 21.

To succeed in the claim the claimant must prove, on the balance of probabilities, that the defendant has breached the principles of administrative law.[162]

Use of the Welsh language 5-45

A hearing before the Administrative Court in Wales is subject to the provisions of s. 22 of the Welsh Language Act 1993 and as such any person addressing the court may exercise their right to speak in Welsh. Under the Practice Direction Relating to the Use of the Welsh Language in Cases in the Civil Courts in Wales, the court may hear any person in Welsh on an ad hoc basis and without notice of the wish to speak in Welsh, providing all parties and the court consent.[163] In practice, the parties should inform the court as soon as possible,[164] preferably when lodging the claim papers. This will allow a judge or the ACO lawyer to make proper directions and allow the Administrative Court Office to make practical arrangements. There are bilingual judges who can consider such claims, but nonetheless, it is likely that an order will be made for simultaneous translation, where a translator appears in court translating into English.[165] The reason for this is that judicial reviews are public hearings, which anyone may attend[166] and watch. For open justice to take place those attending must also be able to understand proceedings.

Judgment 5-46

When the hearing is concluded the judge will either give judgment orally then and there, or sometimes after a short adjournment of a day or two (this is referred to as an *ex tempore* judgment). Alternatively, the judge may reserve judgment. If this option is chosen then the judge will prepare a full written judgment to be 'handed down' at a later date. The hand-down procedure is governed by CPR PD 40E. Two working days before the hand-down date the judge will provide a copy of the judgment to legal representatives in the case.[167] That draft is confidential and any breach of that confidentiality is a contempt of court.[168] The legal representatives

[162] Note, however, the point made later in the chapter under 'remedies' that a claimant may succeed in establishing a breach of the principles of administrative law, but that does not guarantee any remedy, which is within the court's discretion.

[163] Paragraph 1.2 of the Practice Direction Relating to the Use of the Welsh Language in Cases in the Civil Courts in Wales.

[164] Paragraph 1.3 of the Practice Direction Relating to the Use of the Welsh Language in Cases in the Civil Courts in Wales.

[165] This was the format ordered in the only judicial review to date where the claimant requested the hearing be conducted in Welsh: *R (Welsh Language Commissioner)* v *National Savings and Investments* [2014] PTSR D8 and is in line with HMCTS's Welsh language scheme 2013–2016, para. 5.26.

[166] This is the standard practice. Note what is said above in relation to private hearings.

[167] CPR PD 40E, para. 2.3.

[168] CPR PD 40E, para. 2.8.

may then propose any typographical corrections.[169] The final judgment will then be handed down in court. In practice this is simply a five-minute hearing at which the judge will make the final copy available and endorse it. The judge will not read the judgment verbatim. The judgments are then made publicly available to the legal publishers. A copy of every Administrative Court judgment is published at the website *www.bailii.org*, which does not charge a fee to access.

After judgment the parties are obliged to attempt to agree any consequential orders[170] (usually costs and permission to appeal).[171] The parties should submit any agreed order by 12 noon the day before the hand-down date.[172] If the parties can agree a final order then they need not attend the hand-down hearing.[173] If consequential orders cannot be agreed then the judge will decide consequential orders by considering representations. This may be done in one of two ways:

1. the parties may attend court on the date of handing down and make representations orally. The judge will then decide on consequential orders. The parties should inform the ACO in good time if they intend to do this, as time will need to be allocated for the judge to hear representations. Such a hearing would usually last from thirty minutes to an hour, rather than the five minutes set aside for a simple hand down; or

2. the parties may agree a final order that allows them to make written representations within a set time period on consequential orders, which the judge will then consider and, at a later date, make an order based on those written representations alone.

REMEDIES

5-47 There are six remedies available to a successful claimant in judicial review proceedings, all of which are listed in s. 31(1) and (4) of the Senior Courts Act 1981, as well as CPR Part 54:

- CPR 54.2(a) – a mandatory order (formerly known as *mandamus* – prerogative order);
- CPR 54.2(b) – a quashing order (formerly known as *certiorari* – prerogative order);

[169] CPR PD 40E, para. 3.1.

[170] CPR PD 40E, para. 4.1.

[171] See chapter 7 for a discussion of both.

[172] CPR PD 40E, para. 4.2.

[173] CPR PD 40E, para. 5.1.

- CPR 54.2(c) – a prohibiting order (formerly known as *prohibition* – prerogative order);
- CPR 54.3(1)(a) – a declaration;
- CPR 54.3(1)(b) – an injunction;
- CPR 54.3(2) – damages.

Mandatory orders 5-48

A mandatory order is the order the Court can make to compel a public body to act in a particular way. A particularly famous example of a mandatory order can be found in the last decision of the House of Lords (before it reformed as the Supreme Court), *R (Purdy)* v *Director of Public Prosecutions*.[174] In *Purdy*, the claimant, who suffered from a debilitating illness, had declared her wish to travel to a country where assisted suicide was lawful to end her life. She sought information in order to make a decision about whether to ask for her husband's assistance, which the DPP declined to give. The House of Lords determined that the code for Crown prosecutors did not satisfy the requirements of article 8 of the European Convention on Human Rights 1950. The court made a mandatory order requiring the Director of Public Prosecutions to comply with his duty under the Human Rights Act 1998 and promulgate an offence-specific policy identifying the circumstances to be taken into account in deciding whether to begin a prosecution for assisted suicide.

Whilst the discretion of the court is at the centre of what remedy will be applied, mandatory orders are rarely used where a statutory duty has not been breached. Permissive powers exercised contrary to the principles of administrative law are far more likely to be quashed and remitted to the decision maker for determination, as is a decision involving the improper use of discretion, as it may be that the courts will then be seen to fetter the discretion of the public body decision maker. The court will often decline a mandatory order on this basis. See, for example, *R (Van Hoogstraten)* v *Governor of Belmarsh Prison*,[175] where Jackson J (as he then was) refused to make a mandatory order requiring the defendant to allow the claimant's Italian qualified lawyer to make visits to him whilst imprisoned, despite finding that an Italian advocate was a qualified legal adviser within the terms of the Prison Service Rules 1999 and as such refusing access was a breach of the 1999 Rules. Jackson J refused the mandatory order because the Governor was best placed to assess whether that particular legal adviser should be permitted access.

[174] [2010] 1 AC 345.

[175] [2003] 1 WLR 263.

5-49 Quashing order

A quashing order is the order the court may use to declare that the decision challenged has no lawful force and, therefore, does not have effect. The decision is, to use the language of the order, quashed. The quashing order is the remedy sought in the vast majority of judicial review cases, as it will strike down the decision that the claimant contends is unlawful.

Where the decision maker has no power to reconsider the decision (where it is *functus officio*), a quashing order must be sought from the Administrative Court even if the decision maker accepts that the decision is unlawful.[176]

The practice the court will often take after making a quashing order, as outlined in s. 31(5)(a) of the Senior Courts Act 1981 and CPR 54.19(2)(a), will be to remit the matter to the decision maker and direct it to reconsider the matter and reach a fresh decision in accordance with the judgment of the court. An example of this type of order can be found in the majority of cases where the claimant is successful in judicial review. As an illustrative example, see *R (Mavalon Care Ltd)* v *Pembrokeshire County Council*.[177] In *Mavalon*, Beaston J (as he then was) determined that it was appropriate to quash and remit a decision concerning the fee to be paid by a local authority to private residential care home providers. The local authority had failed to have regard to Welsh Government guidance and a previous decision of the Administrative Court giving guidance on the appropriate methodology for calculating residential home fees. As a result the local authority failed to ask itself the right questions and the decision was based on irrelevant factors, which the council took into account as the result of a mistaken appreciation of the position. Consideration of the rate would, after the judgment, have been reconsidered by the local authority with the court directing the defendant as to the proper guidance to consider.

The court has power, under s. 31(5)(b) of the Senior Courts Act 1981 and CPR 54.19(2)(b), to substitute its own decision for the decision that has been quashed. By virtue of s. 31(5A) of the Senior Courts Act 1981, this power is only exercisable against the decisions of the inferior courts or tribunals, only on the grounds of error of law, and only where there is only one possible decision now open to the decision maker (and thus remittal would prove otiose). See, for example, *Newcombe* v *Crown Prosecution Service*.[178] A district judge (magistrates' court) had been wrong to restrict the costs of the claimant, against whom a charge for assault occasioning actual bodily harm had been dismissed. The district judge had restricted the costs on the basis that the claimant had acted unreasonably by not indicating a willingness to be bound over earlier than the day of his trial. However, prior to the complainant's refusal to give evidence on the day of the trial, the prosecution had never suggested that a bind-over would be acceptable.

[176] See *R (Baker)* v *Police Appeals Tribunal* [2013] EWHC 718 (Admin) at paras 26 and 27.

[177] [2012] ACD 45.

[178] [2013] EWHC 2160 (Admin).

As the only option for the Administrative Court was to allow costs there would have been little point in remitting the matter.

Prohibiting order 5-50

A prohibiting order is similar in function to a quashing order, save that it applies to actions that the public body has indicated an intention to take, but has not yet taken. The quashing order is required where the horse has bolted; the prohibiting order shuts the door before it has done so. As a result of its limited application (the horse has usually bolted) and the availability of injunctions, this remedy is in decline. An example of a case where a prohibiting order was needed can be found in *R* v *Dudley Magistrates' Court, ex parte Gillard*,[179] where the court acted to prevent a magistrates' court unlawfully committing the claimant to the Crown Court for trial when the offence alleged was one that was only triable in the magistrates' court.

Declaration 5-51

There are two types of declaration available as a remedy: ordinary declarations and declarations of incompatibility.

Ordinary declaration 5-52

A declaration is a statement by the court as to what the law on a particular point is, or conversely what it is not. Using the declaratory remedy the Administrative Court can examine an act (including an act announced but not yet taken) of a public body and formally declare that it is lawful, or unlawful.[180] A declaration does not have any coercive effect and whilst a public body must note and comply with the declaration, it is not obliged to take any action (unless, of course, another public law remedy is ordered). A declaration can be a remedy on its own,[181] thus giving a statement as to the law but not actually changing the status quo by making a quashing or mandatory order.

The statutory considerations for when a declaration is appropriate can be found in s. 31(2) of the Senior Courts Act 1981. A declaration may be granted if it would be just and convenient for the declaration to be made considering:

a. the nature of the matters,

[179] [1986] AC 442.

[180] When broken down further the declarations take many forms which fall under the banner of lawfulness: declarations as to the validity of decisions, declarations as to the consequences of an action, advisory declarations (whereby the court may give guidance on the effect of an intended future action. For full discussion of the various types of declaration, see H. Woolf et al., *Zamir & Woolf: The Declaratory Judgment* (4th edn) (Sweet & Maxwell, 2011).

[181] CPR 40.20.

b. the nature of the parties against whom relief may be granted, and
c. all the circumstances of the case.

The stipulation above is a somewhat generically phrased provision. As such, in *Re F*,[182] Lord Goff outlined further, more specific principles that ensured that academic (unless there is a point of public law principle to be decided) or unconsidered questions of law could not be subject to declaratory relief:

> [A] declaration will not be granted where the question under consideration is not a real question, nor where the person seeking the declaration has no real interest in it, nor where the declaration is sought without proper argument, e.g. in default of defence or on admissions or by consent.[183]

A good, Welsh example case for ordinary declarations is *R (Clive Rees Associates)* v *Swansea Magistrates' Court*.[184] The Divisional Court found that magistrates had erred in transferring representation orders (commonly known as legal aid) from one firm of solicitors to another where they had failed to consider the relevant statutory test and where there was no reason or explanation given as to why those clients had lost confidence in their original solicitors. However, considering that an order quashing the magistrates' decision would have reinstated the claimant solicitors and would have effected a second change of representation causing additional cost to the public and possibly disruption to the criminal proceedings, the appropriate remedy was declaratory relief, declaring that the decisions transferring the representation orders were made under an error of law.

5-53 Declaration of incompatibility

With the implementation of s. 4 of the Human Rights Act 1998, a new form of declaratory remedy was introduced: the declaration of incompatibility. If the court determines that any Act of the UK Parliament[185] is incompatible with a Convention right (that is to say a right under the European Convention on Human Rights and Fundamental Freedoms 1950 ('ECHR')), it may make a declaration of that incompatibility.[186] Similarly, a declaration may be made in relation to subordinate legislation if it is further satisfied that (disregarding any possibility of revocation) the Act

[182] [1990] 2 AC 1.

[183] [1990] 2 AC 1 at 82.

[184] [2012] ACD 25.

[185] A provision in an Assembly Act which is incompatible with a Convention right is not within competence. A challenge to such a provision on the grounds of incompatibility is therefore a devolution issue as defined in Schedule 9 to GOWA 2006. See 6-22, for the provisions for determining a devolution issue in court proceedings and 4-8 for a discussion of the competence of the National Assembly.

[186] Human Rights Act 1998, s. 4(1) and (2).

of the UK Parliament concerned prevents removal of the incompatibility.[187] The declaration of incompatibility is, in reality, a statutory form of an ordinary declaration. As such, the principles behind ordinary declarations, such as the requirement that a declaration will not be made in hypothetical circumstances, still apply.[188]

The practical effect of a declaration of incompatibility is similar to that of ordinary declarations, in that it has no coercive effect. By virtue of s. 4(6) of the Human Rights Act 1998, a declaration of incompatibility does not affect the validity, continuing operation or enforcement of the provision in respect of which it is given and it is not binding on the parties to the proceedings in which it is made. The declaration acts to inform Parliament of the dichotomy in order that it may act appropriately, thus preserving the sovereignty of Parliament. Declarations of incompatibility are rarely sought and even more rarely granted. Senior judiciary have commented that 'a declaration of incompatibility is a measure of last resort which must be avoided unless it is plainly impossible to do so'.[189]

Examples of situations where a declaration of incompatibility has been made are rare. A fairly famous example can be found in *A* v *Secretary of State for the Home Department*[190] (colloquially known as 'the Belmarsh case'), where it was declared that s. 23 of the Anti-terrorism, Crime and Security Act 2001 was incompatible with articles 5 (right to liberty) and 14 (freedom from discrimination) of the ECHR in that it permitted detention of suspected international terrorists in a way that discriminated on the ground of nationality or immigration status.

The procedure for applying for a declaration of incompatibility in judicial review proceedings can be found in CPR PD 16, CPR 19.4A, CPR PD 19A and CPR PD 54A. The claimant must note the fact that they are applying for a declaration of incompatibility in the remedies section of the claim form, give precise details of the Convention right which has allegedly been infringed, and the provision which is alleged to have infringed the Convention right.[191]

It is submitted that the claimant should consider making the Crown, via the relevant Secretary of State, an interested party from the outset to allow for proper participation. In any event, where an application for a declaration has been made, or of its own volition, the court:

[187] Human Rights Act 1998, s. 4(3) and (4). See, for example, *R (T)* v *Chief Constable of Greater Manchester* [2014] 3 WLR 96 at para. 54 where the Supreme Court declined to strike down the Rehabilitation of Offenders Act 1974 (Exceptions) Order 1975, which made exceptions to the Rehabilitation of Offenders Act 1974 to force the disclosure of spent convictions and cautions in specified circumstances. The primary legislation did not prevent the removal of the incompatibility in the subordinate legislation.

[188] See, for example, *Taylor* v *Lancashire County Council* [2005] 1 WLR 2668 at paras 42–44.

[189] Per Lord Slynn, *R* v *A* [2002] 1 AC 45 at 68.

[190] [2005] 2 AC 68.

[191] CPR PD 16, paras 15.1(2)(a), (c)(i) and (d).

- *may* at any stage (although it appears the permission stage would be the most suitable) consider whether notice[192] should be given to the Crown[193] (presuming the Crown is not already a party); and
- if it is considering making a declaration of incompatibility and the Crown is not already a party, *must* inform the relevant minister and allow them the chance to intervene and make representations.[194]

CPR 19.4A(1) suggests that twenty-one days' notice should be given to the relevant minister to allow them to consider whether they wish to intervene. CPR PD 19A, para. 6.4(2) informs that the notice will be in the form directed by the court but will normally include the directions given by the court and all the statements of case in the claim. The notice must also be served on all parties. The claimant is only required to prepare and serve the notice if directed to do so by the court.[195] Otherwise it is the responsibility of the court.

If the Crown wishes to intervene it must serve written notice of the fact that it wishes to intervene within the time period allowed by the court.[196] The Crown has an automatic right to intervene where it does give such notice.[197]

5-54 Injunctions

An injunction is an order by the court to act in a particular way (a positive injunction) or to refrain from acting in a particular way (a negative injunction). It is a remedy that is not confined to judicial review,[198] although it is available in judicial review. An injunction is a remedy to prevent the commission or the continuance of a wrong in private law. As a public body can commit private wrongs, an injunction can issue against it in public law proceedings. If, for instance, a public body had engaged in an activity which would constitute a nuisance at common law, the decision to do so would be subject to judicial review, and an injunction could prevent the public body from acting upon or continuing to act upon that decision.

[192] Any notice should be served on the relevant department in accordance with the annex to CPR 66 and the Crown Proceedings Act 1947: CPR PD 19A, para. 6.4(1). See Annex D of this work for the relevant addresses.

[193] CPR 54A PD, para. 8.2 and CPR PD 19A, para. 6.1.

[194] Human Rights Act 1998, s. 5(1). Notably, pursuant to s. 5(2) of the 1998 Act, a minister of the UK Government, as well as the devolved administrations in Scotland and Northern Ireland, has a right to intervene once notified under s. 5(1). It appears that this provision is extended to cover the Welsh Ministers by CPR PD 19A, para. 6.4(4).

[195] CPR PD 19A, para. 6.4(3).

[196] CPR PD 19A, para. 6.5.

[197] Human Rights Act 1998, s. 5(1) and CPR 19.4A(2).

[198] Save for an injunction under s. 30(1) of the Senior Courts Act 1981 to prevent someone acting in an office to which they have no entitlement.

The express power to grant injunctions in judicial review proceedings is provided in s. 31(2) of the Senior Courts Act 1981. An injunction may be granted if it would be just and convenient for the declaration to be made considering:

a. the nature of the matters;
b. the nature of the parties against whom relief may be granted; and
c. all the circumstances of the case.

As a matter of practice injunctions tend to be used more as interim orders than final remedies as the same outcome can also be obtained by a mandatory order or a prohibiting order. The advantage that an injunction has over one of the prerogative remedies is that it can be made for a finite period, thus requiring a public body to act, or not to act, in a particular way until a specified date or until it has complied with a particular act.

Damages 5-55

Whilst primarily a private law remedy, the Administrative Court does have power to award and assess damages. The rationale behind this power is that in a case where a public law remedy is sought as well as damages then it would be an excessive use of the parties' and the court's time to have separate proceedings running. As a result the right to seek damages in judicial review proceedings comes with two provisos:

1. the claimant may only seek damages if they are also seeking another public law remedy, not just damages alone;[199] and
2. the claimant may only seek damages if a private law claim for damages on the same basis would have succeeded (had it been brought in the County Court or appropriate division of the High Court).[200]

The second rule backs the principle that there is no right to damages for an unlawful action in public law per se; it is only where the unlawful public law action results in a private law action. Claims for damages will fall broadly into one of four situations:

- the public authority has committed a tort when exercising its functions;[201]

[199] CPR 54.3(2).

[200] Senior Courts Act 1981, s. 31(4).

[201] A common example is the tort of false imprisonment. Public authorities are often required to detain persons and in numerous contexts (criminal, immigration, mental health). Where the public body does so unlawfully in public law terms, they will also have committed the tort of false imprisonment. See *R* v *Governor of Durham Prison, ex parte Hardial Singh* [1984] 1 WLR 704 for details of the principles of public law based false imprisonment.

- the public authority is under some obligation to repay monies paid to it by the claimant;[202]
- the public authority has breached a right under the European Convention on Human Rights and Fundamental Freedoms 1950 and the court considers it just and appropriate to award damages under s. 8(1) of the Human Rights Act 1998;[203]
- the public body has committed an actionable breach of European law.[204]

A discussion of the principles applicable in all of these situations is best left to separate, more specific works.[205]

It should be noted that a frequently used device of the Administrative Court, where the assessment and award of damages is likely to be a lengthy procedure, is to determine the public law question and then transfer the claim under CPR 54.20 to either the County Court or appropriate division of the High Court to determine the question of damages.

Procedural points on remedies

5-56 ### Multiple remedies

The court may grant more than one remedy where it is deemed appropriate to do so, and indeed it often does so; a declaration and a quashing order, or a quashing order and a mandatory order are often made in tandem.

5-57 ### Remedies where the outcome would not be substantially different

If the claimant is successful in judicial review proceedings, but the court considers that it is highly likely that the outcome for the claimant would not be substantially

[202] This is not a commonly requested remedy in the Administrative Court. One example is the repayment of tax unlawfully claimed: see *Test Claimants in the FII Group Litigation* v *Revenue and Customs Commissioners* [2012] 2 AC 337.

[203] Again, an infrequently pursued right, perhaps because most situations where Convention rights will be breached will also be covered by tortuous liability (false imprisonment, nuisance etc.). For an analysis of the relevant provisions, see *R (Anufrijeva)* v *Southwark London Borough Council* [2004] QB 1124. For general discussion, see paras 19-081 to 19-100 of *De Smith's Judicial Review*.

[204] Where a public authority's action both breaches European law and causes some damage (note there must be causation), then damages are payable: see *R* v *Secretary of State for Transport, ex parte Factortame Ltd* (C-48/93) [1996] QB 404 at paras 51 and 52.

[205] A good overview all these principles is given in chapter 19 of *De Smith's Judicial Review*. For specific texts, the following are among some of the leading texts on the subjects: Tort: M. Jones (ed.), *Clerk and Lindsell on Torts* (21st edn) (Sweet & Maxwell, 2015). Law of Restitution and Unjust Enrichment: A. Burrows, *A Restatement of the English Law of Unjust Enrichment* (Oxford University Press, 2013). Human Rights: J. Beatson et al., *Human Rights: Judicial Protection in the United Kingdom* (Sweet & Maxwell, 2008). EU Law: P. Craig and G. De Burca, *EU Law: Text, Cases, and Materials* (6th edn) (Oxford University Press, 2015).

different, the court must refuse to grant any form of relief and must not award damages.[206] The court may only disregard this requirement if it considers it appropriate to do so for reasons of exceptional public interest.[207]

Discretionary remedies 5-58

Save for damages, which retains its private law roots (as discussed above), the public law remedies are discretionary remedies and as such the court is not obliged to grant a remedy at all, even if the claimant is successful in their application for judicial review. There is a presumption that a successful claimant will be granted some form of relief but where it is not fair or just to grant a remedy the court may exercise its discretion not to grant a remedy.[208] In *R* v *HM Coroner for Inner London South District, ex parte Douglas-Williams*[209] the Court of Appeal gave a wide interpretation to the relevant test to be applied when refusing to grant relief, simply stating that it should be 'necessary or desirable to do so in the interests of justice'.[210] In *R (Baker)* v *Police Appeals Tribunal*,[211] Leggatt J outlined[212] four situations where the court may be persuaded not to grant relief:

- Where the claimant has delayed in filing the application for judicial review and the court considers that the granting of the relief sought would be likely to cause substantial hardship to, or substantially prejudice the rights of, any person or would be detrimental to good administration.[213]
- The error of law made by the public body was not material to its decision.[214]

206 Senior Courts Act 1981, s. 31(2A).

207 Senior Courts Act 1981, s. 31(2B).

208 As Sedley J noted in *R* v *Lincolnshire CC, ex parte Atkinson* [1996] 8 Admin LR 529 at 550: 'To refuse relief where an error of law by a public authority has been demonstrated is an unusual and strong thing; but there is no doubt that it can be done'.

209 [1999] 1 All ER 344.

210 [1999] 1 All ER 344 at 347.

211 [2013] EWHC 718 (Admin).

212 [2013] EWHC 718 (Admin) at paras 28–31.

213 Senior Courts Act 1981, s. 31(6).

214 For example, see *R* v *Knightsbridge Crown Court, ex parte Marcrest Properties* [1983] 1 WLR 300. The licensing justices cancelled a licence to run a casino after finding that the licensee had engaged in unlawful conduct. An appeal to the Crown Court was dismissed. On judicial review, it was pointed out that the unlawful conduct had occurred during the period of the previous licence. There had therefore been an error in holding that the premises had been used for an unlawful purpose during the licence period. The court was nevertheless satisfied that, even if this error had not been made, the licence would still have been cancelled because it had been established that the licensee was not a fit and proper person. The licensee had not suffered any injustice as a result of the error and the court declined to make a quashing the order.

- The remedy would serve no useful practical purpose.[215]
- The claimant has suffered no harm or prejudice.[216]

In *Baker*, Leggatt J was referring to quashing orders and was clear that this was not an exhaustive list. These situations do, nonetheless, outline principles that may fairly be applied to the exercise of the discretion to grant relief.

5-59 Orders against the Crown

The prerogative orders (mandatory, quashing and prohibiting orders) and injunctions cannot be made against the Crown directly[217] but they can be made against an officer of the Crown, including a minister.

5-60 Enforcement

Failure to comply with an order of the court granting one of these remedies can be treated as a contempt of court.[218]

5-61 THE ROLE OF THE UPPER TRIBUNAL IN JUDICIAL REVIEW PROCEEDINGS

The Upper Tribunal's judicial review remit

Under the Tribunals, Courts and Enforcement Act 2007 the Upper Tribunal has acquired a judicial review jurisdiction in certain circumstances. The principles of administrative law and judicial review remain relevant to such claims but instead the claim must be conducted in the Upper Tribunal. The Administrative Court has specific power, under s. 31A of the Senior Courts Act 1981, to transfer claims to the Upper Tribunal. Where a claim should have been lodged in the Upper Tribunal it is a mandatory power, but s. 31A also includes a discretionary power to transfer to the Upper Tribunal where the mandatory features are not present. This discretionary power is more often used where questions of fact are relevant and thus the Upper Tribunal's jurisdiction appears more appropriate – for example, cases

[215] For example, see *R* v *North West Thames RHA, ex parte Daniels* [1993] 4 Med LR 364, where the court refused to quash a decision to close a bone marrow unit, despite an unlawful consultation, as staff changes in the unit meant that treatment could not be obtained for the claimant in any event.

[216] For example, see *R (Laporte)* v *Newham London Borough Council* [2004] EWHC 227 (Admin), where the claimant had suffered no prejudice as a result of a procedural error (two allegations, amongst others, of nuisance she was alleged to have committed had not been put to her), since she had been given details of the allegations and had had the opportunity to respond to them and it was held that even without the nuisance the council would have come to the same decision anyway.

[217] Crown Proceedings Act 1947, s. 40.

[218] See *R* v *Poplar MBC, ex parte London CC (No. 2)* [1922] 1 KB 95 and *Re M* [1994] 1 AC 377 for examples of cases where a public body was found to be in contempt for not complying with a prerogative writ.

where the age of a claimant must be determined are fairly routinely transferred to the Upper Tribunal.[219]

The procedural landscape is no longer contained in CPR 54, but instead in the Tribunal Procedure (Upper Tribunal) Rules 2008 ('UTR') and associated practice directions. There are subtle changes to be aware of: for example, judges are referred to in court as 'Sir' or 'Madam',[220] claimants are referred to as applicants, and defendants as respondents. However, the judicial review provisions are very similar to the provisions of CPR 54. As such, it is safe to assume that proceedings will progress in largely the same way as in the Administrative Court (see the overview diagram at Figure 5.1 above). Table 5.1 is a quick guide to the relevant CPR and their corresponding rule under the UTR:

Table 5.1 Judicial review rules (CPR and UTR)

Provision	**CPR**	**UTR**
Application for permission must be lodged promptly and in any Event within three months	54.5(1)	28(2)
Contents of the judicial review papers	54.6	28(4)–(6)
Case management orders can be made by an ACO or UT(IAC) lawyer	54.1A(1)	4(1)
Power for a judge to review an order by a lawyer	54.1A(5)	4(3)
Application for permission must be served within 7/9* days of filing	54.7	28A(2)
Any acknowledgement of service must be filed within 21 days receipt of application for permission†	54.8(2)	29(1)
Right to oral reconsideration where permission is not granted	54.12(3)	30(3)–(4)
Application for oral reconsideration must be served within 7/9/14* days of receipt of notice	54.12(4)	30(5)
No right to reconsideration in 'totally without merit' cases	54.12(7)	30(4A)
Where permission has been granted, detailed response and evidence to be filed within 35 days	54.14(1)	31(2)

* 7 days in the Administrative Court, 9 days in the UT(IAC) and (where applicable) 14 days in the UT(AAC).

† In the UT(IAC), whilst the UTR provides for a 21-day time limit, the time limit is effectively extended to 42 days by the case of *R (Kumar)* v *Secretary of State for the Home Department (Acknowledgement of Service; Tribunal Arrangements) (IJR)* [2014] UKUT 104.

[219] See *R (A)* v *Croydon London Borough Council* [2009] 1 WLR 2557 and *R (FZ)* v *London Borough of Croydon* [2011] PTSR 748.

[220] Although a convention has developed whereby a High Court or Court of Appeal judge sitting in the Upper Tribunal continues to be referred to as 'My Lord/My Lady'.

In the Upper Tribunal (Immigration and Asylum Chamber) ('UT(IAC)') a practice direction has been issued to supplement the above provisions, and keep judicial review procedures in UT(IAC) in line with the procedure in the Administrative Court. The practice direction and its relevant corresponding CPR are outlined in Table 5.2:

Table 5.2 Judicial review rules (CPR and Practice Direction: Immigration Judicial Review in the Immigration and Asylum Chamber of the Upper Tribunal (1 November 2013))

Provision	CPR	PD
Two copies of a paginated and indexed bundle must be filed	PD 54A, para 5.9	5.1
Skeleton argument contents and time limits for filing	PD 54A, paras 15.1–15.3	8.1–8.3
Agreed, paginated and indexed bundle to be provided for the Substantive hearing	PD 54A para 16.1–16.2	9.1

The Upper Tribunal usually sits with a single judge of the Upper Tribunal[221] considering the case, although on occasion it does sit with more than one judge.

The Upper Tribunal, when considering a judicial review, has the power to order all the remedies that the Administrative Court has power to order,[222] including the award of damages.[223] Such an order has the same effect as the corresponding relief granted by the Administrative Court on an application for judicial review[224] and the procedural provisions for those remedies (as discussed above) also apply to the Upper Tribunal.[225]

Whilst the procedural provisions of the Administrative Court and the Upper Tribunal are very similar, there are specific provisions that expressly allocate judicial reviews to the Upper Tribunal. It is appropriate to briefly examine the circumstances in which judicial reviews must be conducted in the Upper Tribunal.

5-62 The Upper Tribunal (Administrative Appeals Chamber)

The Upper Tribunal (Administrative Appeals Chamber) ('UT(AAC)') has possessed a judicial review jurisdiction since 3 November 2008 when the Lord Chief Justice's

[221] The full list of who may sit as an Upper Tribunal judge can be found in ss. 5 and 6 of the Tribunals, Courts and Enforcement Act 2007. More often than not an Upper Tribunal judge will be a judge appointed directly to the Upper Tribunal, a Court of Appeal judge, a High Court judge or a circuit judge.

[222] Tribunals, Courts and Enforcement Act 2007, s. 15(1).

[223] Tribunals, Courts and Enforcement Act 2007, s. 16(6).

[224] Tribunals, Courts and Enforcement Act 2007, s. 15(3).

[225] Tribunals, Courts and Enforcement Act 2007, s. 15(4) and (5).

Practice Direction, *Practice Direction (Upper Tribunal: Judicial Review Jurisdiction)*,[226] pursuant to s. 18(6) of the Tribunals, Courts and Enforcement Act 2007, came into force. The practice direction requires judicial review in the following circumstances to be commenced and determined in the UT(AAC):

a. any decision of the First-tier Tribunal on an appeal made in the exercise of a right conferred by the Criminal Injuries Compensation Scheme in compliance with s. 5(1) of the Criminal Injuries Compensation Act 1995 (appeals against decisions on reviews); and

b. decisions of the First-tier Tribunal where there is no right of appeal to the Upper Tribunal and that decision is not an excluded decision within paragraph (b), (c) or (f) of s. 11(5) of the 2007 Act (appeals against national security certificates or any decision of the First-tier Tribunal that is of a description specified in an order made by the Lord Chancellor).

This direction does not have effect where an application seeks a declaration of incompatibility.

Applications for judicial review in the UT(AAC) can be lodged in Cardiff or London.[227] Whilst UT(AAC) claims can be lodged in Cardiff it should be noted that this is simply a lodging facility and the Cardiff Civil Justice Centre staff will simply forward the claim for processing and administration to the London centre. Hearings can be accommodated in Wales but this must be sought by contacting the London centre, indeed all enquiries should be made to the London centre.

The Upper Tribunal (Immigration and Asylum Chamber) 5-63

The Upper Tribunal (Immigration and Asylum Chamber) ('UT(IAC)') came into possession of a fuller judicial review remit as of 1 November 2013. Before then only a certain class of claims, known as 'fresh claims' cases, were dealt with by the UT(IAC).[228] On 1 November 2013 the Lord Chief Justice's Practice Direction[229] of 29 August 2013 came into force. The practice direction required filing in, or mandatory transfer to, the UT(IAC) of any application for permission to apply for judicial review and any substantive application for judicial review that calls into question:

[226] [2009] 1 WLR 327.

[227] See Annex C for contact details.

[228] See the Lord Chief Justice's Practice Direction, *Practice Direction (Sen Cts: Upper Tribunal: Judicial Review Jurisdiction)* [2012] 1 WLR 16 for the terms of the classes of claims allocated. Note that this practice direction has now been overtaken by the modern provision.

[229] Lord Chief Justice's Practice Direction: Jurisdiction of the Upper Tribunal under s. 18 of the Tribunals, Courts and Enforcement Act 2007 and Mandatory Transfer of Judicial Review applications to the Upper Tribunal under s. 31A(2) of the Senior Courts Act 1981, dated 29 August 2013.

- a decision made under the Immigration Acts[230] or any instrument having effect, whether wholly or partly, under an enactment within the Immigration Acts, or otherwise relating to leave to enter or remain in the UK;
- a decision made of the Immigration and Asylum Chamber of the First-tier Tribunal, from which no appeal lies to the Upper Tribunal.

However, any application which comprises or includes the following does not come under the jurisdiction of the Upper Tribunal:

- a challenge of the validity of primary or subordinate legislation (or of immigration rules);
- a challenge to the lawfulness of detention;
- a challenge to a decision concerning inclusion on the register of licensed Sponsors maintained by the UKBA;
- a challenge to a decision that determines British citizenship;
- a challenge to a decision relating to asylum support or accommodation;
- a challenge to the decision of the Upper Tribunal;
- a challenge to a decision of the Special Immigration Appeals Commission; and
- an application for a declaration of incompatibility under s. 4 of the Human Rights Act 1998.

To retain the principle of access to justice that sparked regionalisation of the Administrative Court,[231] it was decided that the out-of-London ACOs would retain the responsibility for the processing and administration of the UT(IAC) judicial review cases outside London. As such, as of 1 November 2013, the ACO in Wales took on a dual responsibility and it also operates as the UT(IAC) in Wales. The ACO caseworkers are also the UT(IAC) caseworkers and the ACO lawyer for Wales is also a UT(IAC) lawyer for Wales. It is important to emphasise that this only applies with regards to the UT(IAC)'s judicial review jurisdiction. Its appellate jurisdiction (considering appeals from the first-tier tribunal on immigration and asylum cases) remains as it was, that is to say conducted from London.

[230] Defined in Schedule 1 to the Interpretation Act 1978 (which refers to s. 61 of the UK Borders Act 2007) as: Immigration Act 1971, Immigration Act 1988, Asylum and Immigration Appeals Act 1993, Asylum and Immigration Act 1996, Immigration and Asylum Act 1999, Nationality, Immigration and Asylum Act 2002, Asylum and Immigration (Treatment of Claimants, etc.) Act 2004, Immigration, Asylum and Nationality Act 2006, UK Borders Act 2007 and the Immigration Act 2014. See the Practice Direction itself for the transitional provisions relating to the relevant claims lodged in the ACO before 1 November 2013.

[231] See chapter 2 for a discussion of this principle.

The implementation of the UT(IAC)'s fuller judicial review powers represents a huge transfer of work from the ACO to the UT(IAC). The impetus for the change came from the vast numbers of immigration and asylum claims being lodged in the ACO in London: from 1 May 2010 to 30 April 2011 a total of 6,983 immigration and asylum claims were lodged in the ACO in London.[232]

The Upper Tribunal as a defendant in judicial review proceedings 5-64

When the Upper Tribunal acquired a judicial review remit a question was asked by many. Is the Upper Tribunal an equivalent of the High Court or is it an inferior court and thus subject to judicial review? The question was decided by the Supreme Court in *R (Cart)* v *The Upper Tribunal*.[233] The Supreme Court concluded that the Upper Tribunal was subject to judicial review by the Administrative Court but limited to 'second-tier appeals criteria'. In *Cart*, Lady Hale stated:

> [T]he adoption of the second-tier appeals criteria would be a rational and proportionate restriction upon the availability of judicial review of the refusal by the Upper Tribunal of permission to appeal to itself. It would recognise that the new and in many ways enhanced tribunal structure deserves a more restrained approach to judicial review than has previously been the case, while ensuring that important errors can still be corrected. It is a test which the courts are now very used to applying. It is capable of encompassing both the **important point of principle** affecting large numbers of similar claims and the **compelling reasons** presented by the extremity of the consequences for the individual[234]. [Bold emphasis added]

In *PR (Sri Lanka)* v *Secretary of State for the Home Department*[235] the Court of Appeal further defined the second-tier appeals test:

> The emphasis was to be on important points of law or principle. The alternative 'compelling reasons' test … was to be an 'exceptional' remedy, a 'safety valve'. The required value-judgment was entrusted to the court.[236]

It appears that the senior judiciary intend to reserve the process of review of the Upper Tribunal for those cases where an important point of law or principle arises. A litigant or practitioner should, it is submitted, think carefully before relying on the *compelling reasons* test. Certainly, in *PR (Sri Lanka)* the court held that 'there is no case for contending that the nature of an asylum-seeker's case … is a compelling

232 Nason and Sunkin, 'The Regionalisation of Judicial Review' (2013) 76(2) MLR at 239.

233 [2012] 1 AC 663.

234 [2012] 1 AC 663 at para. 57.

235 [2012] 1 WLR 73.

236 [2012] 1 WLR 73 at 85.

reason for giving permission'.[237] The second appeals test now has footing within the CPR at CPR 54.7A(7).

Following the *Cart* decision it became clear that a modified judicial review procedure should be applied to regulate these claims, which have such a high threshold test. The Civil Procedure Rules Committee acted quickly to incorporate CPR 54.7A[238] into the CPR, thus producing a different procedural landscape for those rare cases where judicial review of the Upper Tribunal will be appropriate. CPR 54.7A can be viewed in full at Annex A. There are several differences in procedure of which practitioners and litigants should be aware. The general procedure in CPR 54 will apply, save for the following amendments:

1. When lodging a claim challenging the decision of the Upper Tribunal the application may not include any other claim, whether against the Upper Tribunal or not and any such other claim must be the subject of a separate application.[239]

2. The claim form and the supporting documents must be filed no later than sixteen days after the date on which notice of the Upper Tribunal's decision was sent to the applicant, not the normal three months.[240]

3. If the application for permission is refused on paper without an oral hearing, CPR 54.12(3) (request for reconsideration at a hearing) does not apply and the claim will simply be closed in the Administrative Court[241] (although there is a right of appeal – see the appeals section at 7-28).

4. If permission to apply for judicial review is granted and if the Upper Tribunal or any interested party wishes there to be a hearing of the substantive application, it must make a request for such a hearing no later than fourteen days after service of the order granting permission, in which case the ACO will list a substantive hearing. If no request for a hearing is made within that period, the court will make a final order quashing the Upper Tribunal's decision without a further hearing.[242]

As a result of the combined effect of CPR 54.7A(8) and (9) it is likely that hearings in these types of cases will be very rare.

[237] [2012] 1 WLR 73 at 87.

[238] Collins J has confirmed, in *R (Sharma)* v *Upper Tribunal* [2012] EWHC 3930 (Admin), that this procedure will apply to all claims lodged after 1 October 2012.

[239] CPR 54.7A(2).

[240] CPR 54.7A(3).

[241] CPR 54.7A(8).

[242] CPR 54.7A(9).

THE PLANNING COURT 5-65

On 6 April 2014 a new specialist list in the Queen's Bench Division, known as the Planning Court, came into existence.[243] The new court was implemented to deal with all planning law cases formerly dealt with in the Administrative Court: that is to say judicial review and some statutory appeals and applications (see chapter 6 for details of the procedures in statutory appeals and applications). CPR 54.21(2) states that any judicial review or statutory challenge that involves any of the following matters is allocated to the Planning Court:

- planning permission, other development consents, the enforcement of planning control and the enforcement of other statutory schemes;
- applications under the Transport and Works Act 1992;
- wayleaves;
- highways and other rights of way;
- compulsory purchase orders;
- village greens;
- European Union environmental legislation and domestic transpositions, including assessments for development consents, habitats, waste and pollution control;
- national, regional or other planning policy documents, statutory or otherwise;
- any other matter the judge appointed under rule 54.22(2) considers appropriate.

Further, any case that has been issued or transferred to the Planning Court is allocated to the Planning Court list.

The procedures for claims remain those under the CPR for judicial review (CPR Part 54), statutory applications (CPR Part 8) and statutory appeals (CPR Part 52). As such, this section will not cover the Planning Court procedures; reference can be made to the procedures outlined earlier in this chapter, or in the next. There are some specific differences that those using the Planning Court should be aware of:

- The introduction of tight timetables for the consideration of important cases (known as 'significant cases'),[244] which can be observed in CPR PD 54E. In

[243] CPR 54.22(1) and Civil Procedure (Amendment No. 3) Rules 2014 (SI 2014 No. 610). For a discussion of the importance of expedited timescales in planning cases and the desirability of lodging and hearing of planning cases in the Administrative Court closest to the site location, see I. Dove and F. Patterson, 'The Planning Court: Future Directions' [2015] JPL 1118.

[244] CPR PD 54E, para. 3.1. Significant cases include those that relate to commercial, residential or other developments which have significant economic impact either at a local level or beyond their immediate locality, raise important points of law, generate significant public interest, and, by virtue of the volume or nature of technical material, are best dealt with by judges with significant experience of handling such matters.

fact the ACO in Wales already implemented these timescales under the fast track planning process[245] and the ACO Wales listing policy incorporates the timetable now given the force of the CPR in CPR PD 54E, but does so in relation to all planning cases, not just the significant cases.[246]

- A nominated High Court judge oversees the Planning Court list for all of England and Wales[247] and judges specially appointed by the President of the Queen's Bench Division consider the cases. In practice, the lead planning judge remains in contact with the liaison judge for Wales to ensure that planning cases in Wales are conducted with the proper regard for both the planning timetables and Welsh issues.[248]
- There are discrete forms for the Planning Court,[249] although they are very similar to the forms in the Administrative Court.

As to administration, in Wales the Administrative Court Office doubles up as the Planning Court Office (or perhaps triples up considering the fact that it already doubles up as the UT(IAC) Office). The contact details are the same as the Administrative Court Office and the ACO staff and ACO lawyer act as their equivalents in the Planning Court Office.

CONCLUSION

5-66 The first three chapters sought to establish an historical analysis of the public law powers that Wales has (and indeed has not) enjoyed as well as to highlight the relevant, present day administrative law principles. This chapter has built on that background to analyse the practice and procedure in Wales for judicial review, the principal form of challenge when it is asserted that a public body has breached the principles of administrative law. A number of other forms of such a challenge exist in the Administrative Court and outside it. The next chapter will provide the requisite information to embark upon these alternative challenges.

[245] See *London & Henley (Middle Brook Street) Ltd* v *Secretary of State for Communities and Local Government* [2013] EWHC 4207 (Admin) for a discussion of the short timescales and a warning from Lindblom J (as he then was) that the court will only list/adjourn cases to be heard outside these timescales in exceptional circumstances.

[246] See Annex B for a copy of the ACO Wales listing policy.

[247] CPR 54.22(2).

[248] CPR 54.22(3).

[249] See the Ministry of Justice website for the relevant forms.

Chapter 6

Non-Judicial Review Procedures in the Administrative Court

INTRODUCTION 6-1

Judicial review is the perhaps the most well-known method of challenge to the administrative decisions of public bodies. There are, however, a number of other, less well-known methods of challenge that can be brought in the Administrative Court. Some administrative decisions have an appeals process through the tribunals system, but this chapter will not discuss those appeals as they are numerous.[1] This chapter will discuss those procedures available in the Administrative Court, other than judicial review. An important point to note is that as judicial review is a remedy of last resort[2] these statutory appeals or applications, where available, should be chosen as a method of challenge over an application for judicial review. They may be considered to be an alternative method of challenge and thus act as a bar to judicial review.[3]

PRE-ACTION CONDUCT 6-2

As with judicial review, the parties should attempt to avoid proceedings in the Administrative Court if at all possible. As these cases are not judicial reviews the Judicial Review Pre-Action Protocol does not apply. Instead the Practice Direction – Pre-Action Conduct applies. The practice direction applies to all applications under CPR Part 8[4] and thus covers the majority of the applications in the Administrative Court, but not the appeals under CPR Part 52.

The principles that should govern the conduct of the parties[5] are that, unless the circumstances make it inappropriate, before starting proceedings the parties should:

[1] See 1-24, for an overview of the tribunals system.

[2] See 5-9.

[3] If, in this situation, a judicial review is mistakenly lodged then the court may order that the claim is to continue in the form of a statutory application. See *Cala Homes (South) Limited* v *Chichester District Council* [2000] CP Rep 28.

[4] Practice Direction – Pre-Action Conduct, para. 3.1(1).

[5] Practice Direction – Pre-Action Conduct, para. 6.1.

1. exchange sufficient information about the matter to allow them to understand each other's position and make informed decisions about settlement and how to proceed; and

2. make appropriate attempts to resolve the matter without starting proceedings, and in particular consider the use of an appropriate form of alternative dispute resolution ('ADR')[6] in order to do so.

Under the practice direction, before starting proceedings the claimant should set out the details of the matter in writing by sending a letter before claim to the defendant.[7] The defendant should give a full written response within a reasonable period, preceded, if appropriate, by a written acknowledgement of the letter before claim.[8] A 'reasonable period of time' will vary depending on the matter.[9] The details of what should be in a letter before claim and a response are found in Annex A and Annex B to the practice direction. In practical terms, the letter before claim and the response are quite similar to their counterparts under the judicial review pre-action protocol.

STATUTORY APPLICATIONS

6-3 Identifying statutory applications in the Administrative Court

There are a number of statutes under which public bodies are granted the power to make certain decisions where the statute also contains a procedure to challenge and quash the said decision in the Administrative Court. There are in effect three ways to discover if such a statutory application should be lodged in the Administrative Court:

1. It is an 'application under an enactment giving the High Court jurisdiction to quash or prohibit any order, scheme, certificate or plan, any amendment or approval of a plan, any decision of a Minister or government department or any action on the part of a Minister or government department'.

   The relevant enactment (statute) normally refers to the High Court but as a result of the allocations table following CPR PD 8A, para. 9.4 all applications of this sort (referred to as 'an application to quash',) are assigned to the Administrative Court.

2. The application is expressly assigned to the Administrative Court under the allocations table following CPR PD 8A para. 9.4.

[6] See the discussion of the different types of ADR in 5-14 for further details.

[7] Practice Direction – Pre-Action Conduct, para. 7.1(1).

[8] Practice Direction – Pre-Action Conduct, para. 7.1(2).

[9] Practice Direction – Pre-Action Conduct, para. 7.2.

The allocations table assigns the following challenges to the Administrative Court:

- applications by the Attorney General under s. 42 of the Senior Courts Act 1981 to designate a person as a vexatious litigant;[10]
- applications under Part II of the Mental Health Act 1983, relating to compulsory admission to hospital and guardianship;[11]
- applications by the Attorney General under s. 13 of the Coroners Act 1988 for a fresh inquest;[12]
- applications under s. 54(3) of the Criminal Procedure and Investigations Act 1996 to quash an acquittal that was tainted by witness or juror intimidation.

3. The statute itself or an associated practice direction allocates the application to the Administrative Court.

Not all statutory applications are contained in CPR PD 8A. There are a number of such applications spread across the statute books. The intended claimant should examine the provisions and any associated practice directions to determine whether the application should be allocated to the Administrative Court. Examples are:

- a planning statutory review[13] challenging the decision of a planning authority under one of the following provisions:

  a. s. 287 of the Town and Country Planning Act 1990;
  b. s. 288 of the Town and Country Planning Act 1990;
  c. s. 63 of the Planning (Listed Buildings and Conservation Areas) Act 1990;
  d. s. 22 of the Planning (Hazardous Substances) Act 1990; and
  e. s. 113 of the Planning and Compulsory Purchase Act 2004;

[10] It should be noted that such an application cannot be lodged in Wales, only in the Administrative Court in London, by virtue of the combined effect of CPR PD 8A, para. 16.1 and CPR PD 54D, para. 3.1(5).

[11] Note that some of the provisions in Part II expressly assign the applications to courts other than the Administrative Court, contrary to what is said in CPR PD 8A. For example, applications under s. 29 for appointment by the court of an acting nearest relative are expressly assigned in the 1983 Act to the County Court. As such the primary legislation in the Medical Act 1983 takes precedence over the subordinate legislation in the CPR. Practitioners should examine the statutory provision in question as well as the CPR to ascertain the proper court.

[12] It should be noted that such an application cannot be lodged in Wales, only in the Administrative Court in London, by virtue of the combined effect of CPR PD 8A, para. 19.1 and CPR PD 54D, para. 3.1(5).

[13] Allocated to the Administrative Court by CPR PD 8C. This practice direction also incorporates a discrete procedure which mirrors the judicial review procedure outlined in chapter 5, with two exceptions – namely the statutory time limit to lodge the claim is noted and a provision is incorporated stipulating the planning authorities that the claimant is required to serve with papers.

- applications to extend interim orders made by the Interim Orders Panel or a Fitness to Practice Panel of the General Medical Council under s. 41A(6) of the Medical Act 1983;[14]
- applications to the High Court under the Proceeds of Crime Act 2002 or under RSC Order 115 relating to confiscation orders and civil recovery of unlawful monies;[15] and
- applications under the Prevention of Terrorism Act 2005 relating to control orders.[16]

Applications that fall within this category often have their own distinct procedures within a stand-alone statutory provision or practice direction. As such, litigants and practitioners should be wary of applying the Part 8 procedure that is discussed below for this third class of application. Instead the specifically tailored procedural provisions should be favoured. Where there is no specific procedural provision then the CPR Part 8 procedure discussed below will apply.

6-4 Time limits in statutory applications

The relevant statute will outline the time limit for lodging the claim. In *Pomiechowski* v *Poland*[17] the Supreme Court suggested that reading down the right to a fair trial in article 6 of the ECHR the court should be able to extend time,[18] but only in exceptional circumstances. The Court of Appeal has gone on to examine the principles as to what may be deemed 'exceptional circumstances' to extend time in *Adesina* v *Nursing and Midwifery Council*[19] and *Daniels* v *Nursing and Midwifery Council*.[20] In summary, 'the scope for departure from the … time limit is extremely narrow',[21] so much so that, to date, no applications to extend a statutory time limit have been granted. A claimant should think very carefully before making an application under these principles and certainly must not have contributed to the delay himself.

[14] Allocated to the Administrative Court by virtue of ss. 41A(14) and 40(5) of the Medical Act 1983 and the convention discussed at fn 40 below.

[15] Allocated to the Administrative Court by para. 2.1 of the Practice Direction – Civil Recovery Proceedings in relation to Proceeds of Crime Act 2002 case and by virtue of a Practice Note by Watkins LJ of 22 January 1987 in relation to RSC Ord. 115. It should be noted that such application cannot be lodged in Wales, only in the Administrative Court in London, by virtue of CPR PD 54D, paras 3.1(2) and (3).

[16] Allocated to the Administrative Court by CPR 76.18. It should be noted that such application cannot be lodged in Wales, only in the Administrative Court in London, by virtue of CPR 54D, para 3.1(1).

[17] [2012] 1 WLR 1604.

[18] The Supreme Court originally determined, in *Mucelli* v *Government of Albania* [2009] 1 WLR 276, that statutory time limits could not be extended by the court in any circumstances.

[19] [2013] 1 WLR 3156.

[20] [2015] Med LR 255.

[21] *Adesina* v *Nursing and Midwifery Council* [2013] 1 WLR 3156 at para. 18.

Procedure in statutory applications 6-5

The statutory applications in the Administrative Court apply the same principles of administrative law as the principles that apply in judicial review.[22] As such, when considering what grounds are applicable in a statutory application, reference may be made to the principles of administrative law outlined in chapter 3. It is important to note this and draft grounds of the application based on administrative law principles, not a merits-based review.

As in a judicial review, once the claim papers have been prepared they must be lodged at the Administrative Court Office with the appropriate fee or fee remission form.[23] The Administrative Court Office in Wales can be found in Cardiff Civil Justice Centre.[24] A prospective applicant should also note the terms of the sections on establishing parties and interim applications in chapter 5; they apply equally to these types of claims. The rest of the procedural provisions, however, will differ from those in judicial review.

The first place to check as to the relevant procedure is the relevant statute itself. The statute will cover, in detail that varies from statute to statute, the procedure to be followed. Where the statute outlines a procedure it must be followed, rather than the procedure outlined in the CPR. Where there is no procedure outlined under the statute, or the statute does not cover all aspects of the procedure, then the procedural provisions in Part 8 as well as Practice Direction 8A of the CPR apply and/or fill in the gaps.[25] The following are provisions of note in Part 8:

- **CPR 8.2** The claimant must use the CPR Part 8 claim form, which must:

  a. state that CPR Part 8 applies;
  b. state the question which the claimant wants the court to decide (i.e. what the claimant is challenging) and the remedy which the claimant is seeking and the legal basis for the claim to that remedy (usually to quash the decision challenged);
  c. state under what enactment the claim is being made; and
  d. be verified by a statement of truth in accordance with CPR Part 22.

- **CPR 8.3** The defendant must file an acknowledgement of service[26] not more than fourteen days after service of the claim form and serve the acknowledgement of service on the claimant and any other party. The acknowledgement of service must state:

[22] Confirmed in *R (Newsmith Stainless Ltd)* v *Secretary of State for the Environment, Transport and the Regions* [2001] EWHC Admin 74 and more recently in *Telford and Wrekin Council* v *Secretary of State for Communities and Local Government* [2013] EWHC 1638 (Admin).

[23] See the Ministry of Justice website for the relevant fees and forms.

[24] See Annex C for contact details and opening times.

[25] See the Ministry of Justice website for the relevant fees and forms.

[26] See the Ministry of Justice website for the relevant fees and forms.

a. whether the defendant contests the claim; and
b. if the defendant seeks a different remedy from that set out in the claim form.

- **CPR 8.5**[27] The claimant must file and serve any written evidence on which he intends to rely when he files and serves his claim form. A defendant who wishes to rely on written evidence must also file and serve it when he files and serves his acknowledgement of service. The claimant may, within fourteen days of service of the defendant's evidence on him, file and serve further written evidence in reply.

Where there is no statutory procedure in applications to quash[28] then the Part 8 procedure outlined above is modified in CPR PD 8A, para. 22, which stipulates:

- The time limit for lodging the papers will be specified[29] in the statute. The papers must be served on the relevant government department and any local authority that has made an earlier decision.[30]
- After lodging the application the applicant has fourteen days to file two copies of a witness statement to support the application and attach any exhibits that they intend to rely on in their application.[31] A copy must also be served on any parties to the application.
- Any respondent wishing to oppose the application must file two copies of a witness statement to oppose the application and attach any exhibits that they intend to rely on within twenty-one days of service of the applicant's witness statement.[32] A copy must also be served on any parties to the application.
- The application will be listed as soon as possible after the application form has been lodged, but the hearing will not take place until at least fourteen days after the expiry of the time limit for all parties to lodge documentation.[33] As a result the substantive hearing of the application will normally take place at

[27] However, note the differing procedure in applications to quash, as outlined below, which supersedes CPR 8.5.

[28] Examples of these applications include applications under Schedule 9 to the Road Traffic Regulation Act 1984 to quash a traffic regulation order (see *Trail Riders Fellowship* v *Powys County Council* [2013] EWHC 3144 (Admin)) and under Schedule 15 to the Wildlife and Countryside Act 1981, to quash a decision of an inspector confirming a public path modification order (see *Devine* v *Welsh Ministers* [2011] EWHC 358 (Admin) (Administrative Court); [2011] EWCA Civ 1328 (Court of Appeal)).

[29] As noted in CPR PD 8A, para. 22.3.

[30] See the notes on service of public bodies in chapter 5 at 5-30, which equally apply here, and the addresses for UK Government departments in Annex D.

[31] CPR PD 8A, para. 22.8.

[32] CPR PD 8A, para. 22.9.

[33] CPR PD 8A, para. 22.10.

some point between fifty-six days after the application has been lodged, and another three months thereafter.[34]

It should be noted that (unless the relevant statute requires it) there are no permission hearings or case management hearings in this type of application; the first time the parties will appear in court will be at the final hearing. The parties are expected to liaise with each other and the ACO to ensure that the final hearing progresses as required. Often the case management duties are handled by the ACO lawyer, who has the power to make case management orders under CPR 54.1A. Where a permission hearing is required by statute, as is the case for applications under s. 288 of the Town and Country Planning Act 1990,[35] the hearing will be a short hearing akin to a judicial review permission hearing[36] and it will be listed in accordance with the ACO Wales listing policy on permission hearings.

The substantive hearing will be listed in accordance with the ACO Wales listing policy.[37] The hearing itself is conducted on a very similar basis to the judicial review substantive hearing and the guidance notes on such hearings in chapter 5[38] can be taken to apply to these cases (although not the notes on lodging documents as the different timescales in the statute or CPR Part 8 and PD 8A will apply).

If the claimant is successful then the statute will determine the remedy that may be applied. In the majority of cases the array of public law remedies outlined in chapter 5 are not available and the only option that the court will have is to quash the unlawful decision, thus allowing the respondent public body to reconsider its decision with the court's guidance in mind. The Administrative Court also has a general power to make costs orders in such applications.[39]

GENERAL STATUTORY APPEALS

Identifying statutory appeals in the Administrative Court 6-6

There are a range of appeals that allow for an appeal to the Administrative Court. The most common of such appeals are listed in CPR PD 52D, but as CPR PD 52D, para. 4.1 notes, the list is not exhaustive and does not create, amend or remove any right of appeal. The more common statutory appeals in the Administrative Court, as listed in CPR PD 52D, are:

[34] See the ACO Wales listing policy at Annex B.

[35] See s. 288(4A) of the Town and Country Planning Act 1990.

[36] See chapter 5, at 5-40, for a discussion of permission hearings.

[37] See Annex B.

[38] At 5-44.

[39] Senior Courts Act 1981, s. 51(1). See 7-8 for provisions on costs.

- CPR PD 52D, para. 19.1 – appeals against decisions affecting the registration of architects and health care professionals[40] under the following statutes/statutory instruments:[41]

    a. s. 22 of the Architects Act 1997;
    b. s. 31 of the Chiropractors Act 1994;
    c. s. 29 or s. 44 of the Dentists Act 1984;
    d. art. 38 of the Health Professions Order 2001;
    e. s. 40 of the Medical Act 1983;
    f. ss. 82(3) and 83(2) of the Medicines Act 1968;
    g. s. 12 of the Nurses, Midwives and Health Visitors Act 1997;
    h. art. 38 of the Nursing and Midwifery Order 2001;
    i. s. 23 of the Opticians Act 1989;
    j. s. 31 of the Osteopaths Act 1993;
    k. s. 10 of the Pharmacy Act 1954;
    l. art. 58 of the Pharmacy Order 2010;

- CPR PD 52D, para. 21.1 – appeals under the Extradition Act 2003,[42] relating to the extradition of foreign criminals/suspected criminals;

- CPR PD 52D, para. 26.1 – appeals under s. 289(6) of the Town and Country Planning Act 1990, relating to the decision of a planning inspector on the validity of an enforcement notice;

- CPR PD 52D, para. 26.1 – appeals under s. 65(5) of the Planning (Listed Buildings and Conservation Areas) Act 1990, relating to the decision of a planning inspector on the validity of a listed building enforcement notice;

- CPR PD 52D, para. 27.1 – appeals from decisions of the Law Society (the body that acts as the regulator for all solicitors in England and Wales) or the Solicitors Disciplinary Tribunal;[43] and

- CPR PD 52D, para. 27A.1 – appeals from decisions of the Bar Standards Board (the body that acts as the regulator for all barristers in England and Wales) or

[40] In reality there is nothing in the modern-day procedural provisions (be that statutory, CPR PD 52D or CPR Part 52 generally) that requires these appeals to be heard in the Administrative Court. They continue to do so today by convention.

[41] See 3-4 and 3-5 for an outline of the differences between statutes and statutory instruments.

[42] It should be noted that such appeals cannot be lodged in Wales, only in the Administrative Court in London, by virtue of CPR 54D, para. 3.1(4).

[43] It should be noted that such appeals cannot be lodged in Wales, only in the Administrative Court in London, by virtue of CPR 54D, para. 3.1(6).

Disciplinary Tribunals of the Council of the Inns of Court (the body responsible for administering disciplinary hearings for the Bar).[44]

There are three appeals to the Administrative Court that apply only in Wales. As a result of diverging law between England and Wales, a number of the resulting appellate procedures are diverging. Whilst there are only three at present, it seems likely that more will emerge as the systems continue to diverge. The appeals are:

- appeal against the decision of the Adjudication Panel for Wales, which determines disciplinary proceedings against local authority councillors brought by the Public Services Ombudsman for Wales, under s. 79(15) of the Local Government Act 2000;[45]
- appeal against a decision of the General Teaching Council for Wales to make a disciplinary order under reg. 24 of the General Teaching Council for Wales (Disciplinary Functions) Regulations 2001;[46] and
- appeal against the decision of the Welsh Language Tribunal under s. 59 of the Welsh Language (Wales) Measure 2011.

Relevant procedure in statutory appeals 6-7

The appeal provisions for statutory appeals differ in each case. If conducting a statutory appeal in the Administrative Court there will be, effectively, three places to check for the relevant procedures, which are listed below in order of priority:

1. the statute may have its own statutory procedure which must be followed and so the statute itself is the first port of call;
2. the statutory provisions are often supplemented by express provisions that apply to that type of statutory appeal in the CPR. These supplementary provisions can be found in CPR PD 52D; and

[44] Whilst proceedings relating to the discipline of solicitors must be lodged in the Administrative Court in London, by virtue of CPR 54D, para. 3.1(6), no such provision exists relating to the discipline of barristers. As such, a barrister appealing a decision of the Bar Standards Board or Disciplinary Tribunal may lodge the claim in the Administrative Court in Wales.

[45] An appeal against a decision of the Adjudication Panel for Wales requires permission to appeal (s. 79(16) of the Local Government Act 2000). See *Heesom* v *Public Services Ombudsman for Wales* [2014] EWHC 1504 (Admin) for an appeal under this provision. When the procedure for disciplining local authority councillors changed in England under the Local Government and Public Involvement in Health Act 2007 and subsequently the Localism Act 2011 the changes did not affect Wales as the powers and duties of local authorities and their members is a devolved subject.

[46] The General Teaching Council was abolished in England by the Education Act 2011 and its functions were transferred to the Teaching Agency, an executive agency of the Department of Education. However, this change did not affect proceedings in Wales and the General Teaching Council for Wales as Education is a devolved subject.

3. finally, if the relevant procedural point is not covered by the statute or the express appellate provisions in CPR PD 52D, then the general appellate provisions in CPR Part 52 will apply.

As in a judicial review, once the appeal papers have been prepared they must be lodged at the Administrative Court Office with the appropriate fee or fee remission form.[47] A prospective appellant should also note the terms of the sections on establishing parties and interim applications in chapter 5; they apply equally to these appeals. The rest of the procedural provisions, however, will differ from those in judicial review.

The statute may define the period in which the appellant must lodge the appeal notice.[48] Where the statute is silent on time periods, then the specific provisions in CPR PD 52D are likely to provide a time period to lodge the appellant's notice. Finally, in the absence of a provision in the statute or CPR PD 52D, the appeal must be filed within twenty-one days of the decision under appeal in accordance with CPR 52.4(2)(b). The appellant must serve the appellant's notice on the respondent and on the chairman of the tribunal, Minister of State, government department or other person from whose decision the appeal is brought.[49]

As to general procedure on filing documentation, again it is likely that either the statute itself or CPR PD 52D will give guidance in relation to the specific appeals. Failing any such provisions, the respondent should file a respondent's notice within fourteen days of service of the appellant's notice.[50] The hearing (permission if required, substantive if not) will then be listed in accordance with the ACO in Wales listing policy.[51]

6-8 Appeal or review?

Whether the appeal is limited in its scope or allows a more general right of appeal will depend on the statute under which the appeal is made. The statute may define the terms on which the appeal may be granted. For example, an appeal under s. 289 of the Town and Country Planning Act 1990 (which challenges the decision of a planning inspector on the validity of an enforcement notice) can only be brought on a point of law (that is to say, on administrative law principles only). If the terms are not defined by the relevant statute then the provisions in CPR 52.11(3) apply and the Administrative Court will allow an appeal where the decision was (a) wrong, or (b) unjust because of a serious procedural or other irregularity in

[47] See the Ministry of Justice website for the relevant forms and fees.

[48] CPR PD 52D, para. 3.5 suggests the statutory time limit cannot be extended. However, note the commentary at 6-4 above for a discussion of the very limited circumstances in which statutory time limits can be extended. These principles equally apply to statutory appeals.

[49] CPR PD 52D, para. 3.4(1).

[50] CPR 52.5(4)(b).

[51] See Annex B.

the proceedings. For example, appeals under s. 40 of the Medical Act 1983 (which deal with appeals by doctors against disciplinary decisions made by the Fitness to Practice Panel of the General Medical Council) apply this principle, as confirmed by McCombe J in *Azzam* v *General Medical Council*:[52]

> The court's function is not limited to review of the panel decision but it will not interfere with a decision unless persuaded that it was wrong. The court will, therefore, exercise a secondary judgment as to the application of the principles to the facts of the case before it.[53]

A Welsh example of such a facts-based appeal can be found in s. 79(15) of the Local Government Act 2000 (appeals against decisions of the Adjudication Panel, which considers disciplinary proceedings for local councillors). This appeal no longer applies to disciplinary proceedings for local councillors in England (as historically it did) but the jurisdiction has been retained in respect of the Adjudication Panel for Wales.

Permission in statutory appeals 6-9

Some statutes will require the permission of the Administrative Court to appeal.[54] Where such a provision exists there is no paper permission stage, as there is in judicial review, as CPR Part 52 does not allow for a permission stage to be dealt with on paper. Instead the application for permission will automatically be listed for a short oral hearing. The principles of the judicial review permission hearing in chapter 5[55] can be, more or less, transposed to apply to an oral application for permission to appeal.

Substantive hearing 6-10

If permission is granted or if there is no requirement to obtain permission in the statute then the case will progress to a substantive hearing. As with other procedures in the Administrative Court there is no automatic case management hearing. The parties are expected to liaise with each other and the Administrative Court Office. If necessary, directions can be made by an ACO lawyer or a judge on application by the parties or of the court's own volition.

[52] [2009] LS Law Medical 28. Also confirmed in *Cheatle* v *General Medical Council* [2009] LS Law Medical 299 at para. 15.

[53] [2009] LS Law Medical 28. Also confirmed in *Cheatle* v *General Medical Council* [2009] LS Law Medical 299 at para. 25s.

[54] See, for example, s. 289(6) of the Town and Country Planning Act 1990 – appeals against enforcement notices.

[55] At 5-40.

The hearing itself is conducted on a very similar basis to the judicial review substantive hearing and the guidance notes on such hearings in chapter 5[56] can be taken to apply to these cases (although not the notes on lodging documents as the different timescales in the statute, CPR PD 52D or CPR Part 52 will apply). Subject to any statutory provisions, when the Administrative Court is considering an appeal the appeal is not by way of rehearing and, unless it orders otherwise, the appeal court will not receive oral evidence or evidence which was not before the lower court.[57] Instead the court will base its decision on witness statements, exhibits and the submissions of advocates.

If the appellant is successful in the application then the statute may determine the remedy that is to be applied. Where it does not, the provisions of CPR 52.10(2) will apply whereby the court has power to: affirm, set aside or vary any order or judgment; refer any claim or issue for determination by the lower court or tribunal; order a new trial or hearing; make orders for the payment of interest; and make a costs order.[58]

APPEALS BY WAY OF CASE STATED

6-11 Case stated appeal procedure

An order, judgment or decision of the magistrates' court or Crown Court may be questioned by any party to the proceedings on the ground that it is wrong in law or is in excess of jurisdiction by applying to the magistrates' court or Crown Court to have a case stated for the opinion of the High Court.[59] In *Streames* v *Copping*[60] it was emphasised that the lower court should only agree to state a case where they have made a final determination. May LJ stated:

> [M]agistrates' courts … have no jurisdiction to state a case … unless and until they have reached a final determination on the matter before them, and … this court has no jurisdiction … to consider or determine such a case if justices should nevertheless purport to state one.[61]

[56] At 5-44.

[57] CPR 52.11(2).

[58] The Administrative Court has a general power to make costs orders on appeal in any event under s. 51(1) of the Senior Courts Act 1981. See chapter 7, 7-8, for provisions on costs.

[59] It should be noted that some statutes contain a provision allowing for an appeal by case stated against the decision of a minister, government department or relevant tribunal. It is seldom invoked and as such not discussed here. The procedure for said appeals will be found in the relevant statutes and CPR PD 52E, paras 3.1–3.11.

[60] [1985] QB 920.

[61] [1985] QB 920 at 928.

In that case the magistrates had rejected the contention of the defendant that an information was bad for duplicity but agreed to state a case before they had heard the substantive case. May LJ confirmed that interlocutory challenges must be made by way of judicial review.[62]

The power to appeal by way of case stated is contained in s. 28 of the Senior Courts Act 1981 (for the Crown Court) and s. 111 of the Magistrates' Courts Act 1980 (for the magistrates' court). Unlike other appeals, this appeal begins in the lower court with that court 'stating a case', that is to say the point of law which the Administrative Court will determine, and only after that is done will the matter proceed to the Administrative Court for determination. In the lower court, the procedural provisions relating to criminal proceedings are contained in Part 35 of the Criminal Procedure Rules 2015 ('CrPR'). The procedural provisions relating to civil proceedings are covered by rr. 76 and 81 of the Magistrates' Courts Rules 1981 and by r. 26 of the Crown Court Rules 1982. Once the case is before the Administrative Court then the lower court rules no longer apply and CPR PD 52E applies. The procedure differs depending on whether the case stated is an appeal in a criminal case or a civil case and whether it is an appeal from the Crown Court or the magistrates' court. Figure 6.1 outlines the relevant procedures and time limits.

The application to the lower court[63] to state a case for the opinion of the High Court must be made in writing within twenty-one days of the date of the decision challenged.[64] The time for making the application may be extended by the Crown Court but there is no power to do so in the magistrates' court.[65] The application must specify the decision in issue, specify the proposed question or questions of law or jurisdiction upon which the opinion of the High Court will be sought (i.e. 'Was the judge correct to find [X *proposition of law*]?'), and indicate the proposed grounds of appeal.[66] After making the application, the applicant must forthwith send a copy of it to the parties to the proceedings in the lower court.

If the lower court considers that the application is frivolous, which is defined as 'futile, misconceived, hopeless, or academic',[67] it may refuse to state a case. Such a refusal is the end of the appeal, unless an application for judicial review is made to the High Court, which may by mandatory order require the lower court to state a case.

If the appellant is in custody, once an application has been made to the lower court to state a case, the lower court has the power to grant bail pending the

[62] [1985] QB 920 at 928–9.

[63] See the Ministry of Justice website for the application form.

[64] CrPR 35.2(1)(a), s. 111(1) of the Magistrates' Court Act 1980, r. 26(1) of the Crown Court Rules 1982.

[65] Magistrates' Courts Act 1980, s.111(2).

[66] CrPR 35.2(2)(b).

[67] *R* v *North West Suffolk (Mildenhall) Magistrates Court, ex parte Forest Heath District Council* (1997) 161 JP 401.

Figure 6.1 Case stated procedure

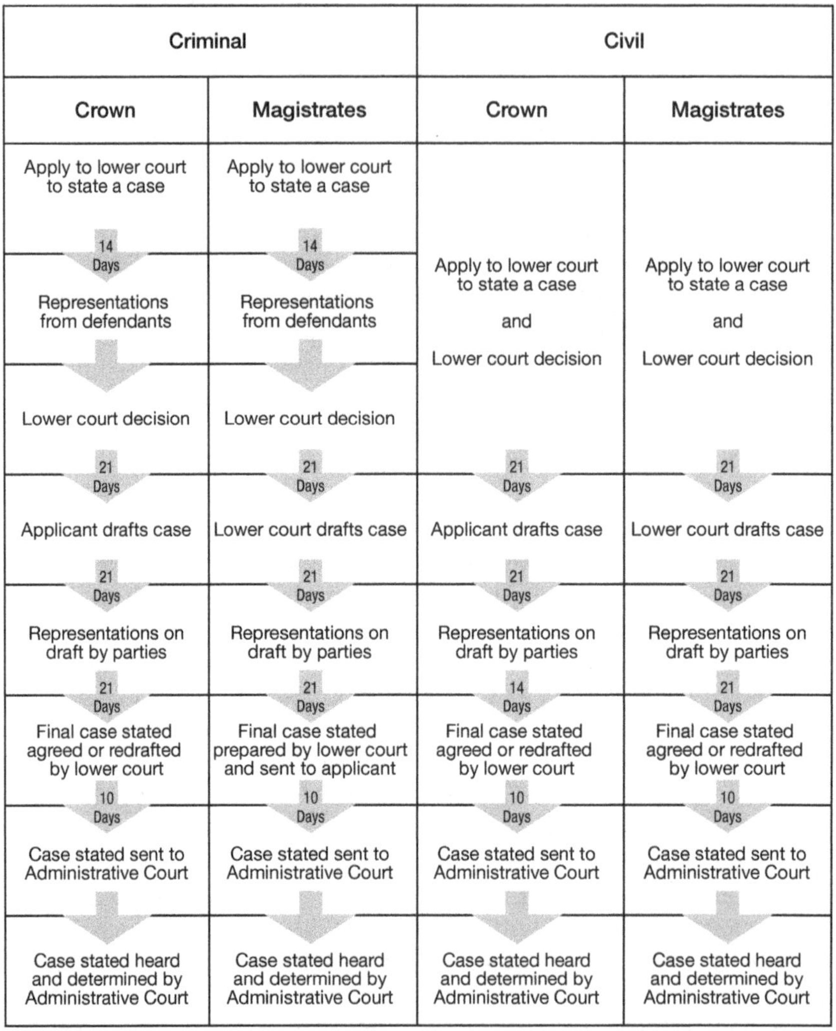

Criminal		Civil	
Crown	**Magistrates**	**Crown**	**Magistrates**
Apply to lower court to state a case	Apply to lower court to state a case		
14 Days	14 Days		
Representations from defendants	Representations from defendants	Apply to lower court to state a case and Lower court decision	Apply to lower court to state a case and Lower court decision
Lower court decision	Lower court decision		
21 Days	21 Days	21 Days	21 Days
Applicant drafts case	Lower court drafts case	Applicant drafts case	Lower court drafts case
21 Days	21 Days	21 Days	21 Days
Representations on draft by parties	Representations on draft by parties	Representations on draft by parties	Representations on draft by parties
21 Days	21 Days	14 Days	21 Days
Final case stated agreed or redrafted by lower court	Final case stated prepared by lower court and sent to applicant	Final case stated agreed or redrafted by lower court	Final case stated agreed or redrafted by lower court
10 Days	10 Days	10 Days	10 Days
Case stated sent to Administrative Court	Case stated sent to Administrative Court	Case stated sent to Administrative Court	Case stated sent to Administrative Court
Case stated heard and determined by Administrative Court	Case stated heard and determined by Administrative Court	Case stated heard and determined by Administrative Court	Case stated heard and determined by Administrative Court

decision of the Administrative Court.[68] If the lower court refuses bail then there is no right of appeal, but the decision may be challenged in the Administrative Court by way of judicial review.[69]

[68] See s. 113(1) of the Magistrates' Courts Act 1980 and s. 81(1)(e) of the Senior Courts Act 1981.

[69] See *R (M)* v *Isleworth Crown Court* [2005] EWHC 363 (Admin) and *R (Allwin)* v *Snaresbrook Crown Court* [2005] EWHC 742 (Admin) for the relevant principles.

Preparing the case stated 6-12

There is no pro forma for how a case stated document (or draft) must be set out. The case stated (and draft) must:[70]

- specify the decision in issue;
- specify the question(s) of law or jurisdiction on which the opinion of the Administrative Court is sought;
- include a succinct summary of the nature and history of the proceedings, the court's relevant findings of fact and the relevant contentions of the parties; and
- if a question is whether there was sufficient evidence on which the court could reasonably reach a finding of fact, that finding must be specified and be accompanied by a summary of the evidence on which the court reached that finding.[71]

Further preparatory guidance was given in *Tuthill* v *Director of Public Prosecutions*,[72] where the court indicated that the Criminal Procedure Rules clearly stated that unless one of the questions on which the opinion of the Administrative Court was sought was whether there was evidence on which the magistrates' court could come to its decision, the case stated should not contain a statement of evidence. If the magistrates set out the facts (and not the evidence) as the rules required, then cases would be dealt with much more quickly, the judgment would be shorter and the parties could properly consider whether it was worth while pursuing the matter. The court also stated that there might be an argument that the court should use its powers to order magistrates' court or HMCTS pay costs incurred where the case stated document did not comply with the relevant rules.

An appellant should be aware of the power to require the appellant to enter into a recognizance[73] to bring the appeal without delay, to submit to the judgment of the High Court and pay such costs as that court may award. A recognizance is effectively a promise to the court and can be backed by a surety (a sum of money which would be forfeited for failure to comply).

70 CrPR 35.3.

71 Except to this extent the draft case must not include an account of the evidence received by the court.

72 [2012] ACD 26.

73 Section 114 of the Magistrates' Courts Act 1980 and r. 26(11) of the Crown Court Rules 1982. The Crown Court also has an inherent power to require a recognizance.

6-13 The case stated in the Administrative Court

Once the final stated case has been received by the appellant from the lower court, it must be forwarded to the Administrative Court Office by the appellant.[74] The case stated document must be accompanied by an appellant's notice,[75] copies of the judgment being appealed (if available), a skeleton argument, and the requisite fee.[76] The respondent may lodge a skeleton argument in response. The documents to be supplied are kept deliberately minimal. This supports the idea that the Administrative Court is simply answering the case put to it by the lower court, not undergoing a detailed appeal and examining all the relevant documents.

The appeal will be listed by the ACO in accordance with the listing policy[77] on substantive hearings. Generally a time estimate of two or three hours is allocated, but this can be varied. The hearing itself is conducted similarly to the judicial review substantive hearing (see chapter 5[78] for details).

Where a case is stated for the opinion of the High Court, the High Court may, if it thinks fit, cause the case to be sent back to the lower court for amendment. Where it does so, the case must be amended accordingly.[79]

The Administrative Court must hear the case and determine the question arising in the case stated. It is confined to the facts as found by the lower court unless those findings are without foundation and, in general, it will not allow a point to be taken in argument before it which was not taken before the lower court. Having determined the question arising in the case stated the Administrative Court must: (1) reverse, affirm or amend the determination in respect of which the case has been stated; or (2) remit the matter to the lower court with the opinion of the High Court, and may make such other order in relation to the matter (including as to costs) as it thinks fit.

HABEAS CORPUS

6-14 Introduction to the writs of habeas corpus

The writ of habeas corpus arises out of an ancient right[80] that it is generally held to have developed to secure the provision of Magna Carta that no freeman be imprisoned save by the judgment of a jury of his peers. It was one of the prerogative writs but it was not included as one of the judicial review remedies when the

[74] The provisions relating to legal aid and representation orders for case stated appeals are discussed at 5-25.

[75] See the Ministry of Justice website for fees and forms.

[76] See the Ministry of Justice website for fees and forms.

[77] See Annex B for a copy of the listing policy.

[78] At 5-44.

[79] Senior Courts Act 1981, s. 28A(3).

[80] For an analysis of the history of the writ see M. Lobban, 'Review essay' (2011) 7(2) Int JLC 257–69.

judicial review procedure was established.[81] As such it retains its distinct procedure. On 6 April 2015 the habeas corpus procedure was brought into the Civil Procedure Rules with the bringing into force of CPR Part 87.[82] Today, there remain three types of habeas corpus:

- *Writ of habeas corpus for release*[83]
  The most famous of the three writs is habeas corpus for release and it is this writ that is most often referred to when simply using the term 'habeas corpus'. It is a long-standing power of the court to order the release of anyone unlawfully detained. In the modern day, applications are still lodged but the practical effect can be obtained through judicial review and a mandatory order.

- *Writ of habeas corpus to give evidence*[84]
  The power to require a prisoner to be produced to give evidence at court. In the modern day most courts have an arrangement with the prison governor whereby the court requests the prisoner be produced at court and the Governor, by convention, arranges the production. As such this writ is rarely sought.

- *Writ of habeas corpus to answer a charge*[85]
  The power to require a prisoner to be produced to answer criminal charges. As above the production procedure normally circumvents use of this writ.

Applications for habeas corpus to give evidence or habeas corpus to answer a charge are considered in accordance with CPR 87.12. The application is made by filing the relevant form, forms 91 and 92 respectively, as outlined in CPR PD 4, with a witness statement or affidavit, which the judge will consider and, if appropriate, grant the writ ordering the detained person be produced.

The rest of CPR Part 87 deals with the procedure for applications for habeas corpus for release. Applications are dealt with in the Administrative Court list by virtue of CPR 87.2(4), unless the application is made in relation to a minor, when it must be made in the Family Division of the High Court.[86]

[81] See 1-32.

[82] See rr. 2(c) and 15 of and Sch. 2 to the Civil Procedure (Amendment No. 8) Rules 2014. The previous procedural provisions were contained in Rules of the Supreme Court Order 54. CPR Part 87 alters the procedure to make it more similar to the modern judicial review procedure, although there are differences. It also updated forms that had gone out of use and removed the Latin from the writ, save for the term habeas corpus, which was thought to be so recognisable a term and so symbolic a right that it should be maintained.

[83] Formerly habeas corpus *ad subjiciendum*.

[84] Formerly habeas corpus *ad testificandum*.

[85] Formerly habeas corpus *ad respondendum*.

[86] Article 3 of the High Court (Distribution of Business) Order 2014.

The application must be made by filing a CPR Part 8 claim form[87] and it must be supported by a witness statement or affidavit.[88] The witness statement or affidavit must state that the application is made at the instance of the person being detained, set out the nature of the detention, and must be made by the detained person.[89] If, however, the detained person is unable to make the witness statement or affidavit, the witness statement or affidavit may be made by some other person on behalf of the detained person and must state the reason why the detained person is unable to make the witness statement or affidavit.[90] Whilst not included in CPR Part 87, it is common sense that the application, witness statement or affidavit should also include the grounds on which the applicant contends the detention is unlawful. The initial application may be made without notice.[91] Further, in urgent cases, the judge may dispense with the requirement that a claim form must be filed, but must give directions for the conduct of the application.[92]

Like judicial review, habeas corpus will not be appropriate where there is another appropriate method of reviewing the validity of the detention. This was the position in *Re Corke*,[93] where an applicant, convicted and sentenced to imprisonment by a magistrates' court, was refused release as he should have appealed rather than applied for habeas corpus.

To be granted a writ of habeas corpus the burden of proof lies on the restrained person to show that the detention is unlawful. If the claimant can make a prima facie case that he is unlawfully detained, he is entitled to a writ of habeas corpus as of right.[94]

6-15 Initial consideration

Initial consideration of the application is similar to the judicial review permission procedure, as outlined in chapter 5, save that there is no right for the respondent to lodge a response or acknowledgement of service. The application will be put before a judge as soon as possible after the papers are lodged. Under CPR 87.3(1) the judge may consider an application for habeas corpus for release initially on papers. In practice, to mirror the judicial review procedure, the Administrative Court Office is likely to arrange for initial consideration on the papers, unless there is good reason why this is not appropriate.

[87] CPR 87.2(1)(a). See the Ministry of Justice website for fees and forms.

[88] CPR 87.2(1)(b).

[89] CPR 87.2(2).

[90] CPR 87.2(3).

[91] CPR 87.2(5).

[92] CPR 87.2(6).

[93] [1954] 1 WLR 899.

[94] See *R* v *Governor of Risley Remand Centre, ex parte Hassan* [1976] 1 WLR 971 at 978.

If an application has not been considered initially on paper, it must be considered by a judge sitting in court.[95] A judge may hear the application otherwise than in court, such as in chambers or by telephone hearing, if no judge is sitting in court when the application needs to be heard.[96] An important point to note is that any application made on behalf of a protected party[97] must initially be considered by a judge otherwise than in court.[98]

Where the judge considers the application for initial consideration on paper the judge may:[99]

a. make an order for the issue of the writ;

b. adjourn the application to a hearing;

c. direct that the application be considered by a Divisional Court;

d. direct that the application continues as an application for permission to apply for judicial review;

e. give such other directions for resolution of the application as may be appropriate; or

f. dismiss the application.

It is important to note that, where the initial consideration takes place on paper, the judge has no power to order that the detained person be released. Where the judge dismisses a paper application, the applicant may request the decision to be reconsidered at a hearing.[100] Such a request must be filed within seven days after service of the order dismissing the application.[101]

Any hearing will be listed in accordance with the judicial review permission hearing section of the ACO Wales listing policy.[102] The only additional proviso within CPR Part 87 is that the applicant and the respondent must be given at least two days' notice of the hearing date.[103] The restrained person will not be produced before the court at this stage unless the court orders they be produced.

Under CPR 87.5, where initial consideration takes place at a hearing, be it a first instance hearing or reconsideration after the application is dismissed on paper, the judge will have all the powers available at the paper stage, but with the added

[95] CPR 87.3(2)(a).

[96] CPR 87.3(2)(b).

[97] Protected parties are defined as persons who lack capacity to conduct proceedings within the meaning of ss. 2 and 3 of the Mental Capacity Act 2005 – see CPR 21.1(2)(c) and (d).

[98] CPR 87.7.

[99] CPR 87.4(1).

[100] CPR 87.4(2)

[101] CPR 87.4(3).

[102] See Annex B to this work.

[103] CPR 87.4(4).

power that the judge may order the detained person be released.[104] It also appears that, as observed in *Re Amand*,[105] the court has power to order the restrained person be released on bail pending the hearing of the issued writ.

6-16 Hearing the issued writ

Where the judge orders that a writ is to be issued it must be issued in practice form 89, as set out in CPR PD 4.[106] The judge will give directions for a date on which the writ should be returned to the court[107] and a hearing will be arranged for that date. The writ must then be personally served on the person to whom it is directed,[108] unless that is not possible when it must be served on a servant or agent of that person at the place where the detained person is being held.[109] The respondent must then return the writ by the date set explaining the cause of the restrained person's detention and the return must be indorsed or annexed to the writ.[110]

At the hearing of the writ the restrained person is to be produced at court by the respondent. The procedure under the old RSC Order 54 provided that the respondent's return would be read and then their counsel would address the court. This would be followed by counsel for the Crown (if appearing), then counsel for the restrained person. In the absence of a formal procedure for the hearing itself in CPR Part 87, the judge will decide how the hearing will take place, but it is submitted that the old procedure will likely be adopted unless inappropriate.

As the prima facie case that the applicant is unlawfully detained has been accepted and the writ has been issued, it is for the respondent who has detained the applicant to make a return justifying it. If the return is good on the face of it then the onus is upon the applicant to show that the detention is unlawful.[111] If the detention is unlawful then an order will be made that the restrained person be discharged from detention; if not then an order will be made that he remain detained.[112]

Failure of the respondent to produce the person at the hearing or to arrange release when ordered is contempt of court and an order for committal for contempt may be sought in accordance with CPR Part 81 (discussed later in the chapter).

[104] See CPR 87.4(5)(g) for the additional power.

[105] [1941] 2 KB 239 at 249.

[106] CPR 87.8(1).

[107] CPR 87.8(2).

[108] CPR 87.9(1).

[109] CPR 87.9(2).

[110] CPR 87.10(1).

[111] See *R* v *Governor of Risley Remand Centre, ex parte Hassan* [1976] 1 WLR 971 at 978.

[112] CPR 87.11(a).

COMMITTAL FOR CONTEMPT

Relevant contempt 6-17

The power to imprison for contempt arises in a number of circumstances in both statute and common law.[113] In certain circumstances that power falls within the jurisdiction of the Administrative Court.

The procedure for applying for committal for contempt in the Administrative Court can be found in CPR Part 81, specifically part III. It should be noted that CPR Part 81 is concerned only with procedure and does not itself confer upon the court the power to make a committal order.[114] Part III of CPR 81 details the procedure for committal applications in relation to interference with the administration of justice in connection with proceedings in the High Court (including the Divisional Court), Court of Appeal, inferior courts,[115] in criminal proceedings, or committal applications otherwise than in connection with any proceedings.[116] Part III is not to apply where the contempt is committed in the face of the court or consists of disobedience to an order of the court or a breach of an undertaking to the court.[117]

Under CPR 81.13(1), where contempt of court is committed in connection with any proceedings then the Administrative Court is, generally, not the correct court to deal with the case. Instead the application should be directed as follows:

a. in the High Court (other than proceedings before a Divisional Court of the High Court), the application for permission may be made only to a single judge of the Division of the High Court in which the proceedings were commenced or to which they have subsequently been transferred;

b. in a Divisional Court, the application for permission may be made only to a single judge of the Queen's Bench Division;

c. in the Court of Appeal, the application for permission may be made only to a Divisional Court of the Queen's Bench Division;

d. in an inferior court, the application for permission may be made only to a single judge of any Division of the High Court; and

e. in criminal proceedings, the application for permission may be made only to a Divisional Court of the Queen's Bench Division.

113 Representation orders are available – see 5-25.

114 CPR 81.2(1).

115 See 1-21 for a discussion of the inferior courts.

116 CPR 81.12(1) and (2).

117 The former of which is dealt with by the instant court in accordance with Part V of CPR 81; the latter is dealt with under Part II of CPR 81.

Where contempt of court is committed otherwise than in connection with any proceedings, the application for permission must be made in the Administrative Court.[118] The circumstances in which contempt of court may consist of conduct interfering with the due administration of justice, but not 'in connection with any proceedings', have sometimes been described as conduct which interferes with justice as a continuing process. The forms of conduct that may arguably fall within the Part III principles (sometimes referred to as the interference principles) are numerous. Examples are contempt under the Contempt of Court Act 1981 by publications which impede or prejudice proceedings, or contempt in the form of making a false statement of truth or disclosure statement without an honest belief in its truth and which otherwise interferes with the administration of justice.[119] A fairly typical example of the type of conduct that can be considered contempt that should be considered in the Administrative Court under these principles can be found in *South Wales Fire and Rescue Service* v *Smith*.[120] The respondent had suffered an accident at work as a result of which he had falsely claimed that he was unable to work. He received severance pay and sick pay over a number of years and made a claim for damages against his employer. He signed statements of truth verifying his inability to work. The respondent later admitted that his claims were false. His employer then brought proceedings for committal for contempt.

The application is usually brought by a person or body (including public bodies) affected by the contempt or which is or may become a party to the proceedings in relation to which the contempt arises.

A point to note is that a committal application may not be discontinued at any stage without the permission of the court.[121]

There is provision to deal with defects or applications that lack merit before the permission stage. CPR PD 81, para. 16.1 states that the court may strike out a committal application if it appears to the court:

1. that the application and the evidence served in support of it disclose no reasonable ground for alleging that the respondent is guilty of a contempt of court;
2. that the application is an abuse of the court's process or is otherwise likely to obstruct the just disposal of proceedings; or
3. that there has been a failure to comply with a rule, practice direction or court order.

[118] CPR 81.13(2).

[119] There are separate provisions in Part VI of CPR Part 81 for dealing with false statements that do not involve an interference with the administration of justice, but where it does CPR 81.17(5) states the proceedings fall under Part III.

[120] [2011] EWHC 1749 (Admin).

[121] CPR PD 81, para. 16.3.

The court may waive any procedural defect if satisfied that no injustice has been caused to the respondent by the defect.[122]

Applying for committal – permission 6-18

To bring an application for committal the applicant must obtain the permission of the court[123] which will be considered at an oral hearing, unless the court otherwise directs on the grounds that an oral hearing is not appropriate.[124] Following *Practice Direction (Committal for Contempt: Open Court)*,[125] there is a presumption that all committal hearings will be public hearings in open court. The listing will take place in accordance with the ACO Wales listing policy on permission hearings[126] and will be listed under the discrete title:[127]

> *Application by [full name of applicant] for the Committal to prison of [full name of the person alleged to be in contempt]*

Under CPR 81.14 the application for permission must be made on a Part 8 claim form[128] which must include:

a. a detailed statement of the applicant's grounds for bringing the committal application;

b. an affidavit setting out the facts and exhibiting all documents relied upon;

c. a penal notice.[129] The form of notice that may be used is to be found at Annex 3 to CPR Part 81.

Further, where the application is made in relation to a false statement, the affidavit evidence in support of the application must:[130]

a. identify the statement said to be false;

b. explain why it is false and why the maker knew the statement to be false at the time it was made; and

122 CPR PD 81, para. 16.2.

123 CPR 81.12(3).

124 CPR 81.14(4). It should be noted that *Practice Direction (Committal for Contempt: Open Court)* [2015] 1 WLR 2195 suggests that holding a private hearing will be exceptional and should not be granted simply because there is a child involved in the case or the parties agree to a private hearing.

125 [2015] 1 WLR 2195.

126 See Annex B for a copy of the listing policy.

127 *Practice Direction (Committal for Contempt: Open Court)* [2015] 1 WLR 2195.

128 See the Ministry of Justice website for fees and forms.

129 CPR PD 81, para. 12(4).

130 By virtue of CPR PD 81, para. 5.2.

c. explain why contempt proceedings would be appropriate.

The claim form and evidence must be served personally on the respondent unless the court otherwise directs,[131] who must, within fourteen days of service file and serve an acknowledgement of service, which may include any appropriate evidence.[132] If the respondent intends to appear at the permission hearing, the respondent must inform the court and applicant at least seven days before the hearing, in writing, and at the same time provide a written summary of the submissions that the respondent proposes to make.[133]

The relevant test that will be applied at the permission hearing was outlined by Gloster LJ in *Stobart Group Ltd* v *Elliott*:[134]

1. there is a strong prima facie case that the allegation will be proven beyond reasonable doubt; and
2. the bringing of contempt proceedings is in accordance with the public interest, proportionality and the overriding objective.[135]

Contempt proceedings are brought in the public interest and the court must consider whether it is appropriate that the person bringing contempt proceedings should act as the guardian of the public interest. Regard is to be had to the strength of the evidence tending to show that the statement was false and known at the time to be false, the circumstances in which it came to be made, its significance, the use to which it was actually put and the maker's understanding of the likely effect of the statement bearing in mind that the public interest lies in making known the dangers of knowingly making false statements in legal proceedings. If the court considers that the applicant is not an appropriate guardian of the public interest, it must consider whether to simply decline to give permission or to decline to give permission and refer the matter to the Attorney General to consider whether to bring proceedings.

In assessing proportionality, the court must have regard to the strength of the case, the value of the claim in respect of which the allegedly false statement was made, the likely costs that would be incurred by each side in pursuing the contempt proceedings and the amount of court time likely to be involved in considering the contempt case.

[131] CPR 81.14(2).

[132] CPR 81.14(3).

[133] CPR 81.14(5).

[134] [2014] EWCA Civ 564 at para. 44. In her judgment, Gloster LJ adopted the dictum of HHJ Pelling QC in the High Court, who summarised the principles as brought together by the key cases on permission in contempt proceedings, principally *Malgar Ltd* v *RE Leach (Engineering) Ltd* [2000] CP Rep 39, *Kirk* v *Walton* [2009] 1 All ER 257, *Berry Piling Systems Ltd* v *Sheer Projects Ltd* [2013] BLR 232, and *KJM Superbikes Ltd* v *Hinton* [2009] 1 WLR 2406.

[135] CPR 1.1(1): 'To deal with cases justly and at proportionate cost'.

Where permission to proceed is given, the court may give such directions as it thinks fit, including, if appropriate, the transfer of the proceedings to another court or a direction that the application be listed for hearing before a single judge or a Divisional Court. Further, the name of the judge who granted permission and the date on which they granted it must be stated on the Part 8 claim form,[136] which will not be issued until the requisite permission has been granted.[137]

The substantive hearing will be listed by the Administrative Court Office to take place on a future date (unless the hearing is transferred). The hearing date must be specified in the claim form or in a notice of hearing attached to and served with the claim form.[138] The substantive hearing may not take place until after fourteen days from service of the claim form on the respondent.

Applying for committal – substantive hearing 6-19

The procedure for the substantive hearing can be found in CPR 81.28 and CPR PD 81. On the hearing date the court may, by virtue of CPR PD 81, para. 15.4, if the committal application is ready to be heard, proceed to hear it. The court also has power to give case management directions with a view to a hearing of the committal application on a future date. This may well be done if the court is not satisfied that the respondent has sufficient information or time to prepare a response.

Unless the court permits it the applicant may not rely on any grounds or evidence other than those set out in the claim papers.[139] The respondent, however, may give oral evidence, whether or not the respondent has filed or served written evidence, and, if doing so, may be cross-examined. Further, with the permission of the court, the respondent may call a witness to give oral evidence whether or not the witness has made an affidavit or witness statement.[140] As well as the parties giving evidence, the court may require or permit any party or other person (other than the respondent) to give oral evidence at the hearing.[141] Further, the court may give directions requiring the attendance for cross-examination of a witness who has given written evidence.[142]

The principles the court will apply when considering contempt were summarised by Gloster LJ in *Stobart Group Ltd* v *Elliott*:[143]

136 CPR PD 81, para. 11(2).

137 CPR PD 81, para. 11(3).

138 CPR PD 81, para. 15.2.

139 CPR 81.28(1).

140 CPR 81.28(2).

141 CPR 81.28(3).

142 CPR 81.28(4).

143 See fn. 134.

1. in order for an allegation of contempt to succeed it must be shown that the alleged contemnor, in addition to knowing that what they said was false, knew that what they said was likely to interfere with the course of justice;
2. the burden of proof is on the party alleging the contempt, who must prove each element identified above beyond reasonable doubt;[144] and
3. a statement made by someone who effectively does not care whether it is true or false is liable as if that person knew what was being said was false.

6-20 The committal warrant

If the court decides the respondent is guilty of contempt then it may order committal of the respondent to prison by issuing a warrant. By virtue of CPR 81.28(5) the court must state, at a minimum, the following in public (even if the application was in private pursuant to CPR 39.2 and *Practice Direction (Committal for Contempt: Open Court)):*[145]

a. the name of the respondent;
b. in general terms, the nature of the contempt of court in respect of which the committal order is being made;
c. the length of the period of the committal; and
d. give reasons for deciding to hold the committal hearing in private (before sitting in private the court must sit in public).

The court ordering committal may, at its discretion, order that execution will be suspended for such period or on such terms or conditions as it specifies.[146] If the order for committal is not suspended then it must be served before or at the time of execution, or, if signed by the judge, within thirty-six hours of execution.[147] A warrant of committal must not be enforced more than two years after the date on which the warrant is issued without further order of the court.[148]

It should be noted that there is provision to order a fine or the seizure of assets in lieu of committal.[149] This is an option most often utilised when the legal person guilty of contempt is a company.

[144] Confirmed in *Phillips* v *Symes* [2003] EWCA Civ 1769 at para. 51 and CPR PD 81, para. 9.

[145] [2015] 1 WLR 2195.

[146] CPR 81.29(1).

[147] CPR 81.30(2).

[148] CPR 81.30(3).

[149] See Part VII of CPR Part 81 for the procedure to apply to seize assets under a writ of sequestration. There is power to fine rather than commit under s. 16 of the Contempt of Court Act 1981. The procedure under CPR Part 81 remains the same.

Discharge/release of a person in custody 6-21

Whilst it is a rarely applied for or acceded to, CPR 81.31 contains a procedure for applying to the court for discharge of the warrant of committal.[150] Under CPR 81.31(2) the application must:

a. be in writing and attested by the governor of the prison (or any other officer of the prison not below the rank of principal officer);

b. show that the person committed to prison for contempt has purged, or wishes to purge, the contempt; and

c. be served on the person who applied for the warrant of committal at least one day before the application is made.

Further, irrespective of any application to discharge the order, s. 258 of the Criminal Justice Act 2003 states that as soon as the person imprisoned for contempt has served half of the sentence, 'it shall be the duty of the Secretary of State to release him unconditionally'.

DEVOLUTION ISSUES IN COURT PROCEEDINGS: PART 2 OF SCHEDULE 9 TO THE GOVERNMENT OF WALES ACT 2006 6-22

Determining a devolution issue is a function that may fall before any court or tribunal in England and Wales. In certain circumstances (as will be discussed below) the Administrative Court can be called upon to determine the issue at first instance or determine a devolution issue upon a reference from another court. This section discusses the general procedure where a devolution issue arises in proceedings at first instance, on appeal, and further to a reference.

Introducing and defining devolution issues 6-23

The Government of Wales Act 2006 ('GOWA 2006') contains provision for raising devolution issues that arise in the courts and tribunals in England and Wales. The procedure for raising such issues in the inferior court, and referring them for determination to a higher court, are outlined in Part 2 of Schedule 9 to GOWA 2006,

[150] CPR 81.31(1).

as enacted by s. 149 of GOWA 2006, and supplemented by the *Practice Direction (Supreme Court: Devolution)*[151] ('The Devolution Practice Direction').[152]

In Schedule 9 to GOWA 2006, a devolution issue is defined in paragraph 1 as:

a. a question whether an Assembly Measure or Act of the Assembly, or any provision of an Assembly Measure or Act of the Assembly, is within the Assembly's legislative competence;

b. a question whether any function is exercisable by the Welsh Ministers, the First Minister or the Counsel General;

c. a question whether the purported or proposed exercise of a function by the Welsh Ministers, the First Minister or the Counsel General is, or would be, within their powers;

d. a question whether there has been any failure to comply with a duty imposed on the Welsh Ministers, the First Minister or the Counsel General; or

e. a question of whether a failure to act by the Welsh Ministers, the First Minister or the Counsel General is incompatible with any of the Convention rights under the European Convention on Human Rights and Fundamental Freedoms 1950.

6-24 Raising a devolution issue

If a devolution issues arises in any court or tribunal proceedings then any party to the proceedings, or the Attorney General or Counsel General, may raise the issue with the court or tribunal, or alternatively, the court or tribunal may raise the issue of its own volition.[153] Once the possibility of a devolution issue arises it is for the court or tribunal in which the issue arises to determine if a devolution issue exists. The court or tribunal may give such directions and hear argument as it considers appropriate to establish whether a devolution issue arises.[154]

A devolution issue is not to be taken to arise merely at the contention of a party to the proceedings. If the court or tribunal before which the proceedings take place deems the issue to be frivolous or vexatious then no devolution issue arises. There is no definition of this term in devolution proceedings. It is submitted that

[151] [1999] 1 WLR 1592. It should be noted that the devolution practice direction has not been fully updated since the implementation of GOWA 2006 and as such still refers to GOWA 1998. When reading the practice direction the procedure should be followed, but references to GOWA 1998 should be read as their corresponding provisions in GOWA 2006. This section of this work updates the terminology as necessary from that used in the practice direction to the equivalent under GOWA 2006.

[152] See GOWA 2006, Sch. 9, Pts 3 and 4 relating to the disposal of Welsh devolution issues arising in Scotland and Northern Ireland.

[153] See para. 2 of Sch. 9 to GOWA 2006 and para. 5 of the *Practice Direction (Supreme Court: Devolution)* [1999] 1 WLR 1592.

[154] Paragraph 6.1 of *Practice Direction (Supreme Court: Devolution)* [1999] 1 WLR 1592.

'frivolous' will most likely be defined as it is in appeal by case stated proceedings: 'futile, misconceived, hopeless, or academic'.[155]

Under para. 5 of Sch. 9 to GOWA 2006, if a devolution issue arises in court proceedings then notice must be given[156] to the Attorney General and Counsel General, unless of course they are already a party to proceedings, and they may take part in proceedings. This provision is supplemented by para. 3.3(1) of the Devolution Practice Direction which informs that both the Attorney General and Counsel General have the right to take part as a party in the proceedings, but only so far as they relate to any devolution issue. If they do not take part, they may require the lower court to refer the devolution issue to a higher court. If the Attorney General or Counsel General became a party to the original proceedings but did not exercise their right to require the devolution issue to be referred to a higher court, and the lower court decided the devolution issue, they have the same rights of appeal as parties in the lower court.

The devolution issue notice must be in form 'DI 1', which can be found at Annex 1 to the Devolution Practice Direction. The notice must state:

- what that devolution issue is clearly and concisely;[157]
- if the devolution issue has arisen in criminal proceedings: (1) whether the proceedings have been adjourned; (2) whether the defendant is remanded in custody; and (3) if the defendant has been remanded in custody and his trial has not commenced, when the custody time limit expires (as per the Prosecution of Offences (Custody Time Limits) Regulations 1987);[158]
- if the devolution issue arises in an appeal, the devolution issue notice must: (1) state that the devolution issue arises in an appeal; (2) identify the court from which the decision is being appealed; and (3) state whether the devolution issue is raised for the first time on appeal; or, if it is not, state that the devolution issue was raised in the court whose decision is being appealed, what decision was reached by that court, and the date of the previous notice to the Attorney General and Counsel General;[159]
- the court considering the issue may, as it considers appropriate, order such additional documents to be served (e.g. the claim form) or additional information to be supplied with the devolution issue notice;[160]

[155] See the discussion of this principle for case stated appeals earlier in this chapter at 6-11.

[156] The court is to serve the devolution notice on both the Attorney General and Counsel General by both fax and post – see para. 7.7 of the Devolution Practice Direction.

[157] Devolution Practice Direction, para. 6.3.

[158] Devolution Practice Direction, para. 7.3.

[159] Devolution Practice Direction, para. 7.4.

[160] Devolution Practice Direction, para. 7.8.

- the devolution issue notice will specify a date which will be fourteen days, or such longer period as the court may direct (to be directed in exceptional circumstances only), after the date of the devolution issue notice as the date by which the Attorney General or the Counsel General must notify the court that they wish to take part.[161]

If the Attorney General or Counsel General wishes to take part in the proceedings they must send to the lower court or tribunal and the other parties (including each other) a notice in the form 'DI 2' shown in Annex 1 to the Devolution Practice Direction. The court or tribunal may give such directions as it considers necessary to allow them to take part.[162] If neither the Attorney General nor the Counsel General notifies the court within the specified time that he or she wishes to take part as a party to the proceedings then the proceedings will continue and the court has no duty to inform them of the outcome of the proceedings, apart from the duty to notify them if the court decides to refer the devolution issue to another court.[163]

The Devolution Practice Direction also contains discrete directions for the lower court or tribunal depending on the nature of the case. These discrete directions do not change the general directions discussed in this work but allow further guidance for the specific lower court or tribunal. The parties should review the following provisions as necessary:

- paragraph 15 – family proceedings in the magistrates' court, the County Court and the High Court;
- paragraph 16 – civil proceedings in the County Court and the High Court;
- paragraph 17 – criminal proceedings in the Crown Court;
- paragraph 18 – criminal and civil proceedings in the magistrates' courts;
- paragraph 19 – appeals to the Court of Appeal (Civil and Criminal Division); and
- paragraph 20 – appeals to the Crown Court.

6-25 Determining whether to refer a devolution issue to the higher court

If the court or tribunal accepts that there is a devolution issue then it may refer the issue to a higher court for determination. An important point to note is the use of the word **may** throughout these provisions. A reference is a voluntary action

[161] Devolution Practice Direction, paras 7.5 and 7.6.

[162] Devolution Practice Direction, paras 8.1 and 8.2.

[163] Devolution Practice Direction, para. 7.10.

to obtain the guidance of the higher court.[164] There are only two circumstances where the lower court **must** refer the devolution issue to a higher court: first, in the case of a tribunal with no further appeal (see below); or, secondly, where the Attorney General or Counsel General requires a reference to be made (also see below). Where the court is not required to make a reference it may determine the devolution issue itself and it may do so based on representations in writing or after oral hearing.

In exercising its discretion as to whether to make a reference, under para. 9.4 of the Devolution Practice Direction, the lower court must have regard to all relevant circumstances and in particular to the following:

1. the importance of the devolution issue to the public in general;
2. the importance of the devolution issue to the original parties to the proceedings;
3. whether a decision on the reference of the devolution issue will be decisive of the matters in dispute between the parties;
4. whether all the relevant findings of fact have been made (a devolution issue will not, unless there are exceptional circumstances, be suitable for a reference if it has to be referred on the basis of assumed facts);
5. the delay that a reference would entail, particularly in cases involving children and criminal cases (including whether the reference is likely to involve delay that would extend beyond the expiry of custody time limits); and
6. the additional costs that a reference might involve.

The court should state its reasons for making or declining to make a reference. If the court decides not to refer the case, it will give directions for the future conduct of the action, which will include directions as to the participation of the Attorney General and Counsel General if they are parties.[165]

If the Attorney General or Counsel General is a party to the proceedings in the lower court or tribunal, either from the beginning of the case or upon serving the DI 2 form, and either of them requires the lower court or tribunal to refer the devolution issue to the higher court, they must as soon as practicable send to the lower court or tribunal and the other parties (including each other) a notice in the form numbered 'DI 3' in Annex 1 to the Devolution Practice Direction.

[164] The ethos is not dissimilar to a reference to the Court of Justice of the European Union, which is discussed in chapter 7 at 7-27.

[165] Paragraphs 9.5 and 9.6 of the Devolution Practice Direction

6-26 Referring a devolution issue

The court to which the devolution issue is referred is determined by virtue of the court referring the issue and the type of case being referred (that is to say a civil or criminal case), as outlined in paras 6 to 10 of Sch. 9 to GOWA 2006:

- a magistrates' court may refer any devolution issue which arises in civil proceedings before it to the High Court, which, by virtue of para. 10.3(4) of the Devolution Practice Direction, is dealt with by the Administrative Court;[166]
- any court except a magistrates' court, the Court of Appeal, the Supreme Court, or the High Court if the devolution issue has been referred to it by a lower court, may refer any devolution issue which arises in civil proceedings before it to the Court of Appeal (Civil Division);
- a tribunal from which there is no appeal must refer any devolution issue which arises in proceedings before it to the Court of Appeal (Civil Division) and any other tribunal may make such a reference;
- a court, other than the Court of Appeal or the Supreme Court, may refer any devolution issue which arises in criminal proceedings before it to the Administrative Court if the proceedings are summary proceedings or the Court of Appeal (Criminal Division)[167] if the proceedings are proceedings on indictment; and
- the Court of Appeal may refer any devolution issue which arises in proceedings before it (unless the devolution issue has been referred to it by a lower court) to the Supreme Court.

A court receiving a reference does not have to serve a devolution issue notice unless it determines that a devolution issue that was not identified by the court making the reference has arisen. In that case the court receiving the reference must serve a devolution issue notice on the Attorney General and Counsel General,

[166] It should be noted that para. 14 of the Devolution Practice Direction gives directions for lodging the reference in Wales but then the papers being referred to the Crown Office (Administrative Court) in London. Paragraph 14 was brought into force before CPR PD 54D and, it is submitted, it is impliedly repealed by CPR PD 54D, which allows the Administrative Court and Administrative Court Office in Wales to have sole charge of Administrative Court matters. See chapter 2 for further discussion.

[167] Paragraph 10.3(c) of the Devolution Practice Direction requires references from Crown Court proceedings on indictment to be filed with the registrar for criminal appeals, which suggests that the reference to the Court of Appeal is to be considered in the Criminal Division. This is contrary to the general rule (discussed at 1-30) that all proceedings not designated to be heard in the Criminal Division are heard in the Civil Division.

which must state what devolution issue has been referred to it, what further devolution issue has arisen, and identify the referring court.[168]

If the decision to refer the devolution issue to a higher court is taken then the form in which the reference must be made can be found in para. 10.3 of the Devolution Practice Direction. The lower court or tribunal must ensure the following:

1. The reference must be in the form numbered 'DI 4' as found in Annex 1 to the Devolution Practice Direction and must set out the following:
   a. the question referred;
   b. the addresses of the parties, except in the case of family proceedings, where the provisions of the Family Proceedings Rules will apply;[169]
   c. a concise statement of the background of the matter including the facts of the case, any relevant findings of fact by the referring court, and the main issues in the case and the contentions of the parties with regard to them;
   d. the relevant law, including the relevant provisions of GOWA 2006; and
   e. the reasons why an answer to the question is considered necessary for the purpose of disposing of the proceedings.
2. Any judgments already given in the proceedings are annexed to the reference.

The lower court or tribunal may order the parties, or one of the parties, to draft the reference. Once drafted and approved the lower court or tribunal will transmit the reference to the relevant higher court, the parties, the Attorney General and the Counsel General. The lower court or tribunal will then stay the proceedings before it until the reference has been determined.[170]

Each person on whom a copy of the reference is served must, within twenty-one days, notify the higher court to which the reference is referred, and the other persons on whom the reference is served, whether they wish to be heard when the court considers the reference. The higher court will give directions containing any further case management directions required and list the substantive hearing to consider the reference.

[168] Devolution Practice Direction, para. 7.2.

[169] See paras 15.2–15.4 of the Devolution Practice Direction.

[170] Paragraph 11 of the Devolution Practice Direction.

6-27 Determining a devolution issue after a reference to the higher court

The hearing itself is conducted on a very similar basis to the judicial review substantive hearing and the guidance notes on such hearings in chapter 5[171] can be taken to apply to these cases (although not the notes on lodging documents as only the documents required under the reference and any other ordered by the court are required). The court will answer the question posed by the reference in a judgment which the lower court or tribunal may consider when determining the case before it.

6-28 CONCLUSION

This chapter has discussed the various procedures, other than judicial review, which may be used to challenge the decisions of public bodies in the Administrative Court. It is of note that Wales has a number of distinct procedures arising out of devolution that apply only to Wales. These range from references to determine devolution issues in the magistrates' court to distinct disciplinary procedures against local authority councillors.

It is likely, or at least it may be submitted, that if the National Assembly, Welsh Government and other Welsh public bodies acquire further, more wide-ranging powers under the devolution settlement, further distinctly Welsh proceedings will necessarily arise. An example of such a developing area can be observed in the aforementioned s. 79(15) of the Local Government Act 2000 (appeals against the decision of the Adjudication Panel for Wales, which considers disciplinary proceedings for local councillors).[172] This appeal no longer applies to disciplinary proceedings for local councillors in England (as historically it did) but the jurisdiction has been retained in respect of the Adjudication Panel for Wales. This represents an early example of divergence of procedure between English and Welsh administrative law checks on public law powers. As well as a useful guide to bringing these proceedings for a practitioner it should be remembered that the procedures which arise in this section may be seen as an indicator as to the extent to which there exists a distinctly Welsh check against distinctly Welsh powers.

171 At 5-44.

172 See *Heesom* v *Public Services Ombudsman for Wales* [2014] EWHC 1504 (Admin) for the only appeal brought under this procedure to date.

Chapter 7

Consequential and Ancillary Orders in the Administrative Court

INTRODUCTION 7-01

This chapter discusses the various consequential and ancillary orders that apply to Administrative Court proceedings. It includes the various orders and actions that a party may seek as part of or to end a case, to apply for as a result of a judgment, or require to enforce orders of the court. The chapter should be treated as supplemental to chapter 5 on judicial review and chapter 6 on statutory appeals and applications in the Administrative Court. It should also be noted that this chapter will not discuss all possible consequential and ancillary orders; the Civil Procedure Rules provide for a great many other orders that may, in niche scenarios, be required. The orders in this chapter are those common or specifically useful provisions for Administrative Court litigants.

ENDING A CASE 7-02

Once a case has been filed then there is a set number of ways to end a claim. They broadly fit into three categories: where the case is determined by the court; where the case is discontinued; and where the case is settled by consent.

Determined by the court 7-03

Perhaps the most obvious way in which a case can be concluded is where the court makes a final determination, and thus an order, which ends the case. In the Administrative Court this will likely be one of the following:

- permission to apply for judicial review or to appeal is refused (either at an oral hearing or, in judicial review, on the papers where the claim is held to be totally without merit or no reconsideration is requested);
- the claim is withdrawn in court by the claimant or an order is made by consent in court;
- the substantive claim or appeal is dismissed; or
- the substantive claim or appeal is allowed.

The ethos of all court proceedings since the implementation of the Civil Procedure Rules and the associated pre-action protocols is to avoid the need for the court to determine the case if at all possible. If the parties can agree to end a case by negotiating a settlement then they should do so. If this can be done, but is done after proceedings have been lodged, then there are set methods of ending a case.

7-04 Discontinuance

A case may be ended by discontinuing it, which may be done at any time.[1] Discontinuance requires the claimant to file a notice of discontinuance[2] and serve it on all parties.[3] The claimant may discontinue the claim in relation to all or some of the parties.[4] Discontinuing is the quickest and simplest way of ending a claim. It also does not attract any court fee. Nonetheless, before discontinuing, a claimant should be aware of a number of key points:

1. The court's permission is required to discontinue where the claimant has obtained an interim injunction[5] or any party has given an undertaking to the court.[6] This will be done simply by filing the notice of discontinuance, referring to the fact that permission is required, and the ACO will forward the notice to a judge to give permission without a hearing (unless the judge orders a hearing and representations).

2. The discontinuance will take effect from the date on which the notice of discontinuance is served on the defendant(s).[7] By filing a notice of discontinuance the claimant accepts that they are liable for the defendant's costs up until that date[8] and a costs order will be deemed to have been made on the standard basis[9] (that is to say that the claimant should pay the defendant any costs which are proportionate to the matters in issue).[10]

   The parties should, as a matter of principle, attempt to agree costs after a claim has been discontinued. This will save recourse to the court as well as time and further costs. If an agreement cannot be reached then the defendant may apply for costs and/or a claimant may apply/cross-apply to reverse the general

[1] CPR 38.2(1).

[2] See the Ministry of Justice website for the fees and forms.

[3] CPR 38.3(1).

[4] CPR 38.2(3).

[5] CPR 38.2(2)(i).

[6] CPR 38.2(2)(ii).

[7] CPR 38.5(1).

[8] CPR 38.6(1).

[9] CPR 44.9(1)(c) – see the costs section below for more details on the basis of assessment.

[10] CPR 44.3(2)(a) – see the costs section below for more details on the basis of assessment and proportionality.

rule that they are liable for costs and claim their costs. Any such application must be made in accordance with the interim applications procedure discussed in chapter 5.[11] The principles that apply during the process of applying for costs are discussed later in this chapter.

3. The discontinuance provisions do not apply to *appeals* in the Administrative Court (that is to say any hearings where CPR Part 52 is the governing procedural provision). CPR PD 52A, para. 6 contains a distinct procedural provision for ending appeals that, whilst similar to discontinuance, is not identical. Under CPR PD 52A, para. 6.1 an appellant who does not wish to pursue an appeal may request the appeal court dismiss the appeal. If such a request is granted it will usually be subject to an order that the appellant pays the costs of the appeal. The language of CPR PD 52A, para. 6.1 refers to a request to dismiss, not an application. As such the ACO will generally accept a written letter detailing why the claim should be dismissed, which will be referred to a judge to consider making an order dismissing the appeal. Such a request can be made in the form of a consent order.[12] The request must be made in the form of a consent order (or at least be accompanied by a letter signed by the respondent stating that the respondent so consents)[13] if the appellant wishes to have the application or appeal dismissed without costs or with an agreed costs order.

Consent orders 7-05

Perhaps the most common way to end a claim without a hearing is for the parties to negotiate a settlement and then lodge a copy of a draft, agreed order with the ACO (accompanied by the requisite fee[14]) for approval by the court. Such an order is referred to as an order by consent or a 'consent order'.[15] The terms of the order can include anything that the parties wish the court to approve, but will generally include the following:

1. The draft order must note (often in the header to the order) that the order is made 'By Consent'.[16]

[11] See 5-31.

[12] CPR PD 52A, para. 6.3.

[13] CPR PD 52A, para. 6.2.

[14] See the Ministry of Justice website for fees.

[15] See Annex G for a pro forma for a consent order in the Administrative Court.

[16] CPR 40.6(7)(b).

2. The draft order must be signed by the legal representative for every party to the claim (including interested parties), or by the party themselves where they are acting in person.[17]

3. Where the claim has been finally determined the consent order must detail the manner of determination.

   The most frequent term used is that the claim is 'withdrawn'. The effect of this is to leave the challenged decision in place (unless the defendant has voluntarily withdrawn the decision, thus removing the claimant's need to obtain the relief of the court) and to end the claim.

   The parties may also agree that the decision of the public body should be quashed.[18] In this situation the defendant has conceded that the decision falls foul of the principles of administrative law and that as a result the decision cannot stand. Where the parties do agree that the order should be quashed then they must also supply a schedule to the consent order detailing the reasons, including legal provisions, as to why the decision should be quashed.[19]

4. The consent order should make provision for determining costs. This is generally done in one of three ways:

   a. by providing for a set sum to be paid between the parties, as agreed by them (e.g. *the claimant is to pay the defendant's costs in the sum of £5000*);

   b. by allowing the parties to agree the quantum of costs after the consent order has been finalised, with a fall-back option of applying for detailed assessment[20] of costs (e.g. *the claimant is to pay the defendant's reasonable costs, to be subject to detailed assessment if not agreed)*; and

   c. by making provision for summary assessment on the papers (e.g. *the claimant must file representations on costs within 14 days, the defendant must file representations on costs 14 days thereafter, the claimant may reply to the response within 7 days thereafter, and the issue of costs will then be determined by a judge on the papers*).[21]

[17] CPR 40.6(7)(c).

[18] See the remedies section in chapter 5, 5-48, for a discussion of quashing orders.

[19] Paragraph 1 of the *Practice Direction (Administrative Court: Uncontested Proceedings)* [2008] 1 WLR 1377.

[20] See the costs section of this chapter below for details as to detailed and summary assessment of costs.

[21] Parties preparing a consent order that deals with costs in this way must ensure the consent order and the representations thereafter conform to the relevant guidance: Guidance as to how the parties should assist the Court when applications for costs are made following settlement of claims for judicial review (December 2013). The timescales in the example in the text above are taken directly from the guidance.

Ending a judicial review in the Upper Tribunal 7-06

As the Upper Tribunal has a judicial review jurisdiction, and the Upper Tribunal (Immigration and Asylum Chamber) has a permanent office in Cardiff, a brief note should be included detailing differences in the above process. The principles above relating to in-court determinations still apply, as do the principles for consent orders, although the rule allowing the Upper Tribunal to approve consent orders is to be found in r. 39(1) of the Tribunal Procedure (Upper Tribunal) Rules 2008 ('UTR'). There is no power under the UTR to discontinue an application. Instead, a similar procedure under UTR 17(1) is to be used which allows the applicant to withdraw the application for judicial review. There is no set form to withdraw a claim and no fee; instead the applicant is required to deliver a written notice of withdrawal to the Upper Tribunal Office.[22] The notice may simply be a letter requesting the claim be withdrawn. The request will need to be approved by either an Upper Tribunal judge or an Upper Tribunal lawyer[23] and, presuming approval is granted, the Upper Tribunal must inform the parties[24] that the application is withdrawn (which is often done by producing an order). Once the application is withdrawn the case is closed. The applicant may apply to reinstate the claim at any point within one month of the date on which the Upper Tribunal received the notice of withdrawal.[25] The UTR does not contain a presumption that the costs of the respondent are to be paid by the applicant (as the CPR in the Administrative Court does). An application for costs can be made by delivering to the Upper Tribunal Office a written application for costs[26] with a schedule of costs. A copy must be sent to the other party. This must be done within one month of the decision determining the proceedings.[27] The other party will then be given the chance to comment on the application[28] before a decision on costs and a costs order is made.

Other points of practice 7-07

The courts have emphasised that the parties have an obligation to inform the court if they believe that a case is likely to settle in advance of the hearing. Such information allows judges and staff to allocate preparation time (which is sparing) accordingly. In *Yell Ltd* v *Garton*[29] the Court of Appeal stated:

[22] UTR 17(1)(a).
[23] UTR 17(2). The UT(IAC) lawyers have been delegated this power under UTR 4(1).
[24] UTR 17(5).
[25] UTR 17(3)–(4).
[26] UTR 10(5).
[27] UTR 10(6).
[28] UTR 10(7)(a).
[29] [2004] CP Rep 29.

> [T]here is a professional obligation on those advising parties to litigation to notify the court if there is a likelihood that judicial time will be wasted in preparing for an appeal which has either been settled or is subject to negotiations which may well lead to settlement. Either way the court needs to be told, and needs to be told as soon as possible.[30]

The importance of full and frank discussion with the ACO in Wales cannot be overemphasised.

As a matter of practice it should be noted that when a case is closed by the ACO in Wales the files are immediately reduced in size for storage (or 'broken up'). Particulars of claim and witness statements are retained on the closed file but all exhibits, written evidence and authorities are confidentially destroyed. The reduced file is retained for two years after the case is closed before it too is confidentially destroyed. If the parties believe there is a need to keep fuller papers on file, or would like full bundles returned to them once the case has been closed, then they should inform the ACO in Wales before the case is closed.

COSTS

7-08 Principles of costs in the Administrative Court – assessing costs

The starting point for consideration of costs in High Court civil cases can be found in s. 51(1) of the Senior Courts Act 1981 and CPR 44.2(1). Costs are within the discretion of the court; as such each case must be considered on its own merits. This said, there are provisions that guide this discretion. There are essentially four stages for the judge assessing costs:

1. liability for costs;
2. the basis of the assessment;
3. the manner of the assessment;
4. quantum of costs.

7-09 Liability for costs

The general rule in all civil litigation on costs is set out in CPR 44.2(2)(a), which states:

> [T]he general rule is that the unsuccessful party will be ordered to pay the costs of the successful party.

In *R (M)* v *Croydon London Borough Council*[31] the Court of Appeal confirmed that the general rules did apply to the Administrative Court and compared judicial

[30] [2004] CP Rep 29 at para. 6.

[31] [2012] 1 WLR 2607 at paras 58–65.

review to 'normal' civil litigation. The court stated that if a defendant conceded, settled or lost the case, and the claimant had complied with the pre-action protocol, then the claimant would generally be entitled to their costs.[32] In *R (KR)* v *Secretary of State for the Home Department*[33] Maurice Kay LJ elaborated on this principle:

> The starting point in [judicial review cases], as in any other costs case, is CPR 44.[2], whereby the court has a discretion as to whether costs are payable by one party to another. The general rule, CPR 44.[2(2)(a)], is that the unsuccessful party will be ordered to pay the costs of the successful party, but the court may make a different order. In deciding what order, if any, to make about costs, the court must have regard to all the circumstances, including the conduct of the parties and whether a party has succeeded on part of his case even if he has not been wholly successful. The conduct of the parties includes conduct before as well as during the proceedings, and in particular the extent to which the parties follow the Practice Direction on Pre-Action Conduct or any relevant preaction protocol. The conduct also includes whether it was reasonable for a party to raise, pursue or contest a particular allegation or issue, the manner in which a party has pursued or defended his case and whether he has wholly or partly exaggerated his claim. These are the details of the provisions set out in CPR 44.[2].[34]

Liability is not necessarily an all or nothing decision and a judge may require the payment of a percentage of the receiving party's costs, thus deciding that the losing party is, for example, 80 per cent liable for the costs. Once liability for costs has been determined the judge can then determine the basis on which costs can be determined.

The basis of the assessment 7-10

The court will not allow costs which have been unreasonably incurred or are unreasonable in amount.[35] In determining whether costs were reasonable the court will have regard to all the circumstances of the case.[36] In particular, the court will

[32] This is a relatively new way of thinking in judicial review, especially in relation to settled cases. The old rule in *R (Boxall)* v *Waltham Forest LBC* [2001] 4 CCLR 258, that 'in the absence of a good reason to make any other order, the fallback position is to make no order for costs' no longer applies. *M* v *Croyden* and *KR* (below) now encapsulate the new way of thinking and have received support in subsequent cases such as *Emezie* v *Secretary of State for the Home Department* [2013] EWCA Civ 733 and *R (Dempsey)* v *Sutton London Borough Council* [2013] EWCA Civ 863.

[33] [2012] EWCA Civ 1555.

[34] [2012] EWCA Civ 1555 at para. 8. The dictum is amended using the square brackets to insert the current CPR provisions.

[35] CPR 44.3(1).

[36] CPR 44.4(1).

give effect to any orders that have already been made.[37] The circumstances of the case will include:[38]

a. the conduct of all the parties, including conduct before, as well as during, the proceedings and the efforts made, if any, before and during the proceedings to try to resolve the dispute;

b. the amount or value of any money or property involved;

c. the importance of the matter to all the parties;

d. the particular complexity of the matter or the difficulty or novelty of the questions raised;

e. the skill, effort, specialised knowledge and responsibility involved;

f. the time spent on the case; and

g. the place where and the circumstances in which work or any part of it was done.

The basis of the assessment is important when determining whether the costs claimed are reasonable. In determining the basis of the assessment the court has two options: on the standard basis or on an indemnity basis.

- *The standard basis*
  Most costs orders are made on this basis. Where a court is silent as to the basis on which it is assessing costs, the presumption is that assessment is on the standard basis.[39] Where the amount of costs is to be assessed on the standard basis, the court will only allow costs that are proportionate to the matters in issue. Where there is doubt as to whether costs were reasonable and proportionate in amount the court will determine the question in favour of the paying party.[40] Costs incurred are proportionate[41] if they bear a reasonable relationship to:

  a. the sums in issue in the proceedings;

  b. the value of any non-monetary relief in issue in the proceedings;

  c. the complexity of the litigation;

[37] CPR 44.4(2).

[38] CPR 44.4(3). It should be noted that CPR 44.4(3)(h) in relation to costs budgeting does not appear in this work. Whilst no case law on the point has been handed down to date the ACO is of the view that the costs budgeting provisions do not apply to the Administrative Court, unless a judge orders otherwise.

[39] CPR 44.3(4)(a).

[40] CPR 44.3(2).

[41] According to CPR 44.3(5).

d. any additional work generated by the conduct of the paying party; and

e. any wider factors involved in the proceedings, such as reputation or public importance.

- *The indemnity basis*
  This basis is reserved as a sort of sanction. The court will apply indemnity costs in those cases where the losing party has obstructed the court's process in some way, normally by failing to comply with the CPR. Where the amount of costs is to be assessed on an indemnity basis, the court will resolve any doubt that it may have as to whether costs were reasonably incurred or were reasonable in amount in favour of the receiving party.[42] Note: there is no requirement that the costs be proportionate, as appears in the standard basis assessment.

Once the court has determined the basis of the assessment it turns to the manner of assessment.

The manner of assessment 7-11

By virtue of CPR 44.6(1), where the court orders a party to pay costs to another party, it may either make a summary assessment of the costs or order detailed assessment of the costs. Where the court does not proceed to summary assessment, and it does not mention the manner of assessment in its costs order then the costs order is presumed to order detailed assessment.[43]

- *Summary assessment*
  Summary assessment involves a judge of the Administrative Court (usually the judge who considered the case) determining the quantum of costs payable by the liable party. This will be done according to the principles outlined above according to the basis of costs.

  To ensure that costs are considered it is imperative that the parties lodge a statement of costs[44] not less than twenty-four hours before the hearing or paper application at which costs will be assessed (unless of course a judge has ordered a different timescale or manner of consideration).[45]

  Whilst not a steadfast rule, summary assessment is usually reserved for those cases where determination of the costs will be a relatively simple exercise as the case is not complex or has not advanced far before the court. Typically (but not always) the Administrative Court will summarily assess a case that has not

[42] CPR 44.3(3).

[43] CPR PD 44, para. 8.2.

[44] See the Ministry of Justice website for the forms.

[45] CPR PD 44, para. 9.5(4)(b). See CPR PD 44, para. 9.5 generally for details to be included in the statement of costs.

passed the permission stage (if one exists in that type of case), be that because permission was refused or because the claim settled.

The court is not entitled to summarily assess the costs of a receiving party who is a child or protected party[46] unless the legal representative acting for the child or protected party has waived the right to further costs.[47]

Unless a judge orders otherwise, any costs order must be complied with within fourteen days of the costs order,[48] although sometimes the parties will agree their own payment terms.[49]

- *Detailed assessment*

  Detailed assessment involves a costs judge considering the claim for costs in accordance with the procedure in CPR Part 47.

  The detailed assessment procedure is generally reserved for more complex or advanced cases where there has been a lot of work done by the parties. In the Administrative Court this generally applies when the parties have proceeded to a substantive hearing. As such, the assessment of the quantum is allocated to a specialist costs judge. The parties are encouraged to attempt to agree costs before submitting a claim for detailed assessment.

  Any application for detailed assessment or correspondence on the subject of detailed assessment is still dealt with by the Administrative Court Office in Wales.[50]

7-12 Applying for costs in the Administrative Court – further principles

The principles of costs having been outlined, it is appropriate to note some cases which have given guidance on the proper procedure in applying for costs in the Administrative Court.

7-13 Deemed costs orders

There are two scenarios in the Administrative Court where costs orders are deemed to be made without an express costs order being made. They are as follows:

- if any orders are silent as to costs and make no provision for how costs are to be assessed, then the court is deemed to have ordered that there be no order for costs[51]; and

[46] See CPR Part 21 for a definition.

[47] CPR PD 44, para. 9.9.

[48] CPR 44.7(1)(a).

[49] As they may do under CPR 2.11.

[50] The Senior Courts Costs Office is not the appropriate office unless the court orders otherwise. See *Public Services Ombudsman for Wales* v *Heesom* [2015] EWHC 3306 (QB).

[51] CPR 44.10(1)(a)(i).

- where the court makes an order granting permission to appeal, an order granting permission to apply for judicial review, or any other order or direction sought by a party on an application without notice, and its order does not mention costs, it will be deemed to include an order for applicant's costs in the case.[52]

A party does have liberty, by virtue of CPR 44.10(3) to apply to set aside the deemed costs order at any point.

Costs following settlement and submissions on the papers 7-14

In *R (M)* v *Croydon London Borough Council*[53] the court considered cases that have settled and costs fall to be determined on the papers. Such cases fall into three categories:

1. where a claimant has been wholly successful;
2. where a claimant has only succeeded in part; and
3. where there has been some compromise which does not actually reflect the claimant's claims.

The court went on to clarify the approach the Administrative Court should take when considering costs in each category:

1. Where a claimant has been wholly successful:

   > [I]t is hard to see why the claimant should not recover all his costs, unless there is some good reason to the contrary. Whether pursuant to judgment following a contested hearing, or by virtue of a settlement, the claimant can, at least absent special circumstances, say that he has been vindicated, and, as the successful party, that he should recover his costs. In the latter case, the defendants can no doubt say that they were realistic in settling, and should not be penalised in costs, but the answer to that point is that the defendants should, on that basis, have settled before the proceedings were issued: that is one of the main points of the pre-action protocols.[54]

2. Where a claimant has only succeeded in part:

   > [T]he court will normally determine questions such as how reasonable the claimant was in pursuing the unsuccessful claim, how important it was compared with the successful claim, and how much the costs were increased as a result of the claimant pursuing the unsuccessful claim. Given that there will have been a hearing, the court will be in a reasonably good position to

[52] CPR 44.10(2).

[53] [2012] 1 WLR 2607.

[54] [2012] 1 WLR 2607 at para. 61.

> make findings on such questions. However, where there has been a settlement, the court will, at least normally, be in a significantly worse position to make findings on such issues than where the case has been fought out. In many such cases, the court will be able to form a view as to the appropriate costs order based on such issues; in other cases, it will be much more difficult. I would accept the argument that, where the parties have settled the claimant's substantive claims on the basis that he succeeds in part, but only in part, there is often much to be said for concluding that there is no order for costs … However, where there is not a clear winner, so much would depend on the particular facts. In some such cases, it may help to consider who would have won if the matter had proceeded to trial, as, if it is tolerably clear, it may, for instance support or undermine the contention that one of the two claims was stronger than the other.[55]

3. Where there has been some compromise which does not actually reflect the claimant's claims:

> [T]he court is often unable to gauge whether there is a successful party in any respect, and, if so, who it is. In such cases, therefore, there is an even more powerful argument that the default position should be no order for costs. However, in some such cases, it may well be sensible to look at the underlying claims and inquire whether it was tolerably clear who would have won if the matter had not settled. If it is, then that may well strongly support the contention that the party who would have won did better out of the settlement, and therefore did win.[56]

7-15 Paper permission stage

In *R (Ewing)* v *Office of the Deputy Prime Minister*,[57] Carnwarth LJ (as he then was) outlined the proper procedure for considering costs when considering permission on the papers.

1. Where a proposed defendant or interested party wishes to seek costs at the permission stage, the acknowledgement of service should include an application for costs and should be accompanied by a schedule setting out the amount claimed.

2. The judge refusing permission should include in the refusal a decision whether to award costs in principle, and (if so) an indication of the amount which he proposes to assess summarily.

55 [2012] 1 WLR 2607 at para. 62.

56 [2012] 1 WLR 2607 at para. 63.

57 [2006] 1 WLR 1260.

3. The claimant should be given fourteen days to respond in writing and should serve a copy on the defendant.
4. The defendant will have seven days to reply in writing to any such response, and to the amount proposed by the judge.
5. The judge will then decide and make an award on the papers.[58]

This procedure is now almost universally used for the paper permission stage. In the event that the claimant renews the application for permission to apply for judicial review then costs are often reconsidered at that stage.

Costs after refusal of permission 7-16

The judge considering costs after refusal of permission will apply the principles for assessing costs as outlined above. There is a key case on Administrative Court costs orders at the permission stage. In *R (Mount Cook Land Ltd)* v *Westminster City Council*,[59] Auld LJ, summed up the additional principles:

> 1) … [A] successful defendant or other party at the permission stage who has filed an acknowledgment of service … should generally recover the costs of doing so from the claimant, whether or not he attends any permission hearing.
>
> 2) … [A] defendant who attends and successfully resists the grant of permission at a renewal hearing should not generally recover from the claimant his costs of and occasioned by doing so.
>
> 3) A court, in considering an award against an unsuccessful claimant of … costs at a permission hearing, should only depart from the general guidance … if he considers there are exceptional circumstances for doing so.
>
> 4) A court considering costs at the permission stage should be allowed a broad discretion as to whether, on the facts of the case, there are exceptional circumstances justifying the award of costs against an unsuccessful claimant.
>
> 5) Exceptional circumstances may consist in the presence of one or more of the features in the following non-exhaustive list:
>
> a) the hopelessness of the claim:
>
> b) the persistence in it by the claimant after having been alerted to facts and/or of the law demonstrating its hopelessness;

[58] [2006] 1 WLR 1260 at para. 47.

[59] [2004] CP Rep 12.

c) the extent to which the court considers that the claimant, in the pursuit of his application, has sought to abuse the process of judicial review for collateral ends – a relevant consideration as to costs at the permission stage, as well as when considering discretionary refusal of relief at the stage of substantive hearing, if there is one; and

d) whether, as a result of the deployment of full argument and documentary evidence by both sides at the hearing of a contested application, the unsuccessful claimant has had, in effect, the advantage of an early substantive hearing of the claim.

6) A relevant factor for a court, when considering the exercise of its discretion on the grounds of exceptional circumstances, may be the extent to which the unsuccessful claimant has substantial resources which it has used to pursue the unfounded claim and which are available to meet an order for costs.

7) The Court of Appeal should be slow to interfere with the broad discretion of the court below in its identification of factors constituting exceptional circumstances and in the exercise of its discretion whether to award costs against an unsuccessful claimant.[60]

7-17 Interveners and costs

Under CPR 54.17 a person may apply to make representations in judicial review proceedings without formally becoming a party. Such a person is commonly referred to as an intervener and, pursuant to s. 87 of the Criminal Justice and Courts Act 2015, there are specific costs consequences for the intervener.

A relevant party, that is to say a claimant or defendant in substantive or permission judicial review proceedings,[61] cannot be ordered to pay an intervener's costs[62] unless there are exceptional circumstances that make such a costs order appropriate.[63] In essence, these provisions will prevent the intervener claiming any costs incurred in the majority of cases, irrespective of the usefulness or necessity of their representations.

Further, the intervener is more likely to be made the subject of an adverse costs order. If the court is satisfied that any one of four conditions, outlined in s. 87(6), is met, the court must order the intervener to pay any costs specified in the application that the court considers have been incurred by the relevant party as a result of the intervener's involvement in that stage of the proceedings.[64] The four conditions are:

[60] [2004] CP Rep 12 at para. 76.

[61] Criminal Justice and Courts Act 2015, s. 87(9) and (10).

[62] Criminal Justice and Courts Act 2015, s. 87(3).

[63] Criminal Justice and Courts Act 2015, s. 87(4).

[64] Criminal Justice and Courts Act 2015, s. 87(5).

- the intervener has acted, in substance, as the sole or principal applicant, defendant, appellant or respondent;
- the intervener's evidence and representations, taken as a whole, have not been of significant assistance to the court;
- a significant part of the intervener's evidence and representations relates to matters that it is not necessary for the court to consider in order to resolve the issues that are the subject of the stage in the proceedings;
- the intervener has behaved unreasonably.

By virtue of CPR 46.15(2) the relevant party may apply for an order under s. 87 and does not have to wait for the court to raise the issue.

As a result of these recently enacted provisions, an intervener must consider their position carefully as they are likely to find themselves at a disadvantage in costs proceedings. A final point to note as an intervener is that if the intervener becomes a relevant party, the costs provisions in s. 87 no longer apply and are deemed never to have applied.[65]

Non-party costs orders 7-18

The court has a discretion under s. 51(1) and (3) of the Senior Courts Act 1981 to make a costs order against a non-party. Such orders are only made exceptionally.[66] The principles for when such orders will be appropriate were outlined by Balcome LJ in *Symphony Group plc* v *Hodgson*,[67] where examples of the types of non-parties which may be made the subject of such orders were included (this is not an exhaustive list):

- where a person has some management of the action, e.g. a director of an insolvent company who causes the company improperly to prosecute or defend proceedings;
- where a person has maintained or financed the action;
- where the court determines that the legal representative, due to his or her conduct, should pay costs;
- where the person has caused the action;
- where the person is a party to a closely related action which has been heard at the same time but not consolidated; and
- group litigation where one or two actions are selected as test action.

Balcome LJ also noted that the trial judge should deal with the application for non-party costs and should treat it with considerable caution. He further emphasised

[65] Criminal Justice and Courts Act 2015, s. 87(11).

[66] As noted by by Balcome LJ in *Symphony Group plc* v *Hodgson* [1994] QB 179 at 192.

[67] [1994] QB 179 at 191–2.

that such an order would be even more exceptional where the non-party could properly have been joined as a party to proceedings. Finally, the non-party should be warned by the applicant at the earliest possibility that costs may be applied for against them.

7-19 Setting aside costs orders

The general rule on setting aside costs orders was established in *R (Jones)* v *Nottingham City Council.*[68] In *Jones*, Collins J held that any costs order in which the parties have had the opportunity to make representations, be that a costs order on the papers or after an oral hearing, is a final costs order. As such there is no power to set it aside and it must be appealed to the Court of Appeal. The Court of Appeal in *R (Bahta)* v *Secretary of State for the Home Department*[69] confirmed that there is power to appeal a High Court costs order (made on paper or at an oral hearing) to the Court of Appeal.

7-20 Protective costs orders[70]

A protective costs order ('PCO') is sometimes known as a 'costs capping order'. It is an order limiting the parties' liability to costs. A PCO will often be made in terms similar to this example:

> A protective costs order is granted. The Claimant's liability for costs will be limited to £5000.00. The Defendant's liability is limited to £35,000.

7-21 Qualifications on when a protective costs order may be granted

An established procedure for making PCOs, arising out of the case of *R (Corner House Research)* v *Trade and Industry Secretary*[71] has been altered by the bringing into force of s. 88 of the Criminal Justice and Courts Act 2015. The 2015 Act introduced some important qualifications on when a PCO may be granted, namely:

- a PCO may only be granted after permission to apply for judicial review has been granted;[72]
- a PCO may only be granted on a claimant's application.[73]

If these criteria are met, the court may advance to consider whether a PCO should be granted.

[68] [2009] ACD 42.

[69] [2011] CP Rep 43.

[70] The relevant provisions of the Criminal Justice and Court Act 2015 came into force on the 8th August 2016. For the procedure before that date and for existing claims lodged before that date, the procedure outlined in *Corner House and Buglife* (discussed below) should be followed.

[71] [2005] 1 WLR 2600.

[72] Criminal Justice and Courts Act 2015, s. 88(3).

[73] Criminal Justice and Courts Act 2015, s. 88(4).

Considerations for a protective costs order 7-22

The key case discussing the principles behind when a PCO should be granted was *R (Corner House Research)* v *Trade and Industry Secretary*.[74] The *Corner House* considerations have now been superseded by the provisions in ss. 88–89 of the Criminal Justice and Courts Act 2015, which give statutory force to many of the *Corner House* principles, and remove others. The principles are:

1. The court may only make a PCO if it is satisfied that:[75]
   a. the proceedings are public interest proceedings;
   b. in the absence of the order, the claimant would withdraw the application for judicial review or cease to participate in the proceedings; and
   c. it would be reasonable for the applicant for judicial review to do so.
2. The court must have regard,[76] when considering whether to make a PCO, to the following:
   a. the financial resources of the parties to the proceedings, including the financial resources of any person who provides, or may provide, financial support to the parties;
   b. the extent to which the applicant for the PCO is likely to benefit if relief is granted to the applicant for judicial review;
   c. the extent to which any person who has provided, or may provide, the applicant with financial support is likely to benefit if relief is granted to the applicant for judicial review;
   d. whether legal representatives for the applicant for the order are acting free of charge;[77] and
   e. whether the applicant for the order is an appropriate person to represent the interests of other persons or the public interest generally.

Public interest proceedings are defined under s. 88(7) as an issue that is the subject of the proceedings, is of general public importance, the public interest requires the issue to be resolved, and the proceedings are likely to provide an appropriate

[74] [2005] 1 WLR 2600.

[75] Further to s. 88(6) of the Criminal Justice and Courts Act 2015.

[76] Further to s. 89(1) of the Criminal Justice and Courts Act 2015.

[77] *Corner House* [2005] 1 WLR 2600, at para. 74, suggested that if those acting for the applicant are doing so pro bono this will be likely to enhance the merits of the application for a PCO. It is submitted that this principle is likely to remain to be the case under s. 89(1)(d) of the Criminal Justice and Courts Act 2015.

means of resolving it. Further, under s. 88(8), the court must have regard to the following when determining whether proceedings are public interest proceedings:

- the number of people likely to be directly affected if relief is granted to the applicant for judicial review,
- how significant the effect on those people is likely to be, and
- whether the proceedings involve consideration of a point of law of general public importance.

Where the court grants a PCO, it must also make a reciprocal PCO, limiting or removing the liability of the defendant to pay the claimant's costs if the claimant is successful.[78]

7-23 Procedure for applying for a protective costs order

Corner House[79] gave guidance on the appropriate procedure for applying for a PCO in the Administrative Court. The Court of Appeal confirmed the *Corner House* procedural principles in *R (Buglife)* v *Thurrock Thames Gateway Development Corp*[80] and added to those principles. Whilst the conditions for making PCOs are now outlined in the Criminal Justice and Courts Act 2015, the 2015 Act only has a small effect on the procedure established in *Corner House* and *Buglife*. The procedure, as outlined in *Corner House*, *Buglife* and the 2015 Act, can be summarised as follows:

1. a PCO should, in normal circumstances, be sought on the face of the initiating claim form;
2. the application must be supported by evidence establishing the PCO criteria, now contained in ss. 88–89 of the Criminal Justice and Courts Act 2015 (see above);[81]
3. if the defendant wishes to resist the making of the PCO it should set out its reasons in the acknowledgement of service. Similarly, any representations on a reciprocal PCO (capping both parties' costs) should be made in the acknowledgement of service;
4. the claimant will be liable for the court fees for pursuing the claim, and will also be liable for the defendant's costs incurred in a successful resistance to an application for a PCO;

[78] Criminal Justice and Courts Act 2015, s. 89(2).

[79] [2005] 1 WLR 2600 at paras 78–81.

[80] [2009] CP Rep 8 at paras 29–31.

[81] The reader should also be aware that certain financial information must be provided with the application – see CPR 46.17 and CPR PD 46 paragraph 10 for evidence requirements.

5. if the judge grants permission to apply for judicial review on the papers the judge will then consider whether to make the PCO on the papers and, if so, in what terms, and the size of the cap on the recoverable costs;

6. if the judge refuses permission to apply for judicial review on the papers then the judge may not make a PCO.[82] If the judge grants permission to apply for judicial review, but refuses to grant the PCO, and the claimant requests that the decision is reconsidered at a hearing (in line with the interim applications procedure),[83] the hearing should be limited to an hour and the claimant will face liability for costs if the PCO is again refused. The paper decision should only be revisited in exceptional circumstances; and

7. the court should not set aside a PCO unless there is an exceptional reason for doing so.

Corner House[84] states that an application for a PCO can be made at any time, although it is discouraged. When the preferred procedure, outlined above, cannot be utilised, a party may still apply for a PCO. In such circumstances the application should be made in accordance with the general application procedure in CPR Part 23, but taking into account the requirements above.[85]

Protective costs order – environmental cases

The Aarhus Convention 7-24

On 25 June 1998, at Aarhus in Denmark, the principles of the Convention on Access to Information, Public Participation in Decision Making and Access to Justice in Environmental Matters ('the Aarhus Convention') were agreed. The Aarhus Convention outlines the obligations of each signatory state to its citizens when challenging decisions made in relation to the environment. The main principle as, far as PCOs are concerned, can be found in article 9(3):

> 3. Each [state] shall ensure that … members of the public have access to administrative or judicial procedures to challenge acts and omissions by private persons and public authorities which contravene provisions of its national law relating to the environment.

The Aarhus Convention also defines what constitutes 'the environment'. Article 2(3) states:

[82] See s. 88(3) of the Criminal Justice and Courts Act 2015 discussed above.

[83] See the interim application procedure in chapter 5, 5-31.

[84] [2005] 1 WLR 2600 at para. 64.

[85] See the interim application procedure in chapter 5, 5-31.

> 3. 'Environmental information' means any information … on:
>
> (a) The state of elements of the environment, such as air and atmosphere, water, soil, land, landscape and natural sites, biological diversity and its components, including genetically modified organisms, and the interaction among these elements;
>
> (b) Factors, such as substances, energy, noise and radiation, and activities or measures, including administrative measures, environmental agreements policies, legislation, plans and programmes, affecting or likely to affect the elements of the environment within the scope of subparagraph (a) above, and cost-benefit and other economic analyses and assumptions used in environmental decision-making;
>
> (c) The state of human health and safety, conditions of human life, cultural sites and built structures, inasmuch as they are or may be affected by the state of the elements of the environment or, through these elements, by the factors, activities or measures referred to in subparagraph (b) above.

7-25 The automatic PCO in environmental judicial reviews

The UK has implemented the terms of the Aarhus Convention by providing for a costs protection procedure in the CPR. Where the claimant[86] believes that their claim comes within the terms of the Aarhus Convention then they should note it in part 6 of the claim form. Where the claimant contends that the Aarhus Convention applies, unless the defendant refutes that assertion, CPR 45.43(1) is taken to apply:

> Subject to rule 45.44, a party to an Aarhus Convention claim may not be ordered to pay costs exceeding the amount prescribed in Practice Direction 45.

The current costs limit is outlined in CPR PD 45, para. 5.1, which stipulates that where the claimant is claiming only as an individual and not as, or on behalf of, a business or other legal person then the limit is £5,000. In all other cases the limit is £10,000. Where a defendant is ordered to pay costs, the limit is £35,000.

Where the defendant intends to refute the assertion that the Aarhus Convention applies (and thus that a CPR 45.43 PCO does not apply) the procedure to challenge the assertion can be found at CPR 45.44:

> **45.44**
> (1) If the claimant has stated in the claim form that the claim is an Aarhus Convention claim, rule 45.43 will apply unless –
>
> (a) the defendant has in the acknowledgment of service filed in accordance with rule 54.8 –

[86] The automatic PCO provisions also apply where the claimant is a public body: see *R (HS2 Action Alliance Ltd)* v *Secretary of State for Transport* [2015] 2 Costs LR 411.

(i) denied that the claim is an Aarhus Convention claim; and
(ii) set out the defendant's grounds for such denial; and
(b) the court has determined that the claim is not an Aarhus Convention claim.

(2) Where the defendant argues that the claim is not an Aarhus Convention claim, the court will determine that issue at the earliest opportunity.

(3) In any proceedings to determine whether the claim is an Aarhus Convention claim –
(a) if the court holds that the claim is not an Aarhus Convention claim, it will normally make no order for costs in relation to those proceedings;
(b) if the court holds that the claim is an Aarhus Convention claim, it will normally order the defendant to pay the claimant's costs of those proceedings on the indemnity basis, and that order may be enforced notwithstanding that this would increase the costs payable by the defendant beyond the amount prescribed in Practice Direction 45.

The standard practice in judicial review claims is for a judge to consider the representations of both parties in accordance with the procedure above when considering permission to apply for judicial review. An order will then be made considering both permission and the existence of any PCO.

Where the applicability of the Aarhus Convention is not disputed the final practice of the court does tend to differ at present. Some judges will expressly note the existence of the Aarhus PCO when considering the application for permission to apply for judicial review; this is probably good practice as it leaves the parties in no doubt. This said, the terms of CPR 45 do not technically require the court to note the existence of the PCO, unless of course the court has had to determine whether a PCO should be granted in accordance with the procedure at CPR 45.44. As such, providing the conditions exist for the PCO to be made and there are no objections to it, the cost cap is automatically in place.

PCOs in environmental non-judicial review cases 7-26

Where a case relating to environmental issues is not a judicial review (usually a statutory application or appeal under ss. 288 or 289 of the Town and Country Planning Act 1990)[87] then the principles in CPR 45.43 do not apply as CPR 45.43 refers expressly to costs protection in judicial reviews. This issue was discussed in *Venn* v *Secretary of State for Communities and Local Government*.[88] In *Venn*, Sullivan LJ considered that environmental challenges brought under s. 288 of the Town and Country Planning Act 1990 were capable of falling within art. 9(3) of Aarhus.[89]

[87] See chapter 6 for statutory appeals and applications in the Administrative Court.

[88] [2014] EWCA Civ 1539.

[89] [2014] EWCA Civ 1539 at para. 17.

However, Sullivan LJ determined that as the CPR was secondary legislation, the court could not circumvent the intention not to provide an automatic PCO regime in Aarhus cases.[90]

Where a PCO is sought in an environmental case that is not a judicial review, the principles in ss. 88–89 of the Criminal Justice and Courts Act 2015 must be applied, with, it is submitted, some modification. The issue of PCOs and environmental cases post-Aarhus first arose in *R (Garner)* v *Elmbridge Borough Council.*[91] The Court of Appeal concluded that to meet its obligations under the Aarhus Convention and Article 10a of Directive 83/337/EEC the standard PCO regime (as established in *Corner House* and *Buglife*) should be modified in the case of planning and environmental decisions. The court (albeit in a decision made before the implementation of the Criminal Justice and Courts Act 2015) held that the public importance and public interest criteria are automatically met where the claim raises environmental matters within the scope of the Aarhus Convention. The Supreme Court, following a reference to the Court of Justice of the European Union ('CJEU'), has given guidance on PCOs under Aarhus in *R (Edwards)* v *Environment Agency.*[92] This guidance was given relating to an application for judicial review made before CPR 45.43 and the Criminal Justice and Courts Act 2015 were implemented. It is submitted, these principles can still be applied to non-judicial reviews. When considering a PCO in an Aarhus case the court may apply the relevant principles with the following further and/or alternative considerations:

> i) First, the test is not purely subjective. The cost of proceedings must not exceed the financial resources of the person concerned nor '*appear to be objectively unreasonable*'...
>
> ii) The [CJEU] did not give definitive guidance as to how to assess what is 'objectively unreasonable'. In particular it did not ... adopt Sullivan LJ's suggested alternative [in *Garner*] of an 'objective' assessment based on the ability of an 'ordinary' member of the public to meet the potential liability for costs. While the court did not apparently reject that as a possible factor in the overall assessment, 'exclusive' reliance on the resources of an 'average applicant' was not appropriate, because it might have 'little connection with the situation of the person concerned'.
>
> iii) The court could also take into account what might be called the 'merits' of the case: that is ... '*whether the claimant has a reasonable prospect of success, the importance of what is at stake for the claimant and for the protection of the environment, the complexity of the relevant law and procedure, the potentially frivolous nature of the claim at its various stages.*'

90 [2014] EWCA Civ 1539 at paras 33–5.

91 [2010] EWCA Civ 1006 at paras 39–40.

92 [2014] 1 WLR 55.

iv) That the claimant has not in fact been deterred for carrying on the proceedings is not 'in itself' determinative.

v) The same criteria are to be applied on appeal as at first instance.[93]

A series of cases, including *Venn* and *Mackman* v *Secretary of State for Communities and Local Government*,[94] have applied the principles established in *Corner House*, *Garner* and *Edwards* to these non-judicial review cases.

REFERENCES TO THE COURT OF JUSTICE OF THE EUROPEAN UNION 7-27

If required, the Administrative Court has power to refer questions on the interpretation of European Union law to the Court of Justice of the European Union ('CJEU'[95]). On such a reference the CJEU has jurisdiction to give preliminary rulings to national courts on the interpretation of the EU treaties, and the validity and interpretation of acts of the member states in that context. The preliminary ruling procedure is aimed at enabling national courts to ensure uniform interpretation and application of European Union law in all the member states.

The CJEU's jurisdiction to grant preliminary rulings is derived in part from the treaties and in part from various conventions and subordinate legislation. In the main the relevant power arises from article 267 of the Treaty on the Functioning of the European Union ('TFEU').[96]

The order referring the question to the CJEU can be made at any stage and it can be made of the court's own initiative or by an application to the Administrative Court for a reference[97] (the procedure is the CPR Part 23 application procedure).[98] The requisite contents of a reference are detailed in CPR PD 68. Parties applying for a reference should also be aware of the terms of the information note published by the CJEU, which appears at Annex 1 to CPR PD 68.

The information note makes three important points of which all parties should be aware:

1. the court *may* refer a question to the CJEU. It is a discretionary procedure;

[93] [2014] 1 WLR 55 at 65 (para. 23 of the judgment).

[94] [2013] EWHC 4435 (Admin).

[95] See chapter 1, 1-37 for discussion of the CJEU, including alternative names for the CJEU.

[96] The Treaty of Lisbon, brought into force on 1 December 2009, made sweeping changes to the constitution of the European Union (as outlined at 1-37). Any references in case law or elsewhere to article 234 of the EC Treaty should be taken to refer to article 267 of the TFEU as article 267 replaced article 234, albeit without amendment.

[97] CPR 68.2.

[98] The interim application procedure, as outlined at 5-31, may be followed.

2. however, where there is no judicial remedy under national law the court *must*, as a rule, refer such a question to the CJEU, unless the CJEU has already ruled on the point (and there is no new context that raises any serious doubt as to whether that case-law may be applied), or unless the correct interpretation of the rule of Community law is obvious; and
3. the preliminary ruling procedure is not a fact-finding procedure. The Administrative Court must determine the facts to which the question applies before referral.

Generally, the Administrative Court will be cautious before acceding to a request to refer a question to the CJEU. The CJEU itself encouraged this caution in *Wiener SI GmbH* v *Hauptzollamt Emmerich*:[99]

> A reference will be most appropriate where the question is one of general importance and where the ruling is likely to promote the uniform application of the law throughout the European Union. A reference will be least appropriate where there is an established body of case law which could readily be transposed to the facts of the instant case; or where the question turns on a narrow point considered in the light of a very specific set of facts and the ruling is unlikely to have any application beyond the instant case. Between those two extremes there is of course a wide spectrum of possibilities; nevertheless national courts themselves could properly assess whether it is appropriate to make a reference, and the Court of Justice, even if it continued to maintain that the decision to refer was exclusively within the discretion of the national courts, could perhaps give some informal guidance and so encourage self-restraint by the national courts in appropriate cases.[100]

Where the Administrative Court decides that a question should be referred to the CJEU the ACO will communicate that fact, along with a copy of the order, to the Senior Master of the Queen's Bench Division. The Senior Master will arrange for the question to be referred[101] but will not do so until the time to appeal the decision to refer the question has passed[102] (there is a right of appeal to the Court of Appeal).[103] Where the Administrative Court does make an order referring the question then the proceedings are automatically stayed until the CJEU has given the preliminary ruling.[104] The case will be reinstated in the Administrative Court

[99] [1997] ECR I-6495.

[100] [1997] ECR I-6495 at para. 20.

[101] CPR 68.3(1).

[102] CPR 68.3(3).

[103] Confirmed in *R (Federation of Technological Industries)* v *Customs and Excise Commissioners* [2004] STC 1424.

[104] CPR 68.4.

once the CJEU has given the preliminary ruling to make a final ruling, having taken the preliminary ruling into account.

APPEALS 7-28

The decisions of the Administrative Court are often subject to an onward right of appeal. The appeal provisions differ depending on the type of case and the stage at which the case is concluded. This section will not examine the method of appealing but will simply detail which appeal routes are available.

Civil judicial review 7-29

All parties have a right of appeal to the Court of Appeal (Civil Division) against a substantive decision or against refusal of permission to apply for judicial review. Permission to appeal is required and it can be granted by the Administrative Court at the hearing where the decision being appealed is made.[105] In the event that permission to appeal is refused by the Administrative Court, a second application can still be made to the Court of Appeal itself in the appellant's notice.[106] The only difference in procedure between appeals from substantive hearings and appeals against refusal of permission to apply for judicial review is the time limits involved. An appeal against a substantive decision must be lodged with the Court of Appeal within twenty-one days of the date of the decision;[107] in permission cases that time limit is reduced to seven days.[108] This is also the case where permission has been refused and the right to renewal has been removed (cases where the Upper Tribunal is the defendant and totally without merit cases),[109] although in these cases the seven-day period begins from the date of service of the order, not the date of the decision.[110]

In rare cases the Administrative Court may grant a certificate allowing the parties to appeal directly to the Supreme Court, thus skipping the Court of Appeal (colloquially called a 'leapfrog appeal').[111]

[105] CPR 52.3(2)(a): note that the application must be made at the hearing – there is no provision to allow for it to be made once the hearing has concluded. The court may adjourn the question of permission to another date or to be considered on written representations, but it must make an order doing so at the time of the hearing.

[106] CPR 52.3(3). See the Ministry of Justice website for forms.

[107] CPR 52.4(2)(b).

[108] CPR 52.15(2).

[109] CPR 52.15(1A).

[110] CPR 52.15(2).

[111] See ss. 12, 13 and 15 of the Administration of Justice Act 1969 for the provisions governing these cases.

7-30 Statutory applications

This category includes all the applications to quash that are made in accordance with the procedure in CPR PD 8A, para. 22 and CPR PD 8C. The provisions are generally identical to those above in relation to substantive, civil judicial reviews. The terms of the relevant statute should be checked to ensure that it does not make alternative provision.

7-31 Statutory appeals

This category includes all statutory appeals that are made in accordance with the procedure in CPR Part 52, save for case stated appeals. Where the appeal in the Administrative Court is one where no permission is required the provisions are identical to those above in relation to substantive, civil judicial reviews. The terms of the relevant statute should be checked to ensure that it does not make alternative provision, for example by excluding any further right of appeal.[112] Where the appeal is one that requires permission to appeal to the Administrative Court (permission being required within the terms of the relevant statute) and permission is refused in the Administrative Court, then there is no further right of appeal.[113]

7-32 Appeal by way of case stated in civil cases

These appeals are those case stated appeals where the appeal is against the magistrates' court or the Crown Court acting in its civil jurisdiction. There is no appeal from the decision of the Administrative Court in a civil case stated appeal, as outlined in *Horseferry Road Justices* v *The Lord Mayor and the Citizens of the City of Westminster*.[114]

7-33 All criminal cases in the Administrative Court (except habeas corpus)

This category will generally include criminal judicial reviews and appeals by way of case stated against the decision of the magistrates' court or Crown Court.

[112] An example of an Administrative Court appeal that does exclude further right of appeal is an appeal under s. 22 of the Architects Act 1997 (disciplinary proceedings against architects). An appeal against the decision of the Administrative Court is expressly excluded by s. 22(7).

[113] *Prashar* v *Secretary of State for the Environment, Transport and the Regions* [2001] 3 PLR 116. The principle was more recently confirmed with regards to appeals under s. 289 of the Town and Country Planning Act 1990 in *Walsall Metropolitan Borough Council* v *Secretary of State for Communities and Local Government* [2013] JPL 1183.

[114] [2004] 1 WLR 195.

There is no right of appeal from the Administrative Court to the Court of Appeal in cases relating to any criminal cause or matter.[115] The only route of appeal from the Administrative Court is to the Supreme Court under a certificate of a point of law, which the claimant must obtain from the Administrative Court.[116] The certificate will be granted by the court where there is an important point of law that requires the determination of the Supreme Court. Any application for leave to appeal to the Supreme Court and for a certificate must be made to the Administrative Court within twenty-eight days of the decision challenged or the date when reasons for the decision are given.[117] An application for leave may be made to the Supreme Court if the Administrative Court refuses leave, but there is no appeal if the Administrative Court refuses to grant a certificate.

In judicial review the right of appeal to the Supreme Court applies only to substantive decisions. There is no appeal from the decision of the court if permission to apply for judicial review is refused.[118]

Habeas corpus 7-34

In an application for habeas corpus in a civil matter the provisions on appeal to the Court of Appeal apply as they would in a substantive application for judicial review. The only difference is that the applicant does not require permission to appeal.[119]

In an application for habeas corpus in a criminal matter, the prohibition on an appeal to the Court of Appeal still applies[120] and as such the only appeal is to the Supreme Court. The applicant does not need a certified point (as with other criminal cases) but does need to apply to the Administrative Court for leave to appeal. If leave to appeal is refused, the applicant can still apply to the Supreme Court for leave.

Committal for contempt 7-35

Where the Administrative Court has made a finding of contempt and ordered committal to prison as a result, the person committed has a right of appeal to the Court of Appeal (Civil Division). There is no need to obtain permission to appeal.[121] Permission is, however, required to appeal a decision not to commit.[122]

[115] Section 18(1)(a) of the Senior Courts Act 1981. See paras 7-22–7-24 of *Archbold: Criminal Pleading, Evidence and Practice* (Sweet & Maxwell, 2014) for a discussion of what constitutes a criminal cause or matter.

[116] Administration of Justice Act 1960, s. 1(2).

[117] Administration of Justice Act 1960, s. 2(1).

[118] *Re Poh* [1983] 1 All ER 287.

[119] CPR 52.3(1)(a)(ii).

[120] Senior Courts Act 1981, s. 18(1)(a).

[121] CPR 52.3(1)(a)(i).

[122] *M* v *M (Breaches of Orders: Committal)* [2006] 1 FLR 1154.

7-36 Reference on a devolution issue

An appeal against a determination of a devolution issue by the High Court or the Court of Appeal on a reference under Schedule 9 to GOWA 2006[123] lies to the Supreme Court but only with permission of the court from which the appeal lies, or the Supreme Court.[124]

ENFORCEMENT AFTER NON-COMPLIANCE WITH AN ORDER OF THE COURT

7-37 When is enforcement appropriate?

Where a judgment or order of the Administrative Court requires some act[125] to be done within a fixed time or an order not to do an act is disobeyed, then the judgment or order may be enforced by an application for a finding of contempt of court and, if appropriate, committal to prison for contempt of court.[126] The procedure can be found in Part II of CPR 81.

As with all civil proceedings, the parties should do all they can to resolve their differences before applying to the court. As a matter of good practice, if at all possible, before applying to the court the party seeking to enforce should inform the defaulting party of their intention to enforce and request the order be complied with, preferably within a set time frame. This is especially important in Administrative Court cases where the defaulting party will usually be a public body. A public body is unlikely not to have complied due to a lack of power or funding. Equally, it is unlikely that there will be bad faith or a vindictive reason for non-compliance. Rather, any non-compliance will likely be due to an oversight or slow administrative progress.

7-38 Requirements before a court may consider committal

Where a finding of contempt is made the court may order that the person guilty of contempt is to be committed to prison. There is provision to order a fine or the seizure of assets in lieu of committal, but that is not discussed in this section as non-compliance will usually apply to public bodies and neither is likely to be appropriate.[127] Before the court will proceed to enforce non-compliance by way

[123] See 6-22.

[124] GOWA 2006, Sch. 9, para. 11.

[125] An act does not include a requirement to pay costs, damages, or deliver goods or their value, all of which have separate enforcement provisions.

[126] CPR 81.4(1).

[127] See Part VII of CPR Part 81 for the procedure to apply to seize assets under a writ of sequestration. There is power to fine rather than commit under s. 16 of the Contempt of Court Act 1981. The procedure under CPR Part 81 remains the same – see 6-17.

of committal the court must be satisfied that the alleged contemnor is aware of the order allegedly breached and is aware of what is required by the order as well as the ramifications of non-compliance. As such, it is prudent for the applying party to ensure the following before applying for committal.

Service of the order 7-39

Enforcement will only be appropriate if the order allegedly not complied with has been served personally on the individual required to comply.[128] The court may dispense with the requirement to serve personally in two scenarios:

- in the case of a judgment or order requiring a person not to do an act, the court may dispense with service if it is satisfied that the person has had notice of it by being present when the judgment or order was given or made or by being notified of its terms by telephone, email or otherwise;[129] and
- in the case of any judgment or order requiring a person to do an act the court may dispense with service, if it thinks it just to do so, or it may make an order in respect of service by an alternative method or at an alternative place.[130]

Clarity of order 7-40

The order must be clear on its face as to precisely what it meant and what it required or forbade.[131] Contempt will not be established where the breach is of an order which is ambiguous, or which does not require or forbid the performance of a particular act within a specified time frame. The person affected must know with complete precision what it is that they are required to do or abstain from doing otherwise there will be no contempt.

Penal notice 7-41

Where the alleged contemnor is an individual or private company, a judgment or order to do or not do an act may not be enforced unless there is prominently displayed, on the front of the copy of the judgment or order, a warning to the person required to do or not do the act in question that disobedience to the order would be a contempt of court punishable by imprisonment, a fine or sequestration of assets.[132] As a result, the judgment or order must have a penal notice endorsed on it as follows (or in words to substantially the same effect):[133]

[128] CPR 81.5(1) and 81.6.

[129] CPR 81.8(1).

[130] CPR 81.8(2).

[131] *Shadrokh-Cigari* v *Shadrokh-Cigari* [2010] 1 WLR 1311 at 1314.

[132] CPR 81.9(1).

[133] CPR PD 81, para. 1.

> If you the within-named [ ] do not comply with this order you may be held to be in contempt of court and imprisoned or fined, or your assets may be seized.[134]

In proceedings in the Administrative Court, it is not the usual practice to include a penal notice on an order against a public body defendant. In *R (JM) v Croydon London Borough Council*,[135] Collins J held that such notice was not needed to enable the court to deal with public bodies by means of proceedings for contempt as the public bodies would seldom find themselves in the position where committal would be contemplated. Collins J considered:

> I do not think that a penal notice is necessary in orders made against a public body. A failure to comply with an order can be dealt with by an application to the court for a finding of contempt and, if necessary, a further mandatory order which may contain an indication of what might happen should there be any further failure to comply. Adverse findings coupled with what would probably be an order to pay indemnity costs should suffice since it is to be expected that a public body would not deliberately flout an order of the court. Were that to happen, the contemnor could be brought before the court and, were he to threaten to persist in his refusal, an order could be made which made it clear that if he did he would be liable to imprisonment or a fine.[136]

If the penal notice is not contained in the original judgment or order then the party wishing to enforce may apply for a further order in the same terms, but containing the penal notice. Such an application should be made in accordance with the procedure in CPR Part 23[137] and can be considered without a hearing, on the papers alone (if appropriate) under CPR 23.8. The new order must then be served personally as discussed above.

Subject to the provisions of Part II of CPR Part 81 and the guidance above, a committal order may be made, and thus the penal notice should reflect:

- in the case of an individual, the individual themselves;
- in the case of a company, any director or other officer of that company;[138] and
- in the case of a public body, an officer of the public body (but only in the specific scenario considered by Collins J above).

[134] This is the exact wording suggested in CPR PD 81. The form is not rigid or prescribed and may be amended, if required, to suit the scenario.

[135] [2010] 1 WLR 1658.

[136] [2010] 1 WLR 1658 at para. 12.

[137] See the interim applications procedure in chapter 5 at 5-31, which may be followed.

[138] CPR 81.4(3).

Applying for a finding of contempt/committal – procedure 7-42

The procedure for applying for a finding of contempt/committal can be found in CPR 81.10, which requires an application to be made in accordance with CPR Part 23 by filing an application notice.[139] Under CPR 81.10(3) and CPR PD 81, the application notice must:

a. set out in full the grounds on which the committal application is made and must identify, separately and numerically, each alleged act of contempt including, if known, the date of each of the alleged acts;[140]

b. be supported by one or more affidavits containing all the evidence relied upon;[141]

c. state that the application is made in the proceedings in question (that is to say the proceedings in which the order being enforced was made) and its title and reference number must correspond with the title and reference number of those proceedings;[142] and

d. contain a prominent notice, similar to a penal notice, stating the possible consequences of the court making a committal order and of the respondent not attending the hearing. The form of the notice can be found at Annex 3 of CPR PD 81.

The application notice and the evidence in support must be served personally on the respondent[143] unless the court dispenses with service (if it considers it just to do so) or makes an order in respect of service for an alternative method of service.[144]

If the applicant wishes to amend the application notice after it has been filed then the permission of the court is required,[145] which in turn requires the filing and serving of an application to amend.[146] A committal application may not be discontinued without the permission of the court.[147]

139 CPR 81.10(1). See the Ministry of Justice website for forms and fees.

140 CPR 81.10(3)(a).

141 CPR 81.10(3)(b).

142 CPR PD 81, para. 13.1.

143 CPR 81.10(4).

144 CPR 81.10(5).

145 CPR PD 81, para. 13.2(2).

146 With a fee and form – see the Ministry of Justice website for fees and forms.

147 CPR PD 81, para. 16.3.

Applying for a finding of contempt/committal – the hearing

7-43 Listing

An application to find the contempt proven and any subsequent committal, fine or seizure of assets must be considered at a hearing in court.[148]

When issuing or filing the application notice, the applicant must obtain from the ACO a date for the hearing of the application.[149] As such, at the time that the application notice is filed, the ACO will list an in-court hearing in accordance with the interlocutory procedure in the ACO Wales listing policy[150] and will be listed under the discrete title:[151]

> Application by [full name of applicant] for the Committal to prison of [full name of the person alleged to be in contempt]

The hearing date must be specified in the application notice or in a notice of hearing attached to and served with the application notice. The hearing date of a committal application must not be less than fourteen days after service of the application notice on the respondent and as such the applicant should not delay service.[152] If the hearing has to be adjourned because this time limit is not capable of being complied with due to late service, costs sanctions are likely to follow.

7-44 The hearing

The procedure for the substantive hearing in CPR 81.28 and CPR PD 81 have been discussed in chapter 6 and apply to these enforcement proceedings.[153] Similarly, the sections on committal warrants and discharge from custody also apply.

7-45 CONCLUSION

This chapter has discussed some of the various consequential and ancillary orders which a litigant in the Administrative Court may need to consider. Some of these procedures – Aarhus Convention PCOs, for example – are little known but do much to advance access to justice, as well as providing procedural clarity for litigants, in Wales as well as in England. Litigants and practitioners should be aware of these provisions as they are likely to be as important to the outcome of the case to the individuals involved, as the point of law considered by the court is to the public.

148 CPR PD 81, para. 13.2(3).

149 CPR PD 81, para. 15.1.

150 See Annex B for the ACO Wales listing policy.

151 *Practice Direction (Committal for Contempt: Open Court)* [2015] 1 WLR 2195.

152 CPR PD 81, para. 15.2.

153 See 6-17.

Annex A

Civil Procedure Rules Part 54

I JUDICIAL REVIEW

Scope and interpretation

54.1
(1) This Section of this Part contains rules about judicial review.

(2) In this Section –
  (a) a 'claim for judicial review' means a claim to review the lawfulness of –
    (i) an enactment; or
    (ii) a decision, action or failure to act in relation to the exercise of a public function.
  (b) [revoked]
  (c) [revoked]
  (d) [revoked]
  (e) 'the judicial review procedure' means the Part 8 procedure as modified by this Section;
  (f) 'interested party' means any person (other than the claimant and defendant) who is directly affected by the claim; and
  (g) 'court' means the High Court, unless otherwise stated.

(Rule 8.1(6)(b) provides that a rule or practice direction may, in relation to a specified type of proceedings, disapply or modify any of the rules set out in Part 8 as they apply to those proceedings)

Who may exercise the powers of the High Court

54.1A
(1) A court officer assigned to the Administrative Court office who is –
  (a) a barrister; or
  (b) a solicitor,

may exercise the jurisdiction of the High Court with regard to the matters set out in paragraph (2) with the consent of the President of the Queen's Bench Division.

(2) The matters referred to in paragraph (1) are –
  (a) any matter incidental to any proceedings in the High Court;
  (b) any other matter where there is no substantial dispute between the parties; and

(c) the dismissal of an appeal or application where a party has failed to comply with any order, rule or practice direction.

(3) A court officer may not decide an application for –
(a) permission to bring judicial review proceedings;
(b) an injunction;
(c) a stay of any proceedings, other than a temporary stay of any order or decision of the lower court over a period when the High Court is not sitting or cannot conveniently be convened, unless the parties seek a stay by consent.

(4) Decisions of a court officer may be made without a hearing.

(5) A party may request any decision of a court officer to be reviewed by a judge of the High Court.

(6) At the request of a party, a hearing will be held to reconsider a decision of a court officer, made without a hearing.

(7) A request under paragraph (5) or (6) must be filed within 7 days after the party is served with notice of the decision.

When this Section must be used

54.2 The judicial review procedure must be used in a claim for judicial review where the claimant is seeking –
(a) a mandatory order;
(b) a prohibiting order;
(c) a quashing order; or
(d) an injunction under section 30 of the Supreme Court Act 1981 (restraining a person from acting in any office in which he is not entitled to act).

When this Section may be used

54.3
(1) The judicial review procedure may be used in a claim for judicial review where the claimant is seeking –
(a) a declaration; or
(b) an injunction.
(Section 31(2) of the Supreme Court Act 1981 sets out the circumstances in which the court may grant a declaration or injunction in a claim for judicial review)

(Where the claimant is seeking a declaration or injunction in addition to one of the remedies listed in rule 54.2, the judicial review procedure must be used)

(2) A claim for judicial review may include a claim for damages, restitution or the recovery of a sum due but may not seek such a remedy alone.

(Section 31(4) of the Supreme Court Act sets out the circumstances in which the court may award damages, restitution or the recovery of a sum due on a claim for judicial review)

Permission required

54.4 The court's permission to proceed is required in a claim for judicial review whether started under this Section or transferred to the Administrative Court.

Time limit for filing claim form

54.5
(A1) In this rule –

'the planning Acts' has the same meaning as in section 336 of the Town and Country Planning Act 1990;

'decision governed by the Public Contracts Regulations 2006' means any decision the legality of which is or may be affected by a duty owed to an economic operator by virtue of regulation 47A of those Regulations (and for this purpose it does not matter that the claimant is not an economic operator); and

'economic operator' has the same meaning as in regulation 4 of the Public Contracts Regulations 2006.

(1) The claim form must be filed –
 (a) promptly; and
 (b) in any event not later than 3 months after the grounds to make the claim first arose.

(2) The time limits in this rule may not be extended by agreement between the parties.

(3) This rule does not apply when any other enactment specifies a shorter time limit for making the claim for judicial review.

(4) Paragraph (1) does not apply in the cases specified in paragraphs (5) and (6).

(5) Where the application for judicial review relates to a decision made by the Secretary of State or local planning authority under the planning acts, the claim form must be filed not later than 6 weeks after the grounds to make the claim first arose.

(6) Where the application for judicial review relates to a decision governed by the Public Contracts Regulations 2006, the claim form must be filed within the time within which an economic operator would have been required by regulation 47D(2) of those Regulations (and disregarding the rest of that regulation) to start any proceedings under those Regulations in respect of that decision.

Claim form

54.6

(1) In addition to the matters set out in rule 8.2 (contents of the claim form) the claimant must also state –

- (a) the name and address of any person he considers to be an interested party;
- (b) that he is requesting permission to proceed with a claim for judicial review; and
- (c) any remedy (including any interim remedy) he is claiming; and
- (d) where appropriate, the grounds on which it is contended that the claim is an Aarhus Convention claim.

(Rules 45.41 to 45.44 make provision about costs in Aarhus Convention claims.)

(Part 25 sets out how to apply for an interim remedy)

(2) The claim form must be accompanied by the documents required by Practice Direction 54A.

Service of claim form

54.7

The claim form must be served on –

- (a) the defendant; and
- (b) unless the court otherwise directs, any person the claimant considers to be an interested party,

within 7 days after the date of issue.

Judicial review of decisions of the Upper Tribunal

54.7A

(1) This rule applies where an application is made, following refusal by the Upper Tribunal of permission to appeal against a decision of the First Tier Tribunal, for judicial review –

- (a) of the decision of the Upper Tribunal refusing permission to appeal; or
- (b) which relates to the decision of the First Tier Tribunal which was the subject of the application for permission to appeal.

(2) Where this rule applies –

- (a) the application may not include any other claim, whether against the Upper Tribunal or not; and
- (b) any such other claim must be the subject of a separate application.

(3) The claim form and the supporting documents required by paragraph (4) must be filed no later than 16 days after the date on which notice of the Upper Tribunal's decision was sent to the applicant.

(4) The supporting documents are –
 (a) the decision of the Upper Tribunal to which the application relates, and any document giving reasons for the decision;
 (b) the grounds of appeal to the Upper Tribunal and any documents which were sent with them;
 (c) the decision of the First Tier Tribunal, the application to that Tribunal for permission to appeal and its reasons for refusing permission; and
 (d) any other documents essential to the claim.

(5) The claim form and supporting documents must be served on the Upper Tribunal and any other interested party no later than 7 days after the date of issue.

(6) The Upper Tribunal and any person served with the claim form who wishes to take part in the proceedings for judicial review must, no later than 21 days after service of the claim form, file and serve on the applicant and any other party an acknowledgment of service in the relevant practice form.

(7) The court will give permission to proceed only if it considers –
 (a) that there is an arguable case, which has a reasonable prospect of success, that both the decision of the Upper Tribunal refusing permission to appeal and the decision of the First Tier Tribunal against which permission to appeal was sought are wrong in law; and
 (b) that either –
 (i) the claim raises an important point of principle or practice; or
 (ii) there is some other compelling reason to hear it.

(8) If the application for permission is refused on paper without an oral hearing, rule 54.12(3) (request for reconsideration at a hearing) does not apply.

(9) If permission to apply for judicial review is granted –
 (a) if the Upper Tribunal or any interested party wishes there to be a hearing of the substantive application, it must make its request for such a hearing no later than 14 days after service of the order granting permission; and
 (b) if no request for a hearing is made within that period, the court will make a final order quashing the refusal of permission without a further hearing.

(10) The power to make a final order under paragraph (9)(b) may be exercised by the Master of the Crown Office or a Master of the Administrative Court.

Acknowledgment of service

54.8

(1) Any person served with the claim form who wishes to take part in the judicial review must file an acknowledgment of service in the relevant practice form in accordance with the following provisions of this rule.

(2) Any acknowledgment of service must be –

(a) filed not more than 21 days after service of the claim form; and
(b) served on –
(i) the claimant; and
(ii) subject to any direction under rule 54.7(b), any other person named in the claim form, as soon as practicable and, in any event, not later than 7 days after it is filed.

(3) The time limits under this rule may not be extended by agreement between the parties.

(4) The acknowledgment of service –
(a) must –
(i) where the person filing it intends to contest the claim, set out a summary of his grounds for doing so; and
(ii) state the name and address of any person the person filing it considers to be an interested party; and
(b) may include or be accompanied by an application for directions.

(5) Rule 10.3(2) does not apply.

Failure to file acknowledgment of service

54.9
(1) Where a person served with the claim form has failed to file an acknowledgment of service in accordance with rule 54.8, he –
(a) may not take part in a hearing to decide whether permission should be given unless the court allows him to do so; but
(b) provided he complies with rule 54.14 or any other direction of the court regarding the filing and service of –
(i) detailed grounds for contesting the claim or supporting it on additional grounds; and
(ii) any written evidence,
may take part in the hearing of the judicial review.

(2) Where that person takes part in the hearing of the judicial review, the court may take his failure to file an acknowledgment of service into account when deciding what order to make about costs.

(3) Rule 8.4 does not apply.

Permission given

54.10
(1) Where permission to proceed is given the court may also give directions.

(2) Directions under paragraph (1) may include –

(a) a stay of proceedings to which the claim relates;
(b) directions requiring the proceedings to be heard by a Divisional Court.

Service of order giving or refusing permission

54.11
The court will serve –
(a) the order giving or refusing permission; and
(b) any directions,

on –
(i) the claimant;
(ii) the defendant; and
(iii) any other person who filed an acknowledgment of service.

Permission decision without a hearing

54.12
(1) This rule applies where the court, without a hearing –
(a) refuses permission to proceed; or
(b) gives permission to proceed –
(i) subject to conditions; or
(ii) on certain grounds only.

(2) The court will serve its reasons for making the decision when it serves the order giving or refusing permission in accordance with rule 54.11.

(3) Subject to paragraph (7), the claimant may not appeal but may request the decision to be reconsidered at a hearing.

(4) A request under paragraph (3) must be filed within 7 days after service of the reasons under paragraph (2).

(5) The claimant, defendant and any other person who has filed an acknowledgment of service will be given at least 2 days' notice of the hearing date.

(6) The court may give directions requiring the proceedings to be heard by a Divisional Court.

(7) Where the court refuses permission to proceed and records the fact that the application is totally without merit in accordance with rule 23.12, the claimant may not request that decision to be reconsidered at a hearing.

Defendant etc. may not apply to set aside

54.13 Neither the defendant nor any other person served with the claim form may apply to set aside an order giving permission to proceed.

Response

54.14
(1) A defendant and any other person served with the claim form who wishes to contest the claim or support it on additional grounds must file and serve –

- (a) detailed grounds for contesting the claim or supporting it on additional grounds; and
- (b) any written evidence,

within 35 days after service of the order giving permission.

(2) The following rules do not apply –

- (a) rule 8.5(3) and 8.5(4) (defendant to file and serve written evidence at the same time as acknowledgment of service); and
- (b) rule 8.5(5) and 8.5(6) (claimant to file and serve any reply within 14 days).

Where claimant seeks to rely on additional grounds

54.15 The court's permission is required if a claimant seeks to rely on grounds other than those for which he has been given permission to proceed.

Evidence

54.16
(1) Rule 8.6 (1) does not apply.
(2) No written evidence may be relied on unless –

- (a) it has been served in accordance with any –
  - (i) rule under this Section; or
  - (ii) direction of the court; or
- (b) the court gives permission.

Court's powers to hear any person

54.17
(1) Any person may apply for permission –

- (a) to file evidence; or
- (b) make representations at the hearing of the judicial review.

(2) An application under paragraph (1) should be made promptly.

Judicial review may be decided without a hearing

54.18 The court may decide the claim for judicial review without a hearing where all the parties agree.

Court's powers in respect of quashing orders

54.19
(1) This rule applies where the court makes a quashing order in respect of the decision to which the claim relates.

(2) The court may –
- (a)
  - (i) remit the matter to the decision-maker; and
  - (ii) direct it to reconsider the matter and reach a decision in accordance with the judgment of the court; or
- (b) in so far as any enactment permits, substitute its own decision for the decision to which the claim relates.

(Section 31 of the Supreme Court Act 1981 enables the High Court, subject to certain conditions, to substitute its own decision for the decision in question.)

Transfer

54.20 The court may
- (a) order a claim to continue as if it had not been started under this Section; and
- (b) where it does so, give directions about the future management of the claim.

(Part 30 (transfer) applies to transfers to and from the Administrative Court)

II PLANNING COURT

General

54.21
(1) This Section applies to Planning Court claims.

(2) In this Section, 'Planning Court claim' means a judicial review or statutory challenge which –
- (a) involves any of the following matters –
  - (i) planning permission, other development consents, the enforcement of planning control and the enforcement of other statutory schemes;
  - (ii) applications under the Transport and Works Act 1992;
  - (iii) wayleaves;
  - (iv) highways and other rights of way;
  - (v) compulsory purchase orders;
  - (vi) village greens;

(vii) European Union environmental legislation and domestic transpositions, including assessments for development consents, habitats, waste and pollution control;
(viii) national, regional or other planning policy documents, statutory or otherwise; or
(ix) any other matter the judge appointed under rule 54.22(2) considers appropriate; and

(b) has been issued or transferred to the Planning Court.

(Part 30 (Transfer) applies to transfers to and from the Planning Court.)

Specialist list

54.22
(1) The Planning Court claims form a specialist list.

(2) A judge nominated by the President of the Queen's Bench Division will be in charge of the Planning Court specialist list and will be known as the Planning Liaison Judge.

(3) The President of the Queen's Bench Division will be responsible for the nomination of specialist planning judges to deal with Planning Court claims which are significant within the meaning of Practice Direction 54E, and of other judges to deal with other Planning Court claims.

Application of the Civil Procedure Rules

54.23 These Rules and their practice directions will apply to Planning Court claims unless this section or a practice direction provides otherwise.

Further provision about Planning Court claims

54.24 Practice Direction 54E makes further provision about Planning Court claims, in particular about the timescales for determining such claims.

Civil Procedure Rules Practice Direction 54A

1.1
In addition to Part 54 and this practice direction attention is drawn to:
- section 31 of the Senior Courts Act 1981; and
- the Human Rights Act 1998.

The Court

2.1
Part 54 claims for judicial review are dealt with in the Administrative Court.

(Practice Direction 54D) contains provisions about where a claim for judicial review may be started, administered and heard.)

2.2
[Omitted]

2.3
[Omitted]

2.4
[Omitted]

3.1
[Omitted]

3.2
[Omitted]

Rule 54.5 – Time limit for filing claim form

4.1
Where the claim is for a quashing order in respect of a judgment, order or conviction, the date when the grounds to make the claim first arose, for the purposes of rule 54.5(1)(b), is the date of that judgment, order or conviction.

Rule 54.6 – Claim form

Interested parties

5.1
Where the claim for judicial review relates to proceedings in a court or tribunal, any other parties to those proceedings must be named in the claim form as interested parties under rule 54.6(1)(a) (and therefore served with the claim form under rule 54.7(b)).

5.2
For example, in a claim by a defendant in a criminal case in the Magistrates' or Crown Court for judicial review of a decision in that case, the prosecution must always be named as an interested party.

Human rights

5.3
Where the claimant is seeking to raise any issue under the Human Rights Act 1998, or seeks a remedy available under that Act, the claim form must include the information required by paragraph 15 of Practice Direction 16.

Devolution issues

5.4
Where the claimant intends to raise a devolution issue, the claim form must:

(1) specify that the applicant wishes to raise a devolution issue and identify the relevant provisions of the Government of Wales Act 2006, the Northern Ireland Act 1998 or the Scotland Act 1998; and

(2) contain a summary of the facts, circumstances and points of law on the basis of which it is alleged that a devolution issue arises.

5.5
In this practice direction 'devolution issue' has the same meaning as in paragraph 1, Schedule 9 to the Government of Wales Act 2006, paragraph 1, Schedule 10 to the Northern Ireland Act 1998; and paragraph 1, Schedule 6 to the Scotland Act 1998.

Claim form

5.6
The claim form must include or be accompanied by –

(1) a detailed statement of the claimant's grounds for bringing the claim for judicial review;

(2) a statement of the facts relied on;

(3) any application to extend the time limit for filing the claim form;

(4) any application for directions.

5.7
In addition, the claim form must be accompanied by

(1) any written evidence in support of the claim or application to extend time;

(2) a copy of any order that the claimant seeks to have quashed;

(3) where the claim for judicial review relates to a decision of a court or tribunal, an approved copy of the reasons for reaching that decision;

(4) copies of any documents on which the claimant proposes to rely;

(5) copies of any relevant statutory material; and

(6) a list of essential documents for advance reading by the court (with page references to the passages relied on).

5.8
Where it is not possible to file all the above documents, the claimant must indicate which documents have not been filed and the reasons why they are not currently available.

Bundle of documents

5.9

The claimant must file two copies of a paginated and indexed bundle containing all the documents referred to in paragraphs 5.6 and 5.7.

5.10

Attention is drawn to rules 8.5(1) and 8.5(7).

Rule 54.7 – Service of claim form

6.1

Except as required by rules 54.11 or 54.12(2), the Administrative Court will not serve documents and service must be effected by the parties.

6.2

Where the defendant or interested party to the claim for judicial review is –

(a) the Immigration and Asylum Chamber of the First-tier Tribunal, the address for service of the claim form is Official Correspondence Unit, PO Box 6987, Leicester, LE1 6ZX or fax number 0116 249 4240;

(b) the Crown, service of the claim form must be effected on the solicitor acting for the relevant government department as if the proceedings were civil proceedings as defined in the Crown Proceedings Act 1947.

(Practice Direction 66 gives the list published under section 17 of the Crown Proceedings Act 1947 of the solicitors acting in civil proceedings (as defined in that Act) for the different government departments on whom service is to be effected, and of their addresses.)

(Part 6 contains provisions about the service of claim forms.)

Rule 54.8 – Acknowledgment of service

7.1

Attention is drawn to rule 8.3(2) and the relevant practice direction and to rule 10.5.

Rule 54.10 – Permission given

Directions

8.1

Case management directions under rule 54.10(1) may include directions about serving the claim form and any evidence on other persons.

8.2

Where a claim is made under the Human Rights Act 1998, a direction may be made for giving notice to the Crown or joining the Crown as a party. Attention is drawn to rule 19.4A and paragraph 6 of Practice Direction 19A.

8.3
[Omitted]

Permission without a hearing

8.4
The court will generally, in the first instance, consider the question of permission without a hearing.

Permission hearing

8.5
Neither the defendant nor any other interested party need attend a hearing on the question of permission unless the court directs otherwise.

8.6
Where the defendant or any party does attend a hearing, the court will not generally make an order for costs against the claimant.

Rule 54.11 – Service of order giving or refusing permission

9.1
An order refusing permission or giving it subject to conditions or on certain grounds only must set out or be accompanied by the court's reasons for coming to that decision.

Rule 54.14 – Response

10.1
Where the party filing the detailed grounds intends to rely on documents not already filed, he must file a paginated bundle of those documents when he files the detailed grounds.

Rule 54.15 – Where claimant seeks to rely on additional grounds

11.1
Where the claimant intends to apply to rely on additional grounds at the hearing of the claim for judicial review, he must give notice to the court and to any other person served with the claim form no later than 7 clear days before the hearing (or the warned date where appropriate).

Rule 54.16 – Evidence

12.1
Disclosure is not required unless the court orders otherwise.

Rule 54.17 – Court's powers to hear any person

13.1
Where all the parties consent, the court may deal with an application under rule 54.17 without a hearing.

13.2
Where the court gives permission for a person to file evidence or make representations at the hearing of the claim for judicial review, it may do so on conditions and may give case management directions.

13.3
An application for permission should be made by letter to the Administrative Court office, identifying the claim, explaining who the applicant is and indicating why and in what form the applicant wants to participate in the hearing.

13.4
If the applicant is seeking a prospective order as to costs, the letter should say what kind of order and on what grounds.

13.5
Applications to intervene must be made at the earliest reasonable opportunity, since it will usually be essential not to delay the hearing.

Rule 54.20 – Transfer

14.1
Attention is drawn to rule 30.5.

14.2
In deciding whether a claim is suitable for transfer to the Administrative Court, the court will consider whether it raises issues of public law to which Part 54 should apply.

Skeleton arguments

15.1
The claimant must file and serve a skeleton argument not less than 21 working days before the date of the hearing of the judicial review (or the warned date).

15.2
The defendant and any other party wishing to make representations at the hearing of the judicial review must file and serve a skeleton argument not less than 14 working days before the date of the hearing of the judicial review (or the warned date).

15.3
Skeleton arguments must contain:

(1) a time estimate for the complete hearing, including delivery of judgment;

(2) a list of issues;

(3) a list of the legal points to be taken (together with any relevant authorities with page references to the passages relied on);

(4) a chronology of events (with page references to the bundle of documents (see paragraph 16.1);

(5) a list of essential documents for the advance reading of the court (with page references to the passages relied on) (if different from that filed with the claim form) and a time estimate for that reading; and

(6) a list of persons referred to.

Bundle of documents to be filed

16.1
The claimant must file a paginated and indexed bundle of all relevant documents required for the hearing of the judicial review when he files his skeleton argument.

16.2
The bundle must also include those documents required by the defendant and any other party who is to make representations at the hearing.

Agreed final order

17.1
If the parties agree about the final order to be made in a claim for judicial review, the claimant must file at the court a document (with 2 copies) signed by all the parties setting out the terms of the proposed agreed order together with a short statement of the matters relied on as justifying the proposed agreed order and copies of any authorities or statutory provisions relied on.

17.2
The court will consider the documents referred to in paragraph 17.1 and will make the order if satisfied that the order should be made.

17.3
If the court is not satisfied that the order should be made, a hearing date will be set.

17.4
Where the agreement relates to an order for costs only, the parties need only file a document signed by all the parties setting out the terms of the proposed order.

Civil Procedure Rules Practice Direction 54D

Scope and purpose

1.1
This Practice Direction concerns the place in which a claim before the Administrative Court should be started and administered and the venue at which it will be determined.

1.2
This Practice Direction is intended to facilitate access to justice by enabling cases to be administered and determined in the most appropriate location. To achieve this purpose it provides flexibility in relation to where claims are to be administered and enables claims to be transferred to different venues.

Venue – general provisions

2.1
The claim form in proceedings in the Administrative Court may be issued at the Administrative Court Office of the High Court at –

(1) the Royal Courts of Justice in London; or

(2) at the District Registry of the High Court at Birmingham, Cardiff, Leeds, or Manchester unless the claim is one of the excepted classes of claim set out in paragraph 3 of this Practice Direction which may only be started and determined at the Royal Courts of Justice in London.

2.2
Any claim started in Birmingham will normally be determined at a court in the Midland region (geographically covering the area of the Midland Circuit); in Cardiff in Wales; in Leeds in the North-Eastern Region (geographically covering the area of the North Eastern Circuit); in London at the Royal Courts of Justice; and in Manchester, in the North-Western Region (geographically covering the Northern Circuit).

Excepted classes of claim

3.1
The excepted classes of claim referred to in paragraph 2.1(2) are –

(1) proceedings to which Part 76 or Part 79 applies, and for the avoidance of doubt –

- (a) proceedings relating to control orders (within the meaning of Part 76);
- (b) financial restrictions proceedings (within the meaning of Part 79);
- (c) proceedings relating to terrorism or alleged terrorists (where that is a relevant feature of the claim); and
- (d) proceedings in which a special advocate is or is to be instructed;

(2) proceedings to which RSC Order 115 applies;

(3) proceedings under the Proceeds of Crime Act 2002;

(4) appeals to the Administrative Court under the Extradition Act 2003;

(5) proceedings which must be heard by a Divisional Court; and

(6) proceedings relating to the discipline of solicitors.

3.2
If a claim form is issued at an Administrative Court office other than in London and includes one of the excepted classes of claim, the proceedings will be transferred to London.

Urgent applications

4.1
During the hours when the court is open, where an urgent application needs to be made to the Administrative Court outside London, the application must be made to the judge designated to deal with such applications in the relevant District Registry.

4.2
Any urgent application to the Administrative Court during the hours when the court is closed, must be made to the duty out of hours High Court judge by telephoning 020 7947 6000.

Assignment to another venue

5.1
The proceedings may be transferred from the office at which the claim form was issued to another office. Such transfer is a judicial act.

5.2
The general expectation is that proceedings will be administered and determined in the region with which the claimant has the closest connection, subject to the following considerations as applicable –

(1) any reason expressed by any party for preferring a particular venue;

(2) the region in which the defendant, or any relevant office or department of the defendant, is based;

(3) the region in which the claimant's legal representatives are based;

(4) the ease and cost of travel to a hearing;

(5) the availability and suitability of alternative means of attending a hearing (for example, by videolink);

(6) the extent and nature of media interest in the proceedings in any particular locality;

(7) the time within which it is appropriate for the proceedings to be determined;

(8) whether it is desirable to administer or determine the claim in another region in the light of the volume of claims issued at, and the capacity, resources and workload of, the court at which it is issued;

(9) whether the claim raises issues sufficiently similar to those in another outstanding claim to make it desirable that it should be determined together with, or immediately following, that other claim; and

(10) whether the claim raises devolution issues and for that reason whether it should more appropriately be determined in London or Cardiff.

5.3
(1) When an urgent application is made under paragraph 4.1 or 4.2, this will not by itself decide the venue for the further administration or determination of the claim.

(2) The court dealing with the urgent application may direct that the case be assigned to a particular venue.

(3) When an urgent application is made under paragraph 4.2, and the court does not make a direction under sub-paragraph (2), the claim will be assigned in the first place to London but may be reassigned to another venue at a later date.

5.4
The court may on an application by a party or of its own initiative direct that the claim be determined in a region other than that of the venue in which the claim is currently assigned. The considerations in paragraph 5.2 apply.

5.5
Once assigned to a venue, the proceedings will be both administered from that venue and determined by a judge of the Administrative Court at a suitable court within that region, or, if the venue is in London, at the Royal Courts of Justice. The choice of which court (of those within the region which are identified by the Presiding Judge of the circuit suitable for such hearing) will be decided, subject to availability, by the considerations in paragraph 5.2.

5.6
When giving directions under rule 54.10, the court may direct that proceedings be reassigned to another region for hearing (applying the considerations in paragraph 5.2). If no such direction is given, the claim will be heard in the same region as that in which the permission application was determined (whether on paper or at a hearing).

Civil Procedure Rules Practice Direction 54E

General

1.1 This Practice Direction applies to Planning Court claims.

How to start a Planning Court claim

2.1 Planning Court claims must be issued or lodged in the Administrative Court Office of the High Court in accordance with Practice Direction 54D.

2.2 The form must be marked the 'Planning Court'.

Categorisation of Planning Court claims

3.1 Planning Court claims may be categorised as 'significant' by the Planning Liaison Judge.

3.2 Significant Planning Court claims include claims which –

a) relate to commercial, residential, or other developments which have significant economic impact either at a local level or beyond their immediate locality;
b) raise important points of law;
c) generate significant public interest; or
d) by virtue of the volume or nature of technical material, are best dealt with by judges with significant experience of handling such matters.

3.3 A party wishing to make representations in respect of the categorisation of a Planning Court claim must do so in writing, on issuing the claim or lodging an acknowledgment of service as appropriate.

3.4 The target timescales for the hearing of significant (as defined by paragraph 3.2) Planning Court claims, which the parties should prepare to meet, are as follows, subject to the overriding objective of the interests of justice –

a) applications for permission to apply for judicial review are to be determined within three weeks of the expiry of the time limit for filing of the acknowledgment of service;
b) oral renewals of applications for permission to apply for judicial review are to be heard within one month of receipt of request for renewal;
c) applications for permission under section 289 of the Town and Country Planning Act 1990 are to be determined within one month of issue;
d) substantive statutory applications, including applications under section 288 of the Town and Country Planning Act 1990, are to be heard within six months of issue; and
e) judicial reviews are to be heard within ten weeks of the expiry of the period for the submission of detailed grounds by the defendant or any other party as provided in Rule 54.14.

3.5 The Planning Court may make case management directions, including a direction to any party intending to contest the claim to file and serve a summary of his grounds for doing so.

3.6 Notwithstanding the categorisation under paragraph 3.1 of a Planning Court claim as significant or otherwise, the Planning Liaison Judge may direct the expedition of any Planning Court claim if he considers it to necessary to deal with the case justly.

Annex B

LISTING POLICY ADMINISTRATIVE COURT OFFICE FOR WALES AND THE WESTERN CIRCUIT

Version 3.1

NOTE ON THE POLICY

This is the third version of the listing policy for the Administrative Court Office ("ACO") based in Cardiff, the first having been implemented on 27 January 2011. This version is updated to include revised practices and particularly to take into account the listing practices in the Planning Court and urgent applications.

This policy applies to all cases handled by the ACO in Cardiff, i.e. cases in the Administrative Court in Wales (including the Planning Court in Wales), and those Western Circuit Administrative Court cases (including Planning Court cases) handled by the office.

The policy is devised by the ACO lawyer and ACO manager as guidance for caseworkers on listing ACO cases. It has the approval of the Queen's Bench Liaison Judge. Parties to cases managed by the ACO in Cardiff may treat this as guidance on how the caseworkers will list cases.

It should be noted that this policy is intended to supplement the general listing policy for all Administrative Court Offices as outlined in Annex C of Practice Statement [2002] 1 All ER 633.

It should further be noted that this policy may be amended in any individual case by judicial order.

1) URGENT AND/OR INTERIM APPLICATIONS AND HEARINGS

1) The interim application process will begin when a claim form and urgent application notice (N461 & N463) or a general application notice (N244 or PF244), as well as the relevant fee, is received by the ACO. If the application requires consideration within a set time period this should be made apparent by the applying party.

2) Under CPR PD 54A paragraph 5.9 and CPR PD 5A paragraph 2.2, the ACO requires the parties to file any urgent or interim application in a hard copy bundle. The only exception in the CPR to this principle is under CPR PD 5A

paragraph 5.3 which allows urgent applications to be filed by fax. However, it is appreciated that on circuit, for urgent claims with a large quantity of documents, it may be impractical to file the claim by fax. In such circumstances, the party making the application should contact the ACO (02920 376460) to discuss whether sending the application by email may be acceptable. If the ACO agrees to receiving the application by email then a hard copy must still be provided to remain compliant with CPR PD 54A paragraph 5.9 and CPR PD 5A paragraph 2.2, but the ACO will not wait for the hard copy before processing the urgent application.

3) Once the ACO agrees to receive the application by email, the applicant will email a copy of the application and/or claim form to the court (administrativecourtoffice.cardiff@hmcts.x.gsi.gov.uk). On receipt, the caseworker will issue the application and process as per points 4–7 below.

4) Once issued, the caseworker will reply to the email and provide the case number. That case number is to be quoted by the applicant on the hard copies of documents that will follow by post.

5) If the application is to be considered on papers, without an oral hearing, the caseworker will send the application to the ACO lawyer to consider initial directions (CPR 54.1A). The ACO lawyer may refer the application to a Judge without making an order. In the absence of the ACO lawyer the caseworker may refer the application to a Judge directly.

6) If the case requires urgent listing the caseworker will consult with the ACO lawyer who will approve a timetable for listing the application. The caseworker will list the case within that timetable and without checking the availability of the parties. A listing notice will be sent by the caseworker, by post, but it may also be sent by fax or email if the parties require early notice of the hearing due to its proximity.

7) If the case does not require urgent listing, then the caseworker will list the case, adopting the process in the permission hearing policy below. At least 3 days' notice of the hearing must be given unless a judicial order provides otherwise.

2) PERMISSION HEARINGS
JUDICIAL REVIEW AND STATUTORY APPEALS & APPLICATIONS

1) Upon receipt of a renewal notice, appeal notice (with the relevant fee) or a Judge's order adjourning permission into Court, the caseworker will proceed to list immediately.

2) The caseworker will either email or telephone counsel's clerks for all sides to request the dates of availability for counsel over the next two months. In Planning Court cases, including appeals against enforcement notices under s 289 Town and Country Planning Act 1990, only dates for the next month will be obtained.[1]

- Only the availability of counsel on the Court record will be checked.
- The listing period will only be extended in exceptional circumstances and with the agreement of the ACO manager or ACO lawyer.
- Unless availability is provided over the phone at the time of the initial contact the clerk will be informed that they must provide availability within 48 hours otherwise the case will be listed, with or without those dates. The caseworker is not required to make a follow up enquiry.

3) If the availability of all counsel correspond, the caseworker will check for judicial availability on those dates. If a Judge is available on the said date(s) then the case will be listed accordingly.

- If counsels' dates do correspond every effort will be made to list on that/ those date(s).
- The caseworker will attempt to list the case in the most geographically appropriate hearing centre, considering judicial availability for that Court centre.
- Only in exceptional circumstances will cases that relate to North Wales not be heard in North Wales. Only in exceptional circumstances will cases that relate to the Western Circuit not be heard at Bristol Civil Justice Centre.

4) If the available dates do not correspond or a Judge is not available then the caseworker will obtain a list of dates when a Judge is available over the next two months (one month for Planning Court cases).[1] The caseworker will inform the clerks of the lack of available dates and inform them of the dates on which a Judge is available. The parties will be asked to agree one of these dates and inform the ACO within 48 hours of the agreed date.

- The sooner the clerks respond the better as judicial availability may change.
- The relevant time limit will not be extended due to the unavailability of counsel alone.

5) Failure to reply within 48 hours will result in the case being listed at the ACO's convenience. When the 48 hour period expires or when the clerks returns the agreed date the caseworker will list the case and send out notices.

[1] Note the time limit can be varied by a judicial order (e.g. – if the order states the hearing must be listed before or after a certain date or within a particular timescale).

- To adjourn or vacate a listed date requires a judicial order which may be obtained via a consent order or a formal application on form N244.

3) SUBSTANTIVE HEARINGS (INCLUDING ROLLED UP HEARINGS) JUDICIAL REVIEW AND STATUTORY APPEALS & APPLICATIONS

1) Upon receipt of a fee to start or continue proceedings (or, for a rolled up hearing, on receipt of an undertaking to pay the appropriate fee if permission is ultimately granted), the caseworker will proceed to list immediately. If the fee was paid at permission stage then the caseworker will begin the listing process on receipt of the order granting permission.

2) The caseworker will either email or telephone counsel's clerks for all sides to request the dates of availability for counsel for the three-month[2] period after the warned list[3] date.

    - When listing the caseworker will always have in mind the target that substantive hearings should be heard within six months of issue.
    - Only the availability of counsel on the Court record will be checked.
    - The listing period will only be extended in exceptional circumstances and with the agreement of the ACO manager or ACO lawyer.
    - Unless availability is provided at the time of the initial contact the clerk will be informed that they must provide availability within 48 hours or the case will be listed, with or without those dates. The caseworker is not required to follow up on the enquiry.

3) If the availability of all counsel correspond, the caseworker will check for judicial availability on that/those date(s). If a Judge is available on the said date(s) then the case will be listed accordingly.

    - If counsels' dates do correspond every effort will be made to list on that/ those date(s).
    - The caseworker will attempt to list the case in the most geographically appropriate hearing centre, considering judicial availability for that Court centre.

[2] Note the time limit can be varied by a judicial order (e.g. – if the order states the hearing must be listed before or after a certain date or within a particular timescale).

[3] The warned list begins on the first day on which the ACO could list the case taking into account the time allowed by the CPR or judicial order for the parties to file documents.

- Only in exceptional circumstances will cases that relate to North Wales not be heard in North Wales. Only in exceptional circumstances will cases that relate to the Western Circuit not be heard at Bristol Civil Justice Centre.

4) If the available dates do not correspond or a Judge is not available then the caseworker will obtain a list of dates when a Judge is available over the relevant three months. The caseworker will inform the clerks of the lack of available dates and inform them of the dates on which a Judge is available. The parties will be asked to agree one of these dates and inform the ACO within 48 hours of the agreed date.
   - The sooner the clerks respond the better as judicial availability may change.
   - The relevant time limit will not be extended due to the unavailability of counsel alone.

5) Failure to reply within 48 hours will result in the case being listed at the ACO's convenience. When the 48-hour period expires or when the clerks returns the agreed date the caseworker will list the case and send out notices.
   - To adjourn or vacate a listed date requires a judicial order which may be obtained via a consent order or a formal application on form N244. A fee is payable on each.

4) DIVISIONAL COURTS

1) Where a party considers that a claim or application should be dealt with by a Divisional Court, then that party should notify the ACO in writing as soon as possible, i.e. usually in or with the claim form or application, or the acknowledgment of service or response to an application.

2) Where a Divisional Court is required for a hearing the relevant process in this policy will continue to apply, i.e. the permission process will apply to permission hearings and the substantive process will apply to substantive hearings.

3) At the stage in the process where the caseworker is required to obtain judicial availability, the caseworker will liaise with the Queen's Bench Liaison Judge as to the proper constitution of the Court and the availability of two (or three) Judges to hear the case.[4]

[4] Due to the relative difficulty of obtaining available dates for two or three Judges the requirement to list before a Divisional Court may be deemed an exceptional circumstance for the purpose of extending the time period for listing referred to in this policy or for a reduced number of days available for listing.

Annex C

CONTACT DETAILS

THE ADMINISTRATIVE COURT OFFICE IN WALES

The Administrative Court Office in Wales
Cardiff Civil Justice Centre
2 Park Street
Cardiff
CF10 1ET
DX 99500 Cardiff 6

Telephone: 02920 376460
Facsimile: 02920 376461

General Email: administrativecourtoffice.cardiff@hmcts.x.gsi.gov.uk
Skeleton Arguments Email: administrativecourtofficecardiff.skeletonarguements @hmcts.x.gsi.gov.uk

Court Hearings Website: http://www.justice.gov.uk/courts/court-lists.

Claims may be lodged in person or by post. When lodging in person the Civil Justice Centre counters are open from 10 a.m. to 2 p.m., but the Administrative Court Office will accept papers up until 4 p.m. A litigant who wishes to lodge papers in person between 2 p.m. and 4 p.m. may do so by ringing the bell next to the counter doors on the first floor. A claim may be lodged by fax but only in an 'unavoidable emergency'.[1] It is submitted that an unavoidable emergency should be considered to be a claim where urgent interim relief is required and there is insufficient time to post or attend the Civil Justice Centre in person. It should be noted that there is no provision to allow claims, even urgent ones, to be lodged by email. Any fees may be paid by cash, cheque made payable to HMCTS, or by credit or debit card. When considering lodging a claim, especially an urgent one, parties are encouraged to contact the Administrative Court Office in Wales on the above number to discuss practical considerations.

[1] CPR PD 5A, paragraph 5.9.

UPPER TRIBUNAL (ADMINISTRATIVE APPEALS CHAMBER)

Upper Tribunal (Administrative Appeals Chamber)
Cardiff Civil Justice Centre
2 Park Street
Cardiff CF10 1ET
DX 99500 Cardiff 6

Or

Upper Tribunal (Administrative Appeals Chamber)
5th Floor Rolls Building
7 Rolls Buildings
Fetter Lane
London EC4A 1NL
DX 160042 STRAND 4

Email: adminappeals@hmcts.gsi.gov.uk
Telephone: 020 7071 5662
Facsimile: 08703 240028

UPPER TRIBUNAL (IMMIGRATION AND ASYLUM CHAMBER)

In summary, claimants wishing to lodge proceedings in the UT(IAC) in Wales should do so as follows:

For the UT(IAC) – Judicial Reviews Only:

Upper Tribunal (Immigration and Asylum Chamber)
Cardiff Civil Justice Centre
2 Park Street
Cardiff CF10 1ET
DX 99500 Cardiff 6

Telephone: 02920 376460
Facsimile: 02920 376461

For UT(IAC) – All non judicial review cases:

Lodging Appeals:

Upper Tribunal (Immigration and Asylum Chamber)
IA Field House
15 Breams Buildings
London EC4A 1DZ

Unless advised otherwise, all other correspondence to:

Upper Tribunal (Immigration and Asylum Chamber)
Arnhem Support Centre
PO Box 6987
Leicester LE1 6ZX

Facsimile: 0116 249 4130

Customer Service Centre (Enquiry Unit) telephone: 0300 123 1711

SENIOR COURTS COSTS OFFICE

Senior Courts Costs Office
Royal Courts of Justice
Strand
London WC2A 2LL
DX 44454 Strand

Telephone: 020 7947 6469/6404/7818
Email: SCCO@hmcts.gsi.gov.uk

COURT OF APPEAL (CIVIL DIVISION)

Civil Appeals Office
Room E307
Royal Courts of Justice
Strand
London WC2A 2LL
DX: 44450 Strand

Telephone Number: 020 7947 7677

SUPREME COURT

The Supreme Court
Parliament Square
London SW1P 3BD
DX 157230 Parliament Sq 4

Telephone Number: 020 7960 1500 or 1900
Facsimile: 020 7960 1901

Annex D

Addresses for Service of Central Government Departments[1]

Government Department	Solicitor for Service
Advisory, Conciliation and Arbitration Service, Board of Trade, Cabinet Office, Commissioners for the Reduction of National Debt, Crown Prosecution Service, Department for Business, Innovation and Skills, Department for Communities and Local Government, Department for Culture, Media and Sport, Department for Education, Department of Energy and Climate Change, Department for Environment, Food and Rural Affairs, Department for Health, Department for International Development, Department for Transport, Department for Work and Pensions, Foreign and Commonwealth Office, Forestry Commissioners, Government Actuary's Department, Government Equalities Office, Health and Safety Executive, Her Majesty's Chief Inspector of Education and Training in Wales, Her Majesty's Treasury, Home Office, Ministry of Defence, Ministry of Justice, National Savings and Investments, Northern Ireland Office, Office for Standards in Education, Children's Services and Skills, Ordnance Survey, Privy Council Office, Public Works Loan Board, Revenue and Customs Prosecutions Office, Royal Mint, Serious Fraud Office, Statistics Board (UK Statistics Authority), The National Archives, Wales Office (Office of the Secretary of State for Wales)	The Government Legal Department, One Kemble Street, London, WC2B 4TS, DX 123242 Kingsway[2]
Crown Estate Commissioners	Legal Director, The Crown Estate, 16 New Burlington Place, London, W1S 2HX
Export Credits Guarantee Department	The General Counsel, Export Credits Guarantee Department, P.O. Box 2200, 2 Exchange Tower, Harbour Exchange Square, London, E14 9GS
Food Standards Agency	Director of Legal Services, Food Standards Agency, Aviation House, 125 Kingsway, London, WC2B 6NH

Government Department	Solicitor for Service
Gas and Electricity Markets Authority	Senior Legal Director, Office of Gas and Electricity Markets, 9 Millbank, London, SW1P 3GE
Her Majesty's Revenue and Customs	General Counsel and Solicitor to Her Majesty's Revenue and Customs, HM Revenue and Customs, South West Wing Bush House, Strand London, WC2B 4RD
Office of Fair Trading	General Counsel, Fleetbank House, 2–6 Salisbury Square, London, EC4Y 8JX
Office of Qualifications and Examinations Regulation (Ofqual)	Head of Legal Ofqual, 1410 Spring Place, Herald Avenue, Coventry Business Park, Coventry, West Midlands, CV5 6UB
Office of Rail Regulation	Director of Legal Services ORR, One Kemble Street, London, WC2B 4AN
Water Services Regulation Authority (OFWAT)	Director of Legal Services and Board Secretary, Water Services Regulation Authority (OFWAT), Centre City Tower, 7 Hill Street, Birmingham, B5 4UA
Welsh Assembly Government	The Director of Legal Services to the Welsh Assembly Government, Cathays Park, Cardiff, CF10 3NQ

[1] Taken from published list by Sir Francis Maude, Cabinet Secretary, on 26 October 2012. Also found at annex 2 to CPR PD 66. The above table has been amended from the 2012 published version for this work to add the Department of Health and the Department for Work and Pensions to the Government Legal Department's remit, thus reflecting the current position for those departments. It also updates by replacing the Treasury Solicitor's Department with the Government Legal Department.

[2] The only exception to this table is when serving the claim form on the Secretary of State for the Home Department in judicial review proceedings in the Upper Tribunal (Immigration and Asylum Chamber). In UTIAC the address for service is Home Office, Status Park 2, 4 Nobel Drive, Harlington, Middlesex, UB3 5EY.

Annex E

Checklist For Judicial Review Documents

No.	Item	Check
1)	Fee or Fee Remission	
2)	Claim Form	
3)	Statement of Facts and Grounds	
4)	Supporting Evidence	
5)	Notice of Decision	
6)	Copies of Statutory Material and Cases Relied Upon	
7)	List of Essential Reading	
8)	Items 2–7 in Paginated and Indexed Bundle (Two copies for ACO, additional copy to serve on each party)	

Annex F

Administrative Court Office in Wales Statistics – 2009–14

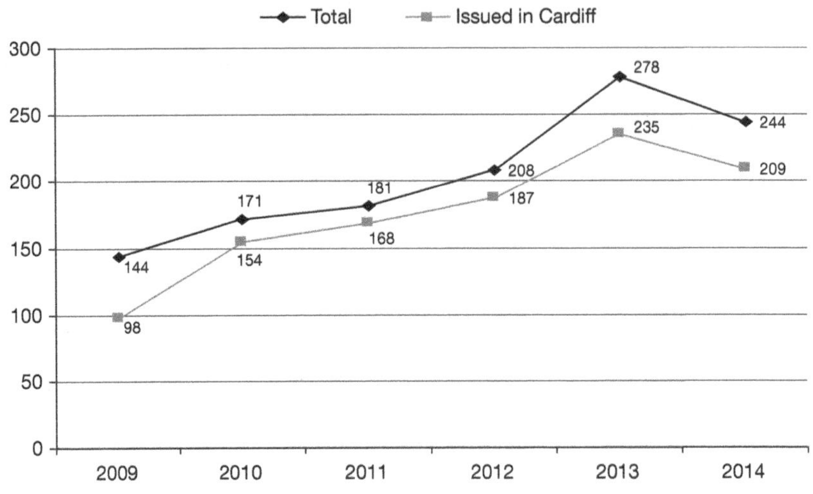

	2009	2010	2011	2012	2013	2014
Total	144	171	181	208	278	244
Issued in Cardiff	98	154	168	187	235	209

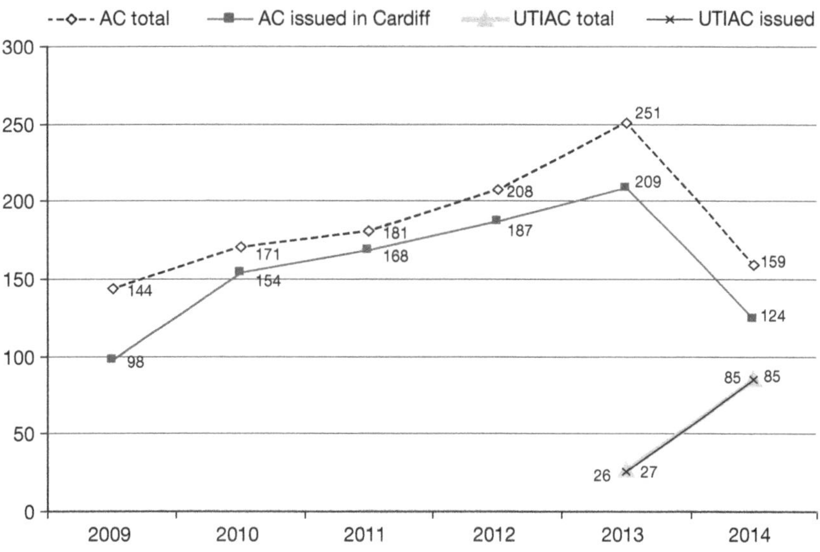

	2009	2010	2011	2012	2013	2014
AC total	144	171	181	208	251	159
AC issued in Cardiff	98	154	168	187	209	124
UTIAC total					27	85
UTIAC issued in Cardiff					26	85

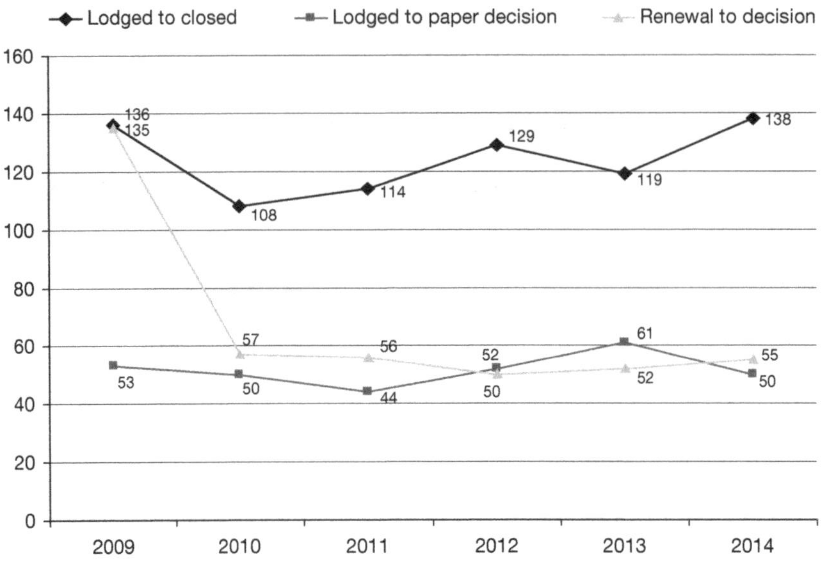

	2009	2010	2011	2012	2013	2014
Average waiting time (days)	136	108	114	129	119	138
Cases closed (under 6 months)	74	139	131	145	207	135
Cases closed (over 6 months)	20	30	26	38	59	49

Notes

The UTIAC Office for Wales/West opened on 1 November 2013 when UTIAC assumed responsibility for the majority of immigration based judicial reviews. Where appropriate, the UTIAC statistics have been separated from the ACO statistics.

* Waiting times are calculated by reference to all cases closed/decisions made within the relevant year, irrespective of what year the case was lodged.

Annex G

Pro Formas

Pro Forma Consent Order

Court Ref: CO/xxxx/20xx

IN THE HIGH COURT OF JUSTICE
QUEENS BENCH DIVISION
ADMINISTRATIVE COURT IN WALES

BETWEEN:

[NAME] **Claimant**

and

[NAME] **Defendant**

CONSENT ORDER

[INSERT OPTIONAL PREAMBLE]

By Consent it is ordered that:

[INSERT TERMS OF CONSENT ORDER]

Name .... Signed ....
Claimant/Claimant's Solicitor

Name .... Signed ....
Defendant/Defendant's Solicitor

Name .... Signed ....
Interested Party/Interested Party's Solicitor

Dated: [INSERT DATE]

Pro Forma Witness Statement

Witness Statement on behalf of: [insert name of claimant/defendant as appropriate]
[Insert initials and surname of witness]
Statement Number: [1st/2nd/3rd etc(of the individual witness)]
[Insert initials of any exhibits referred to]
Date of Statement: [Insert date]

Court Ref: CO/xxxx/20xx

IN THE HIGH COURT OF JUSTICE
QUEENS BENCH DIVISION
ADMINISTRATIVE COURT IN WALES

BETWEEN:

[NAME] **Claimant**

and

[NAME] **Defendant**

WITNESS STATEMENT OF
[INSERT NAME]

[INSERT DETAILS OF WITNESS STATEMENT, EVIDENCE ETC.]

I believe that the facts stated in this witness statement are true.

Name ………………………………………………………

Signed ……………………………………………………..

Date ………………………………………………………

Annex H

THE LEGAL SYSTEM OF ENGLAND AND WALES

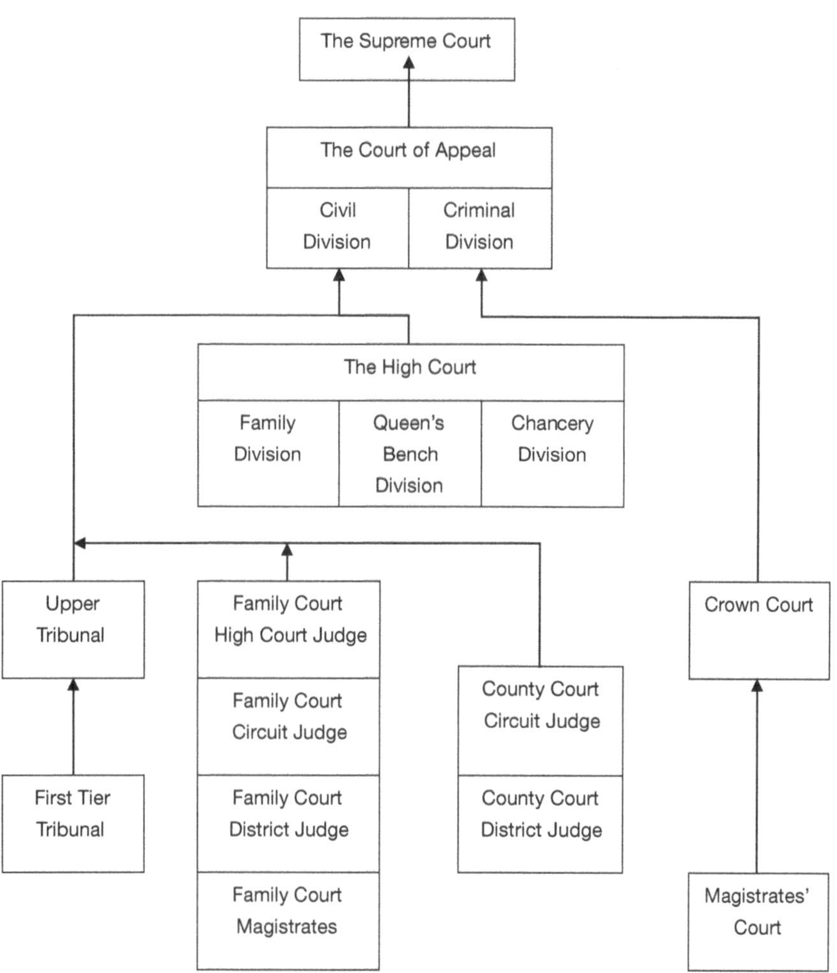

Bibliography

ARTICLES

Arden, M., 'The changing judicial role: human rights, Community law and the intention of Parliament' (2008) 67(3) CLJ 487–507

Bailey, S., 'Taking local government seriously: democracy, autonomy and the constitution' (2009) 68(2) CLJ 436–72

Baksi, C., 'High Court refers firm to SRA after contempt ruling', 9 August 2013, *The Law Society Gazette*

Beatson, J., 'The Scope of Judicial Review for Error of Law' (1984) 4 OJLS 22

Bingham, T., 'The Rule of Law' (2007) 66(1) CLJ 67

Breeze, A., 'Roman Tribunes and Dyfed Kings', *Welsh History Review*, 21/4 (2003)

Campbell, C., 'The Nature of Power as Public in English Judicial Review' (2009) 68(1) CLJ 90–117

Collar, N., 'Judicial Review and alternative remedies – an analysis of recent English decisions' (1991) 10 CJQ 138–51

Cross, T., 'Predispositions, predeterminations and the test for apparent bias: some reflections post National Assembly for *Wales v Condron*' [2007] JPL 1260–73

Costello, K., 'The writ of certiorari and review of summary criminal convictions, 1660–1848' (2012) 128 LQR 443–65

Davies, R., 'In Search of Attitude', *Western Mail*, 4 December 2000

Davies, W., 'Looking Backwards to the Early Medieval Past: Wales and England, a contrast in approaches', *Welsh History Review*, 22/2 (2004)

Dimelow, S. J., 'The interpretation of "constitutional" statutes' (2013) 129 LQR 498–503

Dove, I. and Patterson, F., 'The Planning Court: Future Directions' [2015] JPL 1118

Elliott, M., 'Has the common law duty to give reasons come of age yet?' [2011] PL 56–74

Fordham, M., 'Judicial review: the new rules' [2001] PL 4–10

Gardner, D., 'Local Justice', *Counsel Magazine* (January 2010), 22

Gardner, D., 'Public Law Challenges in Wales: the Past and the Present' [2013] PL 1

Halloran, K., 'Welsh Kings at the English Court', *Welsh History Review*, 25/3 (2011), 297

Harwood, R., 'The Planning Court Comes Into Being' [2014] JPL 699–704

Jarrett, G. and Mann, J., 'The Tribes of Wales', *Welsh History Review*, 4/2 (1968), 161–74

Jenkins, D., 'Legal and Comparative Aspects of the Welsh Laws', *Welsh History Review*, (1963), 51–9

Johnes, M., 'Wales, History, and Britishness', *Welsh History Review*, 25/4 (2011), 596

Jones, T., 'Mistake of Fact in Administrative Law' [1990] PL 507–26

Jones, T. and Williams, J., 'Wales as a Jurisdiction' [2004] PL 78–101

Jolowicz, J. A., 'Practice directions and the Civil Procedure Rules' (2000) 59(1) CLJ 53–61

Jurgens, G. and Van Ommeren, J., 'The public–private divide in English and Dutch law: a multifunctional and context-dependant divide' (2012) 71(1) CLJ 172–99

Kimblin, R. and Dove, I., 'The interpretation of planning policy after *Tesco*' [2012] JPL 1045–52

Lobban, M., 'Review essay' (2011) 7(2) Int JLC 257–69

Laffin, M. and Thomas, A., 'The United Kingdom: Federalism in Denial?' *Publius*, 29/3 (1999), 89–107

Madge-Wyld, S., 'Who may exercise a right of audience in claims for possession in the county court?' (2011) 14(1) JHL 16–21

Masterman, R. and Murkins, J., 'Skirting supremacy and subordination: the constitutional authority of the United Kingdom Supreme Court' [2013] PL 800–20

McHarg, A., 'What is delegated legislation?' [2006] PL 539–61

Nason, S., 'Justice Outside London? Five Years of "Regional" Administrative Courts' [2014] JR 188

Nason, S., 'Regionalisation of the Administrative Court and the Tribunalisation of Judicial Review' [2009] PL 440

Nason, S. et al., 'Regionalisation of the Administrative Court and Access to Justice' [2010] JR 220

Nason, S. and Sunkin, M., 'The Regionalisation of Judicial Review: Constitutional Authority, Access to Justice and Specialisation of Legal Services in Public Law' (2013) 76(2) MLR 223–53

Oliver, D., 'Public law procedures and remedies – do we need them?' [2002] PL 91–110

Pryce, W. T. R., 'Region or National Territory? Regionalism and the idea of the country of Wales, C1927–1998', *Welsh History Review*, 23/2 (2007)

Rawlings, R., 'Hastening slowly: the next phase of Welsh Devolution' [2005] PL 824–52

Roddick, W., 'Law-making and devolution: the Welsh experience' (2003) 3(3/4) LIM 152–7

Scharf, D., 'The duty is to reason why: providing reasons for granting planning permission' [2005] JPL 747–52

Scott, I. R., 'Examination of witnesses in judicial review proceedings' (2002) 21 CJQ 193

Scott, I. R., 'The Law Commission Report on judicial review' (1995) 14 CJQ 97–102

Seneviratne, M., 'A New Ombudsman for Wales' [2006] PL 6–14
Smith, L. B., 'Disputes and Settlements in Medieval Wales: The Role of Arbitration', *English History Review* (1991), 835–60
Sunkin, M. et al., 'Mapping the use of judicial review to challenge local authorities in England and Wales' [2007] PL 545–67
Sunkin, M. and Cornford, T., 'The Bowman Report, access and the recent reforms of the judicial review procedure' [2001] PL 11–20
Trench, A., 'The Government of Wales Act 2006: the next steps on devolution for Wales' [2006] PL 687–96
UK Parliament, 'Living Heritage, Parliament and Europe: The EEC and the Single European Act', April 2013
Unknown author, 'Anglesey council to be taken over, says Carl Sargeant', 16 March 2011, BBC Online
Unknown author, 'Anglesey council: Ministers hand control back to councillors', 23 May 2013, BBC Online
Unknown author, 'Williams Commission report calls for fewer councils', 20 January 2014, BBC Online
Wackham, C., 'Medieval Wales and European History', *Welsh History Review*, 25/2 (2010), 201
Wigley, J., 'Changing times: the importance of proper consultation' [2011] JPL 1447–54
Williams, K., 'Historic 14th century book of Welsh law goes on display', 23 July 2012, Wales Online

BOOKS

Alcock, J. P., *A Brief History of Roman Britain* (Robinson, 2011)
Arnold, C. and Davies, J., *Roman and Early Medieval Wales* (Sutton Publishing, 2000)
Barnes, I., *Mapping History: Classical World* (Eagle Editions Ltd, 2008)
Barnett, H., *Constitutional and Administrative Law* (8th edn) (Routledge, 2011)
Beatson, J. et al., *Human Rights: Judicial Protection in the United Kingdom* (Sweet and Maxwell, 2008)
Bogdanor, V., *Devolution in the United Kingdom* (Updated edn) (Oxford University Press, 2001)
Bradley, A. W. and Ewing, K. D., *Constitutional & Administrative Law* (15th edn) (Pearson Education, 2011)
Burrows, A., *A Restatement of the English Law of Unjust Enrichment* (Oxford University Press, 2013)
Carroll, A., *Constitutional and Administrative Law* (4th edn) (Pearson Education, 2007)
Clayton, R. and Tomlinson, H., *The Law of Human Rights* (2nd edn) (Oxford University Press, 2009)

Craig, P. and De Burca, G., *EU Law: Text, Cases, and Materials* (6th edn) (Oxford University Press, 2015)

Davies, J., *A History of Wales* (Penguin Books, 2007)

Davies, R. R., 'The Identity of "Wales" in the Thirteenth Century', in K. O. Morgan and R. Griffiths (eds), *From Medieval to Modern Wales* (University of Wales Press, 2004)

De La Bedoyere, G., *Roman Britain: A New History* (Thames and Hudson, 2010)

Endicott, T., *Administrative Law* (2nd edn) (Oxford University Press, 2011)

Gower, J., *The Story of Wales* (Random House, 2012)

Halsbury's Laws of England, vol. 1(1) (2001 Reissue), Administrative Law

Halsbury's Laws of England, vol. 8(2) (Reissue), Constitutional Law and Human Rights

Halsbury's Laws of England, vol. 24 (5th edn) (2010), Courts and Tribunals

Halsbury's Laws of England, vol. 69 (5th edn) (2009), Local Government

Halsbury's Laws of England, vol. 71 (5th edn) (2013), Magistrates

Halsbury's Laws of England, vol. 78 (5th edn) (2010), Open Spaces and Countryside

Halsbury's Laws of England, vol. 88A (5th edn) (2013), Rights and Freedoms

Hazel, R., 'Multi-Level Governance', in J. Osmond and B. Jones (eds), *Birth of Welsh Democracy: The First Term of the National Assembly for Wales* (Institute of Welsh Affairs, 2003)

Herbert, T. and Jones, G. E. (eds), *Edward I and Wales* (University of Wales Press, 1988)

Hilliam, D., *Kings, Queens, Bones and Bastards* (Sutton Publishing, 1998)

Howell, R., 'We Were the Welsh Who Fought the Romans, Weren't We?', in H. V. Bowen (ed.), *A New History of Wales* (Gomer Press, 2011)

Jackson, R. (ed.), *Civil Procedure 2013 (The White Book 2013)* (Sweet and Maxwell, 2013)

Jenkins, D., *Hywel Dda – The Law* (Gomer Press, 1986)

Johnes, M., 'What Did Thatcher Ever Do for Wales?', in H. V. Bowen (ed.), *A New History of Wales* (Gomer Press, 2011)

Jones, J. B., 'Welsh Politics Come of Age: The Transformation of Wales Since 1979', in J. Osmond (ed.), *A Parliament for Wales* (Gomer Press, 1994)

Jones, J. G., *Wales and the Tudor State* (University of Wales Press, 1989)

Jones, M. (ed.), *Clerk and Lindsell on Torts* (21st edn) (Sweet & Maxwell, 2015)

Jowell, J., 'The Rule of Law Today', in J. Jowell and D. Oliver (eds), *The Changing Constitution* (4th edn) (Oxford University Press, 2000)

Karl, R., 'How Celtic are the Welsh?', in H. V. Bowen (ed.), *A New History of Wales* (Gomer Press, 2011)

Lang, B., *Administrative Court: Practice and Procedure* (Sweet and Maxwell, 2006)

Lester, A., Pannick, D. and Herberg, J., *Human Rights Law and Practice* (LexisNexis, 2009)

Lieberman, M., *The March of Wales: 1067–1300* (University of Wales Press, 2008)

Lynch, F., Aldhouse-Green, S. and Davies, J. L., *Prehistoric Wales* (Sutton Publishing, 2000)

Lyon, A., *Constitutional History of the United Kingdom* (Cavendish Publishing, 2003)
MacDonald, I. and Toal, R., *MacDonald's Immigration Law and Practice* (8th edn) (Butterworths, 2010)
Manchester, A. H., *A Modern Legal History of England and Wales 1750–1950* (Butterworths, 1980)
Miers, D., 'Law Making', in J. Osmond and B. Jones (eds), *Birth of Welsh Democracy: The First Term of the National Assembly for Wales* (Institute of Welsh Affairs, 2003)
Morgan, K. and Mungham, G., *Redesigning Democracy: The Making of the Welsh Assembly* (Seren, 2000)
Neuberger, D. (ed.), *Civil Court Practice 2013 (The Green Book 2013)* (LexisNexis, 2013)
Osmond, J., 'Re-Making Wales', in J. Osmond (ed.), *A Parliament for Wales* (Gomer Press, 2014)
Owen, A., *Ancient Laws and Institutions of Wales; Comprising Laws Supposed to be enacted by Howel the Good, Modified by subsequent regulations under Natwe Princes prior to the conquest by Edward the First* (Eyre and Spottiswoode, 1841)
Parry, G., *A Guide to the Records of the Great Sessions in Wales* (National Library of Wales, 1995)
Patchett, K., 'The Constitutional Architecture', in J. Osmond and B. Jones (eds), *Birth of Welsh Democracy: The First Term of the National Assembly for Wales* (Institute of Welsh Affairs, 2003)
Pollock, F. and Maitland, F., *History of English Law before the time of Edward I* (2nd edn) (Cambridge University Press, 1968)
Pryce, H., 'Llewellyn the Great and Llewellyn the Last – For Themselves or Wales?', in H. V. Bowen (ed.), *A New History of Wales* (Gomer Press, 2011)
Pryce, H., *The Acts of Welsh Rulers: 1120–1283* (University of Wales Press, 2005)
Pryce, H., 'Were we Welsh or Were we British?', in Bowen, H. V. (ed.), *A New History of Wales* (Gomer Press, 2011)
Rawlings, R., *Delineating Wales: Constitutional, Legal and Administrative Aspects of National Devolution* (University of Wales Press, 2003)
Richardson, J., *Archbold: Criminal Pleading, Evidence, and Practice* (Sweet & Maxwell, 2014)
Ross, D., *Wales: A History of a Nation* (Waverley Books, 2010)
Smith J. B., *Llewellyn Ap Gruffudd, Prince of Wales* (Cardiff University Press, 1998)
Supperstone, M. and Knapman, L., *Administrative Court Practice* (Oxford University Press, 2008)
Turvey, R., *The Lord Rhys: Prince of Deheubarth* (Gomer Press,1997)
Venning, T., *The Kings and Queens of Wales* (Amberley Publishing, 2012)
Watkin, T., *The Legal History of Wales* (2nd edn) (University of Wales Press, 2012)
Wade, H. W. R. and Forsyth, C. F., *Administrative Law* (10th edn) (Oxford University Press, 2009)
Williams, D., 'Sir William Wade Q.C.', in W. Wade (ed.), *The Golden Metwand and the Crooked Cord: Essays in Honour of Sir William Wade* (Oxford University Press, 1998)

Williams, J., 'Legal Wales', in J. Osmond and B. Jones (eds), *Birth of Welsh Democracy: The First Term of the National Assembly for Wales* (Institute of Welsh Affairs, 2003)

Woolf, H. et al., *De Smith's Judicial Review* (7th edn) (Sweet and Maxwell, 2013)

Woolf, H. et al., *Zamir & Woolf: The Declaratory Judgment* (4th edn) (Sweet and Maxwell, 2011)

LECTURES

Arden, M., Welsh Government Legal Services Conference, 9 October 2013, Millennium Centre, Cardiff

Beatson, J., The Administrative Court Event: North Wales, 24 March 2011, Mold Law Courts

Ellis-Thomas, Lord, 'National Assembly, A Year in Power?' 8 July 2000, Institute of Welsh Politics, Aberystwyth

Evans, D. R., 'Devolution and the Administration of Justice', The Lord Callaghan Memorial Lecture 2010, 19 February 2010, Swansea University

Griffiths, J., The Administrative Court Event: North Wales, 24 March 2011, Mold Law Courts

Hazell, R., 'An unstable Union: Devolution and the English Question', State of the Union lecture, 11 December 2000

Hickinbottom, G., 'The Administrative Court in Wales: Evolution or Revolution', The 1st Administrative Court Office for Wales Lecture, 20 February 2014, Law Society Wales Offices

Jarman, M., 'Administrative Court in Wales: Challenges and Opportunities', The 2nd Administrative Court Office for Wales Lecture, 19 November 2014, Swansea University

Jones, C., 'Getting the Devolution Dividend: Legal Wales in the next ten years', 7 May 2009, Cardiff Law School Public Lecture Series

Lloyd Jones, D., 'Law in a Small Nation: Wales and England in a Shared Jurisdiction', Lord Williams of Mostyn Memorial Lecture 2013, 4 July 2013, The Hall, Grey's Inn

Pill, M., 'Address To The Legal Wales Conference', 9 October 2009, Marriott Hotel Cardiff

Tyndall, P., Standards Conference 2013, 19 April 2013, Llandudno

PRIMARY SOURCES

III Parliament Rolls 427 no. 79 (3 November 1399, 1 Henry IV).

A guide to the legislative process in the National Assembly for Wales (Legislation Office of the National Assembly for Wales, May 2011)

Administrative Law: Judicial and Statutory Appeals (Law Com. No. 226)
Administrative Justice and Tribunals Council, Welsh Committee Report, Review of Tribunals Operating In Wales (HMSO, 2010)
All Wales Convention Report ('Jones Parry Report') (2009)
Annual Mid-year Population Estimates, 2011 and 2012 (Office for National Statistics, 8 August 2013)
Archivist's note (Parry, G.), National Library of Wales, Court of Great Sessions in Wales Records
Better Governance for Wales (Cm 6582, 2005)
Devolution: A Decade On. IWA Response to the House of Commons Constitutional Affairs Committee Call for Evidence (Institute of Welsh Affairs, November 2007)
Devolution Guidance Note No. 9 (Ministry of Justice)
Devolution Guidance Note No. 17 (Ministry of Justice)
Empowerment and Responsibility: Legislative Powers to Strengthen Wales ('The Second Report of the Silk Commission'), (Commission on Devolution in Wales, March 2014)
Focusing Judicial Resources Appropriately: The Right Judge for the Right Case (CP 25/05) (Department for Constitutional Affairs, October 2005)
Her Majesty's Courts and Tribunals Service Welsh Language Scheme: 2013–2016
HL *Hansard*, vol. 643, col. WA98 (22 January 2003)
Justice Outside London Report (HMCS, 2007)
Natural Resources Wales: Who We Are and What We Do
Ombudsman's Introduction to the Principles (Parliamentary and Health Service Ombudsman website)
Report: The Future of Legal Services in Wales (Bangor University, 8 July 2013)
Report on Remedies in Administrative Law (Cmnd 6407, 1976)
Report of the Commission on the Powers and Electoral Arrangements of the National Assembly for Wales ('Report of the Richard Commission'), (Cardiff, 2004)
Report of the Commission on Public Service Governance and Delivery ('Report of the Williams Commission') (January 2014)
Results of the National Assembly for Wales Referendum 2011, Paper number: 11/017
Review of the Crown Office List ('The Bowman Report') (Lord Chancellor's Dept, 2000)
Strengthening the Administrative Court in Wales (Joint paper by Public Law Wales and the Standing Committee on Legal Wales, October 2006; available at Appendix G to the *Justice Outside London* Report (2007))
The Boston Manuscript of the Laws of Hywel Dda
The Business of the Courts Committee: Interim Report (Cmd 4265, 1933)
The Constitution Series: 4 – The First Minister and Welsh Minister (National Assembly for Wales, July 2011)
The Counsel General, Evidence to the Richard Commission (December 2002)
The Report of the Royal Commission on the Constitution (Cmnd 5460, 1969–73)
Tribunals for Users – One System, One Service (16 August 2001)

Welsh Assembly Government Representations to the Working Party chaired by Lord Justice May, 25 October 2006 (available at Appendix F to the *Justice Outside London* Report (2007))

Welsh Local Government Association, *Governance in Wales*

Index

A

Aarhus Convention, 7-24
Abuse of Process, Contempt, 6-17
  Urgent Applications, 5-33
Academic Claim, 5-12
Access to Justice, 2-4, 2-5
Acknowledgment of Service, Judicial Review, 5-37
  Statutory Applications, 6-5
Acts of Union, 1-17, 1-18
Adequate Alternative Remedy
  Habeas Corpus, 6-14
  Judicial Review, 5-9, 6-1
Adjudication Panel for Wales, 4-33, 6-6
Administrative Court in Wales
  Establishment, 2-7
  History, 2-2, 2-3, 2-4, 2-6
  Staff, 2-10
  Statistics, 2-7
  Venue, 2-11, 2-12, 2-13, 2-14, 2-1, 2-17
Administrative Court Office
  Generally, 5-1
  History, 1-34
  Lodging Papers, 5-30
Administrative Court Office Lawyer
  Interim Relief, 5-32, 5-33
  Powers, 5-36
  Reconsideration of Orders, 5-36
  Role, 2-10
Administrative Law
  Definition, 3-1
  Generally, 3-2, 3-31
  Human Rights, *see* Human Rights
  Procedural Impropriety, *see* Procedural Impropriety
  Statutory Applications, 6-5
  Unlawfulness, *see* Unlawfulness
  Unreasonableness, *see* Unreasonableness
Advice, 5-21, 5-22, 5-23, 5-27
Amending Claim
  Judicial Review Grounds, 5-41
  Jurisdiction, 6-1
Anonymity, 5-44
Appeals
  Case Stated Appeals, 7-32, 7-33
  Civil Judicial Review, 7-29
  Contempt, 7-35
  Criminal Cases, 7-33
  Generally, 7-28
  Habeas Corpus, 7-34
  Reference to Court of Justice of the European Union, 7-36
  Statutory Appeals, 7-31
  Statutory Applications, 7-30
Architects, 6-6
Arguable Case, 5-39
Assembly Acts
  Competence, 4-7, 4-8, 4-9, 4-10, 4-11, 4-12
  History, 1-42, 1-43
  Interpretation, 4-8, 4-9, 4-10, 4-11, 4-12
  Intervention by Secretary of State, *see* Intervention by the Secretary of State for Wales
  Judicial Review Of, 4-18
  Powers, 4-7
  Reference to Supreme Court, *see* Reference to the Supreme Court
Assembly Commission, Judicial Review Of, 4-18, 4-19
Assembly Measures, History, 1-41
Assembly Members, Judicial Review Of, 4-19
Audi Alteram Partem, *see* Both Sides Must be Heard
Autonomy, 1-16, 1-19, 1-45, 2-4, 2-13, 2-14, 2-19, 4-36, 6-28

B

Bad Faith, 3-14
Bail, Case Stated Appeals, 6-11
Bail, Habeas Corpus, 6-15
Barristers Disciplinary, 6-6

Bars to Judicial Review
  Academic, 5-12
  Adequate Alternative Remedy, 5-9, 6-1
  Generally, 5-8, 5-39
  Public Bodies, 5-11
  Standing, 5-10
  Superior/Senior Courts, 5-13
Better Governance for Wales Paper, 1-40
Bias, 3-15
Both Sides Must be Heard, 3-16
Bundles, 5-30, 5-41
Byelaws
  Confirmation, 4-10, 4-27, 4-30
  Local Government, 4-30
  National Assembly Competence, 4-10

C

Case Stated Appeal
  Bail, 6-11
  Documents, 6-12, 6-13
  Frivolous Applications, 6-11
  Hearing, 6-13
  Listing, 6-13
  Preparing the Case Stated, 6-12
  Procedure, 6-11, 6-13
  Recognizance, 6-12
  Remedies, 6-13
  Representation Orders, 5-25
Case Stated Appeals, Appeals, 7-32, 7-33
Case Titles
  Contempt, 6-18
  Generally, 5-6
Certificate of Service, 5-30
Chiropractors, 6-6
Claim Form
  Contempt, 6-18
  Judicial Review, 5-15, 5-30
  Statutory Application, 6-5
Claimants, 5-2
Committal, *see* Contempt
Companies, 5-2
Consent Order
  Administrative Court Office Lawyer, 5-36
  Generally, 7-5
  Upper Tribunal, 7-6
Constitutional Statutes, 4-10
Consultation, 3-24
Contempt
  Abuse of Process, 6-17
  Appeals, 7-35
  Burden of Proof, 6-18, 6-19
  Case Titles, 6-18
  Claim Form, 6-18
  Committal, 6-19, 6-20
  Discharge of Committal, 6-21
  Discontinuance, 6-17
  Documents, 6-18
  Enforcement, *see* Enforcement
  Generally, 6-17, 7-8
  Listing, 6-18
  Permission to Apply, 6-18
  Procedure, 6-17, 6-18, 6-19, 6-20, 6-21, 6-22
  Proportionality, 6-18
  Public Interest, 6-18
  Representation Orders, 5-25
  Service, 6-18
  Substantive Hearing, 6-19
Coroners, 6-3
Corporations, 5-2
Costs
  Consent Orders, 7-5
  Deemed Costs Order, 7-13
  Detailed Costs Assessment, 7-11
  Discretion, 7-8
  Indemnity Costs, 7-10
  Interveners, 7-17
  Liability, 7-9
  Non-Partys, 7-18
  Paper Permission, 5-39, 7-15, 7-16
  Protective Costs Orders, *see* Protective Costs Orders
  Setting Aside, 7-19
  Settlement and Assessment, 7-14
  Standard Costs, 7-10
  Summary Costs Assessment, 7-11
Council of Wales, 1-15, 1-38
Councils, *see* Local Government
County Court
  Generally, 1-22
  Judicial Review Of, 5-3
Court of Appeal
  Appeals to, *see* Appeals
  Generally, 1-30
Court of Justice of the European Union
  Generally, 1-37

Reference to Court of Justice of the European Union, *see* Reference to Court of Justice of the European Union

Courts
County Court, *see* County Court
Court of Appeal, *see* Court of Appeal
Court of Justice of the European Union, *see* Court of Justice of the European Union
Crown Court, *see* Crown Court
European Court of Human Rights, *see* European Court of Human Rights
Family Court, *see* Family Court
High Court, *see* High Court
Inferior Courts, *see* Inferior Courts
Magistrates' Court, *see* Magistrates
Superior Courts, *see* Superior Courts
Supreme Court, *see* Supreme Court

Crown Court
Case Stated Appeals, 6-11
Generally, 1-28
Superior Court, 5-13

Crown Office, 1-33

D

Damages, 5-47, 5-55
Decentralisation, 2-5, 2-6, 2-13, 2-17, 2-19
Declaration, 5-47, 5-51, 5-52
Declaration of Incompatibility, 5-47, 5-51, 5-53
Deemed Costs Order, 7-13
Defendants
Judicial Review, 5-3
Public Bodies, *see* Public Bodies
Delay, 3-19
Dentists, 6-6
Detailed Costs, 7-11
Devolution
Administrative Court in Wales, 2-19
History, 1-38, 1-39, 1-40
Devolution Issue
Definition, 6-23
Judicial Review, 5-30
Devolution Reference
Definition, 6-23
Frivolous, 6-24
Generally, 6-22, 6-23
Hearing, 6-27
Notice, 6-24
Raising a Devolution Issue, 6-24
Reference, 6-25, 6-26, 6-27
Directions
Administrative Court Office Lawyer, 5-36
Substantive Claim, 5-41
Disclosure, 5-16
Discontinuance
Contempt, 6-17
Generally, 7-4
Statutory Appeals, 7-4
Discretion
Costs, 7-8
Fettering Discretion, 3-22
Remedies, 5-58
Divisional Court
Generally, 1-29
Substantive Claim, 5-41, 5-44
Wales, 2-9
Documents
Case Stated Appeals, 6-12, 6-13
Contempt, 6-18
Extending/Abridging Time, 5-36
Judicial Review, 5-30
Substantive Claim, 5-41
Duty of Candour, 5-16

E

Either-Way Offences, 1-21
Ending a case
Administrative Court, 7-2, 7-3, 7-4, 7-5, 7-7
Upper Tribunal, 7-6, 7-7
Enforcement
General Principles for Committal, *see* Contempt
Non-Compliance with an Order, 5-60, 7-37, 7-38, 7-39, 7-40, 7-41
Procedure, 7-42, 7-43, 7-44
Enforcement Notice, 6-6
English Kings
Edward I, 1-11, 1-12, 1-13
Edward IV, 1-14
Henry III, 1-10, 1-11
Henry VII, 1-17
Henry VIII, 1-17
Richard III, 1-17

Environment
- Natural Resources Wales, 4-34
- Protective Costs Orders, 7-24

Equality Duties, 3-10

European Convention on Human Rights
- Duties, 3-11
- History, 1-36
- In Domestic Law, 3-25
- History, 1-36
- In Domestic Law, 3-30

European Court of Justice, *see* Court of Justice of the European Union

European Law
- Direct Effect, 3-12
- Duties, 3-12
- History, 1-37
- Proportionality, 3-19

European Union, 1-37

Evidence
- Habeas Corpus, 6-14
- Judicial Review, 5-44

Executive
- Local Government, 4-29
- Wales, 4-20

Extradition, 6-6

F

Fair Process, *see* Procedural Impropriety

Family Court
- Family Division, 1-29
- Generally, 1-23

Fettering Discretion, 3-22

First-tier Tribunal, 1-25

Forms, 5-15

Funding, 5-21, 5-22, 5-23, 5-24, 5-25

G

General Teaching Council for Wales, 6-6

Great Sessions, 1-18

Group Representation, 5-2

H

Habeas Corpus
- Adequate Alternative Remedy, 6-14
- Appeals, 7-34
- Bail, 6-15
- Burden of Proof, 6-14, 6-16
- Evidence, 6-14
- For Release, 6-14, 6-15, 6-16
- History, 1-14, 6-14
- Initial Consideration, 6-15
- Introduction, 6-14
- Listing, 6-15
- Minors, 6-14
- Reconsideration, 6-15
- Substantive Hearing, 6-16
- To Answer a Charge, 6-14
- To Give Evidence, 6-14
- Urgent Applications, 6-14
- Writ, 6-16

Hearings
- Case Stated Appeals, 6-13
- Devolution Reference, 6-27
- Reconsideration, 5-40
- Substantive Judicial review, 5-44

High Court
- Chancery Division, 1-29
- Family Division, 1-29
- Generally, 1-29
- Queen's Bench Division, 1-29

Human Rights
- Absolute Rights, 3-26
- Disclosure, 5-16
- European Convention on Human Rights, *see* European Convention on Human Rights
- European Court of Human Rights, *see* European Court of Human Rights
- Freedom from Discrimination, 3-28
- Freedom from Forced Labour, 3-27
- Freedom from Punishment without Authority, 3-26
- Freedom from Slavery, 3-26
- Freedom from Torture, 3-26
- Freedom of Assembly, 3-28
- Freedom of Expression, 3-28
- Freedom of Thought, Conscience, and Religion, 3-28
- Generally, 3-25
- In Domestic Law, 3-25
- Limited Rights, 3-27
- National Assembly Competence, 3-25, 4-7, 4-12
- Necessity, 3-29
- Proportionality, 3-29
- Qualification Principles, 3-29
- Qualified Rights, 3-28

Right to a Fair Hearing, 3-27
Right to Education, 3-27
Right to Enjoyment of Possessions, 3-28
Right to Free Elections, 3-28
Right to Liberty and Security, 3-27
Right to Life, 3-26
Right to Marry, 3-27
Right to Private Life, 3-28
Standard of Review, 3-25

I

Illegality, *see* Unlawfulness
Indemnity Costs, 7-10
Indictment, 1-28
Inferior Courts
Devolution Reference, 6-23
Generally, 1-20, 1-21
Quashing Orders, 5-49
Inherent Powers
Public Bodies, 3-4
Setting Aside Orders, 5-39
Witnesses, 5-44
Injunction, 5-47, 5-54
Interested Parties, 5-4
Interim Relief
During Claim, 5-34
Listing, 5-32, 5-35
Lodging Claim, 5-32
Orders, 5-31
Pre-Action, 5-32
Reconsideration, 5-35
Statutory Appeals, 6-7
Statutory Applications, 6-5
Urgent Consideration, *see* Urgent Applications
Interveners
Costs, 7-17
Generally, 5-5
Intervention by the Secretary of State for Wales, 4-17, 4-19
Irrationality, *see* Unreasonableness
Irrelevant Matters, *see* Relevant Matters

J

Judges
Liaison Judge, 2-9
Upper Tribunal, 5-61
Wales, 2-9
Western Circuit, 2-18
Judgment, 5-46
Judicial Review
Acknowledgment of Service, *see* Acknowledgment of Service
Appeals, 7-29, 7-33
Assembly Acts, 4-18
Bars to Judicial Review, *see* Bars to Judicial Review
Bundles, 5-30
County Court, 5-3
Devolution Issue, 5-30
Disclosure, 5-16
Documents, 5-30
Duty of Candour, 5-16
Evidence, 5-44
Generally, 5-1, 5-7, 5-29
Interim Relief, *see* Interim Relief
Judgment, 5-46
Local Government, 4-31
Lodging the Claim, 5-30
National Assembly, 4-19
National Park Authority, 4-35
Natural Resources Wales, 4-34
Ombudsman, 4-33
Permission, *see* Permission to Apply for Judicial Review
Planning Court, 5-65
Remedies, *see* Remedies
Rolled Up Hearing, 5-39
Service, 5-30
Standing, 5-10
Time Limits, 5-17, 5-18, 5-19, 5-20
Totally Without Merit, 5-39
Upper Tribunal, *see* Upper Tribunal
Urgent Applications, *see* Urgent Applications
Welsh Government, 4-22
Judicial System, 1-20
Jurisdiction
Amending Claim, 6-1
Appellate, 3-2
England and Wales, 3-1
Outside of Jurisdiction, 3-3
Supervisory, 3-2
Upper Tribunal, 5-61, 5-62, 5-63
Juror Intimidation, 6-3
Justice Outside London Report, 2-5, 2-6, 2-8, 2-11, 2-18
Justices of the Peace, *see* Magistrates

K

Kilbrandon Report, 1-38

L

Legal Aid, 5-24, 5-25
Legal Personality, 5-2
Legislation
  Assembly Acts, *see* Assembly Acts
  Assembly Measures, *see* Assembly Measures
  Primary, *see* Primary Legislation
  Secondary, *see* Secondary Legislation
Legislative Competence Order, 1-41, 1-42
Legitimate Expectation
  Consultation, 3-24
  Generally, 3-20
Listing
  Case Stated Appeals, 6-13
  Contempt, 6-18
  Habeas Corpus, 6-15
  Interim Relief, 5-32, 5-35
  Reconsideration, 5-40
  Statutory Applications, 6-5
  Substantive Judicial Review, 5-43
Local Authority, *see* Local Government
Local Government
  Byelaws, 4-30
  Claimant, 4-27, 5-3
  Defendant, 5-3
  Functions, 4-28, 4-29
  Generally, 4-27
  Guidance, 4-29
  Judicial Review Of, 4-31
  National Park Authority, 4-35
  Ombudsman, 4-33
  Planning Statutory Review, 4-31
  Powers, 4-27, 4-28
  Service, 5-30
  Statutory Appeals, 4-31

M

Magistrates
  Case Stated Appeal, 6-11
  Generally, 1-21
Mandatory Order, 5-47, 5-48
Marcher Lords, 1-9
McKenzie Friends, 5-28
Medical Appeals, 6-6
Medical Applications, 6-3
Mental Health, 6-3
Mistake of Fact, 3-2

N

National Assembly for Wales
  Competence, 4-7, 4-8, 4-9, 4-10, 4-11, 4-12
  History, 1-39, 1-42
  Intervention by Secretary of State, *see* Intervention by the Secretary of State for Wales
  Judicial Review Of, 4-18, 4-19
  Powers, 1-43, 4-7
  Reference to Supreme Court, *see* Reference to the Supreme Court
National Park Authority, 4-35
Natural Justice
  Audi Alteram Partem, 3-16
  Bad Faith, 3-14
  Bias, 3-15
  Both Sides Must be Heard, 3-16
  Generally, 3-13
Natural Resources Wales, 4-34
No Substantially Different Outcome
  Permission, 5-39
  Remedies, 5-57
Non-Compliance with an Order, *see* Enforcement
Non-Party Costs Orders, 7-18

O

Ombudsman
  Adequate Alternative Remedy, 5-9
  Generally, 4-33
Opticians, 6-6

P

Parliamentary Sovereignty, 1-39, 4-7
Parties
  Adding/Removing, 5-36
  Judicial Review, 5-2, 5-3, 5-4, 5-5
  Statutory Appeals, 6-7
  Statutory Applications, 6-3, 6-4, 6-5
Partnerships, 5-2
Permission to Appeal, 6-9
Permission to Apply for Contempt, 6-18

Permission to Apply for Judicial Review
  Bars to Judicial Review, 5-8, 5-9, 5-10, 5-11, 5-12, 5-13, 5-39
  Costs, 5-39, 7-15, 7-16
  Forms, 5-30
  Generally, 5-38, 5-39
  No Substantially Different Outcome, 5-39
  Orders, 5-39
  Paper Application, 5-39
  Reconsideration, 5-39, 5-40
  Rolled Up Hearing, 5-39
  Set Aside, 5-39
  Test, 5-39
  Totally Without Merit, 5-39
Pharmacists, 6-6
Planning Court, 5-65
Planning Statutory Review
  Local Government, 4-31
  Statutory Applications, 6-3
Powers
  Acting Within Powers, 3-4
  Inherent Powers, *see* Inherent Powers
  Public Body, *see* Public Body
Pre-action Orders, 5-32
Pre-action Protocol
  Judicial Review, 5-14
  Statutory Appeals and Applications, 6-2
Prerogative Orders, *see* Prerogative Writs
Prerogative Writs
  Certiorari, 1-14
  Generally, 1-14, 1-32, 5-47
  Habeas Corpus, *see* Habeas Corpus
  Mandamus, 1-14
  Prohibition, 1-14
Primary Legislation
  Definition, 3-4
  National Assembly for Wales, 4-7
Private Hearing, 5-44
Private Law
  Damages, 5-47, 5-55
  Generally, 3-1
  Injunction, 5-47, 5-54
Procedural Impropriety
  Consultation, 3-24
  Fettering Discretion, 3-22
  Generally, 3-21
  Reasons, 3-23
Procedure
  Case Stated Appeals, 6-11, 6-13
  Contempt, 6-17, 6-18, 6-19, 6-20, 6-21, 6-22
  Judicial Review, *see* Judicial Review
  Statutory Appeals, 6-7
  Statutory Applications, 6-5
Proceeds of Crime, 6-3
Prohibiting Order, 5-47, 5-50
Promise, *see* Legitimate Expectation
Proportionality
  Contempt, 6-18
  European Law, 3-19
  Human Rights, 3-29
  Unreasonableness, 3-19
Protective Costs Orders, Environmental Law, 7-24, 7-25, 7-26
Protective Costs Orders
  Generally, 7-20, 7-21, 7-22
  Procedure, 7-23
Public Body
  Bars to Judicial Review, 5-11
  But For Test, 4-2
  Claimants, 5-2
  Definition, 4-2
  Examples of, 4-3
  Functions, 4-2, 4-3
  Generally, 4-2
  Local Government, *see* Local Government
  National Assembly for Wales, *see* National Assembly for Wales
  National Park Authority, 4-35
  Natural Resources Wales, 4-34
  Ombudsman, 4-33
  Principles, 4-2
  Private Persons, 4-4
  Public Services Ombudsman for Wales, 4-33
  UK Government, 4-5
  Wales, 4-1
  Welsh Government, *see* Welsh Government
  Welsh Ministers, *see* Welsh Ministers
Public Duties
  Equality Duties, 3-10
  Statutory Duties, 3-9
Public Hearing, 5-44
Public Law
  Definition, 3-1
  Generally, 3-2
Public Policy, 3-7

Public Sector Equality Duty
Generally, 3-10
Wales, 3-10
Welsh Language, 3-10
Public Services Ombudsman for Wales, 4-33

Q

Quashing Order
Judicial Review, 5-47, 5-49
Statutory Application, 6-3

R

Ram Docterine, 3-4
Reasons
Procedural Impropriety, 3-22
Unreasonableness, 3-18
Recognizance, 6-12
Reconsideration
Administrative Court Office Lawyer Orders, 5-36
Habeas Corpus, 6-15
Interim Relief, 5-35
Permission to Apply for Judicial Review, 5-39, 5-40
Reference, Devolution Reference, *see* Devolution Reference
Reference to Court of Justice of the European Union
Appeals, 7-36
Generally, 7-27
Reference to Supreme Court
Judicial Review Of, 4-19
National Assembly Competence, 4-9, 4-10, 4-11, 4-12
Procedure, 4-13, 4-14, 4-15, 4-16
Relevant Matters, 3-5
Remedies
Case Stated Appeals, 6-13
Contempt, 5-60
Crown, 5-59
Damages, 5-47, 5-55
Declaration, 5-47, 5-51, 5-52
Declaration of Incompatibility, 5-47, 5-51, 5-53
Discretionary Remedies, 5-58
Enforcement, 5-60
Forms, 5-30
Generally, 5-47
Injunction, 5-47, 5-54
Mandatory Order, 5-47, 5-48
Multiple Remedies, 5-56
No Substantially Different Outcome, 5-57
Prohibiting Order, 5-47, 5-50
Quashing Order, 5-47, 5-49
Statutory Appeals, 6-10
Representation, 5-21, 5-22, 5-23, 5-24, 5-25, 5-26
Representation Orders, 5-25
Resources, 3-7
Richard Commission, 1-40
Rolled Up Hearing, 5-39
Romans, 1-3
Royal Prerogative, 3-4
Rule of Law, 3-4

S

Secondary Legislation
Byelaws, *see* Byelaws
Definition, 3-4
Local Government, *see* Byelaws
Statutory Instrument, 3-5
Welsh Government, 4-21, 4-25
Secretary of State for Wales
Generally, 1-38
Intervention, 4-17
Senior Courts, *see* Superior Courts
Service
Acknowledgment of Service, 5-37
Claim Papers, 5-30
Contempt, 6-18
Settlement
Consent Orders, *see* Consent Orders
Costs Assessment, 7-14
Skeleton Argument, 5-41, 5-42
Solicitors Disciplinary, 6-6
Specific Disclosure, 5-16
Standard Basis Costs, 7-10
Standing, 5-10
Statute of Rhuddlan, 1-12, 1-13
Statute of Wales, *see* Statute of Rhuddlan
Statutory Appeals
Adjudication Panel for Wales, 6-6
Appeals, 7-31
Architects, 6-6
Barristers Disciplinary, 6-6

Chiropractors, 6-6
Dentists, 6-6
Discontinuance, 7-4
Enforcement Notice, 6-6
Extradition, 6-6
General Teaching Council for Wales, 6-6
Generally, 6-6
Interim Relief, 6-7
Local Government, 4-31
Medical Appeals, 6-6
Opticians, 6-6
Parties, 6-7
Permission to Appeal, 6-9
Pharmacists, 6-6
Procedure, 6-7
Remedies, 6-10
Solicitors Disciplinary, 6-6
Standard of Review, 6-8
Substantive Hearing, 6-10
Welsh Language Tribunal, 6-6
Statutory Applications
Administrative Law, 6-5
Appeals, 7-30
Coroners, 6-3
Generally, 6-3
Identifying, 6-3
Interim Relief, 6-5
Juror Intimidation, 6-3
Listing, 6-5
Medical Applications, 6-3
Mental Health, 6-3
Parties, 6-5
Planning Statutory Review, 6-3
Procedure, 6-3, 6-4, 6-5
Proceeds of Crime, 6-3
Quashing Order, 6-3
Terrorism, 6-3
Time Limits, 6-4, 6-5
Vexatious Litigant, 6-3
Statutory Instrument, 3-5
Subordinate Legislation, *see* Secondary Legislation
Substantive Hearing
Contempt, 6-19
Documents, 5-41
Evidence, 5-44
Habeas Corpus, 6-16
Judicial Review, 5-44
Skeleton Argument, 5-41, 5-42
Statutory Appeals, 6-10
Without a Hearing, 5-44
Summary Costs, 7-11
Summary Offences, 1-21
Superior Court, Crown Court, 5-13
Superior Courts
Bars to Judicial Review, 5-13
Generally, 1-20, 1-28
Supreme Court
Generally, 1-31
Reference to the Supreme Court, *see* Reference to the Supreme Court

T

Terrorism, 6-3
Time Limits
Judicial Review, 5-17, 5-18, 5-19, 5-20
Statutory Applications, 6-4, 6-5
Totally Without Merit, 5-39
Transfer
Minded to Transfer, 2-16
Upper Tribunal, 5-36
Transfer of Functions Orders, 1-39, 4-21
Treaty of Aberconwy, 1-11
Treaty of Lisbon, 1-37
Treaty of Maastricht, 1-37
Treaty of Montgomery, 1-10, 1-11
Treaty of Oxford, 1-11
Treaty of Rome, 1-37
Treaty of Woodstock, 1-11
Tribes of Wales, 1-3
Tribunals
First-tier Tribunal, *see* First-tier Tribunal
Generally, 1-20, 1-24
Quashing Orders, 5-49
Upper Tribunal, *see* Upper Tribunal
Welsh Tribunals, 1-27

U

Ultra-Vires, *see* Unlawfulness
Unincorporated Associations, 5-2
Unitary Authorities, *see* Local Government
Unlawfulness
Acting Within Powers, 3-4
Bad Faith, 3-14